BLACKSTONE'S GUIDE TO

The Consumer Rights Act 2015

BLACKSTONE'S GUIDE TO

The Consumer Rights
Act 2015

Denis Barry

Edward Jenkins QC

Daniel Lloyd

Ben Douglas-Jones

Charlene Sumnall

OXFORD
UNIVERSITY PRESS

OXFORD
UNIVERSITY PRESS

Great Clarendon Street, Oxford, OX2 6DP,
United Kingdom

Oxford University Press is a department of the University of Oxford.
It furthers the University's objective of excellence in research, scholarship,
and education by publishing worldwide. Oxford is a registered trade mark of
Oxford University Press in the UK and in certain other countries

© Denis Barry, Edward Jenkins, Daniel Lloyd, Ben Douglas-Jones, and Charlene Sumnall 2016

Published in the United States of America by Oxford University Press
198 Madison Avenue, New York, NY 10016, United States of America

British Library Cataloguing in Publication Data
Data available

Library of Congress Control Number: 2015957372

ISBN 978–0–19–872611–1

Printed in Great Britain by
Ashford Colour Press Ltd, Gosport, Hampshire

This book is dedicated to our parents, children, and loved ones.

Denis Barry
Edward Jenkins QC
Daniel Lloyd
Ben Douglas-Jones
Charlene Sumnall

Preface

The Consumer Rights Act 2015 ('the Act') has been a long time in the making. There have been a number of initiatives over the last few years to codify, simplify, and modernize consumer law. However, the Act in its current form is really the result of three recent events.

Firstly, the decision of the Supreme Court on the law of unfair terms and the core terms exemption in the now infamous 'bank charges' case.[1] The question at issue in that case was the interpretation of the core terms exemption under the old Unfair Terms in Consumer Contracts Regulations 1999[2] ('UTCCRs'). The UTCCRs state that a term of a contract cannot be assessed for fairness if it is written in plain and intelligible language, AND it relates either to the 'definition of the main subject matter of the contract' or to the 'adequacy of the price or remuneration, as against the goods or services supplied in exchange'.[3] The case revolved around how these provisions applied to particular banking charges, including overdrafts. The Supreme Court found that the terms of the contract between the banks and consumers allowing for those excess overdraft charges to be levied did fall within the core terms exemption. Those terms could not be challenged for fairness, as the Supreme Court deemed that they related to the adequacy of the price to be paid for the services being provided.

The Supreme Court judgment in favour of the banks set in chain a process. It started with a report from the Law Commission on the need for consumers to have greater clarity on what charges they would have to pay for the services they were buying. It has ended in a significant change to the core terms exemption by including a requirement for core terms to be prominent if they are not to be assessable for fairness.

Secondly, the failure of the Consumer Rights Directive, which was the most amended Directive in history, to fulfil its original purpose of applying to all areas of consumer contracts. The Consumer Rights Directive became so politically charged that it was not possible for the European Member States to reach agreement on proposals regarding unfair contract terms, consumer guarantees, and remedies. Thus, the Consumer Rights Directive, when it was enacted, was much reduced in scope. It mainly comprised a re-write of the law on distance selling and the need for greater amounts of information to be made available to consumers before they were legally bound.

---

[1] *Office of Fair Trading v Abbey National Plc and ors* [2010] 1 AC 696.
[2] SI 1999/2083, repealed by the Act.
[3] See reg. 6(1) and (2) of SI 1999/2083.

The failure of the Consumer Rights Directive, billed as a comprehensive re-statement of consumer law, created a vacuum. As a result, the British government of the time decided to proceed with the Act and legislate directly on areas that the European legislative process had failed to address. It also allowed the government to address for the first time in a comprehensive fashion the issue of digital content. The government had been concerned for some time that consumers who buy digital content online do not have the same protection as consumers who buy the same content on physical media, an example being a CD Rom. After widely consulting, the government decided to adopt wholesale the law as it applies to the sale of physical goods to the sale of digital content online. It is the first time a European Member State has legislated directly on such an important question.

The third problem was the right for consumers to bring collective actions under the previous section 47B of the Competition Act 1998. It had been used once by Which? in their action against JJB for replica football shirts. Only 130 consumers signed up for the compensation, which was less than 0.1 per cent of those affected; hence the changes to the Competition Act, more procedural than substantive, but far-reaching nonetheless.

The Act, as well as addressing the issues above, represents an attempt to codify and simplify consumer law. It re-states the law on the sale of goods and the supply of services. It sets out detailed rules on the sale of digital content based on the law as it applies to the sale of goods. The Act also sets out the law on unfair contract terms with some significant changes. In addition, the Act makes a number of important changes to consumer law enforcement, under which regulators have significantly enhanced powers. There are also substantial changes in the area of competition law enforcement which are designed, optimistically, to have far-reaching effects.

So, although the Act is a codification and simplification Act, it contains a lot of new legislation that will have to be tested in the courts. It is by no means the final word in any of the large number of areas that it covers; save, we hope, for the regulation of unwrapped bread.

The book sets out the chapters and sections of the Act. It provides in each chapter background on why the changes have been made, an explanation of how the different sections of the Act work and inter-relate and, where appropriate, some commentary on how the Act might work in practice.

We have each practised in the area of consumer law over many years. It is an area of law that has rapidly evolved over the last thirty years and is continuing to do so. As experienced practitioners in consumer law, we have had extensive experience over the years in dealing with many issues in contentious and non-contentious contexts.

We decided to write the book because we are all passionate about how consumer law should work in practice. It is an area of great debate and will no doubt continue to be so over the coming years.

It is a matter of considerable regret that many consumers are likely to continue to have no idea what their consumer rights are, that those who enforce consumer rights are facing very severe funding problems, and that the gap between consumers and the courts (because of access to justice) remains as wide as ever. We note with wry amusement that, in the competition sphere, the Act obliges sums of money unclaimed by some rather particular claimants to be given to the Access to Justice Foundation. It is, to put it very mildly, rather a shame that that is necessary.

In writing the book we would like in particular to thank Gaynor Jeffrey, Lara Mustafa, Laura Harbridge, and Harriet Knighton at the Department of Business, Innovation and Skills who have always been very helpful in explaining the policy positions underlying many of the provisions in the Act. We would also like to thank some of our peers including, in particular, Kate Cook at BT, John Davidson-Kelly at Osborne Clark, Lisle Alden at BSkyB, and Kate Vernon at DLA Piper, whose ideas and insights have been very helpful. Oxford University Press have been helpful, professional, and patient throughout, as have the staff at 5 Paper Buildings, in particular Dale Jones.

Finally we would like to thank as authors of the book our husbands, wives, children, and loved ones who have put up with us spending many long hours at weekends putting this book together, and without whose patience and understanding we would not have been able to complete this guide to the Act. This book is dedicated to them and the emotional support they have provided us over many years, and in particular the last eighteen months.

Denis Barry
Edward Jenkins QC
Daniel Lloyd
Ben Douglas-Jones
Charlene Sumnall

Contents—Summary

Contents

Contents

Contents

Contents

Table of Cases

Table of Legislation

Australia

Table of European Cases

Table of Secondary Legislation

Table of European Legislation

List of Abbreviations

ADR	Alternative Dispute Resolution
BERR	Department for Business, Enterprise and Regualtory
BIS	Business, Innovation and Skills
CA	Competition Act 1998
CAT	Competition Appeal Tribunal
CCA	Consumer Credit Act 1974, as amended
CCRs	Consumer Contracts (Information, Cancellation and Additional Charges) Regulations 2013
CDPA	Copyright Designs and Patents Act 1988
CJEU	Court of Justice of the European Union
CMA	Competition and Markets Authority
CPO	Collective Proceedings Order
CPRs	Consumer Protection from Unfair Trading Regulations 2008
CPUTR	Consumer Protection from Unfair Trading Regulations 2008
CPUTs	Consumer Protection (Amendment) Regulations 2014
CRA	Consumer Rights Act 2015
CRD	Consumer Rights Directive
CSD	Consumer Sales Directive
EA	Enterprise Act 2002
ECRs	Electronic Commerce (EC Directive) Regulations 2002
EEA	European Economic Area
ERRA	Enterprise and Regulatory Reform Act 2013
EU	European Union
EULA	End User Licence Agreement
FCA	Financial Conduct Authority
FOS	Financial Ombudsman Service
ICO	Information Commissioners
ODR	Online Dispute Resolution
OfCom	Office of Communications
OfGem	Office of Gas and Electricity Markets
OFT	Office of Fair Trading
PSRs	Provision of Services Regulations 2009
RIPA	Regulation of Investigatory Powers Act 2000

SGA	Sale of Goods Act 1979
SGITA	Supply of Goods (Implied Terms) Act 1973
SGSA	Sale of Goods and Services Act 1982
TFEU	Treaty on the Functioning of the European Union
UCTA	Unfair Contract Terms Act 1977
UTCCRs	Unfair Terms in Consumer Contracts Regulations 1999
UTD	Unfair Contract Terms Directive

1

INTRODUCTION

A. PURPOSE OF THE LEGISLATION

1. What the Act is Trying to Achieve

The Act does quite a large number of things at the same time. It is principally, but   1.01
not exclusively, concerned with the relationships between businesses and consumers. It brings into UK law[1] various European Directives,[2] and relies to an extent on
European law concepts, whilst simultaneously reforming and codifying existing
UK consumer law. It codifies the law regarding digital content for the first time,[3]
makes the law about unfair contract terms clearer,[4] and provides a new draft of
enhanced measures for consumer regulators to use against rogue traders. It codifies
the law for both goods[5] and services,[6] and sets out the powers for those involved
in consumer law enforcement.[7] It reforms the work of the Competition Appeal
Tribunal[8] in striking and potentially exciting ways. There are some reforms to
the secondary ticketing market,[9] the law regarding premium rate services, letting
agents, and higher education providers. Most vitally of all, it amends the weights
and measures regarding unwrapped bread.

It was described as 'a major part of the government's reform of UK consumer law   1.02
and is predicted to boost the economy by £4 billion over the next decade by streamlining complicated law from 8 pieces of legislation into one place'. It was hoped that
consumers would be better informed and protected.[10]

---

[1] We are afraid that for reasons of space this book does not cover the law in Scotland.
[2] Directives 99/44/EC and 93/13/EEC and some of 2011/83/EU, 2001/95/EC, 98/27/EC, and also
parts of EC Regulations 2006/2004 and 765/2008.
[3] Ch 3 of the Act.
[4] Part 2 of the Act.
[5] Ch 2 of the Act.
[6] Ch 4 of the Act.
[7] s. 77 and Sch 5 of the Act.
[8] Part 3 Ch 2 and Sch. 8 of the Act.
[9] Ch 5 of the Act.
[10] Department for Business, Innovation and Skills ('BIS') press release on Royal Assent.

1.03   The objectives of the Act were set out in a rather pithy paragraph by Dr Vince Cable at Second Reading:

> In conclusion, the Bill represents a radical and far-reaching set of reforms designed to streamline the law, making it clearer and more accessible. It will enhance consumer rights and deregulate for business. It will benefit consumers by reducing the time and cost of finding out how to deal with problems. It will protect consumers from the small print in contracts and increase the redress they get when things go wrong. It will benefit businesses by reducing the need for ongoing legal advice, and it will save legitimate businesses from losses from anti-competitive practices. The benefits are substantial. They will create more confident consumers, who in turn will be more likely to try new and innovative goods and services, which in turn will create a more responsive and vibrant UK economy.[11]

2. Structure of the Act

1.04   The structure of the Act is set out in the Explanatory Notes and summarized in Table 1.1.

Table 1.1 Structure of the Act

Part 1	i.	Sets out the standards that goods must meet.
	ii.	Consolidates and aligns the currently inconsistent remedies available to consumers for goods supplied under different contract types, such as sale, work and materials, conditional sale, or hire purchase.
	iii.	Sets a time period of thirty days in which consumers can reject sub-standard goods and be entitled to a full refund.
	iv.	Limits the number of repairs or replacements of sub-standard goods before traders must offer some money back.
	v.	Sets limits on the extent to which traders may reduce the level of refund (where goods are not rejected initially) to take account of the use of the goods the consumer has had up to that point.
	vi.	Introduces a new category of digital content.
	vii.	Introduces tailored quality rights for digital content.
	viii.	Introduces tailored remedies if the digital content rights are not met.
	ix.	Introduces a new statutory right that if a trader provides information in relation to a service, and the consumer takes this information into account, the service must comply with that information.
	x.	Introduces new statutory remedies when things go wrong with a service.
	xi.	Makes it clear that consumers can always request these rights and remedies when a trader supplies a service to them.
Part 2 including Schedules 2, 3, and 4	i.	Consolidates the legislation governing unfair contract terms in relation to consumer contracts, which currently is found in two separate pieces of legislation, into one place, removes anomalies and overlapping provisions in relation to consumer contracts.
	ii.	Makes clearer the circumstances when the price or subject matter of the contract cannot be considered for fairness and in particular makes clear that, to avoid being considered for fairness, those terms must be transparent and prominent.
	iii.	Clarifies the role and extends the indicative list of terms which may be regarded as unfair (the so-called 'Grey List').

---

[11] House of Commons Hansard Debates 28 January 2004 at Col 776.

Part 3 including Schedules 5, 6, 7, 8, 9, and 10	i.	Consolidates and simplifies the investigatory powers of consumer law enforcers in relation to the listed legislation and sets them out in one place as a generic set.
	ii.	Clarifies the law so that trading standards are able to work across local authority boundaries as simply and efficiently as possible.
	iii.	Introduces new powers for public enforcers to seek, through applying to the civil courts:
		a) Redress for consumers who have been disadvantaged by breaches of consumer law;
		b) Remedies from traders who have breached consumer law to improve their compliance and reduce the likelihood of future breaches; and/or
		c) Remedies to give consumers more information so they can exercise greater choice and help improve the functioning of the market for consumers and other businesses.
	iv.	Includes a power for the Secretary of State to extend the use of the enhanced consumer measures to private designated enforcers providing certain conditions are met and subject to safeguards on their use.
	v.	Clarifies the maximum penalties that the regulator of premium rate services can impose on non-compliant and rogue operators.

It is obvious that the relationships between consumers and businesses are multi-farious and often complex. It is our view that the success of this piece of legislation will depend to a very large extent on the access that consumers have to justice in order to exercise these rights. Whether and how it is in fact possible for consumers to fully exercise their consumer rights is essentially a political question.[12] The aims are certainly laudable, but it may be that the legislation will fall into the trap iden-tified by Jonathan Swift nearly 400 years ago: 'Laws are like cobwebs, which may catch small flies, but let wasps and hornets break through.'[13]   1.05

3. History

The history of consumer law is a vast topic and plainly outside the scope of any such guide as this.[14] It is, however, worth pointing out that the ideas contained in this Act have been several decades in gestation. Some of the more knotty problems that legislation in this field inevitably must deal with include: 1.06

(1) The extent to which consumers are able to exercise the rights that they have;

(2) The extent to which it is desirable for the state to interfere in the invisible hand of the market;

(3) The extent to which the courts should be concerned with concepts of fairness in contract law;

---

[12] And one that the authors of this work do not necessarily agree about!

[13] Jonathan Swift, 'A Critical Essay on the Faculties of the Mind' in *Miscellanies in Prose and Verse* (London: John Morphew, 1709).

[14] For further reading on this interesting topic see G. Howells and S. Weatherill, *Consumer Protection Law* (UK: Ashgate Publishing, 2nd edn, 2005), and in particular Ch 1.

(4) The extent to which consumers are able to absorb the information that they have been given.

1.07   The Act is also a combination of European law and UK law. With the former, the policy objectives are necessarily more explicit than has been traditional in the common law of contract.

4. EU Policy Objectives

1.08   By the 1970s there was a clear desire at EU level to grow the appeal of the Community away from economic affairs and into the social sphere. As much was made explicit in 1975 with the Council Resolution of the EEC for a consumer protection and information policy. The Annex to that document provided a list of five (very) basic rights:[15]

(1) The right to protection of health and safety;

(2) The right to protection of economic interests;

(3) The right to redress;

(4) The right to information and education;

(5) The right to representation (the right to be heard).

1.09   In 1985 there was a Commission Paper entitled 'A New Impetus for Consumer Protection Policy'.[16] It concluded that nothing like as much as was hoped had been achieved. It was suggested that an unfortunate argument had become popular that the promotion of consumer rights was an activity which should only be pursued in times of economic growth, and that the protection of consumer interests would represent a burden on business. The paper did not accept that argument. It would be fair to observe that this argument still has a fair number of supporters.

1.10   One of the counter arguments put forward was that reliable and safe goods for consumers assisted in maintaining the Community's share of trade against competing external producers.[17] Stephen Weatherill suggests that there was then a certain amount of competence creep in the consumer law area by the EU institutions. The breakthrough arrived in the Maastricht Treaty that created a separate title on Consumer Protection, now article 169:

In order to promote the interests of consumers and to ensure a high level of consumer protection, the Union shall contribute to protecting the health safety and economic interests of consumers, as well as to promoting their right to education and to organize themselves in order to safeguard their interests.[18]

---

[15] Official Journal 195/C92/1. See S. Weatherill, *EU Consumer Law and Policy* (UK: Elgar European Law, 2005) Ch 1.

[16] COM (85) 314 para. 5.

[17] *EU Consumer Law and Policy*, Ch 1 para. 16.

[18] Treaty on the Functioning of the European Union ('TFEU') art. 169 (ex art. 153 TEC).

There is no doubt about the importance of EU law in the context of consumer law. 1.11
In *OFT v Purely Creative* the High Court explained the approach that must be taken:

Domestic regulations designed to implement EU directives, and in particular maximum har-
monisation directives, must be construed as far as possible so as to implement the purposes
and provisions of the directive. The interpretation of words and phrases is neither a matter of
grammars nor dictionaries, nor even a matter of the use of those phrases (or of the underlying
concepts) in national law. If similar words and phrases are used in the directive itself, then they
must be interpreted both in the directive and in the implementing regulations by means of a
process of interpretation which is independent of the member state's national law and, for that
matter, independent of any other member state's national law. For that purpose the primary
recourse of the national court is to the jurisprudence of the ECJ.[19]

The current policy report from the Commission on EU Consumer Policy dates 1.12
from 2014.[20] There are behavioural studies into the conduct of consumers in a
number of different areas, including the extent to which consumers can make an
informed choice under a proposed Common European Sales Law. It is also proposed to study consumer attitudes to reading, understanding, and accepting terms
and conditions. It is plain that the Commission has concerns that have remained
since the *Oceano Grupo*[21] case in 2000:

The system of protection introduced by the Directive is based on the idea that the consumer is
in a weak position vis-à-vis the seller or supplier, as regards both his bargaining power and his
level of knowledge.

How this sits with what is sometimes described as the classical law of contract[22] is 1.13
a nice point. However, the position of the government in passing the Act was clear,
and closer to the thinking of the Commission than the tradition described below.

5. Common Law Contractual Tradition

The high water-mark was the observation of Sir George Jessel in 1875 that: 1.14

If there is one thing which more than another public policy requires it is that men of full age
and competent understanding shall have the utmost liberty of contracting, and that their contracts entered into freely and voluntarily shall be held sacred and shall be enforced by Courts of
Justice.[23]

Similarly, in the competition area, the influential Chicago school has been very 1.15
critical of interventionist policies, particularly when they have come from the government as distinct from the courts.[24]

---

[19] *OFT v Purely Creative* [2011] EWHC 106 (Ch) per Mr Justice Briggs para. 40.
[20] European Commission Report on Consumer Policy 2014.
[21] [2002] 1 CMLR 43.
[22] Hugh Collins, *The Law of Contract* (Cambridge: Cambridge University Press, 2003) Ch 1.
[23] *Printing and Numerical Registering Co v Sampson* (1875) LR 19 Eq. 462, 465.
[24] See discussion in Howells and Weatherill, *Consumer Protection Law*, p. 79.

1.16   Hugh Collins has described the tension between the common law contractual tradition and the way in which contract law has developed:

> This traditional conception of contract law persists in part because of the need to preserve the integrity and, hence, the legitimacy of this closed doctrinal system of thought. Its doctrinal integrity helps to achieve legitimacy, because the law can be presented as objective and neutral, not as a matter of politics or preference, but a settled body of rules and principles, legitimated by tradition and routine observance, and applied impartially and fairly to all citizens.[25]

1.17   The common law has moved on quite a lot since the 1980s. The courts are now concerned with concepts of fairness. As Lord Steyn observed (in the context of the unfair contract terms), the purpose of the European law was 'to enforce community standards of decency, fairness and reasonableness in commercial transactions'.[26]

1.18   Regulation does not come without a cost, as Lord Diplock said in *Tesco v Nattrass*:[27] 'the price to the public of the protection afforded to a minority of consumers might well be an increase in the costs of goods and services to consumers generally'.

6. Sources and Consultations

1.19   The Act has had a long gestation. There have been a large number of consultations which have informed the way in which it has been drafted. The main consultation documents are listed in Table 1.2. There were a number of pieces of domestic law that have been amended. There are a number of Directives and Regulations that have been implemented in part or in full.[28]

Table 1.2 **List of main consultation documents**

PART 1	Davidson Report HM Treasury 2006.
	http://webarchive.nationalarchives.gov.uk/+/http://www.hm-treasury.gov.uk/d/davidson_review281106.pdf
	Law Commission No. 317.
	http://www.lawcom.gov.uk/wp-content/uploads/2015/03/lc317_Consumer_Remedies_Faulty_Goods.pdf
	Consolidation and simplification of UK consumer law, BIS 2010.
	https://www.gov.uk/government/uploads/system/uploads/attachment_data/file/31838/10-1255-consolidation-simplification-uk-consumer-law.pdf

---

[25] Hugh Collins, *The Law of Contract* (Cambridge: Cambridge University Press, 2003) p. 7.

[26] *D-G of Fair Trading v First National Bank plc* (HL) [2002] 1 AC 481, 500.

[27] [1971] 2 All ER 127, 151h.

[28] See Explanatory Notes para. 8 and following, which has a very helpful summary of the assorted amendments.

	Consumer Rights in Digital Products, BIS 2010.
	https://www.gov.uk/government/uploads/system/uploads/attachment_data/ file/31837/10-1125- consumer-rights-in-digital-products.pdf
	Enhancing consumer confidence by clarifying consumer law.
	https://www.gov.uk/government/uploads/system/uploads/attachment_data/ file/31350/12-937- enhancing-consumer-consultation-supply-of-goods-services-digital.pdf
PART 2	The Law Commission No. 292.
	http://www.lawcom.gov.uk/wp-content/uploads/2015/06/lc292_Unfair_Terms_In_ Contracts.pdf
PART 3	Enhancing consumer confidence through effective enforcement, BIS, March 2012.
	https://www.gov.uk/government/uploads/system/uploads/attachment_data/ file/31534/12-543- enhancing-consumer-confidence-effective-enforcement-consultation.pdf
	Civil enforcement remedies – consultation on extending the range of remedies available to public enforcers of consumer law.
	https://www.gov.uk/government/uploads/system/uploads/attachment_data/ file/32713/12-1193- civil-enforcement-remedies-consultation-on-extending.pdf
	Private actions in competition law: a consultation on options for reform.
	https://www.gov.uk/government/uploads/system/uploads/attachment_data/ file/31528/12-742- private-actions-in-competition-law-consultation.pdf

By the time the Act had its second reading, the Secretary of State had two **1.20** principal objectives to meet two broad problems. In competition law, the problem was that businesses believed that the current regime for private actions was too slow and costly; as a result, consumers did not obtain redress when they had been harmed by anti-competitive behaviour. In respect of consumers, they could not be expected to be confident when they did not understand their rights or entitlements if something were to go wrong. There is no doubt that the government took a fairly paternalistic view of the consumer, consistent with the direction of travel in EU law.

B. IS THE ACT GOING TO BE EFFECTIVE?

1. Access to Justice

One of the central problems in the area of consumer law is the extent to which the **1.21** individual consumer can access any of the various rights which are contained in the Act. Most consumer claims are for sums of money that are generally too small to be worth litigating. It is not to be unduly cynical to observe that there are businesses

7

in the UK that are aware of that reality. In 2012, Consumer Focus estimated that out of 6.4 million consumer complaints made to businesses, 2 million were unresolved.[29] It remains to be seen what steps will be taken to make consumers aware of and confident in their consumer rights.

1.22   The Act provides and codifies consumer rights, and then codifies and enhances enforcement of those rights. Part 1 of the Act provides various consumer rights in respect of goods (Chapter 2), digital content (Chapter 3), and services (Chapter 4). In Parts 2 and 3 the Act aspires to deal with enforcement.

1.23   Part 2 and Schedule 2 codify the law regarding unfair terms. They set out the circumstances in which the fairness of contractual terms can be considered by the courts. Schedule 3 provides the ways in which enforcers can regulate unfair terms. That works on both the individual level, in that a consumer can cite the Schedule to demonstrate that the relevant contractual term may be regarded as unfair, and at the enforcement level, in that the relevant regulators may consider complaints about terms or notices said to be unfair.

1.24   Part 3 then deals with other kinds of consumer protection for larger groups of consumers. Section 79 and Schedule 7 provide enhanced consumer measures so that breaches of consumer law can be dealt with more effectively by enforcers. This involves amendments to Part VIII of the Enterprise Act 2002, which provided orders for infringing breaches of EU or domestic law behaviour which could be sought by enforcement bodies. The remedies available have been 'enhanced': including redress; compliance; and choice measures.[30]

1.25   Section 81 and Schedule 8 are designed to widen the types of competition cases that the Competition Appeal Tribunal ('CAT') is able to deal with, to provide for opt-in collective action and opt-out collective settlements, and to provide a voluntary redress scheme in respect of competition cases.[31]

2. Alternative Dispute Resolution

1.26   The government is hopeful that the changes to alternative dispute resolution ('ADR') will provide remedies for the missing consumers who do not pursue their rights.[32] A consultation was published in November 2014[33] in which it was proposed that the Trading Standards Institute will act as a competent authority to ensure that ADR schemes in the non-regulated sectors function properly. The start-up costs will be funded, and then the operation costs will be covered by fees charged to the certified ADR providers. Effectively, it is hoped that the costs of investigating such

---

[29] 'Consumer Detriment 2012' available at <http://www.consumerfocus.org.uk/publications/consumer-detriment-2012>.

[30] See Ch 8.

[31] See Ch 9.

[32] See the Alternative Dispute Resolution for Consumer Disputes (Competent Authorities and Information) Regulations 2015 (SI 2015/542), large parts of which are in force, and some of which are likely to be in force in October 2015.

[33] <https://www.gov.uk/government/uploads/system/uploads/attachment_data/file/377522/bis-14-1122-alternative-dispute-resolution-for-consumers.pdf>.

disputes will not be the responsibility of hard-pressed trading standards officers (and the ratepayers who pay for them) but those who are involved in individual disputes. This could be described as a form of privatization of the problem. There are echoes of this approach in the reforms to competition law as well: the state agencies sharing enforcement with individual consumers or their representatives.

However, simultaneously there have been substantial cutbacks to trading standards departments throughout the country.[34] A survey carried out by National Trading Standards and the Trading Standard Institute concluded that most trading standards departments have been cut by an average of 40 per cent since 2010. There is also a chronic problem with regional differences. The number of trading standards officers per service varied from 0.5 to 48, with apparently little reference to the size of the areas they serve or the number of businesses. 1.27

C. SIMULTANEOUS CHANGES TO CONSUMER LAW

1. The Practical Problem

The Explanatory Notes are explicit about the purpose of the Act: 1.28

There is general agreement across business and consumer groups that the existing UK consumer law is unnecessarily complex. It is fragmented, and in places unclear, for example where the law has not kept up with technological change or lacks precision or where it is couched in legalistic language. There are also overlaps and inconsistencies between changes made by virtue of implementing European Union ('EU)' legislation alongside unamended pre-existing UK legislation.[35]

To be blunt, that position will remain the same. The Act has not consolidated all of the relevant legislation into one place. What might be regarded as 'consumer law' more broadly includes the law on product and service liability and consumer safety, as well as the law on consumer credit. They all remain distinct areas with their own (at times pointlessly complex) legislative regimes. To that extent, the Act represents rather a wasted opportunity. 1.29

An example of the various types of consumer law legislation can be seen in the Statutory Instruments that accompany the changes to Part VIII of the Enterprise Act 2002.[36] 1.30

The Act is also part of various other wider reforms to the consumer legislation framework. The Consumer Contracts (Information, Cancellation and Additional Charges) Regulations 2013 and the Consumer Rights (Payment Surcharges) Regulations 2012 have implemented the Consumer Rights Directive. In the competition sphere, the replacement of the Office of Fair Trading ('OFT') by the Competition and Markets 1.31

---

[34] See e.g. <http://www.tradingstandards.uk/extra/news-item.cfm/newsid/1464>.
[35] Explanatory Notes para. 5.
[36] See, in particular, Ch 8 and The Enterprise Act 2002 (Part 8 Domestic Infringements) Order 2003 and the Enterprise Act 2002 (Part 8 Community Infringements UK Laws) Order.

Authority ('CMA') is likely to have a growing impact. The criminal law on cartels has been substantially reformed.[37]

1.32　In particular, the Consumer Protection from Unfair Trading Regulations 2008[38] (which are now the primary vehicle for the prosecution of consumer offences) were also amended[39] and Part 4A came into force in October 2014.[40] They provide for a right of redress in circumstances where a trader is involved in a misleading action or an aggressive practice. In those circumstances, the consumer can unwind the contract, apply for damages and have a discount. It is difficult to see why these Regulations could not, for example, have been incorporated into a more cohesive set of enhanced consumer measures (see Chapter 8).

D. POLICY CHOICES

1. Choices Made by Consumers

1.33　A focus on the rights of consumers is to an extent predicated on a particular model of an economic system:

> Producers have to sell their goods to consumers in order to survive. They will only be able to sell to consumers what consumers want to buy. Consumer preference will dictate what is made available. Producers compete. Consumers choose. The 'invisible hand' of producers behaving in response to consumer preference organises the market. The survival instinct among producers which is instilled by the mechanism of competition will ensure an efficient allocation of resources. Given the stimulus of competition, resources will not be wasted.[41]

1.34　As the authors of that quotation recognize, that system is as alluring as it is unrealistic. In particular, it is very doubtful whether or not consumers know as much as they should about the goods, services, and digital content that they are purchasing. Recent work in cognitive and social psychology has shown the extent to which risks are over- or under-estimated by consumers, and of course that effects the extent to which consumers can make choices which are not particularly rational.[42] As J. Hanson and D. Kysar wrote in 1999:

> Our central contention is that the presence of unyielding cognitive biases makes individual decision makers susceptible to manipulation by those able to influence the context in which decisions are made. More particularly, we believe that market outcomes will be heavily influenced, if not determined, by the ability of one actor to control the format of information, the presentation of choices, and, in general, the setting within which market transactions occur. Once one

---

[37] See Archbold, *Criminal Pleading, Evidence and Practice* (London: Sweet and Maxwell, 2015) 30–25.

[38] Consumer Protection from Unfair Trading Regulations 2008 (SI 2008/1277).

[39] SI 2014/870.

[40] The details are outside the scope of this work.

[41] Howells and Weatherill, *Consumer Protection Law*, p. 1.

[42] Daniel Kahnemann, *Thinking Fast and Slow* (London: Penguin, 2012).

accepts that individuals systematically behave in non-rational ways, it follows from an economic perspective that others will exploit those tendencies for gain.[43]

In conclusion, it is perhaps worth considering whether a focus on consumer rights should be a priority at the present time at all: 1.35

A sober look at our world shows that the degree of human intervention, often in the service of business interests and consumerism, is actually making our earth less rich and beautiful, ever more limited and grey, even as technological advances and consumer goods continue to abound limitlessly.[44]

---

[43] J. Hanson and D. Kysar, 'Taking Behaviouralism Seriously' (1999) 112 *Harvard Law Review* 630.
[44] Pope Francis, 'Laudato Si' (2015) para. 34.

2

KEY DEFINITIONS

A. OVERVIEW

This Act applies to agreements between traders and consumers which are contracts. 2.01
At its most basic level, for a contract to be formed under the law of England and
Wales or Northern Ireland there needs to be an offer and acceptance (i.e. one party
must express a willingness to contract on certain terms and the other party must
agree to those terms); and there must be 'consideration', which is to say that both
sides must offer something to the other (for example, money in return for goods).
A contract could be implied by conduct of the parties; for example, by jumping
into a black cab and stating your destination, this conduct would be taken as an
agreement that the taxi driver will take you to your destination and that you will
pay a price for it.

The scope of the Act's application to contracts is actually set out in section 1; sub- 2.02
sections (3) to (6) set out the position with regard to 'mixed contracts'. Examples of
mixed contracts include contracts involving the supply of both goods and services
(for example, a car service where parts are fitted) or digital content and a service
(for example, supplying and installing anti-virus software). In such contracts under
the Act, the service element of the contract attracts service rights and remedies, the
goods elements attract goods rights and remedies, and the digital content elements
attract the digital content rights and remedies. Subsection (3) therefore makes clear
that, for such mixed contracts, it will be relevant to look at the rights and remedies
for each element of the mixed contract. In most cases it will be relevant to look at
the appropriate chapter of the Act (Chapter 2 for goods, Chapter 3 for digital content, and Chapter 4 for services). For particular mixed contracts (goods and installation services and goods and digital content) see sections 15 and 16.

The Act sets out the rights and obligations which arise in such contracts. 2.03

One of the Government's main legislative aims was to align, as far as possible, 2.04
the definitions of certain key terms across the Act and other consumer laws, such
as the Consumer Contracts (Information, Cancellation and Additional Charges)
Regulations 2013 which implement Directive 2011/83/EU of the European
Parliament and of the Council on consumer rights (commonly known as the
Consumer Rights Directive ('CRD')) in regulations made under the European

Communities Act 1972,[1] in order to facilitate easier interpretation and clearer application of the law. These terms are 'trader', 'consumer', 'business', 'goods', and 'digital content'. To ensure as much consistency as possible, the definitions of these key terms in the Act are based largely on the definitions within the CRD.[2] They are not, therefore, all consistent across all UK Acts.[3]

2.05   These key definitions are set out separately from the general interpretation section (section 59) because they are important to understanding the scope of the Act. 'Service' is also a key concept but it is not defined by the Act; nor was it defined in the Sale of Goods and Services Act 1982 ('SGSA').

2.06   Insofar as 'services' is concerned, it is perhaps worth highlighting that, while that term is not defined, the Act does not apply to certain services: the Act does not cover contracts of employment or apprenticeships and, where there is legislation that gives more detailed provision about rights or duties of particular services, that legislation will take precedence over the provisions in Chapter 4 (the services chapter of the Act). The services chapter also partially implements article 5 (consumer information for contracts other than distance or off-premises contracts) and article 6 (consumer information and right of withdrawal for distance and off-premises contracts) of the CRD; however certain sectors, such as financial and gambling services, are exempt from those provisions.

B. KEY DEFINITIONS

2.07   Section 2 sets out the definitions:

(1) These definitions apply in this Part (as well as the definitions in section 59).

(2) "Trader" means a person acting for purposes relating to that person's trade, business, craft or profession, whether acting personally or through another person acting in the trader's name or on the trader's behalf.

(3) "Consumer" means an individual acting for purposes that are wholly or mainly outside that individual's trade, business, craft or profession.

(4) A trader claiming that an individual was not acting for purposes wholly or mainly outside the individual's trade, business, craft or profession must prove it.

(5) For the purposes of Chapter 2, except to the extent mentioned in subsection (6), a person is not a consumer in relation to a sales contract if—

(a) the goods are second hand goods sold at public auction, and

(b) individuals have the opportunity of attending the sale in person.

(6) A person is a consumer in relation to such a contract for the purposes of—

---

[1] Note: a small number of the CRD's provisions are implemented in the Act.

[2] See reg. 4 which defines 'consumer' and 'trader' and reg.5 which includes the other definitions including 'business', 'goods', and 'digital content'.

[3] E.g. 'goods' under s. 18 of the SGSA as *goods* includes all personal chattels,…; and in particular "goods" includes emblements, industrial growing crops, and things attached to or forming part of the land which are agreed to be severed before the transfer [bailment or hire] concerned or under the contract concerned'.

(a) sections 11(4) and (5), 12, 28 and 29, and

(b) the other provisions of Chapter 2 as they apply in relation to those sections.

(7) "Business" includes the activities of any government department or local or public authority.

(8) "Goods" means any tangible moveable items, but that includes water, gas and electricity if and only if they are put up for supply in a limited volume or set quantity.

(9) "Digital content" means data which are produced and supplied in digital form.

1. Trader

A trader is a person acting for purposes relating to his or her trade, business, craft, or profession, whether acting directly or through another person acting in the trader's name or on the trader's behalf. Examples would be a trader who subcontracts part of a contract, or a company on whose behalf the employees make contracts with customers. This will render a trader liable for the acts of his staff and agents (including sub-contractors).[4]   2.08

Consequently a holding company could be a 'trader' and thus can be liable for the acts of its subsidiaries.[5]   2.09

A 'person' here is not only a natural person, but also a legal person, which includes companies, charities, unincorporated associations and arms of national and local government and public authorities (and the reference to a 'person' can also include more than one person). So where such entities are acting for purposes relating to their trade, business, craft, or profession, they are caught by the definition of trader.   2.10

The trader definition does not include those selling at car boot sales, school fairs, and at public auction of second hand goods[6] when acting for the purposes of their everyday activity of trade, business, craft, or profession. There is no qualification in section 2(7) that limits a trader to someone acting commercially. The definition therefore includes charities.   2.11

The Act does not specifically state whether abnormal commercial activities of a trader would be caught, such as selling off its old computers on a one-off basis. Presumably this is still activity for the purposes of the company's trade, as the computers belong to the company and the profits will be channelled back into it. Unlike the definition of 'sole trader' for VAT purposes, there is no requirement of commerciality in determining whether someone is a trader.   2.12

The definitions of trader and consumer in the Consumer Rights (Payment Surcharges) Regulations 2012 (2012/3110), reg. 2, are broadly the same as in the Act: 2.13

"consumer" means an individual acting for purposes which are wholly or mainly outside that individual's trade, business, craft or profession; "trader" means a person acting for purposes

---

[4] An example in the Explanatory Notes to the Act (para. 35) makes reference to building contracts. This may not be a helpful example as art. 3(3)(f) of the CRD excludes contracts 'for the construction of new buildings, the substantial conversion of existing buildings and for rental of accommodation for residential purposes'.

[5] *R v SSE Plc* [2013] EWCA Crim 539. This was a case on the Consumer Protection from Unfair Trading Regulations 2008.

[6] See the interplay between s. 2(5) and (6).

relating to that person's trade, business, craft or profession, whether acting personally or through another person acting in the trader's name or on the trader's behalf.

2. Consumer

2.14 A consumer can only be an individual. There is no protection for corporations or those buying on behalf of corporations in the Act.

2.15 There was an attempt to broaden the definition of consumer to include small businesses that had less than ten employees.[7] The Government pointed out that the case for small businesses to be treated as consumers had been considered in 2008 and 2012, and that the Business, Innovation and Skills Committee acknowledged that all business groups preferred to retain the current distinction between a business and a consumer. It was further pointed out that this was consistent with the position in European law.[8]

2.16 An individual is a consumer if he is acting for purposes wholly or mainly outside that individual's trade.

> If people use something wholly or mainly as a consumer, they do not lose those protections if they also occasionally use the things for business. For example, if they buy a kettle for their house and occasionally work from home, even if they use it while they are working, because it is wholly or mainly used for their personal use, consumer rights relating to that kettle are not undermined.[9]

2.17 Conversely, a sole trader operating from a private dwelling who buys a printer, of which 95 per cent of the use is for the purposes of the business, is not likely to be held to be a consumer (and therefore the rights in this Part will not protect that sole trader, but they would have to look to other legislation. For example, if the sole trader were buying goods, they would have to look to the SGA for protections about the quality of the goods).[10] A professional buying a laptop for work is therefore not a consumer within the meaning of the Act.

2.18 However, it is for the trader to prove that an individual is not a consumer. The standard of proof is the balance of probabilities.

2.19 Under old case law this would be strictly applied i.e. there really must be no connection to trade etc. However, recital (17) in the preamble to the CRD makes it plain that trade etc. need only not be the predominant purpose which may water down the meaning of 'mainly' in section 2(3):

> The definition of consumer should cover natural persons who are acting outside their trade, business, craft or profession. However, in the case of dual purpose contracts, where the contract is concluded for purposes partly within and partly outside the person's trade and the trade

---

[7] Hansard House of Commons Public Bill Committee 13 February 2014 at Col 83.
[8] Hansard House of Commons Public Bill Committee 13 February 2014 at Col 94.
[9] House of Commons Public Bill Committee 13 February 2014 at Col 103.
[10] Explanatory Notes to the Act, para. 36.

purpose is so limited as not to be predominant in the overall context of the contract, that person should also be considered as a consumer.

In the High Court decision in *OFT v Foxtons*[11] under the Unfair Terms in 2.20 Consumer Contracts Regulations 1999, the court accepted that there could be a category of a consumer landlord. This was a concession made by Foxtons, to a description by the Office of Fair Trading ('OFT') of landlords who either let the property whilst abroad, rented out part of their property, or for whom the property was part of a pension plan or long-term saving.

In *R (On the application of Bluefin Insurance Ltd) v Financial Ombudsman* 2.21 *Service*,[12] the court interpreted the scope of a similar definition of 'consumer'. There, the *Financial Services Handbook* defined a consumer as 'any natural person acting for purposes outside his trade, business or profession'. Bluefin was authorized to provide insurance broking services under the Financial Services and Markets Act 2000. L was a company director and Bluefin had acted for L in obtaining a directors' and officers' insurance policy in respect of the company. The question was whether L was a consumer for the purposes of the Handbook, and therefore entitled to complain to the Financial Ombudsman. The court held that the definition of 'consumer' required a specific finding of objective fact. The claim against L was in respect of his allegedly wrongful acts when acting as a director. The policy benefited him as an insured person in relation to his acting in the capacity of a company director. Those acts were therefore in the course of his trade, business, or profession. There had been no proper basis on which the Financial Ombudsman Service ('FOS') could have concluded that L's purposes were outside his trade, business, or profession. The fact that he made his complaint to the FOS in his personal capacity, in respect of his personal loss, was not sufficient to cause him to fall within the definition of a consumer. As a matter of precedent fact, L was not an eligible complainant and did not fall within the compulsory jurisdiction of the FOS.

In *Gruber v Bay Wa AG*,[13] the European Court of Justice was asked for a pre- 2.22 liminary ruling as to whether a contract for the supply of goods intended partly for private and partly for business use could be regarded as a consumer contract for the purposes of the Brussels Convention 1968. Article 13 of the Convention defines a 'consumer' as a person acting 'for a purpose which can be regarded as being outside his trade or profession'.

In that case, it was held that the benefit of those provisions could not be relied on 2.23 by a person who concluded a contract for a purpose that was partly concerned with his trade or profession and was therefore only partly outside it. The only exception to that general rule would be where the link between the contract and the trade or profession was so slight as to be marginal and therefore played only a negligible role in the context of the supply in respect of which the contract was concluded, when

---

[11] [2009] EWHC 291 (Ch) para. 28.
[12] [2014] EWHC 3413 (Admin).
[13] (C-464/01) [2006] QB 204.

considered in its entirety. It was for the person wishing to rely on the derogation to show that, in a contract with a dual purpose, the business use was only negligible. It was then for the court seised to decide whether the contract was intended, to a non-negligible extent, to meet the needs of the trade or profession of the person concerned or whether the business use was merely negligible. For that purpose, the national court had to take into consideration not only the content, nature, and purpose of the contract, but also the objective circumstances in which it was concluded. If the objective evidence was not sufficient to demonstrate that the supply in question had a business purpose that was more than negligible, that contract should, in principle, be regarded as a consumer contract. However, as the protective scheme under articles 13 to 15 represented a derogation, the court was also obliged in such a case to determine whether:

…the other party to the contract, acting in good faith, could reasonably have been unaware of the private purpose of the supply because the supposed consumer had in fact, by his own conduct with respect to the other party, given the latter the impression that he was acting for business purposes.[14]

2.24   In *Francesco Benincasa v Dentalkit Srl* the European Court further held that:

…in order to determine whether a person has the capacity of a consumer, a concept which must be strictly construed, reference must be made to the position of the person concerned in a particular contract, having regard to the nature and aim of that contract, and not to the subjective situation of the person concerned…the self-same person may be regarded as a consumer in relation to certain transactions and as an economic operator in relation to others.

Consequently, only contracts concluded for the purpose of satisfying an individual's own needs in terms of private consumption come under the provisions designed to protect the consumer as the party deemed to be the weaker party economically. The specific protection sought to be afforded by those provisions is unwarranted in the case of contracts for the purpose of trade or professional activity, even if that activity is only planned for the future, since the fact that an activity is in the nature of a future activity does not divest it in any way of its trade or professional character.

Accordingly, it is consistent with the wording, the spirit and the aim of the provisions concerned to consider that the specific protective rules enshrined in them apply only to contracts concluded outside and independently of any trade or professional activity or purpose, whether present or future.[15]

2.25   *Benincasa* was considered in the High Court in *Standard Bank London Limited v Apostolakis (No 1)*[16] in which a civil engineer and his wife had entered into a foreign exchange contract. Longmore J held that it was a consumer contract, although the transactions involved were substantial. The defendants were not engaged in the trade of foreign exchange trading. They were using their income in what they hoped would be a profitable manner.

---

[14] Para. 51.
[15] *Francesco Benincasa v Dentalkit Srl* (C-296/95) [1997] ETMR 447, paras 16–18.
[16] [2002] CLC 933.

Even if the individual is not a consumer for the purposes of the Act, he will still   2.26
have the protection of other rights under other Acts. Thus, if someone purchases a
work uniform that is faulty or not appropriate for use in the course of their trade
etc., they still have recourse against the seller under the Sale of Goods Act 1979 and
the Unfair Contract Terms Act 1977 ('UCTA').[17]

Consequently it is suggested that the courts will favour a restrictive interpreta-   2.27
tion of 'consumer' especially if the 'trader' would have no means of knowing of the
buyer's 'consumer' status.

If a group of consumers contract for goods, services, or digital content, they are   2.28
not left without protection. For example, if one consumer makes all the arrangements for a group to go to the theatre or on holiday, depending on the circumstances, each member of the group may be able to enforce his or her rights, or the
person who made the arrangements would have to enforce the rights on behalf
of the group.[18]

Section 2(5) of the Act excludes (for some purposes) from the definition of   2.29
consumers those acquiring second hand goods at an auction which they have the
opportunity to attend in person. This derives from the CRD (article 1(3)), and the
previous definition of 'dealing as a consumer' under the UCTA. This exclusion
applies to the goods provisions in Chapter 2 only, other than those derived from the
CRD (as the scope of the CRD is not subject to this exclusion)—its application is
set out in subsection (6) and in the relevant clauses.

A sales contract, mentioned in section 2(5), is further defined in section 5 itself   2.30
(see Chapter 3 on Goods).

3. Business

The 'business' of a 'trader' includes the activities of government departments and   2.31
local and public authorities as set out in section 2(7), which means that contracts to
supply by these bodies will be subject to the Act.

The Explanatory Notes to the Act suggest that 'business' will include not-for-profit   2.32
organizations, such as charities, 'mutuals' (which is not defined), and co-operatives,
which means that these bodies may come within the definition of a 'trader' if they
execute supply contracts with consumers. For example, if a charity shop sells t-shirts
or mugs, they would be acting as a 'trader'.

The Sale of Goods Act 1979 ('SGA') defines 'business' in section 61(1). It 'includes   2.33
a profession and the activities of any government department (including a Northern
Ireland department) or local or public authority'. This is broadly similar to the
definition in the Act, but the word 'profession' appears in the definition of 'trader'
rather than the definition of 'business'.

---

[17] For contracts between businesses, the Supply of Goods (Implied Terms) Act 1973, the Sale of Goods
Act 1979, the Supply of Goods and Services Act 1982, the Sale and Supply of Goods Act 1994, and the
Unfair Contract Terms Act 1977.
[18] Explanatory Notes, para. 36.

4. Goods

2.34   Section 2(8) sets out the key definition: 'goods'. This derives from article 2(3) of the CRD. Essentially 'goods' means anything physical which you can move ('any tangible moveable item'). Therefore, Chapter 2 of Part 1 (the Goods Chapter) does not apply to purchases of immovable property such as land or a house. However, this subsection makes it clear that the supply of water, gas, and electricity by the privatized statutory undertakers do not count as the supply of 'goods' within the meaning of the Act unless the water, gas, and electricity is put up for sale in a limited volume or set quantity. Examples of such sales contracts would be for the supply of gas cylinder, a bottle of water, or a battery. Section 3 contains further provision on the scope of the contracts for goods covered by the Act.

2.35   During the passage of the Bill, the Minister, Jenny Willott, stated:

"Goods" means any tangible, moveable items; water, gas, and electricity are included only if they are supplied in a limited volume or a set amount. That definition is consistent with those in the regulations that implement the consumer rights directive. We also want to be clear that a set amount of such commodities more obviously constitutes goods than larger or unlimited amounts supplied as part of an ongoing service of providing utilities.[19]

2.36   Under the SGA, 'goods' include all personal chattels other than things in action and money. This includes emblements,[20] industrial growing crops, and things attached to or forming part of the land which are agreed to be severed before sale or under the contract of sale; and includes an undivided share in goods.

5. Digital Content

2.37   The definition of digital content in section 2(9) is the same as the definition in article 2(11) of the CRD, namely, 'data which are produced and supplied in digital form', and the definition in the Consumer Contracts (Information, Cancellation and Additional Charges) Regulations 2013 (SI 2013/3134). This broad definition was presumably designed to 'future-proof' the Act against inevitable technological changes. It must be read in conjunction with recital (19) in the preamble to the CRD. Data includes computer programs and software: the recital gives helpful, non-exhaustive examples of such content: computer programs, applications, videos, games, texts, or music. This data will be digital content no matter how it is accessed. It also states that content supplied on a tangible medium such as a CD should be considered as goods with the meaning of the CRD.

2.38   However, where digital content is not supplied on a tangible medium, then the relevant contract for such content is not to be classified as a sales or a service contract. This means that ownership does not have to pass and as such a 'licence' to use

---

[19] House of Commons Public Bill Committee 13 February 2014 at Col 101.
[20] Vegetable products which are the annual result of agricultural labour.

the content will be caught by the Act. The detailed rules concerning such contracts are set out in Chapter 4.

The creation of a category of digital content in the Act does not affect the treatment of digital content in any other legislation.   2.39

During debates, the Minister, Jenny Willott, said[21] that: 2.40

"Digital content" means data produced and supplied in digital form. That is important, because different rights attach to digital content compared with, for example, digital devices, which are goods and may include some digital content. Overall, the definitions are consistent with those used in the regulations that implement the consumer rights directive, so the legislation creates a coherent framework of consumer protection 12.

6. Services

'Services' are not defined in section 2 and the only assistance in the Act is in section 48(2), which states that the Act does not apply to a contract of employment or apprenticeship. However, the CRD in article 3 lists a series of contracts to which the Directive does not apply: 2.41

- social services
- healthcare
- gambling
- financial services
- the creation, acquisition, or transfer of immovable property or of rights in immovable property
- the construction of new buildings or substantial conversions
- package travel, package holidays, and package tours
- timeshare, long-term holiday product, resale, and exchange contracts which, in accordance with the laws of Member States, are established by a public office-holder who has a statutory obligation to be independent and impartial and who must ensure, by providing comprehensive legal information, that the consumer only concludes the contract on the basis of careful legal consideration and with knowledge of its legal scope
- food and drink supplied to homes by rounds-men
- passenger transport services (with certain exceptions) concluded with telecommunications operators through public payphones for their use or concluded for the use of one single connection by telephone, internet, or fax established by a consumer.

The courts will undoubtedly have due regard to that article when construing the ambit of the Act.   2.42

---

[21] Hansard House of Commons Public Bill Committee 13 Febuary 2014 at Col 101.

3

GOODS

A. OVERVIEW

1. Background

The background to the provisions about goods is summarized in the Explanatory Notes.[1]   **3.01**

Initially it was the courts that recognised that a person buying goods has certain clear and justified, but sometimes unspoken, expectations. The courts developed a body of case law which gave buyers rights when these expectations were not met. This case law was then made into legislation that protected buyers when buying goods…The EU has also legislated to protect consumers and so the UK legislation has been amended to incorporate this European legislation; sometimes this has been implemented in domestic law without resolving inconsistencies or overlaps.

The antecedent legislation provided that goods had to meet certain standards, and that   **3.02** the trader must have had the right to sell (or hire) the goods. These standards, such as being of satisfactory quality, or corresponding to their description, were treated as 'implied terms' of the contract, and were categorized as either 'conditions' of the contract or 'warranties'. Where there was a breach of an implied term that was a condition, the consumer could choose either to treat the contract as terminated, or to continue with the contract but claim damages. Most statutory implied terms were categorized as conditions.

Implied terms regarding goods being free from third parties' rights were categorized   **3.03** as 'warranties'. Where there was a breach of a warranty, the consumer may have had a claim for damages.

The antecedent legislation also provided for particular statutory remedies, such as   **3.04** repair or replacement, where certain implied terms were breached in contracts other than for hire or hire purchase. This regime has long been criticized as overly complex and inaccessible.[2]

The Davidson Report (HM Treasury, 2006) examined the transposition of   **3.05** European Directives into domestic law, and concluded that UK law on the sale

---

[1] Explanatory Notes paras 6 and 7.
[2] See, in particular, 2009 Law Commission and Scottish Law Commission, 'Consumer Remedies for Faulty Goods'; 2010 Department for Business, Innovation and Skills ('BIS'), 'Consolidation and Simplification of UK Consumer Law', 2012 BIS Consultation,

of goods was unnecessarily complex.[3] There were several consultations and reports considering how the law on goods could be clarified and simplified.

3.06   The Consumer Rights Act 2015 ('CRA') implements parts of the Consumer Rights Directive (2011/83/EU) ('CRD'), including the following provisions (that relate to goods):

- For all contracts where a trader provides goods, services, or digital content to a consumer, the trader must provide certain information, for example on the main characteristics of the goods, before the consumer is bound by the contract;

- Specific consumer cancellation rights (the 'cooling off periods') concluded at a distance or off premises.

2. Changes to Existing Legislation

3.07   The following table from the Explanatory Notes (Table 3.1) also sets out how the provisions in the existing legislation which cover trader-to-consumer contracts only will be repealed.[4]

Table 3.1 Changes to existing legislation

Supply of Goods (Implied Terms) Act 1973	Replaced by provisions in the Act.
Sale of Goods Act 1979	For business-to-consumer contracts this is mainly replaced by the Act, but some provisions still apply, for example, rules which apply to all contracts of sale of goods (essentially, sales of goods for money), regarding matters such as when property in goods passes. This still applies to business-to-business contracts.
Supply of Goods and Services Act 1982	For business-to-consumer contracts, this is replaced by the Act. It is amended so that it covers business-to-business contracts only.
Sale and Supply of Goods Act 1994	Replaced by provisions in the Act.
Sale and Supply of Goods to Consumers Regulations 2002	Replaced by provisions in the Act.

B. CHAPTER 2

1. Summary of Changes

3.08   Chapter 2 sets out the rights of a consumer when a trader supplies goods under contract. These are in effect contractual rights; if they are breached, there has been a breach of contract.

---

[3] See Explanatory Notes para. 17.
[4] See Explanatory Notes para. 24.

There are the following statutory remedies: 3.09

- A right to reject the goods within an initial period;
- A right to repair or replacement, and a subsequent right to a reduction in the price (keeping the goods);
- A right to reject the goods for a refund (subject to deduction for use in some cases).

The trader cannot limit or exclude liability for breaches of the above rights in   3.10
most cases.

There is clarification that the statutory remedies do not prevent the consumer   3.11
claiming other remedies from the trader where they are available according to general contract law. For example, the new statutory remedies do not prevent claims for damages, specific performance, or to treat the contract as at an end.

Section 2(8) makes it plain that 'goods' means any tangible moveable items, but   3.12
that includes water, gas, and electricity if and only if they are put up for supply in a limited volume or set quantity.[5] Therefore, the Act does not apply to purchases of immovable property, such as land. Certain utilities *are* included: for example a gas cylinder, a bottle of water, or a battery.

Under section 61(1) of the Sale of Goods Act 1979 ('SGA'), goods included 'all   3.13
personal chattels other than things in action and money'. 'Personal chattels' means any things that are not real property; i.e. a leasehold interest in land or other similar real property rights. However, personal chattels must also be tangible, and not merely choses in action. This excludes, for example, intellectual property rights in patents, trademarks, copyrightable material, and securities and debts.

In *Re Sugar Properties (Derisley Wood) Ltd* (1987) 3 BCC 88, divided shares in   3.14
two stallions were considered to be choses in action and not goods or personal chattels for the purposes of the Bills of Sale Acts. *Benjamin's Sale of Goods* opines that: 'There is no reason why this ruling should not be regarded as still authoritative in that context'.[6]

C. WHAT GOODS CONTRACTS ARE COVERED?

1. Section 3

Section 3(1): This chapter applies to a contract for a trader to supply goods to a   3.15
consumer—'a contract to supply goods' (section 3(4))—if it is:

- A sales contract;
- A contract for the hire of goods;

---

[5] See, in particular, the Explanatory Notes at para. 38.
[6] See Michael G. Bridge (ed.), *Benjamin's Sale of Goods* (London: Sweet and Maxwell, 2014, 9th edn) para. 1–081.

- A hire-purchase agreement;
- A contract for transfer of goods (section 3(2)).

3.16   Section 3(5): Contracts to supply goods include:

- Contracts entered into between one part owner and another;
- Contracts for the transfer of an undivided share in goods;
- Contracts that are absolute and contracts that are conditional.

3.17   This includes mixed contracts (section 3(7)).

3.18   Chapter 2 applies in most cases where a trader supplies (or agrees to supply) goods to a consumer under a 'contract for the supply of goods'. It does not apply to certain specified contracts.[7] For example, a contract for a trader to supply coins or notes to a consumer for use as currency is not a 'contract for the sale of goods',[8] although coins and notes supplied, for example, to a collector, are captured by Chapter 2. Also excluded are items sold by execution or authority of law[9] which removes from the scope of Chapter 2 goods sold, for example, by an official authorized to sell off the property of a bankrupt. This echoes the CRD[10] and the Consumer Sales Directive (1999/44/EC) ('CSD').[11]

3.19   A contract intended to act as a mortgage, or other security, is excluded from Chapter 2 (section 3(3)(c)), as is a contract not supported by consideration other than being executed as a deed (section 3(3)(d)).

3.20   See further section 3(5): Contracts for the supply of goods fall within the scope of Chapter 2 if they involve the transfer of a share in the goods, whether between current part-owners, or one current owner and a third party.

2. Ownership of Goods

3.21   In this chapter, ownership of goods means the general property in goods, not merely a special property. For the time when ownership of goods is transferred, see in particular the following provisions of the SGA (which relate to contracts of sale (Table 3.2)):

Table 3.2 Ownership of goods

Section 16	Goods must be ascertained
Section 17	Property passes when intended to pass
Section 18	Rules for ascertaining intention
Section 19	Reservation of right of disposal
Section 20A	Undivided shares in goods forming part of bulk
Section 20B	Deemed consent by owner to dealings in bulk goods.

---

[7] s. 3(3).
[8] s. 3(3)(a).
[9] s. 3(3)(b).
[10] art. 2(3).
[11] art. 12(b).

The effect of this provision is to preserve the case law relating to these sections 3.22 in the SGA.

Section 16 provides: 'Goods must be ascertained. Subject to section 20A below 3.23 where there is a contract for the sale of unascertained goods no property in the goods is transferred to the buyer unless and until the goods are ascertained.' The SGA does not define 'ascertained goods'. In *Re Wait* [1927] 1 Ch. 606 at 630, Lord Atkin said that '"Ascertained" probably means identified in accordance with the agreement after the time a contract of sale is made, and I shall assume that to be the meaning.'

Section 17 provides that: 3.24

17.— Property passes when intended to pass.
  (1) Where there is a contract for the sale of specific or ascertained goods the property in them is transferred to the buyer at such time as the parties to the contract intend it to be transferred.
  (2) For the purpose of ascertaining the intention of the parties regard shall be had to the terms of the contract, the conduct of the parties and the circumstances of the case.

The five rules for ascertaining this intention are set out in section 18, in some 3.25 detail. All can be overridden by a different intention if such is expressed by the parties. They are examined in specialist textbooks on the subject.[12]

Section 19 contains a reservation of right of disposal: 3.26

(1) Where there is a contract for the sale of specific goods or where goods are subsequently appropriated to the contract, the seller may, by the terms of the contract or appropriation, reserve the right of disposal of the goods until certain conditions are fulfilled; and in such a case, notwithstanding the delivery of the goods to the buyer, or to a carrier or other bailee or custodier for the purpose of transmission to the buyer, the property in the goods does not pass to the buyer until the conditions imposed by the seller are fulfilled.
(2) Where goods are shipped, and by the bill of lading the goods are deliverable to the order of the seller or his agent, the seller is prima facie to be taken to reserve the right of disposal.
(3) Where the seller of goods draws on the buyer for the price, and transmits the bill of exchange and bill of lading to the buyer together to secure acceptance or payment of the bill of exchange, the buyer is bound to return the bill of lading if he does not honour the bill of exchange, and if he wrongfully retains the bill of lading the property in the goods does not pass to him.

Reservation has the effect that the seller retains both legal and the equitable title 3.27 to the goods. However, it would appear, by virtue of section17, that the effect of section 19 can be negated in whole or in part if the parties so agree in the instrument.

A common reservation is that the price be paid before property passes as a matter 3.28 of law. As in all contractual matters, the question of intention to make a reservation is to be determined from all the circumstances, including the behaviour of

---

[12] See, e.g., *Benjamin's Sale of Goods*, paras 5–016 onwards; and H. Beale (ed.), *Chitty on Contracts* (London: Sweet and Maxwell, 2014, 31st edn) paras 43–171 onwards.

the parties and the terms of the instrument. It need not be an express reservation within the document itself.

3.29   By section 19(1), the seller can override the presumption in section 18 rule 5(2). Delivery is thereby not deemed to be an unconditional appropriation of the goods to the contract.

3.30   Section 20 deals with the passing of risk:

(1)   Unless otherwise agreed, the goods remain at the seller's risk until the property in them is transferred to the buyer, but when the property in them is transferred to the buyer the goods are at the buyer's risk whether delivery has been made or not.

(2)   But where delivery has been delayed through the fault of either buyer or seller the goods are at the risk of the party at fault as regards any loss which might not have occurred but for such fault.

(3)   Nothing in this section affects the duties or liabilities of either seller or buyer as a bailee or custodier of the goods of the other party.

(4)   In a case where the buyer deals as consumer…subsections (1) to (3) above must be ignored and the goods remain at the seller's risk until they are delivered to the consumer.

3.31   By virtue of subsection (4), the general rule that risk passes with property does not apply where the buyer is a consumer.

3.32   Sections 20A and 20B deal with bulk goods and divided shares in such goods. Section 20A provides an exception to the rule in section 16 that property cannot pass in unascertained goods:

(1)   This section applies to a contract for the sale of a specified quantity of unascertained goods if the following conditions are met—

(a)   the goods or some of them form part of a bulk which is identified either in the contract or by subsequent agreement between the parties; and

(b)   the buyer has paid the price for some or all of the goods which are the subject of the contract and which form part of the bulk.

(2)   Where this section applies, then (unless the parties agree otherwise), as soon as the conditions specified in paragraphs (a) and (b) of subsection (1) above are met or at such later time as the parties may agree—

(a)   property in an undivided share in the bulk is transferred to the buyer, and

(b)   the buyer becomes an owner in common of the bulk.…

3.   Sales Contracts

3.33   The definition of sale contract[13] derives from the CRD. Under a sales contract, a trader transfers (or agrees to transfer) ownership of goods to the consumer, and the consumer pays (or agrees to pay) the price (section 5). This means that for a contract to be a sales contract, the goods must have a monetary price.

---

[13]   s. 5.

4. Contracts for the Hire of Goods

Under a contract for the hire of goods,[14] the trader gives (or agrees to give) the 3.34
consumer possession of the goods with the right to use them, subject to the terms
of the contract, for a period determined in accordance with the contract. This is
consistent with the definition under sections 6 and 11G of the Supply of Goods and
Services Act 1982 ('SGSA') (save that it applies only to trader-consumer contracts).

5. Hire-Purchase Agreements

A contract is a hire-purchase agreement[15] if, under the contract, goods are hired by 3.35
the trader in return for periodical payments by the consumer.

Ownership of the goods will transfer to the consumer if the terms of the contract 3.36
are complied with, and:

(1) The consumer exercises an option to buy the goods;

(2) Any party to the contract does a specified act; or

(3) A specified event occurs.

This is consistent with the definitions in section 189 Consumer Credit Act 1974 3.37
and section 15 Supply of Goods (Implied Terms) Act 1973 ('SGITA') (save that it
applies only to trader-consumer contracts). A hire-purchase agreement is an agreement for the bailment of goods for hire with an option to purchase. This is explicitly
not a contract for the sale of goods and as such has never been of the type that falls
under the SGA.

6. Contracts for the Transfer of Goods

Under a contract for transfer of goods,[16] the trader transfers ownership of the 3.38
goods to the consumer, but there is no monetary value assigned to the goods. The
consumer provides (or agrees to provide) some consideration other than by paying
a monetary price. This is a narrower category than 'transfer' under section 1 SGSA.

D. WHAT STATUTORY RIGHTS ARE THERE UNDER A GOODS CONTRACT?

1. Goods to be of Satisfactory Quality

Sections 9 to 18 set out the requirements that the goods supplied, or the trader, 3.39
must meet. Some sections specify that the contracts are to be treated as containing

---

[14] s. 6.

[15] s. 7.

[16] s. 8.

terms that the requirements will be met (for example, the requirement that the goods are of satisfactory quality).[17] These requirements must be met even if neither party refers to them in the contract.

3.40   Goods provided under a contract for the supply of goods (section 3) must be of satisfactory quality. This means the goods must meet the standard that a reasonable person would consider satisfactory, taking account of:

- The description of the goods;
- The price or other consideration for the goods (if relevant—so that a lower standard might be expected of cheap or disposable goods); and
- All the other relevant circumstances.

3.41   'All the other relevant circumstances' includes 'any public statement about the specific characteristics of the goods made by the trader, the producer or any representative of the trader or the producer';[18] in particular, any public statement made in advertising or labelling.[19] However, such statements are not to be considered as relevant if the trader was not, and could not reasonably have been expected to be, aware of the statement, or if the statement was withdrawn or corrected before the contract was made.[20] The statement will also not be relevant if it could not have influenced the consumer's decision to contract for the goods.[21]

3.42   Section 9(3) gives a non-exhaustive list of aspects that may be relevant when considering whether the goods are satisfactory:

- Fitness for all the purposes for which goods of that kind are usually supplied;
- Appearance and finish;
- Freedom from minor defects;
- Safety;
- Durability.

3.43   This corresponds to section 14 SGA, section 10 SGITA, and sections 4, 9, 11D, and 11J SGSA, insofar as they relate to satisfactory quality in trader-consumer contracts.

3.44   The quality of the goods may be treated as included as a matter of custom (section 9(8)).

3.45   Specifically excluded from this term to be read into the contract is anything which makes the quality unsatisfactory which:

- Is specifically drawn to the consumer's attention before the contract is made;

---

[17] s. 9.
[18] s. 9(5).
[19] s. 9(6).
[20] s. 9(7).
[21] s. 9(7)(c).

- Examination ought to reveal, where the consumer has examined the goods before the contract is made; and
- Would have been apparent on a reasonable examination of the sample (under a contract to supply goods by sample—even if the consumer did not actually examine the sample).

Sections 9, 10, 13, 14, and 15 re-transpose article 2 CSD regarding conform- 3.46
ity of goods with the contract, previously found in the Sale and Supply of Goods
to Consumers Regulations 2002 (SI 2002/3045) which amended the SGA and
the SGSA.

2. Goods to be Fit for Particular Purpose

Goods must be fit for a particular purpose if the consumer contracts for these 3.47
goods for a specific purpose.[22] The consumer must make this purpose known to
the trader prior to the contract being made, though this can be done expressly or
by implication. It does not matter whether that purpose is one for which the goods
are usually supplied.

Section 3(3) does not apply if the circumstances show that the consumer does 3.48
not rely, or it would be unreasonable for the consumer to rely, on the skill or judgment of the trader (or credit broker).

This corresponds to section 14(3) SGA, section 10(3) SGITA, and sections 3.49
4(4)–(6), 9(4)–(6), 11D(5)–(7), and 11J(5)–(7) SGSA, insofar as they apply to
trader-consumer contracts.

Section 10(2) extends the 10(3) requirement to transactions in which the con- 3.50
sumer makes the purpose known to a credit broker, but contracts with another
party. There is no additional obligation on the consumer to make the purpose
known to the credit provider.

Sections 9 and 10 adopt several principles from section 14 SGA. 'Satisfactory 3.51
quality' is a phrase found in section 14(2) SGA. Fitness for purpose is also dealt
with in that section, which provides, in part:

14.— Implied terms about quality or fitness.

(1) Except as provided by this section and section 15 below and subject to any other enact-
     ment, there is no implied term about the quality or fitness for any particular purpose of
     goods supplied under a contract of sale.
(2) Where the seller sells goods in the course of a business, there is an implied term that the
     goods supplied under the contract are of satisfactory quality.
(2A) For the purposes of this Act, goods are of satisfactory quality if they meet the standard
     that a reasonable person would regard as satisfactory, taking account of any description of
     the goods, the price (if relevant) and all the other relevant circumstances.

---

[22] s. 10(3).

31

(2B) For the purposes of this Act, the quality of goods includes their state and condition and the following (among others) are in appropriate cases aspects of the quality of goods—
  (a) fitness for all the purposes for which goods of the kind in question are commonly supplied,
  (b) appearance and finish,
  (c) freedom from minor defects,
  (d) safety, and
  (e) durability.

(2C) The term implied by subsection (2) above does not extend to any matter making the quality of goods unsatisfactory—
  (a) which is specifically drawn to the buyer's attention before the contract is made,
  (b) where the buyer examines the goods before the contract is made, which that examination ought to reveal, or
  (c) in the case of a contract for sale by sample, which would have been apparent on a reasonable examination of the sample.

(2E) A public statement is not by virtue of subsection (2D) above a relevant circumstance for the purposes of subsection (2A) above in the case of a contract of sale, if the seller shows that—
  (a) at the time the contract was made, he was not, and could not reasonably have been, aware of the statement,
  (b) before the contract was made, the statement had been withdrawn in public or, to the extent that it contained anything which was incorrect or misleading, it had been corrected in public, or
  (c) the decision to buy the goods could not have been influenced by the statement. . . .

(3) Where the seller sells goods in the course of a business and the buyer, expressly or by implication, makes known—
  (a) to the seller, or
  (b) where the purchase price or part of it is payable by instalments and the goods were previously sold by a credit-broker to the seller, to that credit-broker, any particular purpose for which the goods are being bought, there is an implied term that the goods supplied under the contract are reasonably fit for that purpose, whether or not that is a purpose for which such goods are commonly supplied, except where the circumstances show that the buyer does not rely, or that it is unreasonable for him to rely, on the skill or judgment of the seller or credit-broker. . .

3.52   The interpretation of section 14 SGA has been the subject of much case law over the years. The principle is a well-established one and is a matter of fact to be determined in the circumstances of the case.

3.53   Where the goods are capable of use for a number or range of purposes, liability will depend upon whether the parties specified a special purpose within that range. If so, the suitability must be for that purpose. In the absence of such specification, it must be suitable for any purpose reasonably foreseeable.

3.54   Even if the buyer has had an opportunity to examine the goods before purchase, this does not mean that the warranty does not exist. In *Henry Kendall & Sons v William Lillico Ltd* [1969] 2 AC 31, the buyer was able to rely on the seller's skill and judgment even though the buyer himself had a degree of expertise in the same industry. However, the provision does not apply where the seller can rebut the buyer's claim of reliance, or (as section 14(3) provides), 'where the circumstances show that the buyer does not rely, or that it is unreasonable for him to rely, on the seller's skill or judgment'.

If no 'particular purpose' is indicated by the buyer, it has been held that the goods must be suitable for their usual purpose. In *Preist v Last* [1903] 2 KB 148, the buyer of a hot-water bottle successfully sued because it later burst. The seller sought to argue that the predecessor to section 14 would not apply because the buyer had not specified the particular purpose for which he required it. The court said, at 152–3:   3.55

[T]he judge has inferred that the article was bought by the plaintiff, and sold by the defendant, for the specific purpose of being used as a hot-water bottle. The argument addressed to us with reference to the terms of s. 14, sub-s. 1, of the Sale of Goods Act, 1893, was that, the sub-section requiring that the particular purpose for which the article is purchased should be made known to the seller, this can only be done by something beyond what is contained in the recognised description of the article itself.... The argument appears to be that the purpose for which this article was sold was merely the ordinary purpose of use as a hot-water bottle, and, that being its ordinary purpose, the case is not brought within the words "makes known to the seller the particular purpose for which the goods are required". I do not think that this contention is sound.... There are many goods which have in themselves no special or peculiar efficacy for any one particular purpose, but are capable of general use for a multitude of purposes. In the case of a purchase of goods of that kind, in order to give rise to the implication of a warranty, it is necessary to shew that, though the article sold was capable of general use for many purposes, in the particular case it was sold with reference to a particular purpose. But in a case where the discussion begins with the fact that the description of the goods, by which they were sold, points to one particular purpose only, it seems to me that the first requirement of the sub-section is satisfied, namely, that the particular purpose for which the goods are required should be made known to the seller. The fact that, by the very terms of the sale itself, the article sold purports to be for use for a particular purpose cannot possibly exclude the case from the rule that, *where goods are sold for a particular purpose, there is an implied warranty that they are reasonably fit for that purpose* (emphasis added).

3. Goods to be as Described

Every contract to supply goods by description is to be treated as including a term that the goods will match the description.[23] Goods may be supplied by description even if they are available for the consumer to inspect and select, for example on a shop shelf (section 11(3)).   3.56

This corresponds to section 13 SGA, section 9 SGITA, and sections 3, 8, 11C, and 11I SGSA, insofar as they relate to trader-consumer contracts.   3.57

If the supply is by sample and description, the bulk of the goods must match both the sample and the description (section 11(2)).   3.58

---

[23] s. 11.

3.59 Section 11(4), (5): Certain information relating to the main characteristics of goods required by articles 5.1(a) and 6.1(a) CRD provided by the trader forms part of the contract, and any change to that information will not be effective unless expressly agreed between the trader and consumer.

4. Other Pre-Contract Information Included in Contract

3.60 Where information is provided to the consumer pursuant to the Consumer Contracts (Information, Cancellation and Additional Charges) Regulations 2013, regulations 9, 10, or 13, that information is to be treated as included as a term of the contract to supply goods.[24] (This captures the information to be provided under articles 5.1 and 6.1 CRD other than that relating to the main characteristics of the goods, which falls under section 11 above.) As above, any change to this information is not effective unless expressly agreed between the trader and consumer.

5. Goods to Match a Sample

3.61 If a consumer enters into a contract with a trader to supply goods by reference to a sample of the goods, the final goods must match the sample.[25] Deviation is permitted insofar as it is brought to the consumer's attention before the contract is made (section 13(2)(a)). The goods must be free from any defect that makes their quality unsatisfactory and that would not be apparent on a reasonable examination of the sample (section 13(2)(b)).

3.62 This differs from section 14 (Goods to Match a Model Seen or Examined), as a sample is usually only a representative part of the whole goods. The example given in the Explanatory Notes is to a consumer buying curtains after having seen a swatch of the material.[26]

3.63 This corresponds to section 15 SGA, section 11 SGITA, and sections 5, 10, 11E, and 11K SGSA (insofar as they relate to trader-consumer contracts).

6. Goods to Match a Model Seen or Examined

3.64 Every contract to supply goods by reference to a model of the goods seen or examined by the consumer before entering into the contract is to be treated as including a term that the goods will match the model.[27] Deviation is permitted where that is brought to the consumer's attention prior to entering into the contract.

3.65 The example given in the Explanatory Notes is: a consumer views a television in a shop, but receives a boxed television from the stockroom. The model received

---

[24] s. 12.
[25] s. 13.
[26] Explanatory Notes para. 74.
[27] s. 14.

must match the model that was viewed (subject to the consumer being informed of any differences).[28]

7. Installation as Part of Conformity of the Goods with the Contract

Goods do not conform to a contract to supply goods if.[29]   3.66

- Installation of the goods forms part of the contract;
- The goods are installed by the trader or under the trader's responsibility; and
- The goods are installed incorrectly.

8. Goods Not Conforming to Contract if Digital Content Does Not Conform

Where goods include digital content, and that digital content does not conform to   3.67
the contract, the goods are to be taken to not conform to the contract.[30]

This applies irrespective of the nature of the relationship between the digital   3.68
content and the rest of the goods.

9. Trader to Have the Right to Supply the Goods

Every contract to supply goods is to be treated as including a term that the trader   3.69
must have the right to sell or transfer the goods at the time the sale, transfer, or hire
takes place.[31] (This section corresponds to section 12 SGA, section 8 SGITA, and
sections 2, 7, 11B, and 11H SGSA.)

Such contracts are to be treated as including the term that the goods are free   3.70
from any charge or encumbrance not disclosed to the consumer, and will remain so
until ownership is transferred.

For hire contracts, the consumer is entitled to enjoy quiet possession of the goods   3.71
for the period of hire agreed. The consumer's use may only be interrupted by the
owner, or third party, if the consumer was informed of that person's rights before
entering into the contract (section 17(3)).

This term will not be read into a contract if the contract, or the circumstances   3.72
when the contract was entered into, imply that the trader and consumer intended
that only limited title would be transferred. However, the contract will be treated
as including a term that the trader must disclose to the consumer all charges or
encumbrances known to him, but not known to the consumer, before entering into
the contract (section 17(4), (5)). This does not affect the trader's rights to repossess
the goods as provided for in the contract (section 17(8)).

---

[28] Explanatory Notes para. 77.
[29] s. 15.
[30] s. 16.
[31] s. 17.

3.73   Under the equivalent provision in section 12 SGA, the seller's liability if he does not have title is strict liability. It does not matter whether he knew of the lack of title or whether it was due to his error. Where the seller does not have title, the buyer may reject the goods under the contract or, if he has already purchased them, he may reclaim the price he paid. He is naturally entitled to damages in any event.

3.74   In *Niblett v Confectioners' Materials Co Ltd* [1921] 3 KB 387 the claimants purchased condensed milk in tins from a firm which dealt in confectioners' materials. The price included insurance and freight from New York to London. Payment was to be made in cash on receipt of the shipping documents. The buyers received the documents and paid the price. However, the goods arrived bearing the name 'Nissly', which constituted an infringement of a registered trade mark. The goods were detained by customs officials and the buyers were obliged to remove the name in order to get possession of the goods and could only sell them at a loss without any distinctive mark. The court held that the defendants did not have a right to sell the goods at the time when the property was to pass.

3.75   Scrutton LJ said: 'The defendants impliedly warranted that they had then a right to sell them. In fact they could have been restrained by injunction from selling them, because they were infringing the rights of third persons. If a vendor can be stopped by process of law from selling he has not the right to sell'.[32]

3.76   The goods were at the time subject to an intervention by a third party who had the power to stop the sale entirely.

10. No Other Requirement to Treat Term about Quality of Fitness as Included

3.77   Unless there is an express term concerning the quality of the goods, or their fitness for a particular purpose, the contract should not be treated as including any term except those expressly included in the contract, and those set out in sections 9, 10, 13, and 16 (goods to be of satisfactory quality, fit for particular purpose, to match a sample, and where digital content does not conform to contract).[33] This corresponds to section 14(1) SGA in relation to trader-consumer contracts.

E. WHAT REMEDIES ARE THERE IF STATUORY RIGHTS UNDER A GOODS CONTRACT ARE NOT MET?

1. Consumer's Rights to Enforce Terms about Goods

3.78   Sections 19–26 set out the remedies that apply if the consumer's statutory rights above are not met.[34] Sections 19, 24, and 25 re-transpose article 3 CSD, originally

---

[32] At p. 398.
[33] s. 18.
[34] s. 19.

transposed by the Sale and Supply of Goods to Consumers Regulations 2002, which amended the SGA and the SGSA.

Under section 19, depending on the statutory right breached, the consumer 3.79 may have:

• A short-term right to reject;

• A right to replacement or repair, or if this is not possible, or does not remedy the fault;

• A right to have the purchase price reduced (and keep the goods); or

• A final right to reject the goods.

Goods must conform to requirements stated in the contract, and to requirements 3.80 read into the contract under sections 9 to 16.

Section 19(2): There is a general exception where 'it has its origin in material sup- 3.81 plied by the consumer', i.e. the rights to which section 19(1) gives rise will not be available where the goods' failure to conform to the contract stems from a failure of materials supplied by the consumer.

The section is similar to section 48F SGA. That section dealt with 'conformity 3.82 with the contract', and specified that 'For the purposes of this Part, goods do not conform to a contract of sale if there is, in relation to the goods, a breach of an express term of the contract or a term implied by section 13, 14 or 15 above'. The CRD contains more detailed provisions on conformity.

Under section 19(1), the bases for non-conformity give rise to the following rem- 3.83 edies (see Table 3.3: references to numbers in brackets are to section numbers):

Table 3.3 Remedies

Non-conformity	Remedy
Goods to be of satisfactory quality (9)	Short-term right to reject (20–22) Right to repair or replacement (23) Right to a price reduction or the final right to reject (20, 24)
Goods to be fit for particular purpose (10)	Short-term right to reject (20–22) Right to repair or replacement (23) Right to a price reduction or the final right to reject (20, 24)
Goods to be as described (11)	Short-term right to reject (20–22) Right to repair or replacement (23) Right to a price reduction or the final right to reject (20, 24)
Goods to match a sample (13)	Short-term right to reject (20–22) Right to repair or replacement (23) Right to a price reduction or the final right to reject (20, 24)

(Continued)

Table 3.3 (*Continued*)

Non-conformity	Remedy
Goods to match a model seen or examined (14)	Short-term right to reject (20–22) Right to repair or replacement (23) Right to a price reduction or the final right to reject (20, 24)
Goods with digital content (16)	Short-term right to reject (20–22) Right to repair or replacement (23) Right to a price reduction or the final right to reject (20, 24)
Installation as part of conformity with the contract (15), or breach of requirements stated in the contract	Right to repair or replacement (23) Right to a price reduction or the final right to reject (20, 24)
Other pre-contract information included in the contract (12)	Right to recover from the trader the amount of any costs incurred by the consumer as a result of the breach, up to the amount of the price paid, or the value of other consideration given for the goods (19(5))
Right to supply the goods, etc. (17)	Right to reject (20, 24)

2. Table of Remedies

3.84   The availability of these remedies is subject to particular rules for delivery of the wrong quantity (section 25) or instalment deliveries (section 26). Section 28 deals with remedies for breach of a term relating to the delivery of goods.

3.85   Nothing in Chapter 2 of the Act prevents the consumer from seeking other remedies, such as specific performance, or for breach of contract, including breach of a term read into the contract under Chapter 2. However, the consumer cannot recover more than once for the same loss.

3.86   Claims for breach of contract are subject to a limitation period of six years from the date of the breach in England and Wales. The consumer therefore has six years to pursue a claim for a breach of one of his statutory rights. However, a claim will only arise if one of the rights has been breached.

3.87   There is a useful example in the Explanatory Notes: a consumer cannot seek a remedy for a fault arising in a cheap kettle five years after it was purchased, as a reasonable person might not expect a kettle of that quality to last that long.[35]

3.88   Section 19(14): If a fault arises within six months of delivery, it is presumed to have been present at the time of delivery, unless it is established that the goods did conform to the contract on that day, or this presumption is incompatible with the nature of the goods or the particular fault. This subsection corresponds to section 48A(3) and (4) SGA and section 11M(3) and (4) SGSA.

---

[35] Explanatory Notes para. 105.

3. Right to Reject

The consumer exercises his right to reject[36] if he indicates to the trader that he is 3.89
rejecting the goods and treating the contract as at an end (section 20(5)). This indication must be clear, but there is no prescribed form.

From the time this indication is made, the trader has a duty to give the consumer 3.90
a refund (subject to subsection (18)), and the consumer has a duty to make the
goods available for collection by the trader, or return them as agreed (though the
trader must bear any reasonable costs of returning them, other than costs incurred
by the consumer in returning them in person to the place where the consumer took
physical possession of them).

If the consumer paid money for the goods under the contract, the trader must 3.91
refund the same amount of money. The trader must give the refund using the same
means of payment as used by the consumer, unless the consumer expressly agrees
otherwise (section 20(16)).

If the consumer transferred anything else under the contract, he is entitled to 3.92
receive back the same amount of what was transferred, or receive the thing in its
original state if it cannot be substituted.

There is no entitlement to receive a refund where a thing transferred under the 3.93
contract by the consumer cannot be given back in its original state (section 20(18)),
or where the thing cannot be divided so as to pay back to the consumer the part to
which he is entitled. Where there is no entitlement to receive a refund, or because
of the limits of that entitlement, the consumer may claim damages instead:

Where a toy is bought with vouchers, it would be possible to return equivalent vouchers, rather
than the actual vouchers transferred by the consumer. The trader gives the consumer a microwave in exchange for the consumer's fridge-freezer. If the fridge-freezer is still available in
an unchanged state, this could be returned as a 'refund'. Otherwise, a refund would not be
possible.[37]

If the contract is for the hire of goods, the refund due extends only to anything 3.94
paid or transferred for the period of hire that the consumer does not get because
the contract is treated as at an end (section 20(13)) i.e. the consumer cannot claim
a refund for hire that the consumer enjoyed.

If the contract is a hire-purchase agreement, or conditional sales contract, the 3.95
consumer is entitled to a refund only for the part of the price paid (section 20(14)).

A refund under section 20 must be given without undue delay, and in any event 3.96
within fourteen days of the trader agreeing that the consumer is entitled to a refund
(section 20(15)).

The right to reject has not previously been set out in such statutory detail. 3.97
However, it is clear from section 15A SGA that a breach of section 13, 14, or 15

---

[36] s. 20.
[37] Explanatory Notes para. 114.

does give the buyer the right to reject unless the buyer is not a consumer and the breach is so slight that it would be unreasonable for the buyer to reject the goods.

3.98   A valid rejection requires 'a clear notice that the goods are not accepted and at the risk of the vendor': *Graanhandel T Vink BV v European Grain & Shipping Ltd* [1989] 2 Lloyd's Rep. 531 at 533.

3.99   It has been held that a buyer must reject the goods within a reasonable time, and must not cause by any delay unnecessary prejudice to the seller: *Manifatture Tessile Laniera Wooltex v J B Ashley Ltd* [1979] 2 Lloyd's Rep. 28.

3.100   As to where the risk lies in respect of rejected goods, see *Benjamin's Sale of Goods*, 9th edn, paras 6–011: 'If goods are rightfully rejected, but the seller neglects or refuses to collect them, the buyer would appear thereafter to be an involuntary bailee, being liable only for deliberate injury to the goods or for gross negligence, but not for ordinary negligence'.

3.101   If they have been damaged or destroyed and this arises from the very defect complained of, the risk is clearly on the seller.

3.102   The buyer is not bound to return the goods to the seller (section 36 SGA) but simply needs to tell the seller that he is rejecting them. However, he cannot then exercise a lien over the goods against repayment of the price: *J L Lyons & Co Ltd v May & Baker Ltd* [1923] 1 KB 685.

3.103   The buyer can waive the right to reject, by expressing an intention not to reject and to be content with damages. This is known as an affirmation of the contract and:

seems to be based on the rule that a person must elect or choose between inconsistent rights . . . [I]f the seller's breach can be regarded as continuing, as in an instalment contract, the buyer may be able to treat this as a fresh act or acts of repudiation, unless there is some reliance on the affirmation making it inequitable to do so. Similarly, a buyer who rejects cannot thereafter insist on delivery.[38]

3.104   A waiver may be express or implied, but it requires knowledge of the breach waived. This is subject to statutory provisions whereby acts or omissions are deemed to constitute acceptance regardless of the buyer's knowledge.

3.105   It should be noted that the Act does not make provision as to the meaning or circumstances of 'acceptance', unlike in section 35 SGA.

4. Partial Rejection of Goods

3.106   The consumer may reject some or all of the goods that do not conform to the contract, but cannot reject goods that do conform (section 21(1)).

3.107   If any of the goods form a commercial unit, the consumer cannot reject only some of the goods. A unit is a 'commercial unit' if division of the unit would 'materially impair the value of the goods or the character of the unit' (section 21(4), (5)).

---

[38] *Benjamin's Sale of Goods*, 9th edn, paras 12–039.

As above, partial rejection must be indicated to the trader in a way that is clear enough to be understood.   3.108

The goods must be returned etc. as above.   3.109

The right of partial rejection was first introduced in 1994, in section 35A SGA. It has received very little attention in subsequent case law.   3.110

5. Time Limit for Short-term Right to Reject

The consumer loses his or her short-term right to reject[39] at the end of thirty days after: 3.111

- Ownership (or possession, in the case of a contract for hire, hire-purchase agreement, or conditional sales contract) has been transferred to the consumer; and
- The goods have been delivered; and
- Where the contract requires the trader to install the goods, or take some other action to enable the consumer to use them, the trader has notified the consumer that that has been done (e.g. fitting double-glazed windows).

The time limit is shorter for perishable goods, and lasts only as long as it would be reasonable to expect those goods to last (section 22(4)).   3.112

If the consumer requests or agrees to the repair or replacement of goods, the time limit pauses for the duration of the 'waiting period' (section 22(6)). The 'waiting period' starts when the consumer requests or agrees to the repair or replacement. It ends when the goods are returned to the consumer (section 22(8)). The consumer then has the remainder of the period, or seven days, whichever is longer, to exercise the short-term right to reject (section 22(7)).   3.113

6. Right to Replacement or Repair

Where the consumer has the right to repair or replacement,[40] and requires that the trader repairs or replaces the goods, the trader must: 3.114

- Do so within a reasonable time, and without significant inconvenience to the consumer; and
- Bear any necessary costs incurred in doing so.

What is a 'reasonable time' and 'significant inconvenience' is to be determined in the light of the nature of the goods and the purpose for which they were acquired (section 23(5)). The consumer must give the trader a reasonable time to repair or replace the goods unless giving the trader that time would cause the consumer significant inconvenience (section 23(6)).   3.115

---

[39] s. 22.
[40] s. 23.

3.116   The consumer cannot require the repair or replacement if that remedy is impossible. Similarly, the consumer cannot require replacement if that is disproportionate in comparison to repair, and vice versa (section 23(3)). The chosen remedy will be disproportionate in comparison to the other if it imposes comparatively unreasonable costs on the trader. Whether the cost is unreasonable will be determined taking into account:

- The value of the goods if they conformed to the contract;
- The significance of the deviation from the contract; and
- Whether the other remedy could be effected without significant inconvenience to the consumer (section 23(4)).

3.117   'Repair', in relation to goods that do not conform to a contract, means to make the goods conform to a contract (section 23(8)).

3.118   Under the similar provisions of the SGA, the election between repair and replacement belongs with the buyer. The seller has no right to demand that the remedy be either one of these in preference to the other. Note however, that the court can order that one remedy is more appropriate than another. The comparative expense to which the seller may be put is not itself a reason for finding that the buyer's demand is disproportionate within section 48B(4) SGA. The agreement to repair is itself a new transaction between the parties and arguably requires the seller to specify what repairs will be made, and how long it will take.

3.119   Replacement cannot be effected where it is simply impossible to do so, for example if the goods are second hand, unique, or hard to source, or if the reason for the non-conformity is in fact that all goods of that specification would be unsuitable for the purpose that the buyer requires.

3.120   Under the SGA, the buyer is required to co-operate with all reasonable steps to ensure that the seller can fulfil the repair or replacement demand. If the buyer suffers loss as a result of waiting for the goods to be repaired or replaced, he may claim for additional consequential losses.

3.121   The risk attaching to the goods belongs with the seller whilst the goods are being repaired or replaced.

3.122   In *J H Ritchie Ltd v Lloyd Ltd* [2007] 1 WLR 670, the House of Lords considered the question whether, although the buyer had agreed to a repair being made on the goods, he still retained the right to reject. The appellants, R, purchased agricultural machinery from L which proved to be defective. The parties agreed that L would take the equipment back with a view to investigation and possible repair. L repaired the equipment and advised R that it was ready for collection. L refused to tell R what the problem had been, despite repeated requests, stating only that it had been repaired to 'factory gate' standard. When R discovered by other means what the problem had been, they became concerned about the fact that they had operated the equipment while it had been defective, which might have affected other parts in the equipment. R were also concerned about the possible effects of the events on the manufacturer's guarantee period. Accordingly, they rejected the equipment.

The House of Lords held that section 35(6)(a) SGA impliedly included terms 3.123 governing the relationship of the parties when it was arranged that the equipment should be taken away and inspected. Thus, when L took the equipment away, the parties entered into a separate inspection and repair agreement. It must have been an implied term of that agreement that, so long as L was duly performing its obligations under it, R were not to exercise their right to rescind the contract of sale. The right to reject would be lost when a buyer decided to accept the goods or was deemed to have accepted them. That was a right of election which he could not be expected to exercise until he had the information that he needed to make an informed choice. Since L was the company that supplied the defective equipment in the first place, R were entitled to insist on being told what L had discovered. L's refusal to supply the information amounted to a material breach of the inspection and repair agreement, entitling R to rescind it and to refuse to collect the equipment. Once R had rescinded the inspection and repair agreement, there was nothing to prevent them from exercising the right to rescind the sale contract.

7. Right to Price Reduction or Final Right to Reject

The rights to a price reduction, or to reject the goods and obtain a partial refund,[41] 3.124 are generally available if repair or replacement has not been possible, or has not remedied the fault.

The right to a price reduction may be up to the full amount of the price (or thing 3.125 transferred). However, the right to a price reduction does not apply if what the consumer is required to transfer cannot be divided up as necessary, or given back in its original state. It is irrelevant whether the item to be transferred has in fact been transferred.

A consumer must choose whether to exercise his right to a price reduction, or the 3.126 final right to reject, but not both. He may exercise one of these rights only where the goods do not conform after repair or replacement, the trader failed to repair or replace the goods within a reasonable time and without significant inconvenience, or under section 23(3) the consumer cannot require repair or replacement (section 24(5)).

There has only been repair or replacement if the consumer has requested this, and the 3.127 trader has delivered the goods or made them available to the consumer (section 24(6)).

If the consumer exercises his final right to reject, any refund may be reduced to 3.128 take account of the use the consumer has had of the goods since they were delivered (section 24(8)), excluding any time when the consumer had the goods only because the trader failed to collect them as agreed (section 24(9)).

If the final right to reject is exercised within six months of delivery of the goods, 3.129 the consumer will receive a full refund, unless the goods are a motor vehicle, or as specified by the Secretary of State.

The remedy of price reduction did not exist before its statutory introduction in 3.130 the SGA in 2003. The buyer keeps the goods and affirms the contract, but the price

---

[41] s. 24.

is adjusted to reflect the correct value of the goods retained, taking into account its non-conformity. The goods must still be suitable for purpose.

3.131   Commentary on the equivalent provision in the SGA observes that:

> the remedy of price reduction will not be "appropriate" as is required by s.48E(3) if the goods are unable to perform the main function or purpose for which the buyer acquired them. In the case of defective quality, a price reduction is likely to be appropriate when the defect in the quality of the goods relates to an aspect of the goods which does not impede their use as intended by the buyer. For more serious defects in quality, the remedy of replacement or of termination (rescission) will be more appropriate.[42]

3.132   Rescission is also only available if there is no scope for repair or replacement. Again, it appears that the choice of remedy lies with the buyer. It has been observed that 'A powerful right to reject exists in any case at common law and it is not likely that the right to rescind under the [SGA] will prove particularly useful'.

3.133   Section 48C(3) SGA requires a reduction of the price to take account of any use the buyer has made of the goods prior to rescission. However, this does not apply if rescission is made at common law and not under section 48C.

F. OTHER RULES ABOUT REMEDIES

1. Delivery of Wrong Quantity

3.134   This corresponds broadly with section 30 SGA. The consumer may reject goods if the wrong quantity is delivered,[43] but he must pay the contract rate for them if the goods are accepted (section 25(1), (2)). Where the trader delivers a greater quantity of goods than agreed, the consumer may reject some or all of the goods (section 25(3)). The consumer rejects the goods by indicating that to the trader in a way that is clear enough to be understood (section 25(5), (6)).

3.135   Under section 30 SGA, the buyer does not have a right to reject where the wrong quantity is delivered 'if the shortfall or, as the case may be, excess is so slight that it would be unreasonable for him to do so'.

3.136   As for the requirement that the buyer must indicate a rejection to the seller, see *Graanhandel T Vink BV v European Grain & Shipping Ltd* [1989] 2 Lloyd's Rep. 531. The buyer paid for the goods but later rejected them on the grounds that they were contaminated and not genuine. The seller purported not to accept the rejection. Initial analysis certified that the goods were correctly described, and the buyer then sold the goods notwithstanding their earlier rejection. Further analysis then certified that the goods were not genuine, and the buyer again tried to reject them. It was held that, by reselling the goods, the buyer had 'unequivocally accepted the goods' and was not entitled to any remedy.

---

[42] See *Benjamin's Sale of Goods*, 9th edn, paras 12–093.
[43] s. 25.

2. Instalment Deliveries

This corresponds broadly to section 31 SGA. Under a contract to supply goods, the consumer is not bound to accept delivery by instalments[44] unless that has been agreed (section 26(1)). **3.137**

If the consumer does agree for the goods to be delivered by instalments, which are to be paid for separately, and one or more of the deliveries is defective, the consumer may have the right to reject the goods in a particular instalment, or in respect of the whole contract (section 26(3)). The right that applies depends on the terms of the contact and the circumstances of the case (section 26(4)). **3.138**

Conversely, the trader may be entitled to treat the whole contract as at an end, or have a claim for damages if it is a severable breach, if the consumer neglects or refuses to take delivery of, or pay for, one or more instalments (section 26(6)). This, too, depends on the terms of the contract and the circumstances of the case (section 26(7)). **3.139**

Section 26 specifies that a 'defective delivery' does not include failing to comply with section 28. **3.140**

The parties can agree to delivery by instalments either expressly or impliedly. For an example of an implied agreement, see *Howell v Evans* (1926) 134 LT 570. The contract there provided that thirteen engravings purchased by the buyer were 'to be sent to me as published'. This was by implication, and of necessity, an agreement to delivery in instalments. **3.141**

A contract for the delivery of goods by instalments is not a series of separate contracts. This is so even if the contract expressly provides that each delivery is to be treated as a separate contract. In *Ross T Smyth & Co Ltd v TD Bailey Son & Co* [1940] 3 All ER 60 it was said that such sections are merely 'subsidiary sections, which generally have effect upon questions of performance. There is still only one contract and one contract quantity, though, for certain purposes, particular instalments or shipments and parcels may be treated in separation from the others'. **3.142**

G. OTHER RULES ABOUT REMEDIES UNDER GOODS CONTRACTS

1. Delivery of Goods

This implements article 18 CRD. Unless the trader and consumer have agreed otherwise, any sales contract is to be treated as including a term that the trader must deliver the goods to the consumer (section 28(2)). **3.143**

Unless otherwise agreed, the trader must deliver the goods without undue delay, and in any event within thirty days after the contract is entered into. **3.144**

If the trader does not deliver the goods within thirty days, or as otherwise agreed, the consumer may specify an appropriate further period for the trader to deliver **3.145**

---

[44] s. 26.

the goods (section 28(7)). If the goods are not delivered within this period, the consumer may treat the contract as at an end section (28(8)).

3.146   Where the trader has refused to deliver the goods, and in all the circumstances delivery of the goods within the relevant period was essential, and the consumer told the trader this before the contract was entered into, the consumer may treat the contract as at an end (section 28(6)). In those circumstances, the consumer does not have to give the trader a second opportunity to deliver the goods. (Explanatory Notes examples: wedding dress, birthday cake; paragraph 153).

3.147   If the consumer treats the contract as at an end, the trader must reimburse all payments made under the contract without undue delay (section 28(9)).

3.148   If the consumer is entitled to treat the contract as at an end, but chooses not to do so, that does not prevent the consumer from cancelling the order for any of the goods, or rejecting goods that have been delivered. If the consumer takes this course, the trader must reimburse all payments made under the contract in respect of any goods cancelled or rejected without undue delay. (One exception: as above, the consumer must reject the whole of a commercial unit, or none.)

3.149   Equivalent provisions concerning delivery in the SGA also define 'delivery'. In section 61(1), 'delivery' means 'voluntary transfer of possession from one person to another'. Delivery may be actual or constructive.[45] Actual delivery is effected when possession is transferred. Constructive delivery is effected 'without any change in the actual possession of the thing delivered, as in the case of delivery by attornment (i.e. acknowledgement) or symbolic delivery'. Constructive or symbolic delivery might, for example, be represented by giving the buyer a key to a place where the goods are stored.

3.150   Non-delivery of goods results in an action for damages, although specific performance can be ordered instead.

3.151   Mere late delivery has not, in the past, been enough to constitute a sufficiently serious breach of contract to entitle the buyer to reject. By virtue of section 28, where time is of the essence in the circumstances of the contract, the breach will entitle the buyer to reject. Where time is not of the essence and goods are not delivered in time, the buyer may specify an appropriate period by which the goods should be delivered. If they are not then delivered, the buyer is able to treat the contract as at an end: see subsections (6) to (8).

2. Section 29: Passing of Risk

3.152   This section requires that a sales contract be treated as including provisions as to where risk relating to the good lies before and after transfer of physical possession to the consumer. The goods remain at the trader's risk until they come into the physical possession of the consumer, or a person identified by the consumer to take possession of the goods (section 29(2)). However, if the consumer stipulates that the trader must use a carrier of the consumer's choosing, and that carrier was not

---

[45] See *Benjamin's Sale of Goods*, 9th edn, paras 43–275.

offered by the trader, the risk transfers to the consumer at the time the goods are passed to the carrier (section 29(3), (4)).

3. Goods under Guarantee

This replaces regulation 15 of the Sale and Supply of Goods to Consumers Regulations 2002, which transposed the CSD, and regulation 15 implemented article 6 of the CSD.   3.153

Any guarantee[46] provided in relation to goods takes effect at the time the goods are delivered as a contractual obligation (section 30(3)). The guarantor must ensure that the guarantee meets certain conditions: 3.154

(a) the guarantee sets out in plain and intelligible language the contents of the guarantee and the essential particulars for making claims under the guarantee,
(b) the guarantee states that the consumer has statutory rights in relation to the goods and that those rights are not affected by the guarantee, and
(c) where the goods are offered within the territory of the United Kingdom, the guarantee is written in English.
(5) The contents of the guarantee to be set out in it include, in particular—
    (a) the name and address of the guarantor, and
    (b) the duration and territorial scope of the guarantee.

The guarantor or any other person who offers to supply to consumers goods which are the subject of the guarantee must provide the consumer with a copy of the guarantee on request within a reasonable time (section 30(6), (7)).   3.155

A 'guarantee' means an undertaking given by the guarantor in the course of his business to the consumer without extra charge. The undertaking is that, if the goods do not meet the specifications set out in the guarantee or any associated advertising, the consumer will be reimbursed for the price paid for the goods, or the goods will be repaired, replaced, or handled in any way.   3.156

If the guarantor fails to comply with one of these requirements, the enforcement authority may apply to the court for an injunction.   3.157

H. CAN A TRADER CONTRACT OUT OF RIGHTS AND REMEDIES?

1. Liability that Cannot be Excluded or Restricted

This prevents traders from contracting out of the consumer's statutory rights:[47]   3.158

(1) A term of a contract to supply goods is not binding on the consumer to the extent that it would exclude or restrict the trader's liability arising under any of these provisions—
    (a) section 9 (goods to be of satisfactory quality);

---

[46] s. 30.
[47] s. 31.

   (b) section 10 (goods to be fit for particular purpose);

   (c) section 11 (goods to be as described);

   (d) section 12 (other pre-contract information included in contract);

   (e) section 13 (goods to match a sample);

   (f) section 14 (goods to match a model seen or examined);

   (g) section 15 (installation as part of conformity of goods with contract);

   (h) section 16 (goods not conforming to contract if digital content does not conform);

   (i) section 17 (trader to have right to supply the goods etc);

   (j) section 28 (delivery of goods);

   (k) section 29 (passing of risk).

3.159   Any term of a contract to supply goods is not binding on the consumer to the extent that it seeks to prevent the consumer from having access to the statutory rights and remedies, or makes exercising those rights less attractive, either by making it more difficult and onerous to do so, or by placing the consumer at a disadvantage after doing so:

   (2) That also means that a term of a contract to supply goods is not binding on the consumer to the extent that it would—

      (a) exclude or restrict a right or remedy in respect of a liability under a provision listed in subsection (1),

      (b) make such a right or remedy or its enforcement subject to a restrictive or onerous condition,

      (c) allow a trader to put a person at a disadvantage as a result of pursuing such a right or remedy, or

      (d) exclude or restrict rules of evidence or procedure.

3.160   It is possible to contract out of the protection that the trader must have the right to transfer possession for hire contracts, though this is subject to the requirement for terms to be fair (section 63).

3.161   The new provision differs from that under section 55 SGA, whereby implied terms could be negatived or varied by the parties. This is subject to the terms of the Unfair Contract Terms Act 1977 ('UCTA'), which has a very significant effect on the parties' freedoms under section 55. Thus, section 6(1) UCTA provides that liability for breach of the obligations arising from section 12 SGA cannot be excluded or restricted by reference to any contract term. Subsections (2) and (3) prevent or otherwise limit any exclusion or restriction of liability for breach of the obligations arising from sections 13, 14, and 15 SGA.

2. Contracts Applying Law of Non-EEA State

3.162   Parties to a contract may agree that the contract is to be governed by the law of a particular country. However, where the sales contract has a close connection with the United Kingdom, certain provisions of Chapter 2 will apply regardless of that choice. Section 32 reads:

(2) The exceptions are—

    (a) sections 11(4) and (5) and 12 (information provided in accordance with Consumer Contracts (Information, Cancellation and Additional Charges) Regulations 2013);

    (b) sections 28 and 29 (Delivery of goods and passing of risk);

    (c) section 31(1)(d), (j) and (k) (Liability that cannot be excluded or restricted: sections 12, 28, and 29).

4

DIGITAL CONTENT

A. OVERVIEW

Digital goods are big business. According to the Governement Department for   4.01
Business Innovation and Skills ('BIS'), more than £1 billion was spent in 2012
on downloaded films, music, and games. The global market is said to be worth
£200 billion. Digital content as defined encompasses a diverse range of products
and services, including computer software, films, music, games apps, and e-books.
They can be accessed in a variety of ways through the internet and through physical
media. But the government has never explicitly legislated on digital content before.
The Act represents the first occasion when Parliament has sought to grapple with
legislating for digital content as a category distinct from goods and services. So
what is digital content?

The definition of digital content is set out in section 2(9) of the Act: 'Digital   4.02
content means data which are produced and supplied in digital form'.

The definition is the same as can be found in article 2(5) of the Consumer Rights   4.03
Directive[1] ('CRD'). Recital (19) in the preamble to the CRD is a little more helpful
and goes into greater detail as to the nature of digital content where it states:

Digital content means data which are produced and supplied in digital form, such as com-   4.04
puter programs, applications, games, music, videos or texts, irrespective of whether they are
accessed through downloading or streaming, from a tangible medium or through any other
means. Contracts for the supply of digital content should fall within the scope of this Directive.

See the Digital Content Business Guidance: 'The scope of the digital content   4.05
category is broad and not limited to particular means of content transmission or by
the way in which digital content is packaged or paid for'.

The policy of the government was made plain during the second reading:[2]   4.06

On digital content, because most consumer law has been in place for a long time, since long
before the advent of digital content, there is significant legal uncertainty about what rights

---

[1] Directive 2011/83/EU.
[2] Hansard House of Lords 1 July 2014, per Viscount Younger of Leckie.

apply here. This uncertainty harms consumers and business, first, because consumers do not know how to go about resolving problems with digital content and, secondly, in contrast, some consumers may think that they are entitled to a remedy that the business does not think it is obliged to provide under the current law. This situation is unacceptable in a market that is both of a substantial size—around £200 billion—and still developing.

4.07   The solution posited by the government is as follows:

We are introducing a set of quality rights tailored specifically to digital content. For example, where a trader provides an update to digital content previously supplied, this update must not lower the quality of the original digital content. If it does, the trader must provide appropriate remedies to the consumer. Note that the onus in this example is on the trader because that is the person the consumer paid for the digital content. This in turn will raise consumer confidence to try new products, because consumers will be clearer about what they are entitled to if something goes wrong. This is good for businesses, too, because it makes it easier for new firms and innovative businesses to compete successfully for a share of the market.

4.08   BIS has issued Guidance on Digital Content entitled 'Consumer Rights Act: Digital Content Guidance for Business' ('the Guidance'). The Guidance declares that for the avoidance of doubt digital content does not include online shopping or services delivered online (such as online banking). For example, the Guidance states:

Digital content is not online shopping. Online shopping is just one method by which digital content can be obtained, just as it is a method by which goods can be obtained – so a physical book bought online is not digital content, it is goods.

Digital content is not services delivered online, such as online banking or the website for online grocery shopping. In the same way as the use of a physical bank is not seen as the supply of goods, the use of an online bank is not the supply of digital content. The exception is where a consumer has separately paid for an online banking app – the app itself would be digital content.[3]

4.09   The Guidance also sets out a series of answers to hypothetical 'frequently asked questions' to enable consumers and traders alike to understand how the Act will work in practice.

4.10   What was the mischief that this part of the Act was designed to meet? The practical problem was that the existing definitions of goods under the Sale of Goods Act 1979 ('SGA') were not sufficiently broad to include 'intangible media'. That produced perverse results, such as a consumer purchasing a music CD having more protection than someone downloading the same through Itunes or similar.

4.11   The resulting uncertainty undermined consumer and business confidence. The Labour government of 2005 to 2010 recognized this difficulty in its 2009 White Paper *A Better Deal for Consumers*.[4] A commitment was made to improve the level of protection for consumers in contracts for the sale of digital content by ensuring that the core principle of consumer protection applied to such contacts.

---

[3] p. 5 of the Guidance.
[4] <https://www.gov.uk/government/uploads/system/uploads/attachment_data/file/238580/7669.pdf>.

The Coalition Government continued with that policy and commissioned 4.12
Professor Bradgate to write a report ('the Bradgate Report')[5] on how the government should legislate for digital content in light of the unsatisfactory state of the
existing law and the lack of certainty that consumers and business alike had regarding the legal rules that pertained to the sale of digital content.

The Bradgate Report contains a detailed discussion of how the existing law treats soft- 4.13
ware and digital content. It came to the conclusion, after an analysis of the leading cases,[6]
that there is a lack of clarity as to whether or not the law treats software as services or as
goods. Importantly, Bradgate noted that there was no significant body of consumer case
law as consumers were unlikely to litigate over the amounts in their contracts.

The conclusion reached was that since the policy was to increase the level of pro- 4.14
tection for consumers in the sale of digital content, the sale of goods regime should
be applied to the sale of digital content whether it is supplied online or on a tangible
medium (for example, a CD).

In reaching this conclusion, Professor Bradgate immediately recognized the diffi- 4.15
culties inherent in such an approach. Where physical goods are sold in a business-to-
consumer context, consumers ordinarily take title to the goods concerned and
physically own them. The same is not true when a consumer buys digital content
on a non-physical medium, i.e. where it is streamed or downloaded to their device,
as Professor Bradgate recognizes in paragraph 26 of his Report, where he says:

On the other hand it is probably not a sale in the strictest sense because the parties do not intend
a transfer of property in the digital content as such, but rather the grant of a non-exclusive licence
of the digital content, together with a transfer of property in any physical item supplied. However,
the correct legal analysis is probably not appreciated by the average consumer who is likely to say "I
have a copy of 'Football Manager 2010'", or "I own a recording of Beethoven's 5th on CD" rather
than "'I have a licence to run 'Football Manager 2010'" or "I own a CD with Beethoven's 5th on it".

The existing sale of goods regime therefore contains detailed provisions around 4.16
goods being fit for purpose, as described, without encumbrance on title and further
provisions around delivery etc. However, this approach does not work in the context of digital content where the consumer is not taking actual title to the content
he is buying. He is, rather, buying a contractual licence to use that digital content
for his own personal use. Consumers rarely acquire title to the content they are
purchasing. The Bradgate Report acknowledges the difficulty where it says:

The grant of the end user licence is central to the supply of a digital product. First, it is clear the
copyright holder does not transfer ownership ("property") of the software program to the end
user; the transaction is, essentially, one for the grant of a contractual licence. As the law presently
stands it is therefore not a contract for the sale of goods.[7]

---

[5] Bradgate, R. (2010) 'Consumer rights in digital products: A research report prepared for the UK
Department for Business, Innovation and Skills.'
[6] Including *International Computers Ltd v St Albans District Council* [1996] 4 All ER 481 and *Beta
Computers Europe Limted v Adobe Systems Limited* 1996 SLT 604.
[7] Bradgate, para. 90, p. 37.

4.17   However, Professor Bradgate saw no reason not to apply a sale of goods type approach to digital content, as can be seen where he says, at paragraph 28 of his Report: 'there is no existing legal constraint which would prevent the extension of the definition of "goods" to make it explicit that digital content such as computer software is goods.'

4.18   In the absence of any such constraints Professor Bradgate, throughout his Report, gravitates towards adopting the approach set out in the SGA on the basis that this will give consumers greater levels of protection when they are buying digital goods and certainty as to their rights, which they do not have in the absence of the Act. This is despite the fact that traders cannot sell what they do not have. And this is where the difficulties may occur.

4.19   A trader who is selling digital content is usually selling only a licence to use that content, and then only the licence he himself has permission to sell from the original rights holder. The original holder will have rights which are governed by and provided for by the Copyright, Designs and Patents Act 1988 ('CDPA').

4.20   By giving the consumer rights against the final retailer, there is a real danger that the Act may inadvertently cut across a wide range of existing contractual relationships. If the consumer is given statutory rights against the final retailer, it may well be the case that the trader may not be able to honour those rights if he has been unable to procure those same rights from the original copyright holder.

4.21   So, despite acknowledging some of the difficulties with this approach, the Bradgate Report makes a very clear recommendation that the SGA regime should be applied to the sale of digital products in order to give consumers a greater degree of certainty and a higher level of protection. In its summary on page 30, the Bradgate Report states:

In summary, if the government is to make good its commitment to providing purchasers of digital products with a high level of protection, equivalent to that provided to purchasers of traditional products, it must provide them with rights at least equivalent to the buyer of goods under a sale contract governed by the SGA. They must therefore have rights equivalent to those provided by sections 12 to 14 of the SGA. The potency of those sections as measures protective of the consumer derive from the fact that:

- They are classed as conditions so that any breach allows the buyer to reject the goods and demand a refund;
- They are easy to prove and establish; liability for their breach is strict; they cannot be excluded nor liability for their breach limited;
- They provide a remedy against the retailer who will generally be relatively accessible to the consumer; and
- They are familiar to and understood by consumers and retailers alike.

If consumers are to be given equivalent rights in relation to digital products, either the existing regime must stretch to accommodate digital products, or a new, parallel, no less effective regime must be established alongside the existing SGA regime.[8]

---

[8] Bradgate, p. 30.

The Act follows exactly this approach in the digital content sections. BIS has 4.22
also made it clear in numerous forums that, as they have adopted wholesale the
approach recommended by Professor Bradgate, the existing case law on the SGA
should also be applied to the new sections that deal with digital content. The Act
has therefore brought the law on the sale of digital content in line with the level of
protection offered to consumers when they buy physical goods.

B. POTENTIAL DIFFICULTIES

But as we shall see below, this approach is not without difficulty. The SGA provi-   4.23
sions around quality rights etc. were first codified into statute in the Sale of Goods
Act 1893 to reflect the position that had already been reached through numerous
common law cases decided by that time. In 1893, virtually all sales of goods, in a
business-to-consumer context, took place either face-to-face or by mail order cata-
logue. The sections were therefore drafted with those situations in mind.

But these same sections are strained when one considers the manner in which   4.24
digital content is sold to consumers online. The vast majority of these contracts
are for standard products where the consumer is buying a *licence* to use the digital
content without having any right to either re-sell it or modify it. The consumer, furthermore, has limited ability to communicate with the trader other than through
the online means that are made available. This is all very different from buying a
pound of potatoes for thruppence in the local green grocer in 1893.

The Act has defined digital content in line with the definition used in the CRD[9]   4.25
i.e. content supplied in a digital form. The advantage of such an approach is that the
law will capture *all* digital content as supplied in the future, irrespective of advances
in technology or on which platforms content is supplied.

The disadvantage is that even within this definition there are several very impor-   4.26
tant categories of digital content contracts that do not easily sit within the type
of transaction contemplated by the SGA provisions. So, for example, it is quite
straightforward to buy a film on line to rent or 'own', as the case may be. One can
click on the screen, watch the film being downloaded and view it at a later date.
This kind of digital content contract is not time critical. The absence of time criti-
cality can also be said to apply to contracts for the sale of music online, or television
content over satellite (which is content provided in a digital form).

Where time is a critical factor, these provisions will not work so effectively. So,   4.27
for example, in the world of online gaming or in app purchases, time is often a
critical factor. Consumers will not be worrying about their statutory rights when
rushing to purchase a magic potion in World of Warcraft or a hammer in Candy
Crush saga. Exactly how the quality rights (defined in sections 34, 35, and 36 of the
Act) will be applied in these contexts is an interesting and open question.

---

[9] Directive 2011/83/EU art. 2(11) and the Consumer Contracts (Information, Cancellation and
Additional Charges) Regulations 2013 reg. 5.

4.28   A good example is given in paragraph 179 of the Explanatory Notes in the context of assessing how much compensation the consumer may be entitled to:

In contrast, for a game which the consumer has played for five months and which is exhibiting a minor bug at a later stage in the game play (e.g. a character "floats" instead of "runs"), the consumer has already had some enjoyment from playing the game and the bug does not prevent the game from being played, the appropriate amount might be quite a small proportion of the amount paid. If a single film failed to stream satisfactorily, as part of a monthly subscription, the appropriate amount may reflect the portion of the monthly subscription that could be ascribed to that film.

C. WHAT DIGITAL CONTENT CONTRACTS ARE COVERED BY CHAPTER 3?

1. Contracts Covered by this Chapter

4.29   Section 33 defines the contract as having the following elements:

- It is between a trader and a consumer;
- For a price paid by the consumer; or
- Free with goods or services or other digital content for which the consumer pays a price. This includes 'references to the consumer using, by way of payment, any facility for which money has been paid'.

4.30   As the Guidance elucidates:

Question. Does this mean that if I sell tangible digital content (e.g. on a disk) then I have to provide different remedies to a trader who sells the same digital content as a download?

Yes. The quality of the digital content will be judged against the same quality rights. But if the digital content is faulty then if it is supplied on a disk, the goods will be faulty and so the goods remedies will apply.

4.31   Section 33(5) provides that the Secretary of State may by order provide for the chapter to apply to other similar contracts if he thinks that it is appropriate to do so because of significant detriment caused to consumers under contracts of the kind to which the order relates. This is in acknowledgement of the commercial value that personal data now has to many different businesses. It may well be that digital content which is provided free may eventually be covered by the chapter. The reason is as follows.

4.32   If a consumer does not have to pay for digital content but in exchange provides personal data about herself, the data provided is often of significant commercial value to the trader, who is then able to monetize it. As a result, several consumer groups, including Which?, had lobbied for the provisions in Chapter 3 to apply also to contracts for digital content where the content was provided free of charge. BIS have decided not to adopt the approach set out by Which and others but to reserve to themselves the power to extend the scope of Chapter 3 should there be sufficient evidence of consumer harm in the future.

2. Different Kinds of Licences

As set out above, many forms of digital content are subject to an End User Licence 4.33
Agreement ('EULA'), as most digital content is protected by the law of intellectual
property. If a consumer had to tick a box to agree terms before buying a download,[10]
the courts would almost certainly find that there was a contract. These are called
'click wrap' licences.

The case of 'browse wrap' licences may be different. Those are where the consumer 4.34
is told that, by downloading material, he will have been taken to have agreed to the
owner's terms and conditions, but the consumer does not need to take any action
and there is no box or icon to click. The example given by the Law Commission
was the BBC website.[11] Their view is that the courts would not find that licences of
this type have contractual status, which was the conclusion reached in two cases in
the United States.[12]

'Shrink wrap licences' are a more complex category, where a consumer buys 4.35
software on a CD Rom from a retailer. Often, the licence agreement is only
obvious after the goods have been purchased and installed. The legal effect is
complex because the consumer will already have entered into a contract with the
retailer to buy goods before finding out about the terms of the licence. The Law
Commission indicated that the question was outside the terms of their project
and that the shrink wrap licence may disappear before its legal status is ever
conclusively resolved.

The Explanatory Notes suggest that all three types of licence would be subject to 4.36
Part 2 of the Act (Unfair Terms) and any terms in the relating to limiting liability
could be held to be unfair.

D. THE QUALITY RIGHTS

1. Section 34: Digital Content Must be of Satisfactory Quality

Every contract has an implied term that the quality of the digital content is satis- 4.37
factory. These provisions deliberately echo section 14 SGA. That term is defined
in the following ways. That consumers experience problems with digital content
was highlighted during the course of the passage of the Bill through the House of
Lords.[13]

The content of digital content is satisfactory if it meets the standard that a rea- 4.38
sonable person would consider satisfactory.[14] That rather circular definition is given

---

[10] <http://lawcommission.justice.gov.uk/docs/unfair_terms_in_consumer_contracts_appendices.pdf>.
[11] <http://www.bbc.co.uk/terms/>.
[12] *Specht and Others v Netscape Communications Corp and America Online Inc* 306 F.3d 17 (2d Cir.
2002) and *Ticketmaster Corp v Tickets.com, Inc* 2000 WL 525390, at 3 (C.D.Cal. March 27, 2000).
[13] Hansard debate on 20 October 2014, GC 177 and following.
[14] s. 34(2).

slightly sharper focus by the addition of the following matters which must be 'taken into account':

- Any description of the digital content;
- The price;
- All the other 'relevant circumstances'.

4.39   It also includes the following important definitions.[15] In appropriate cases, aspects of the quality of digital content will include:

- Fitness for all the purposes for which digital content of this kind is usually provided;
- Freedom from minor defects;
- Safety;
- Durability.

4.40   Furthermore, something cannot make the quality of the digital content unsatisfactory if:

- It is specifically drawn to the consumer's attention before the contract is made; or
- Where the consumer examines the digital content before the contract is made, that examination ought to have revealed it; or
- Where the consumer examines a trial version (before the contract is made) it would have been apparent on a reasonable examination of the trial version.[16]

4.41   It is important to emphasize that, whilst the wording of section 34(3) follows exactly the wording that appears in section 9(3) of the Act, there is a difference between how these two sections are intended to operate in practice. This became clear during the parliamentary debates as the Act went through its legislative passage. It became clear that the government accepted that digital content involves very different kinds of goods from the goods covered in Chapter 2 of the Act:

We have acknowledged in the Explanatory Notes that it is the norm to encounter some bugs in a complex game or piece of software on release. A reasonable person might not expect that type of digital content to be completely free from minor defects. We will also highlight this point in business and consumer guidance when implementing the Bill. That guidance is being written in consultation with industry and consumer stakeholders. The Bill team confirmed this when we went through it again just before this session.[17]

4.42   The government made it plain that it did not wish to provide additional definitions about what 'relevant circumstances' might be, but preferred to deal with that in the guidance.[18]

---

[15] s. 34(3).
[16] s. 34(4).
[17] Hansard House of Lords 20 October 2014, GC 184 per Baroness Jolly.
[18] See also other debates during the passage of the Bill. Hansard House of Commons 27 February 2014 at Col 304; Hansard House of Lords 19 November 2014 at Col 513.

The Guidance posits the difference between two space invaders games, one at 69p 4.43
and one at £30, and points out that price is relevant to the standard a reasonable person
would consider satisfactory. The graphics in the latter would be expected to be better.
Both games, however, should respond to the player's use of the controls.

The Explanatory Notes draw attention to the importance of consideration and how 4.44
the price paid for digital content can have a material impact on whether or not it is of
satisfactory quality. At paragraph 178, the Explanatory Notes say: 'this quality standard is flexible to allow for the many different types of digital content. For example, the
reasonable expectations of quality for a 69p app would not be as high as for one worth
£5.99.'

At paragraph 179, the Explanatory Notes go on to say:

> for example a reasonable person might expect a simple music file to be free from minor defects so
> that a track which failed to play to the end would not be of satisfactory quality. However, it is the
> norm to encounter some bugs in a complex game or piece of software on release so a reasonable
> person might not expect that type of digital content to be free from minor defects. Consequently
> the application of the quality aspect 'freedom from minor defects' to digital content will depend on
> reasonable expectations as to quality.

A reasonable consumer would therefore expect there to be some minor defects in 4.45
complex products such as games or software, so such defects should not necessarily
mean that the digital content is not of satisfactory quality. A reasonable consumer may
legitimately expect other types of digital content, such as an MP3 file, to be free from
minor defects.

2. Relevant Circumstances

The relevant circumstances[19] include any public statement about the specific char- 4.46
acteristics of the digital content made by the trader or the producer. This includes
any public statement made in advertising or labelling.

However the 'public statement' referred to above is not a 'relevant circumstance' 4.47
if the trader can show that when the contract was made any one of the following
five circumstances existed:[20]

- The trader was not aware of the statement;
- The trader could not reasonably have been aware of the statement;
- The statement had been publicly withdrawn; or
- To the extent that it contained anything which was incorrect or misleading, it
  had been publicly corrected;
- The consumer's decision to contract for the digital content could not have been
  influenced by the statement.

---

[19] s. 34(5)–(7).
[20] See the Guidance, which gives the example of an online description in a foreign language.

4.48   The section also applies to the acts of agents. If a person is acting as an agent, the above provisions apply to him unless:

- The other person is not providing the digital content in the course of a business; and
- The consumer knows that fact; or
- Reasonable steps are taken to bring it to the consumer's attention before the contract is made.

E. THIRD PARTIES

4.49   The Guidance gives a pithy analysis of the responsibilities of traders in the Questions and Answers:

Question: How can I be responsible for the quality of digital content that I didn't produce?
- In the same way that shopkeepers are liable for the quality of the goods sold in their shops, a supplier of digital content is liable for the quality of the digital content even if they did not produce it;.
- The consumer has the right to go back to the person who they paid for the digital content to get a remedy.
- If you have had to compensate the consumer for faulty digital content that you did not produce, you will have to go back to the supplier of that digital content for redress (if available).

Am I liable if my digital content contains some third party software that is later found to have an inherent security weakness (e.g. the heartbleed bug)?
- To be of satisfactory quality, digital content must meet the standards a reasonable person would consider satisfactory taking into account all relevant circumstances.
- The security of digital content is a relevant circumstance that could form part of the judgement of whether digital content is of satisfactory quality.
- The fact that you did not know about the security weakness when you supplied the digital content would not change that position.
- This is the same as with goods: a trader may not know that a component of their goods – say a hinge on a box – had an inherent weakness or latent defect when they sold the goods, but that would not make any difference to the judgement as to whether the goods were of satisfactory quality or not.
- The first tier remedy for faulty digital content would be a repair or a replacement, so once a consumer noted a vulnerability, you would be required to offer a repair (an update) or replacement that would fix the vulnerability.

A consumer pays for an MMO game, but when they play it in the online mode, the server is completely unreliable and keeps crashing. As a result their experience of the game does not meet their expectations.
- The consumer would be entitled to a remedy from you. If another trader is responsible for the servers on which the game is played, you may have the option to seek compensaiton from them if your contract with them says you can. If the consumer has another contract with the

trader who provides the server, perhaps through a monthly subscription, they would also have the option of claiming a remedy from that trader, for example if the service is not provided with reasonable care and skill, although they could not recover twice for the same loss.

1. Section 35: Digital Content Must be Fit for a Particular Purpose

The contract is to be treated as including a term that the digital content is reason- 4.50
ably fit for that purpose, whether or not that is a purpose for which digital content of that kind is usually provided. The contract **is only** to be treated in that way in the following two sets of circumstances.

If before the contract is made the consumer makes known to the trader (expressly 4.51
or by implication) any particular purpose for which the consumer is contracting for the digital content (subsection 1).

If the content was previously sold by a credit-broker to the trader: 4.52

- The consideration or part of it is a sum payable by instalments; and
- Before the contract is made, the consumer makes known to the credit-broker (expressly or by implication) any particular purpose for which the consumer is contracting for the digital content (subsection 2).

If either of the provisions above apply, the contract is to be treated as including a 4.53
term that the digital content is reasonably fit for that purpose, whether or not that is a purpose for which digital content of that kind is usually supplied (subsection (3)).

But the contract is not to be so treated if the circumstances show that the con- 4.54
sumer does not reply, or it is unreasonable for the consumer to rely on the skill or judgment of the trader or credit-broker.

F. QUALITY RIGHTS: PRE-CONTRACT INFORMATION AND MODIFICATION

It is not absolutely clear how section 35 relates to section 34(4). A trader can protect 4.55
himself by drawing the consumer's attention to particular aspects of the quality of the digital content before the contract is made under section 34(4). Similarly, the consumer is able to protect himself by making known to the trader the particular purpose for which he is contracting. Which of the two sections trumps the other?

To understand how the clause is to operate, we must turn to the leading cases 4.56
under section 14 SGA. Section 14 SGA is re-stated in section 10 of the Act. Section 35 of the Act follows exactly the corresponding wording in section 10 of the Act. Therefore, logically, the contract will not include such a term where the trader makes it clear that the goods are not reasonably fit for a particular purpose that the consumer has made known to the trader, and it would therefore be unreasonable for the consumer to rely upon the trader's representations.

The Explanatory Notes to the Act support this approach. According to the 4.57
Explanatory Notes, 'made known' implies that the trader must be aware of the

consumer's intentions: 'For example, an email sent to a trader immediately before downloading an app is unlikely to fulfil the "makes known" requirement, whereas an email discussion with a trader would.'

4.58   The Explanatory Notes[21] reflect the current common law position as set out in the most recent authority from the Court of Appeal *BSS Group plc v Makers* (UK) [2011] EWCA Civ 809. Rimer LJ, citing previous cases, sets out the questions arising under section 14(3) SGA as being:

- Whether the buyer, expressly or by implication, made known to the vendor the purpose for which the goods were being bought;
- If so, whether they were reasonably fit for that purpose;
- If they were not reasonably fit for that purpose, whether the vendor has shown
  - that the buyer did not rely upon its skill and judgment; or
  - if he did, that it was unreasonable for him to do so.

4.59   In *Henry Kendall v William Lillico & Sons Limited* [1969] 2 AC 31, Lord Reid explained that the purpose must be stated with sufficient particularity to enable the seller to exercise his skill and judgment in making or selecting the appropriate goods.

4.60   However, it is difficult to assess how section 35(3) will be applied in practice as the vast majority of digital content is sold, not on bespoke terms, but on standard terms for stated purposes. The examples are legion. Taking the following four categories of digital content to illustrate the point: Game purchases, apps from app stores, film or music downloads, and computer software.

1. Game purchases: Many products are bought and sold to allow players to move through the levels of the game or to augment the powers that their particular character or avatar may have. But very rarely in these scenarios would players have the ability to negotiate a bespoke piece of software to be fit for a particular purpose. In fact, speed is often of the essence and what will matter more to players is obtaining the item needed in good time for the purposes of the game. Applying the questions set out by Rimer LJ to this scenario will produce some interesting results in relation to the goods that are bought. Of course they must be of merchantable quality and be as described etc. But it is difficult to imagine a scenario in a fast-moving game where the consumer could in any meaningful sense make known to the trader the purpose for which a digital product is being bought, and be able to rely upon a term being implied into the contract that the digital product will be fit for that purpose, in light of the limited interactive communication that usually exists between trader and consumer in an online gaming scenario.

2. Apps bought in an app store, be it Apple IOS or Android: It is quite usual for consumers to place as much reliance upon what other consumers who have bought the app may say about it as upon the statements made by the seller of the app. Apps by definition are not bespoke to a consumer's needs but are sold on

---

[21] And the Guidance, which gives the example of an email sent by a consumer.

the basis of being standard products that all consumers can buy. There is never an opportunity to request that the app provided is fit for a particular purpose, as these stores are not set up in such a way as to allow for a such an interaction between trader and consumer.

3. Films: The Explanatory Notes to the Act make it clear that there can be no implied term as to the artistic merit of the work that is being sold but that it must of course be able to be seen and viewed as intended.

4. Software: Where software on consumers' devices or computers is regularly updated by internet service providers (ISPs), or the likes of Apple and Microsoft, to make sure that it continues to work effectively and secures the device against possible security threats. Nowhere in these interactions is there the possibility for the consumer to make known to the trader the purpose for which the software is to be used. It is therefore unlikely that sections 34 and 35 will be engaged on a regular basis, as they will apply only to a very small number of consumer contracts for digital content where the consumer is able to make known to the trader the specific purpose for which the digital content is being used.

In this context, the concept of reliance will presumably have limited applica- 4.61 tion: *Ashington Piggeries Ltd v Christopher Hill Limited* [1972] AC 441, at 477G, per Lord Guest; and, also at 505B to C, where Lord Diplock pointed out that:

a buyer who has made known the purpose of his proposed purchase and had selected a seller who made it his business to supply goods which are used for purposes of that kind will thereby convey to the seller that he is relying on the seller's skill and judgment to ensure that the goods are fit for that particular purpose. Whilst the drawing of an inference of reliance was easier in a case in which the buyer had stated his purpose expressly, that was not a necessary precondition of the drawing of such an inference.

So, where a consumer sends an e-mail stating a particular purpose (which was 4.62 not a usual purpose for the goods or digital content in question) and then without waiting for a response goes ahead and buys the goods or digital content online, it is unlikely that the consumer will be able to say that the contract contains an implied term that the digital content is fit for that particular purpose.

It is unlikely that section 35(3) of the Act would be breached in these circum- 4.63 stances, as the trader would be able to argue, inter alia, that:

(1) The consumer may not have made known his purpose to the trader, particularly if the time interval was such that the trader could not have been aware of the purpose at the time the contract was made;

(2) In some circumstances, the consumer will not have explained the purpose with sufficient particularity for the trader to exercise skill and judgement;

(3) The trader has not responded in any way and so has not exercised any skill and judgment or selected the goods or digital content for the consumer; and

(4) The consumer did not rely on the trader's skill and judgment in these circumstances since his decision was made before the trader responded (and in some

cases before the trader could have responded, again dependent on the time interval); and that

(5) If the consumer did rely on the skill and judgment of the trader, it was unreasonable for him to do so.

4.64   Conversely, if the consumer makes known the purpose for which the digital content is to be used through either an online chat forum, or via social media, or email exchange, or even a telephone call, in such a way that the trader is drawn into making representations about the digital content being sold, then it is for the seller to prove either that the consumer has not relied upon the trader's representations, or alternatively that it would be unreasonable for the consumer to rely upon the seller's representations in the specific context of what has been said or written about the digital content by the seller.

1. Section 36: Digital Content Must be as Described

4.65   Every contract to provide digital content is to be treated as including a term that the digital content will match any description of it given by the trader to the consumer. This is the same as section 13 SGA. This is an important right in the digital content where people may not be able to view the content before buying the full version.

4.66   If the consumer examines a trial version before the contract is made, it is not sufficient that the digital content simply matches or is better than the trial version. The digital content must still match the description if it is given by the trader to the consumer (subsection (2)).

4.67   As the Explanatory Notes make plain:

> The policy intention is that matching the description should mean that the digital content should at least do what it is described as doing. It is not intended that "matches the description" should mean that the digital content must be exactly the same in every aspect. This clause would not, for example prevent the digital content going beyond the description, as long as it also continues to match the description. This is particularly relevant for updates that may enhance features or add new features. As long as the digital content continued to match the original product description, additional features would not necessarily breach this right.[22]

4.68   The Guidance emphasizes that the descriptions must comply with other relevant legislation such as the Consumer Protection from Unfair Trading Regulations 2008, and that the Consumer should cross refer to the Competition and Markets Authority ('CMA') Guidance.

2. Section 37: Other Pre-Contract Information Included in Contract

4.69   The Consumer Contracts (Information, Cancellation and Additional Charges) Regulations 2013 (the CCRs) brought the CRD into force. It is made plain by section 36(3) that certain provisions of the Schedules to that statutory instrument are to be

---

[22] Explanatory Notes para. 185.

included as terms of the contract.[23] The purpose of that Directive is to harmonize consumer distance and off-premises contracts (recital (4)) in order to develop the internal market. It is perceived that the growth in cross-border distance sales has been limited, and that the discrepancy for internet sales compared to other types of trade has been marked compared to direct selling.

It repealed two important Regulations: The Consumer Protection (Distance Selling) Regulations 2000[24] and the Cancellation of Contracts made in a Consumer's Home or Place of Work Regulations 2008.[25]   4.70

The CRD makes it plain that Member States may decide to extend the application of the rules of the CRD to legal persons or to natural persons who are not consumers within the meaning of the CRD, such as non-governmental organizations, start-ups, or small and medium-sized enterprises. The application of the CRD to digital content is made explicit in recital (19) in the preamble thereto.   4.71

The CRD makes a distinction between three types of contracts: 4.72

(1) Distance contract (in simple terms[26]) means a contract in which the trader and consumer are not simultaneously present. The definition is the same as the Distance Selling Regulations;

(2) Off-premises contracts are contracts where the parties are present but not at the business premises of the trader;

(3) On-premises contracts are all contracts which are not distance or off-premises contracts.

Within the UK Regulations, if regulations 9 (on-premises contracts), 10 (off-premises contracts) or 13 (distance contracts) **require** the trader to provide information to the consumer before the contact becomes binding, that information is to be regarded as part of the contact and is legally binding on the trader unless both the consumer and trader expressly agree to it being changed. The list is lengthy and is set out in Table 4.1 below.   4.73

Table 4.1 Pre-contract information

CONSUMER INFORMATION FOR CONTRACTS OTHER THAN DISTANCE OR OFF-PREMISES CONTRACTS	
The identity of the trader, such as his trading name, the geographical address at which he is established, and his telephone number.	Schedule 1(b).
The total price of the goods or services inclusive of taxes, or where the nature of the goods or services is such that the price cannot reasonably be calculated in advance, the manner in which the price is to be calculated, as well as, where applicable, all additional freight, delivery or postal charges or, where those charges cannot reasonably be calculated in advance, the fact that such additional charges may be payable.	Schedule 1(c).

(Continued)

---

[23] This is emphasized in the Guidance.
[24] SI 2000/2334.
[25] SI 2008/1816.
[26] See reg. 2 of the The Consumer Contracts (Information, Cancellation and Additional Charges) Regulations 2013 for the full definition.

Table 4.1 (*Continued*)

Where applicable, all additional delivery charges or, where those charges cannot reasonably be calculated in advance, the fact that such additional charges may be payable.	Schedule 1(d).
Where applicable, the arrangements for payment, delivery, performance, and the time by which the trader undertakes to deliver the goods or to perform the service.	Schedule 1(e).
Where applicable, the trader's complaint handling policy.	Schedule 1(f).
In the case of a sales contract, a reminder that the trader is under a legal duty to supply goods that are in conformity with the contract.	Schedule 1(g).
Where applicable, the existence and the conditions of after-sales services and commercial guarantees.	Schedule 1(h).
The duration of the contract, where applicable, or, if the contract is of indeterminate duration or is to be extended automatically, the conditions for terminating the contract.	Schedule 1(i).

CONSUMER INFORMATION AND RIGHT OF WITHDRAWL FOR DISTANCE AND OFF-PREMISES CONTRACTS

The identity of the trader, such as his trading name.	Schedule 2(b).
The geographical address at which the trader is established and the trader's telephone number, fax number and e-mail address, where available, to enable the consumer to contact the trader quickly and communicate with him efficiently.	Schedule 2(c).
Where the trader is acting on behalf of another trader, the geographical address and identity of that other trader.	Schedule 2(d).
If different from the address provided in accordance with paragraph (c), the geographical address of the place of business of the trader, and, where the trader acts on behalf of another trader, the geographical address of the place of business of that other trader, where the consumer can address any complaints.	Schedule 2(e).
The total price of the goods or services inclusive of taxes, or where the nature of the goods or services is such that the price cannot reasonably be calculated in advance, the manner in which the price is to be calculated.	Schedule 2(f).
Where applicable, all additional delivery charges and any other costs or, where those charges cannot reasonably be calculated in advance, the fact that such additional charges may be payable.	Schedule 2(g).
In the case of a contract of indeterminate duration or a contract containing a subscription, the total costs per billing period or (where such contracts are charged at a fixed rate) the total monthly costs.	Schedule 2(h).
The cost of using the means of distance communication for the conclusion of the contract where that cost is calculated other than at the basic rate.	Schedule 2(i).
The arrangements for payment, delivery, performance, and the time by which the trader undertakes to deliver the goods or to perform the services.	Schedule 2(j).
Where applicable, the trader's complaint handling policy.	Schedule 2(k).
Where a right to cancel exists, the conditions, time limits, and procedures for exercising that right in accordance with regulations 27 to 38.	Schedule 2(l).
Where applicable, that the consumer will have to bear the cost of returning the goods in case of cancellation and, for distance contracts, if the goods, by their nature, cannot normally be returned by post, the cost of returning the goods.	Schedule 2(m).
That, if the consumer exercises the right to cancel after having made a request in accordance with regulation 36(1), the consumer is to be liable to pay the trader reasonable costs in accordance with regulation 36(4).	Schedule 2(n).

Where under regulations 28, 36, or 37 there is no right to cancel, or the right to cancel may be lost, the information that the consumer will not benefit from a right to cancel, or the circumstances under which the consumer loses the right to cancel.	Schedule 2(o).
In the case of a sales contract, a reminder that the trader is under a legal duty to supply goods that are in conformity with the contract.	Schedule 2(p).
Where applicable, the existence and conditions of after-sale customer assistance, after-sales services, and commercial guarantees.	Schedule 2(q).
The existence of relevant codes of conduct, as defined in regulation 5(3)(b) of the Consumer Protection from Unfair Trading Regulations 2008, and how copies of them can be obtained, where applicable.	Schedule 2(r).
The duration of the contract, where applicable, or, if the contract is of indeterminate duration or is to be extended automatically, the conditions for terminating the contract.	Schedule 2(s).
Where applicable, the minimum duration of the consumer's obligations under the contract.	Schedule 2(t).
Where applicable, the existence and the conditions of deposits or other financial guarantees to be paid or provided by the consumer at the request of the trader.	Schedule 2(u).
Where applicable, the possibility of having recourse to an out-of-court complaint and redress mechanism, to which the trader is subject, and the methods for having access to it.	Schedule 2(x).

The Guidance explains that the consumer must be given information of inter- 4.74
operability (compatibility) of the digital content with hardware and software that
he is aware of or can reasonably be expected to be aware of prior to sale.

3. Table of Pre-Contract Information

Section 37 of the Act means that not only is the information about the main char- 4.75
acteristics functionality and compatibility of the digital content legally binding
upon the trader by virtue of section 36(3) but all the other information provided
by the trader under Schedules 1 and/or 2 to the CCRs is also to be treated as part
of the contract, for example the requirement set out in paragraph k of Schedule 2
to the CCRs to provide (where applicable) information about the 'trader's complaint
handling policy'. Whatever information is provided pursuant to that requirement
the becomes legally binding on the trader.

Importantly, a change to any of that information, made before entering into the 4.76
contract or later, is not effective unless expressly agreed between the consumer and
the trader (section 37(3)). If the trader and consumer do expressly agree a change
the description of the digital content, the consumer would not subsequently be
entitled to a remedy if the digital content did not meet the original description but
did meet the agreed, changed description.

The Guidance explains that the fourteen-day cooling-off period does not apply 4.77
to sealed audio, video, and software products once unsealed, or once digital content
has been streamed or downloaded.

4. Section 38: Modification of the Contract

Section 38 makes it plain that, other than the provisions of sections 36 and 37, a 4.78
contract to provide digital content is not to be treated as including any term about

quality or fitness for purpose unless the term is expressly included in the contract. However, express terms about quality and fitness can be included and the section allows for interaction with other pieces of legislation.

5. Section 39: Supply by Transmission and Facilities for Continued Transmissions

4.79 This is an important provision. It is concerned with the interplay involving digital content and third parties. The content must be of satisfactory quality, fit for a particular purpose and as described *at the point where it reaches the consumer's device, or if earlier a trader with whom the consumer has contracted.* See subsection (2). The Guidance makes this clear where it says:

> When is digital content "supplied" to the consumer?

> For the purposes of this Act, the digital content is "supplied" to the consumer at the point it reaches the consumer's device or an independent trader such as an Internet Service Provider (ISP) or Mobile Network Operator (MNO), who the consumer has contracted with for a service to deliver the digital content to their device, whichever is sooner.

> If you are supplying the consumer with more than one item of digital content under your contract with them (e.g. if you offer a subscription service), each item of digital content is supplied at the point it reaches the consumer's device or an independent trader within the contractual control of the consumer (e.g. their ISP) whichever is sooner.[27]

4.80 The Explanatory Notes provide the following explanation:

> Where digital content fails to meet the quality standards because of a problem with the consumer's device or with the delivery service supplied by an independent trader with whom the consumer has contracted (e.g. ISP, mobile network provider, cable provider), T would not be liable for the failure to meet the quality standards as that trader (T) cannot be at fault in any way for the problem and has no way of rectifying it. If the problem is with the consumer's network access provider, then this service provider is liable under the services provision of the Bill if, for example, the service is not provided with reasonable care and skill (see Chapter 4). However, where the digital content fails to meet the quality standards because of a problem for which T or an intermediary in the contractual control of T (either directly or indirectly) is responsible, then T will be liable. This is similar to the rules on the passing of risk for goods (clause 29) which provide that the trader carries the risk for the goods purchased until they come into the physical possession of the consumer, unless the delivery is arranged by the consumer in which case the consumer takes the risk for the delivery of the goods.[28]

4.81 Subsections (3) to (7) apply to the following circumstances: if there is a contract to supply digital content, and after the trader has supplied the content the consumer is to have access under the contract to a processing facility under the arrangements made by the trader. Examples would include a music streaming facility or a massively multiplayer online game. Subsection (5) provides that, for such content,

---

[27] See p. 5 of the Guidance.
[28] Explanatory Notes para. 194.

the consumer should be able to use their digital content in the way described for a reasonable period of time, unless a time is already specified in the contract.

Sections 34, 35, and 36 (the quality rights) apply to all digital content transmitted to the consumer on each occasion under the facility. Subsection 7 provides that breach of subsection (5) would give the consumer access to the remedies under section 42.   4.82

6. Section 40: Modifications

Digital content is of course different because manufacturers and traders can change or update digital content after the initial provision of the digital content. This is a good thing. Requiring consent for every update would not make any sense. Section 40 does not prevent a trader or third party updating the digital content, provided that the original contract made that plain. Any such provision would be assessable for fairness pursuant to Part 2 of the Act (Unfair Terms) in any event.   4.83

If there are any updates, the digital content must still meet the quality rights pursuant to sections 34 to 36. Any claim on the grounds that the digital content does not conform to the quality rights is to be treated as arising at the time when the digital content was originally supplied, and not at the time of the modification. Therefore, any claim for breach of this provision must be brought within six years of the date the digital content was first supplied, which is a (very) long time in the context of digital content.   4.84

See paragraph 198 of the Explanatory Notes: 4.85

It is for a consumer to prove that the digital content is faulty. Where a consumer has not identified a fault (and therefore not requested a repair or replacement), but a general update is sent in any case to the consumer, this does not necessarily mean that the quality rights were breached nor that the update constitutes a repair or replacement.

7. Section 41: Trader's Right to Provide Digital Content

Every contract for digital content presumes that the trader has the right to provide the content to the consumer (section 41). This obviously includes intellectual property rights. If the trader does not have the right to supply the digital content at all, the consumer will be entitled to a refund. See section 45 of the Act.   4.86

G. REMEDIES

1. Section 42: What Remedies are there if Statutory Rights under a Digital Content Contract are not Met?

The Explanatory Notes include the following helpful table:[29]   4.87

---

[29] Explanatory Notes para. 101.

Table 4.2 Consumer's statutory rights and remedies

Consumer's statutory rights being breached	Remedies that may apply
Digital content to be of satisfactory quality (section 34).	• The right to repair or replacement (section 43); • If repair or replacement are not possible or do not resolve the fault within a reasonable time or without causing significant inconvenience to the consumer, the right to a price reduction (section 44).
Digital content to be fit for particular purpose (section 35).	• The right to repair or replacement (section 43); • If repair or replacement are not possible or do not resolve the fault within a reasonable time or without causing significant inconvenience to the consumer, the right to a price reduction (section 44).
Other pre-contractual information (section 37).	• The right to recover costs incurrent as a result of the breach (section 42).
Trader's right to supply digital content (section 41).	• The right to a refund (section 45).
Remedy for damage to device or other digital content (section 46)[30]	The trader must either: • Repair the damage; or • Compensate the consumer with an appropriate payment (section 46).

4.88   If the digital content does not conform to the rights in section 36 (satisfactory quality), section 37 (fit for purpose), and section 38 (to be as described), then the consumer has various rights.

4.89   The first is a right to repair or replacement (section 43); the second a right to a price reduction (section 44) (where the consumer has bought digital content on physical media they may in addition have rights flowing from section 16 of the Act).[31] Those two types of remedy are similar to some of those available to a consumer of goods, with the notable difference that there is no right to *reject* digital content as there is where goods do not conform with a contract.

4.90   Unlike the position with the corresponding sections dealing with goods, there are no strict limits on the number of repairs or replacements. The policy behind this is that restricting the number of repairs could create an incentive for some consumers to report minor problems in order to proceed to a price reduction. It is nonetheless possible that a consumer will be caused 'significant inconvenience' after a single repair or replacement.

4.91   There is no right to reject substandard digital content because it often cannot (unlike many goods) be returned. This is where section 16 comes in. If the digital content is sold on a tangible medium (for example, a digital camera, or as a disk), the consumer will be able to exercise the goods remedies under section 16 of the Act.

---

[30] The Guidance gives quite detailed assistance with this topic.
[31] See Ch. 3 above.

Section 42(4) deals with the position where pre-contract information pursuant 4.92
to section 37 has not been complied with. This remedy is similar to the remedy of a
price reduction under section 44 of the Act. The Explanatory Notes explained that
it is anticipated that this section will have more limited application, since section 37
is only concerned with information under the Consumer Contracts (Information,
Cancellation and Additional Charges) Regulations 2013, which do not in fact
describe the digital content itself.

Sections 42, 43, and 44 do not prevent the consumer from exercising the other 4.93
remedies available to him which are set out in section 42(7):

(a) Claiming damages;
(b) Seeking to recover money paid whether the consideration for payment of the money has
     failed;
(c) Seeking specific performance;
(d) Seeking an order for specific implement;
(e) Relying on the breach against a claim by the trader for the price.

Any claim for damages would generally be the difference between the value of 4.94
the goods, service or digital content received by the consumer and the value had
there not been a breach. A person cannot recover damages for loss which was not
caused by the breach (of the term required by the Bill) or which was not reasonably
foreseeable; nor can the consumer recover for loss which he could reasonably have
acted to limit or mitigate.[32]

The burden would be on the consumer to prove that the digital content is faulty, 4.95
but importantly, if the consumer can (within the first six months) prove that the
digital content was faulty, it is assumed that the fault was present on the day it was
supplied (section 42(8)) unless this is inconsistent with the type of alleged fault or
the trader proves to the contrary.

2. Section 43: Right to Repair or Replacement

Where the consumer has the right to repair or replacement of the digital content, 4.96
then the trader must do so within a reasonable time, but without causing significant
inconvenience to the consumer and bear any necessary costs in so doing. These
include the costs of labour, materials, and postage.[33] What is a reasonable time or
significant inconvenience is to be determined by taking account of the nature of the
content and the purpose for which it was obtained or accessed.[34]

The consumer cannot specify either repair or replacement if a particular remedy 4.97
(the repair *or* the replacement) is impossible or disproportionate compared to the
other of those remedies. The definition of a disproportionate remedy is one which
imposes costs on the trade which are unreasonable taking into account the value

---

[32] Explanatory Notes para. 204.
[33] s. 43(2).
[34] s. 43(5).

of the digital content, the significance of the lack of conformity to the rights in the Act, and whether the other remedy could be effected without significant inconvenience to the consumer.

4.98 The Explanatory Notes provide a helpful example:[35]

> For example, a downloaded music file is very low cost to the trader and can be delivered very quickly, and a replacement file would similarly be very quick and easy to provide. In this example, therefore, a reasonable time would be very short and any measure of inconvenience would similarly be very low. However, for an expensive, complicated piece of software which may require a patch to bring it in line with the contract (i.e. it may need to be repaired rather than replaced) the process might be expected to take longer. But, if the digital content was obtained with a specific purpose in mind, for example, when a consumer has paid an extra amount to have early access to an online multi-user game but the server crashed and so the consumer was not able to access the game early, a repair or replacement may not be possible so the consumer would be entitled to a price reduction of an appropriate amount.

4.99 It is important to note that the trader does not get to choose the appropriate remedy. Having said that, if a consumer chooses to have the digital content *repaired*, he cannot then require it to be *replaced* if a reasonable time has not been given to repair it, and the converse is also true.[36]

4.100 The Guidance deals with the overlap between updates and repairs:

> A repair is something that you provide in response to a consumer identifying a fault, that is, a breach of the quality rights. Under the Act, if a consumer shows that the quality rights are not complied with, they can ask you to repair the digital content so that it does meet the quality rights. If you issue a general update and it does ensure that the digital content meets the quality rights, then this will be enough to count as a repair. A repair does not have to be bespoke for an individual consumer – it just has to rectify the fault (that is, make it comply with the quality rights).

3. Section 44: Right to Price Reduction

4.101 The right to a price reduction means the right to require the trader to reduce the price to the consumer by an appropriate amount. The right may only be exercised in two sets of circumstances:

(1) If the consumer cannot require repair or replacement because of the disproportionate cost involved; or

(2) The trader is in breach of the requirement of section 43(2)(a) to do so within a reasonable time and without significant inconvenience to the consumer.

4.102 The right to the refund must be given without undue delay and in any event within fourteen days beginning with the day on which the trader agrees that the consumer is entitled to one, the same method of payment must be used, and the

---

[35] para. 209.
[36] s. 43 (6)–(7).

trader must not impose any fee.[37] The Explanatory Notes foresee circumstances in which this repayment could be in the form of digital currencies, such as bitcoins. The government expects the reduction in price here to reflect the difference in value between what the consumer paid for the content and what he actually receives.

If only a portion of the digital content is affected, then it is only necessary to reduce the price by the same proportion. If a consumer pays a monthly subscription to download five movies per month and one movie fails to download, and the download cannot be repeated, an appropriate price reduction may be one-fifth of the monthly subscription.[38]   **4.103**

4. Section 45: Right to a Refund

The right to a refund gives the consumer the right to receive a refund from the trader of all money paid for the digital content. If the breach only applied to some of the digital content provided under the contract, the right only extends to that part.[39] There are similar provisions about the speed and type of payment.   **4.104**

5. Section 46: Compensation for Damage to Device or Other Digital Content

A consumer is entitled to payment from a trader if: **4.105**

- The trader provides digital content to the consumer under a contract;
- The digital content causes damage to a device or to other digital content;
- The device or digital content that is damaged belongs to the consumer;
- The damage is of a kind that would not have occurred if the trader had exercised reasonable care and skill.[40]

What constitutes reasonable care and skill will be judged against the standards of the profession and what is reasonable will depend on the particular circumstances.   **4.106**

It would, of course, be open to a consumer who received a virus to bring proceedings for negligence, as the explanatory notes anticipate.[41] The purpose of this section is to engage the principles behind a claim for negligence but to limit the type of loss that can be claimed. It applies to all digital content contractually supplied even it is free. The consumer is entitled to the costs of replacing the device or the digital content that is damaged.[42]   **4.107**

---

[37] s. 44(4)–(6).
[38] Example taken from the Guidance.
[39] s. 45(2).
[40] s. 46(1).
[41] See also Hansard House of Lords 20 October 2014, Col. GC 205.
[42] s. 46(3).

4.108.   The consumer's rights regarding digital content forms part of the contract between the trader and the consumer. A consumer can therefore enforce a remedy for up to six years after the consumer receives the digital content.[43]

4.109   Generally speaking, it is the responsibility of the consumer to prove that digital content did not meet the requirements of the Act at the time of supply. However, where the issue arises within six months starting on the day of supply, there is an assumption that the digital content failed to meet the requirements at the time of supply.[44]

H. CAN A TRADER CONTRACT OUT OF RIGHTS AND REMEDIES?

1. Section 47: Liability that Cannot be Excluded or Restricted

4.110   A term of a contract to provide digital content cannot exclude or restrict the trader's liability arising under the following sections:

- Section 34 (quality of digital content);
- Section 35 (fitness for a particular purpose);
- Section 36 (description);
- Section 41 (trader's right to provide digital content);
- Section 46 (compensation for damage to other digital content).

4.111   This also means that a term of a contract cannot do the following:[45]

- It cannot exclude or restrict a right or remedy in respect of a liability under a provision listed in that subsection;
- It cannot make a right or remedy in this chapter, or its enforcement, subject to a restrictive or onerous condition;
- It cannot allow a trade to put a person at a disadvantage as a result of pursuing such a right or remedy.

4.112   Schedule 3 of the Act, which pertains to the enforcement of the law on unfair contract terms, makes specific references to section 47. If a complaint is made about an attempt to exclude or restrict liability in digital contents contracts, Schedule 3 applies. See Chapter 6 below.

4.113   Liability for damage to the consumer's device or other digital content can be restricted or excluded to the extent that such contract terms would be judged as fair under Part 2 of the Act.

---

[43] Limitation Act 1980.
[44] s. 42(9).
[45] s. 47(2).

I. INFORMATION ABOUT ALTERNATIVE
DISPUTE RESOLUTION

The Alternative Dispute Resolution ('ADR') Directive is in force on 9 July 2015. 4.114

The detailed provisions of the ADR Directive are outside the scope of this 4.115
guide.[46] However, under the Online Dispute Resolution ('ODR') Regulations
2015, from January 2016 there is a requirement that there must be a link to the
ODR platform.[47]

---

[46] For further information, please refer to the following statutory instruments: the Alternative Dispute Resolution for Consumer Disputes (Competent Authorities and Information) Regulations 2015 (SI 2015/542) and the Alternative Dispute Resolution for Consumer Disputes (Amendment) Regulations 2015 (SI 2015/1392).

[47] There are very useful materials on this topic provided by the Civil Justice Council. See <https://www.judiciary.gov.uk/wp-content/uploads/2015/02/Online-Dispute-Resolution-Final-Web-Version1.pdf>.

5

SERVICES

A. SUMMARY AND BACKGROUND

Chapter 4 of the Act covers contracts for service between a trader and consumer. 5.01
It re-states the existing law, but also introduces some important changes to address
certain policy considerations. The chapter sets out in order which contracts are covered, what a consumer's statutory rights are, what remedies have now been created
and the fact that a trader may not contract out of a consumer's rights and remedies
as provided under the Act.

More specifically, the chapter sets out what rights the consumer has when he or 5.02
she contracts for the provision of services from a trader and that these rights are
contractual. Therefore, if the trader breaches those statutory rights, the trader is in
breach of contract.

When or if a trader breaches those rights, he or she is liable to provide to the 5.03
consumer certain statutory remedies that have been enshrined in statute for the first
time. In addition to the statutory remedies that have been created, the consumer
also has the right to pursue any actions in common law that may arise under the
contract. These common law remedies exist side-by-side with the new statutory
remedies.

If a trader seeks to exclude his or her liability under the contract for a breach of a 5.04
consumer's statutory rights or remedies, any such term that the trader purports to
rely upon shall be deemed to be automatically unfair and comprise part of the black
list (see Chapter 6 on Unfair Contract Terms).

The Act effectively repeals the Supply of Goods and Services Act 1982 ('SGSA') 5.05
in so far as it applies to contracts for service between traders and consumers.
However, the Act incorporates and re-states much of the law contained within
the SGSA, with some important additions. Unlike the SGSA, the Act does away
with the concept of implied terms, as such language is considered to be arcane
and overly legalistic when considering consumer contracts for service. However,
the Act retains and restates the duty on traders to provide services with reasonable
care and skill.

The Act also introduces certain new statutory rights for consumers: firstly, that 5.06
traders will be legally bound in the contracts they provide for services, by any

statement they make either about the services, or about themselves; secondly, that consumers now have two new statutory remedies for any breach by traders of their statutory duties, which will be treated as breach of contract. These remedies comprise the right to a repeat performance and the right to a price reduction.

5.07   These changes reflect the recommendations set out in the Report commissioned by the Government Department for Business Innovation and Skills ('BIS') in 2010 entitled 'Consolidation and Simplification of UK Consumer Law'[1] ('the Report'). The Report's stated aim was to see how 'consumer contract law could be simplified, streamlined by separating out into a coherent package the legal provisions affecting consumers, and rationalised by adopting more appropriate terminology.'[2] The Report also argues that: 'With regard to remedies for services, it is also necessary to make these clearer and more accessible by incorporating them in the new consolidating statute (the Act).'[3]

5.08   The new rights set out for consumers in the Act reflect in large part the recommendations set out in the Report commissioned by BIS. However, it should be noted that the statutory rights that have been created do not necessarily represent a substantial change in the content of the law as it relates to the provision of services to consumers under contract, but attempt to make it easier for consumers to understand their rights and to exercise them and for traders to understand their obligations. But, in doing so, there are some important changes that have been made which may result in the Act creating new rights for consumers that may have unforeseen consequences, as we shall note below.

B. ON OUTCOME-BASED LIABILITY STANDARDS

5.09   It should be noted that the government ultimately rejected the recommendation set out in the Report to introduce an outcome-based liability standard for service contracts. The Report had recommended that fault-based liability led to confusion for traders and consumers alike and left consumers in a position where they did not know if they had a remedy for breach of contract where they had not benefitted from the outcome that was originally paid for. However, BIS ultimately decided to keep the existing law in place for service contracts, where it is therefore incumbent on the consumer to show that the trader has acted without reasonable care and skill in order to be entitled to a remedy.

5.10   The Report noted that, where goods were supplied under a services contract, they were subject to strict liability standards, whereas consumers had no such guarantees

---

[1] See <https://www.gov.uk/government/uploads/system/uploads/attachment_data/file/31838/10-1255-consolidation-simplification-uk-consumer-law.pdf>.
[2] Report, para. 1.1.
[3] Report, para 1.42.

for the standards to which services performed under contract should be delivered. BIS noted in the Report at paragraph 1.17:

The present law is too complex and uncertain. The fault standard can be problematic for consumers who may not feel they are obtaining value for money or that the law is meeting their reasonable expectations. In particular there seems to be an unnecessary divergence from the strict liability standard adopted for goods, especially as many services are increasing standardised.

The government's rejection of this proposal was set out very clearly at an early stage in the legislative process. In the House of Commons on 28 January 2014, the Parliamentary Under-Secretary of State for Business, Innovation and Skills, Jenny Willott, said in support of the government's decision not to introduce outcome-based liability standards, that: **5.11**

As part of the consultation ahead of the Bill, the Government asked for comments on additional proposals to move the services regime closer to the regime for goods by introducing an outcome-based quality standard for certain services, but the responses that we received gave a wide range of views, including contradictory views on whether an outcome-based standard would be easier to understand...Government feel that the evidence does not fully support the conclusion that they [BIS] came to and we have decided to stick with the current legal position requiring reasonable care and skill rather than introducing an outcomes-based quality standard. The current system is understood and it seems easier to apply, rather than introducing a new system that could be complicated and subjective, particularly as there are strong views on either side.[4]

The proposal by BIS set out in the Report was not a new one. The debate about aligning the regime between goods and services, so that consumers have the same rights in relation to contracts for goods as they do for services, has been going on for some time. The law on the sale of goods gives consumers certain objective verifiable rights that can be exercised, and which effectively impose a strict liability standard on traders to ensure that goods do comply with the statutory requirements now restated in Chapter 2 of the Act. This compares to the law on services, which is not so much about the standard to which a service is delivered or the result that is thereby achieved, but how it is delivered i.e. with reasonable care and skill. **5.12**

The issue was highlighted in the third edition of *Cranston's Consumers and the Law* where it says: **5.13**

Previous editions of this work have made a strong case for abandoning the reasonableness test and replacing it with strict liability for defective services....The central argument is that it is very difficult to know whether professional services or repairs to goods have been carried out to a standard of reasonable care and skill or not. There is also the difficulty of proving the breach of the standard.[5]

---

[4] House of Commons Hansard Debates 28 January 2014 (pt 0003) 15 March 2015, p. 5.
[5] C. Scott and J. Black, *Cranstons' Consumers and the Law* (London: Butterworths, 2000, 3rd edn) p. 202.

5.14   If the Act had introduced such a standard, it would mean that a service would have to meet either an objective standard, or at the very least a standard that would have been reasonably expected. The BIS Committee argued in the Report that introducing such a standard would have aligned the law on goods and services and thereby created more certainty for traders and consumers alike. The BIS Committee also anticipated the possibility that traders might negate such a standard by introducing long and complex disclaimers into their contracts. The BIS Committee in response argued in the Report that such a development could have been met with the adoption of a reasonable person test, i.e. that the outcome would be that which a reasonable person would expect, irrespective of what a disclaimer may have stated.

5.15   The government rejected the BIS Committee proposals set out in the Report. It considered that there was insufficient evidence of benefit to consumers, when weighed against the potential costs that would be incurred by traders, for introducing an outcome-based liability standard. The government stated in its response ('the Response') that the reasonable person test would be unsatisfactory: '...because of the subjective element of many services it may not be clear what a reasonable person might expect in different circumstances'.[6] The Response also went on to say that, although case law would build up over time to clarify in law the meaning of an outcome-based liability standard, case law is difficult for traders and consumers to follow in practice. Accordingly, the adoption of an outcome-based liability standard would create greater uncertainty for traders and consumers alike, without the promise of any consumer benefit later.

5.16   The Response further stated that merely aligning the regime between goods and services for its own sake is not sufficient by itself to introduce a reform that, in the opinion of the government, would not actually increase the level of consumer protection. The statement on page 26 of the Response illustrates this: 'the Government also recognises that differences in regimes are still sometimes necessary to ensure there are not unintended consequences. For example, applying a time limit to the short term right to reject goods could not be applied with the same meaning to services. It is therefore not a sufficient argument in itself.'[7] This position was again rehearsed by Jenny Willott, in the Public Bill Committee hearing on 4 March 2014:

We agree that if a trader says it will achieve a certain outcome that it does not then achieve, that can be incredibly frustrating for the consumer. That is why the Bill introduces a new

---

[6] Consumer Rights Bill: Statement on Policy Reform and Responses to Pre-Legislative Scrutiny Presented to Parliament by the Secretary of State for Business, Innovation and Skills by Command of Her Majesty <https://www.gov.uk/government/uploads/system/uploads/attachment_data/file/274912/bis-14-566-consumer-rights-bill-statement-on-policy-reform-and-responses-to-pre-legislative-scrutiny.pdf>.
[7] Response, p. 26.

statutory right. Members need only to look to clause 50, which makes it clear that where a trader gives information about itself or the service it provides and the consumer takes that into account, the trader must comply with that information and if not, the consumer has statutory remedies available. We debated at length this morning the ability of someone to learn to drive after a certain number of driving lessons, or to lose a certain amount of weight. Those are good illustrations of why the Government do not want to introduce a quality standard as such. Instead, clause 50 will be a much better way of addressing the concerns hon. Members have raised.[8]

C. COMMENT

Chapter 4 of the Act represents another step into the ongoing regulation of business-to-consumer service contracts. It introduces greater levels of protection than have been allowed for previously by introducing statutory rights and remedies into contracts for the provision of services for the first time. The changes made here are following the prevailing wind in consumer legislation. The law remains blind to the actual value exchange that takes place between consumer and trader (save for where the contract fails to stipulate a price) but seeks to protect the consumer by placing ever more obligations upon the trader, and by moving towards ever-greater levels of transparency.   5.17

The debates have moved a long way from the 1990s, when consumer protection legislation was very much in its infancy after the mass privatizations of the 1980s. Prior to the 1980s, utilities provided services in accordance with certain statutory requirements laid down by secondary legislation. After privatization, different sectoral regulators were set up to oversee liberalization and consumer protection. Those regulators have now established detailed sectoral regulatory regimes covering service providers in many different sectors. Traders complying with those requirements will also be subject to the obligations that are placed upon them by the Act. The introduction of statutory rights and remedies into consumer contracts for services is the latest step in that journey, but absent strong public enforcement or an affordable agency through which a consumer may exercise his or her rights, one has to question the extent to which these reforms will be effective and really have an impact on the operation of business-to-consumer contracts. In this context, the Directive on Alternate Dispute Resolution (Directive 2013/11/EU), in force from October 2015, and the Online Dispute Resolution Regulation (EU Regulation No 524/2013), in force from January 2016, may be of greater significance in allowing consumers to access justice and exercise these newly created rights in a meaningful way.   5.18

---

[8] Hansard: House of Commons Public Bill Committee: Consumer Rights Bill, 4 March 2014 , p. 25.

D. WHAT SERVICE CONTRACTS ARE COVERED?

1. Section 48: Contracts Covered by this Chapter

5.19   This section sets out which contracts are covered by Chapter 4. The section follows the same structure as set out in the corresponding section in the SGSA. However, unlike the SGSA, this section makes it clear that the Act only applies to contracts for service entered into between a trader and consumer, and defines these as 'a contract to supply a service'. The Act does not apply to contracts for service between consumers or between traders. The SGSA continues to apply to those kinds of contracts. Section 48 also follows the corresponding provision in the SGSA, in that it applies to contracts for service between a trader and consumer where an agent employed by the trader is supplying the service.

5.20   The section expressly excludes contracts of employment, which are governed by the Employment Rights Act 1996. The second part of section 48 sets out the express powers that may be exercised by the Secretary of State, by use of a statutory instrument, to disapply certain provisions of this chapter to contracts specified in that statutory instrument. This repeats the corresponding provision in the SGSA. Under that provision, the Secretary of State has in the past disapplied the relevant parts of the SGSA to contracts for services provided by: an advocate in a court or tribunal; a company director; a building society and the management of a provident society; and to services provided by an arbitrator. It is not clear at the time of writing whether or not these statutory instruments will remain in force, so as to disapply the relevant provisions of Chapter 4 of the Act to those same categories of service contracts.

5.21   Section 48(8) requires that a statutory instrument disapplying certain provisions of Chapter 4 to certain contracts for service must be laid before both Houses of Parliament before being legally effective. At the time of writing, no statutory instruments had been issued under section 48 of the Act.

E. WHAT ARE A CONSUMER'S STATUTORY RIGHTS?

1. Section 49: Service to be Provided with Reasonable Care and Skill

5.22   Under the corresponding provision of the SGSA, implied into every contract for service is a term stating that the trader will carry out the service with reasonable care and skill. Under section 49 of the Act, this concept of implied terms is done away with and replaced in effect with a scheme of statutory guarantees. The relevant revised wording in section 49(1) says, instead: 'Every contract to supply a service is to be treated as including a term that the trader must perform the service with reasonable care and skill'. The underlying intention here, as originally stated in the Report commissioned by BIS, was to move away from legalistic language which consumers could not reasonably be expected to understand and move towards a more straightforward modern construction that would allow consumers to better understand their rights where the trader has not performed his service with reasonable care and skill.

It remains to be seen if this will make the law easier to understand for consumers when exercising their statutory rights, especially as there is no further guidance on what reasonable care and skill actually means in practice. This omission can be forgiven, however, in that the Act is merely attempting in this context to re-state the law with greater clarity than before. The Explanatory Note to the Act makes this clear, with explicit references to how existing case law should still be relevant in determining, as a question of fact, whether or not a service has been provided with reasonable care and skill. It is important to note that, for the trader, regardless of the outcome of the service provided, if he has not provided that service with reasonable care and skill he will have breached the consumer's statutory rights and may be liable to provide the consumer with the statutory remedies provided for by sections 54, 55, and 56 of the Act.

The Act therefore gives the consumer a statutory right to have services performed 5.24 with reasonable care and skill, irrespective of the actual outcome of that service being provided. Section 49(2) contemplates a consumer having a right to the new statutory remedies set out in sections 55 and 56 of the Act where the trader is in 'breach of a term that this section requires to be treated as included in a contract'. There will be a range of factors that will be taken into account by a court in determining whether or not a service has been performed with reasonable care and skill, in line with existing case law.

The Explanatory Notes, at paragraph 244, state that the reason for this is to allow 5.25 the standard to be flexible between different industries and sectors, and to permit the courts to take into account existing case law on the meaning of this term. This approach also allows the court to take into account different standards and codes of practice that may apply in different sectors.

The leading cases on reasonable care and skill suggest that the trader must use 5.26 the reasonable skill expected of a competent person providing services of a similar nature. But the standard may vary, depending on who is providing the service, how much is being paid for it and what, therefore, the consumer could reasonably expect. For example, in *Philips v William Whitley Ltd* [1938] All ER 566, a jeweller piercing an ear is subject to a lower standard of care than a medical practitioner offering the same service. But if a business holds itself out as performing a service to a certain standard, the trader warrants that it has those skills and may therefore be held to a higher standard. See, for example, *Kimber v William Willett Ltd* [1947] 1 All ER 36, where expert carpet layers were held not to have performed their service with reasonable care and skill when the carpet they had laid had been left in a dangerous condition in premises which they knew to be occupied, even where the occupiers present exercised reasonable care.

In *Stewart v Ravells Garage* [1952] 1 All ER 1191, it was held that a garage carrying 5.27 out a motor repair was liable for the defective work carried out by a sub-contractor where the consumer had consented to that sub-contractor doing the work, unless the consumer chose the sub-contractor himself and did not place reliance upon the statements made by the trader.

5.28   In *Perry v Sharon Development Co Ltd* [1937] 4 All ER 390, it was held that a newly constructed house had to be completed in a workmanlike manner and contain all fittings, including water taps and baths that had been installed, and walls that had been plastered.

2. Section 50: Information about the Trader or Service to be Binding

5.29   This section represents a significant departure from the SGSA, in which there is no corresponding provision. The section introduces two new statutory rights for consumers that may have a significant impact on the terms under which traders provide services to consumers. Firstly, section 50 introduces a statutory right for consumers to have included as a term of the contract any statement made by the trader about the services or the trader, whether made orally or in writing. Secondly, the section operates so as to give effect to article 6 of the Consumer Rights Directive ('CRD'),[9] arguably beyond what the CRD allows for, by setting out that any information delivered to the consumer before the contract is entered into becomes a term of the contract and cannot be changed subsequently without the consumer 'expressly' agreeing to any such change.

3. Section 50(1) and Invitation to Treat

5.30   Section 50(1) of the Act has potential in its operation to raise questions over the law, as it distinguishes between an invitation to treat and a legally binding offer. But let us turn first to the underlying policy reasons for introducing this change. According to paragraph 246 of the Explanatory Notes, 'there may be consumer detriment where a trader may say something to a consumer, which the consumer then relies on, but which the trader later does not comply with' *and*:

> Secondly, for certain contracts, the 2013 Regulations[10] mandate that certain information must be made available by a trader to a consumer before the consumer is bound by a contract. To enable enforcement of those Regulations, the Act makes clear that these pieces of information will form part of the contract – so that the service must be provided as stated in the information – which cannot be altered unless the parties expressly agree otherwise (although it may not be necessary to do so where the pre-contract information itself reflects the fact that the particular potential changes envisaged may be made).

5.31   To achieve these two underlying policy objectives, section 50(1) states that: 'Every contract to supply a service is to be treated as including as a term of the contract anything that is said or written to the consumer, by or on behalf of the trader, about

---

[9] See Directive 2011/83/EU.
[10] The Consumer Contracts (Information, Cancellation and Additional Charges) Regulations 2013 (SI 2013/3134).

the trader or the service, if (a) it is taken into account by the consumer when deciding to enter into the contract, or (b) it is taken into account by the consumer when making any decision about the service after entering into the contract'.

The potentially wide ranging effect of this section is immediately qualified by the provision that follows, section 50(2), which says:
5.32

Anything taken into account by the consumer as mentioned in subsection (1)(a) or (b) is subject to—(a) anything that qualified it and was said or written to the consumer by the trader on the same occasion, and (b) any change to it that has been expressly agreed between the consumer and the trader (before entering into the contract or later).

The operation of section 50(1) in practice may undermine the certainty in the law on the distinction between invitation to treat and offer. For a contract to be legally binding, there must be an offer, acceptance and consideration. It is trite law to say that the courts therefore distinguish an offer from what is known as an 'invitation to treat' by objectively asking if the party intended to be legally bound by their statement to make an offer capable of acceptance. But under this statutory regime a statement, if made, is legally binding unless it is qualified on 'the same occasion', irrespective of whether or not the trader making the statement intended to be legally bound by it.
5.33

So whether or not an advert contains a legally binding offer capable of acceptance by the consumer is treated very much as a question of fact to be determined by whether or not the statement made was one by which the trader intended to be legally bound, or intended just to start negotiation. But under section 50 of the Act, the trader is legally bound by any statement he makes about either himself or the service, and which is taken into account by the consumer when entering into the contract or making any decision about the service after entering into the contract, save to the extent that the trader qualifies it 'on the same occasion'.
5.34

This would suggest that, unless the trader qualifies any statement made immediately at the time of making it, then that statement may become legally binding on the trader and may be included as a 'term of the contract'. But the trader may have no control over which statements the consumer chooses to take into account when entering into the contract. So whether or not the trader intended to be legally bound by a statement, it is for the consumer to determine which statements are legally binding upon the trader. This represents a potentially significant shift in the law towards creating new levels of protection for the consumer which may, however, have unintended consequences in the longer term for traders in the statements they choose to make. Traders will inevitably have to be more careful and circumspect, and may need to restrict themselves to statements they are absolutely sure they can comply with, as such statements will become a term of the contract where the consumer has taken them into account when making their decision.
5.35

How the Act will interact with The Consumer Protection (Amendment) Regulations 2014[11] ('CPUTs') remains to be seen. Although the concept of
5.36

---

[11] The Consumer Protection (Amendment) Regulations 2014 (SI 2014/870).

'transactional decision' which lies at the heart of the CPUTs is not mentioned in section 50, it is clear from the wording used that the section is very wide-ranging and intended to apply to any statement made by the trader which 'is taken into account by the consumer when deciding to enter into the contract'. In this context, traders need to be aware of how this section may operate in practice so as to create potential new liabilities to which the trader was not subject under the old SGSA (see paragraph 5.57 below on section 54 of the Act and which remedies for breach of section 50(1) by the trader may apply).

5.37   Traders also need to be aware that where they make statements about themselves which are not related to the service, these statements also become legally binding and form part of the contract for the supply of service to the consumer. Where these statements have become part of the contract, traders need to be aware that if they are then 'breached', the consumer will be entitled to claim a statutory remedy, in the form of a price reduction, from the trader (see paragraph 5.57 below on section 54 of the Act).

4. Changing Pre-Contractual Information

5.38   Section 50(3) goes on to say: 'any information provided by the trader in accordance with regulation 9, 10 or 13 of the Consumer Contracts (Information, Cancellation and Additional Charges) Regulations 2013 (SI 2013/3134) is to be treated as included as a term of the contract'. In doing so, section 50(3) merely repeats the provisions in the underlying CRD in relation to pre-contractual information that must be provided to a consumer before he is legally bound by the contract he is entering into.

5.39   However, the Act goes one step further, and arguably introduces a level of protection not allowed for in the CRD as a maximum harmonization Directive, where at section 50(4) the Act says: 'A change to any of the information mentioned in subsection (3), made before entering into the contract or later, is not effective unless expressly agreed between the consumer and the trader'.

5.40   The difficulty here is that article 6 of the underlying CRD contemplates and allows for 'pre-contract' information to be changed with the express agreement of the consumer before the contract is entered into. The recitals to the CRD contemplate a situation where the trader and consumer would have to expressly agree to any change in the pre-contractual information before the contract is entered into. For example, recital (35) in the preamble to the CRD says: 'The information to be provided by the trader to the consumer should be mandatory and should not be altered. Nevertheless, the contracting parties should be able to expressly agree to change the content of the contract subsequently concluded, for instance the arrangements for delivery'.

5.41   This is reflected in the guidance to the CRD, published by DG Justice, where at paragraph 4.2.5 it says: 'The provisions under Article 6(5) would not apply to any changes made by the trader to the terms of the contract after the contract has been concluded. The Unfair Contract Terms Directive 93/13/EEC14 would be relevant regarding such changes'.[12] It is also reflected in the guidance issued by BIS on Digital Content and the Competition and Markets Authority on Unfair Terms ('CMA Guidance'). The CMA Guidance emphasizes, at paragraphs 1.55 and 1.56 and at paragraphs 6.25 through to 6.29, the need to bring to the consumer's attention any changes that may be made to the contract before the consumer becomes legally bound by it and the legal difficulties of ensuring that such clauses comply with the requirements of the Act.

5. Unilateral Right to Vary

But these guidance documents both contemplate a situation where a unilateral right to vary may be exercised by the trader, provided it is narrowly drafted and brought to the consumer's attention, to address the imbalance thereby created between trader and consumer. Paragraph 23 of Schedule 2 to the Act suggests that such clauses will be fair if the trader is required to inform the consumer with reasonable notice and the consumer is free to dissolve the contract if he or she does not agree to the change that has been proposed. The Unfair Contract Terms Directive 1993 and Part 2 of the Act are designed to protect consumers from traders acting unilaterally to the detriment of consumers to the point where consumers suffer a significant imbalance. However, they explicitly allow for the fact that many traders will need to rely upon unilateral variation clauses. But the drafting of section 50(3) and (4) of the Act would appear, if interpreted literally, to prevent any unilateral right of variation being exercised by a trader unless the trader can show that this unilateral right of variation was part of the 'pre-contractual' information that the trader made available to the consumer before the contract was entered into. The CMA Guidance would appear to support this approach. Clarity on this point will be important for traders and regulators in the light of section 57 of the Act, which effectively makes it illegal for traders to contract out of the statutory remedies and rights that the Act provides for. See paragraph 5.72 below on section 57 of the Act.

5.42

6. Section 51: Reasonable Price to be Paid for a Service

This section repeats the principles set out in section 15 of the SGSA, but in keeping with much of the rest of the Act it does so by updating and modernizing the language used so that the law is clearer to consumers.

5.43

Most contracts for the supply of services will include a price, especially where those contracts are governed by the CRD and the associated Consumer Contracts (Information, Cancellation and Additional Charges) Regulations 2013. The section therefore only applies where the consumer has not paid a price for the services, the contract neither fixes a price nor sets out how a price may be calculated for the services, and anything that is included under section 50 does not state what the

5.44

---

[12] <http://ec.europa.eu/justice/consumer-marketing/files/crd_guidance_en.pdf>.

price is. If this is the case then the contract is treated as including a term that the consumer must pay a reasonable price for the service and no more.

5.45   As to what is a reasonable price, the section only states that a reasonable price is a question of fact and therefore leaves it open to the courts to work out what will be the best approach on a case by case basis. But paragraph 255 of the Explanatory Notes gives the following example:

> If a home owner engages a plumber to fix an urgent leak, he/she may not take the time to discuss the price before fixing the problem. The price might not be in the contract if the plumber did not know the problem before he/she arrived to fix it. If the leak was fixed in ten minutes and with only a £50 replacement part, the consumer has the right not to receive a bill for £1000, even though they did not negotiate the price in advance.

7. Section 52: Service to be Performed Within a Reasonable Time

5.46 As with section 51, this section only operates where the contract is silent as to the time frames within which a service must be performed. It corresponds to section 14 SGSA, which performed a similar role.

5.47   Where the contract does not state the time frame within which the service must be performed, and there is no information arising under section 50 as to when the service is to be performed, then the contract is deemed to contain a term that the trader must perform the service within a reasonable time. The section operates so as to give the consumer the right to have the service performed within a reasonable time where no time has been agreed. But what is a reasonable time is a question of fact and will fall to the courts to be decided on a case by case basis.

8. Section 53: Relation to Other Law on Contract Terms

5.48 Section 53 works so as to ensure that the Act operates without prejudice to other rules of law or enactments that may set down a stricter rule on the trader. The section goes on to make the services provisions contained in Chapter 4 of the Act subject to other enactments that define or restrict rights, duties, or liabilities arising in connection with a service. What are other rules of law and enactments? A rule of law is considered to be any rule of the common law that may apply in any given set of circumstances.[13] Enactments are defined in section 59 of the Act so as to include any primary or subordinate legislation, which is defined in the Interpretation Act 1978 as 'Orders in Council, orders, rules, regulations, schemes, warrants, byelaws and other instruments made or to be made under any Act'.

5.49   Section 53 corresponds to section 16 SGSA. In practice, it means that the Act applies alongside sector-specific legislation that may apply in certain indus-tries. Traders therefore need to be aware that, in addition to compliance with the

---

[13] Explanatory Notes para. 260.

provisions of the Act, more detailed sectoral regulation will continue to apply depending on the nature of the service they are supplying.

In certain sectors such as financial services, communications, utilities, and   5.50
energy, detailed sectoral regulations apply to traders offering such services that often provide much greater detail as to the standard of care to which services must be provided, beyond the test of reasonable care and skill that applies under the Act. Traders providing services that are subject to more detailed sectoral regulation will also be subject to the provisions of the Act, in the same way as traders operating in unregulated sectors.

Section 53 is the method by which the government intends to define the relation-   5.51
ship between the new rules on services in the Act and any sector-specific rules. As it states, this provision means that the sector-specific legislation applies alongside the sections set out in Chapter 4 of the Act. The government has declined to include any express carve-out for particular sectors, despite different stakeholders arguing that their particular service sector should be exempt from the provisions set out in the Act, based on already being subject to detailed sector-specific regulation. For example, the Law Society argued for an express carve-out for legal services in oral evidence to the BIS Committee.

In effect, this means that any existing enactment or rules of law which impose   5.52
stricter duties on traders will continue to stay in force and are not watered down or diminished by the provisions of the Act. Section 53(2) of the Act makes this clear. Where Parliament has legislated previously in an industry or service sector and has decreed that particular rules should apply there, then those rules will take priority over anything stated in the Act. The only example of sector-specific legislation given is financial services in paragraph 259 of the Explanatory Notes. But it should be noted that detailed sector-specific regulations exist now in many different sectors, including utilities, transport, and communications, in addition to financial services.

It is notable that the services provisions within Chapter 4 are the only ones   5.53
in the Act that allow for the imposition of stricter duties by way of a rule of law. Chapter 2 on Goods and Chapter 3 on Digital Content do not contain any equivalent provisions. However Chapter 2 does contain sections that make terms about quality and fitness for purpose, in relation to goods, subject to any enactment.

F. SUMMARY OF A CONSUMER'S STATUTORY RIGHTS

So under the Act the consumer now has the following statutory rights in relation to   5.54
contracts entered into for the provision of services by traders. Consumers have the right to have services:

• performed with reasonable care and skill;
• performed within a reasonable time frame.

5.55   In addition, consumers now have the right to treat as incorporated into the contract as a term any information provided by the trader about the service or the trader that is not qualified at the time of providing that information, and that the consumer has relied upon when making a decision (a) to enter into the contract; or (b) about the service after entering into the contract. Consumers also have the right to only pay a reasonable price for the service where the contract fails to stipulate what the price should be.

G. WHAT ARE A CONSUMER'S REMEDIES UNDER THE ACT?

5.56   The creation of statutory remedies under the Act for the consumer to exercise where a trader is in breach of any of sections 49 to 52 of the Act is a new development in the law and a significant departure from the SGSA, in which there are no corresponding rights. The Act effectively creates two new statutory remedies under section 55 (repeat performance) and section 56 (right to a price reduction), for a consumer to exercise where a contract for service has not been performed in conformity with the contract or with a consumer's statutory rights. Section 54 sets out the principle that a consumer has a statutory right to enforce terms in a contract for services and the operation of the section governs the circumstances under which the consumer may require either repeat performance or a price reduction.

1. Section 54: Consumer's Rights to Enforce Terms about Services

5.57   Section 54 sets out which of the two statutory remedies may apply in relation to any breach of sections 49, 50, and 52 by the trader, but also makes clear that the consumer's right to remedies that may arise at common law remain unaffected. Depending on the nature of the breach by the trader, the consumer will have access to two new statutory remedies that have no corresponding provision under the SGSA.

5.58   Where a trader fails to perform the service with reasonable care and skill, or fails to perform the service in line with information that is provided by the trader and which, by virtue of section 50, is now a term of the contract, the consumer has the the right to repeat performance (section 55) and if that is not possible the right to a price reduction (section 56). Where the trader is in breach of a term that arises under section 50 of the Act and which relates to the trader but not to the service, the consumer is entitled to a price reduction (section 56).

5.59   In this context, traders may need to take much more care in relation to statements they may make about themselves for reasons of corporate PR etc., if in fact those statements are not actually true and a consumer can show that he or she has taken those statements into account when entering into the contract with the trader.

5.60   By way of illustration, consumers will often contract with traders on the basis of their publicly stated adherence to certain corporate social responsibility standards or on the basis that they behave ethically. Under the Act, if a consumer can show that he relied on such statements when making a decision to enter into a service contract with a trader, then he will be entitled to a price reduction from the trader in relation to that service contract where he can show that the trader has breached those 'terms', even though the fact of breaching those terms has had no bearing on the level of service that the trader has continued to supply to the consumer. More specifically, for example, a consumer may have entered into a service contract with an energy company on the basis of how much 'clean' energy it had publicly stated it supplied. If that statement turned out to be untrue, then the consumer might be entitled to a price reduction from that trader even though there had been no diminishment in the quality of service provided.

If the trader is in breach of the requirements arising under section 52, namely per-   5.61
formance of the service within a reasonable time, the consumer is entitled to a price reduction under section 56. The Act sets out no remedies for a breach by the trader of section 51 (reasonable price to be paid for the service). But as section 51 is drafted so as to impose a duty on the consumer to pay a reasonable price for the service and no more, where the contract is silent on price, section 51 contains in effect its own remedy. So if the trader under section 51 does demand a sum of money in considera-tion that is too high, the consumer's remedy is effectively to enforce his or her rights under section 51 to pay no more than what is reasonable in the circumstances.

Section 54 goes on to explain that these new statutory remedies operate without   5.62
prejudice to any remedies the consumer may have under the existing common law. These remedies are specified in section 54(7) and include: the right to claim dam-ages; the right to seek specific performance; the right to recover monies paid to the trader; and the right to treat the contract as at an end. In exercising any of these specific common law remedies, the consumer must have regard to the existing rules governing their administration.

Damages: In a contract between a trader and consumer where the consumer is   5.63
able to show that his statutory rights have been breached, the consumer is entitled to claim damages on a restitutionary basis, i.e. an award of damages may be made to put the consumer back in the position he would have been in had the breach not occurred. This is provided that the consumer can show that the losses he has suffered are reasonably forseeable as a consequence of the breach, and that he has taken all necessary steps to mitigate or avoid suffering losses, in respect of which he may not otherwise be able to make a claim. The court may of course make an award of aggravated damages where the consumer has suffered mental distress as a result of the trader's breach.

In *Jarvis v Swan Tours Ltd* [1973] QB 233, a holiday maker, Mr Jarvis, obtained   5.64
sums in compensation greater than he had paid for the holiday to reflect the dis-appointment he experienced as a result of his Swiss skiing holiday not being as originally described. This included the bar not being open most nights, an absence of full length skis, the lack of a welcome party and the lack of any delicious Swiss cakes promised for tea. The award of damages made reflects the difficulty in con-sumer contracts of applying conventional tests when it comes to damages, as the contracts will often contain an element of satisfaction for the consumer which, when not obtained, cannot be compensated for by merely returning the original sum of money paid.

5.65   Specific performance: Where damages might not be an adequate remedy, the consumer may seek an order from the court for specific performance of the contract. The remedy of specific performance is an equitable remedy and does not arise as a right at common law. It is unlikely to be granted in a contract for personal services: where to do so would cause the defendant unnecessary hardship; where the contract is too vague to be enforced; where specific performance is impossible; where the contract could be terminated by either party at will; where the claimant (the consumer) has misbehaved and does not have clean hands; or where the contract itself was unconscionable.

5.66   The Act effectively puts the consumer in the position where he has the right to tiered remedies when a trader has breached his statutory rights. So where a trader either fails to provide a service with reasonable care and skill, or fails to provide a service in line with the information that the trader provided about the service, then the consumer may elect to have the service performed again (repeat performance). Where repeat performance is not possible or cannot be done in a reasonable time without causing the consumer serious inconvenience, the consumer has a right to have the price payable for service reduced (price reduction). The consumer is also entitled to claim a price reduction where the service is not performed within a reasonable time frame, or where the trader is in breach of a statement he has made about himself but not the service, and which the consumer has taken into account when entering into the contract, thus making it a term of the contract. Alternatively, the consumer may elect to pursue any of the remedies he may have at common law. Table 5.1 summarizes the remedies a consumer may obtain against a trader for a breach of sections 49, 50, and 52 of the Act.

Table 5.1 Consumer's statutory rights and remedies

Consumers' statutory right being breached	Remedies that apply
Service not performed with reasonable care and skill (section 49)	The right to ask for a repeat performance (sections 54 and 55) and, if that is impossible, or not done in a reasonable time without inconvenience: The right to a reduction in price (sections 54 and 56)
Service not performed within a reasonable time (section 52)	The right to a reduction in price (sections 54 and 56)
Service not performed inline with information provided concerning the service (section 50)	The right to ask for a repeat performance (sections 54 and 55) and, if that is impossible, or not done in a reasonable time without inconvenience: The right to a reduction in price (sections 54 and 56)
Service not performed inline with information provided concerning the trader (section 50)	The right to a reduction in price (Sections 54 and 56)

H. TABLE OF CONSUMER'S STATUTORY RIGHTS
AND REMEDIES THAT APPLY

1. Section 55: Right to Repeat Performance

Where this remedy applies, the consumer has the right to require the trader to 5.67
repeat performance of the contract to the extent necessary to ensure conformity
with the original contract. When exercising this remedy, the consumer has the
right to require the trader to repeat the performance within a reasonable time frame
without suffering significant inconvenience, and for the trader to bear any necessary costs in doing so. Section 54 of the Act makes clear that significant inconvenience or necessary costs are to be determined by taking into account the nature of
the service and the purposes for which it is provided. But where repeat performance
is not possible, the consumer has no right to require repeat performance under the
Act as a remedy.

How would repeat performance work in practice in a contract for continuous 5.68
supply, such as a contract between a consumer and trader for the supply of water
to domestic premises, in the event of the water supply either being inadvertently
cut off or being contaminated? In those circumstances, the trader's remedy to the
consumer would be the restoration of supply as soon as possible, following repair of
the water supply. Provided the service was then repeated in a reasonable time at the
trader's cost without causing the consumer signicant inconvenience, the trader will
have discharged his statutory duty to repeat performance. If the trader was unable
to repeat performance with a reasonable time, or without causing the consumer significant inconvenience, the consumer would then be entitled to a price reduction.

Similarly with contracts for services bespoke to the consumer, under the terms 5.69
of which a trader is providing a service which will result in the consumer acquiring ownership, use of and/or title to a physical good that the trader has made for
him; or alternatively, a contract under which the consumer will have acquired a
new skill which he paid the trader to teach him. Another example might be where
a trader fails in a contract for building services to complete the work paid for with
reasonable care and skill, or in line with the information incorporated into the contract by virtue of section 50 of the Act. Where the trader in these examples is able
to repeat performance without causing significant inconvenience to the consumer
and within a a reasonable time, the trader will have provided the statutory remedy
required of him. Requiring repeat performance in these situations is a meaningful
remedy capable of exercise by the consumer and performance by the trader.

2. Section 56: Right to a Price Reduction

The right to repeat performance is logically prior to the right to claim a price 5.70
reduction. Section 56 makes it clear that where a consumer has a right to require
repeat performance, he may only exercise his right to a price reduction where repeat

performance itself is not possible. Repeat performance may not be possible where the trader is unable to repeat performance in conformity with the original contract. Alternatively, the consumer may be entitled to a price reduction where the trader fails to repeat the performance within a reasonable timeframe and/or without causing the consumer to suffer significant inconvenience.

5.71   When exercising the right to a price reduction, the consumer may be entitled to require the trader to reduce the price by an appropriate amount. This might in the circumstances be a full refund. Where the trader agrees that the consumer does have a right to a price reduction and the amount to be refunded has been further agreed, then the trader must refund the consumer within fourteen days of the agreement being reached between them. Furthermore, the trader must refund the consumer using the same means of payment as that originally used by the consumer, unless the consumer expressly agrees otherwise, and the trader is expressly prohibited from imposing any fee on the consumer in respect of the refund.

I. CAN A TRADER CONTRACT OUT OF STATUTORY RIGHTS AND REMEDIES UNDER A SERVICES CONTRACT?

1. Section 57: Liability that Cannot be Excluded

5.72   Section 57 of the Act serves to prevent traders from 'contracting out' of the consumer's statutory rights as established under sections 49, 50, 51, and 52. So the trader is not able to rely upon any term in his contract with the consumer that may exclude the liability of the trader to perform the service with reasonable care and skill (section 49), or in conformance with the information provided to the consumer (section 50). The only exception to this principle is where the trader can show that he either qualified the information he provided to the consumer or expressly agreed a contract variation with the consumer (section 50(2)). In such circumstances, under section 50(2) a trader may exclude his liability for statements made where those statements are either qualified or superseded by a revised agreement with the consumer.

5.73   Section 57 also makes it clear that a trader cannot limit his liability for breach of a consumer's rights under sections 49 (reasonable care and skill), 50 (statements legally binding), 51 (reasonable price to be paid for a service), and 52 (service to be performed in a reasonable time), to less than the contract price paid. Of course, the trader can avoid liability under either of sections 51 and 52 by expressly disapplying them through stating both the price that is payable for the service and the time frame within which the service will be performed. In such circumstances, the trader will then be liable to the consumer for the information he has provided (price for the service and time by which the service will be performed) under section 50 of the Act, in relation to which the trader will not be able to exclude liability.

5.74   As section 57(3) of the Act makes it clear that the trader cannot limit his liability to the consumer for breaches of the consumer's rights under sections 49 to 52 to less than the total contract price, does this mean that the trader can limit his liability to no *more* than the contract price? Logically, it will be possible for traders to draft terms into their contracts that do limit (but do not exclude) their liability to the consumer to no more than the contract price paid. But it should be noted that any terms that do restrict the trader's liability to the contract price and no more will most likely be subject to a test of fairness under the unfair contract terms provisions in Part 2 of the Act.

Section 57(6) makes it clear that any agreement with the consumer to send dis- 5.75 putes to arbitration is not to be treated by itself as excluding liability for breaching a consumer's statutory rights for the purposes of the Act. However, it should be noted that under paragraph 20 of Schedule 2 to the Act, any term that requires a consumer to take disputes to arbitration may fall to be considered as unfair. There is, of course, a difference between a trader and a consumer mutually agreeing to refer their disputes to arbitration, as contemplated by this section, and a contract clause that obliges the consumer to seek arbitration to resolve disputes. Not only would such a clause risk being assessable for fairness under Part 2 and Schedule 2 of the Act, but it could also be construed as excluding a trader's liability for breaches of the consumer's statutory rights under the Act, if the trader sought to rely upon the clause to prevent the consumer from either claiming his statutory remedies or from pursuing any remedy he would otherwise have at common law.

6

UNFAIR CONTRACT TERMS

A. BACKGROUND

The legislation that governs unfair contract terms is the Unfair Contract Terms Act 1977 ('UCTA'). It has a wider scope than just the business-to-consumer relationships that are governed by this Act.   6.01

Since the Unfair Terms in Consumer Contract Regulations 1999 ('UTCCRs') were passed they have enabled consumers to challenge most non-negotiated terms of a contract on the grounds that they are unfair. Those Regulations brought into force the Unfair Contract Terms Directive ('UTD').[1]   6.02

The effect of the Act on the UCTA is to amend it to make plain that the latter Act applies to business-to-business and consumer-to-consumer contracts only.   6.03

The effect of the Act on the UTCCRs is that they are replaced by the Act.   6.04

The background history reflects the tension between two interpretations of the economic interests of consumers. In the battle between the advocates of consumer rights and the supporters of free competition, the latter emerged victorious in the Council of Ministers. As Professor Hugh Collins neatly expressed it:[2]   6.05

The Directive does not require consumer contracts to be substantively fair, but it does require them to be clear. Clarity is essential for effective market competition between terms. What matters primarily for EC contract law is consumer choice, not consumer rights.

The purpose of the UTD has been described as follows: 6.06

The system of protection introduced by the Directive is based on the idea that the consumer is in a weak position vis-a-vis the seller or supplier, as regards both his bargaining power and his level of knowledge. That leads to the consumer agreeing to terms drawn up in advance by the seller or supplier without being able to influence the content of those terms...Such an imbalance

---

[1] Council Directive 93/13/EEC.

[2] Professor Hugh Collins, 'Good Faith in European Contract Law' (1994) 14(2) *OJLS* 229 cited in *OFT v Abbey National* [2010] 1 AC 696 at para. 44.

between the consumer and the seller or supplier may only be corrected by positive action unconnected with the actual parties to the contract.[3]

6.07 The UTD is not designed to protect consumers from entering into disadvantageous contracts. The consumer is deemed to be adequately protected with regard to the main subject matter through competition.[4] But the Court of Justice of the European Union ('CJEU') has emphasized that the enforcement of the UTD should deter the further use of unfair terms. That may mean group enforcement actions before an unfair term is actually used:

> The deterrent nature and dissuasive purpose of the measures to be adopted, together with their independence from any particular dispute mean, as the Court held, that such actions may be brought even though the terms which it is sought to have prohibited have not been used in specific contracts, but have only been recommended by suppliers and sellers or their associations.[5]

6.08 There is an obvious tension between the contracting parties' freedom to arrange their own affairs and the need for statutory intervention in favour of consumer protection. One of the ways in which the UTD achieves that it is by article 4(2):

> Assessment of the unfair nature of the terms shall relate neither to the definition of the main subject matter of the contract nor to the adequacy of the price and remuneration, on the one hand, as against the services or goods supplied in exchange, on the other, in so far as these terms are in plain intelligible language.

6.09 The rationale behind this article is that it would be a bar to freedom of contract for the court to determine whether the essence of the contract and the price of the contract were fair. The equivalent Australian legislation describes these elements as the main subject matter and the 'upfront price payable'.[6]

6.10 Spain, however, has omitted this exemption in its entirety, because Member States may go beyond the minimum harmonization requirements of the UTD by adopting more stringent measures to protect consumers. Members States still have a level of discretion in this area.[7]

B. AIMS OF THIS PART

6.11 Part 2 of the Act is described as having the following aims in the Explanatory Notes:

---

[3] *Oceano Grupo Editorial SA v Murciano Quintero* (Joined Cases C-240-244/98) [2000] ECR I-4941, paras 25, 27.

[4] Per AG Trstenjak in *Caja de Ahhors* (C-484/08) [2010] ECR I-04785.

[5] *Commission v Italy* (C-372/99) [2002] ECR I-819.

[6] Competition and Consumer Law 2010 Sch. 2 s. 26.

[7] The Law Commission explained that it had not been able to discern a common trend among Member States on how the UTD had been implemented and applied (*Unfair Terms on Consumer Contracts Issues* para. 7.75).

- Consolidates the legislation governing unfair contract terms in relation to consumer contracts, which currently is found in two separate pieces of legislation, into one place, and removes anomalies and overlapping provisions in relation to consumer contracts.

- Makes clearer the circumstances when the price or subject matter of the contract cannot be considered for fairness, and in particular makes clear that to avoid being considered for fairness, those terms must be transparent and prominent.

- Clarifies the role of and extends the indicative list of terms which may be regarded as unfair (the so-called 'Grey List') (see Table 6.1).

In 2005, the two Law Commissions published a joint report on unfair terms.   6.12
In 2012 the Department of Business Innovation and Skills ('BIS') asked them
to review the report.

The Law Commissions explained that in reaching their proposals they had to   6.13
consider the following factors:

(1) The law should be compatible with European Union law. As the UTD is a minimum harmonization measure, the UK may not provide a lower standard of consumer protection;

(2) Although our proposals may go beyond what is strictly required by the UTD, we should not gold-plate the UTD to the extent that it imposes significant costs on traders;

(3) The law should be compatible with the grey list set out in Schedule 2 of the UTCCRs. We think the intention of the UTD is that the exemption should not apply to these terms;

(4) The law should preserve consumer rights under UCTA;

(5) The CJEU has stressed that implementing legislation must be 'precise and clear'. Stakeholders have asked for more certainty over the meaning of the exemption, though that certainty is not always easy to deliver.

The aim of the Law Commission (consistent with the UTD) was to ensure   6.14
that consumers knew what they had to pay and what they would receive in
return. The starting point should be the same as the UTD, namely to distinguish between terms which are subject to competition and those which are buried in 'small print'. They give a helpful description of 'small print' in consumer
contracts. It is not just about font size, but, for example, legal jargon and inadequate signposting.

Their proposals also considered whether a term was transparent and promi-   6.15
nent. If so, it should not be assessed for fairness. The reason is that it will be
subject to competitive pressures. If hidden in a document in such a way that
even an observant and circumspect consumer is unlikely to read it, it should not
contain unfair surprises. 'Transparent' should be defined as in plain and intelligible language, readily available and, if in writing, legible.

The test of prominence should refer to the average consumer test, which is   6.16
widely used in European consumer law. It refers to a hypothetical consumer who

is 'reasonably well informed, reasonably observant and circumspect'.[8] As a result, a term would be prominent if it were presented in such a way that the average consumer would be aware of it. The more unusual or onerous the term, the more prominent it would need to be.

C. THE GUIDANCE

6.17 Parliament has published guidance.[9] There is detailed guidance as well as two Competition and Markets Authority ('CMA') publications aimed at smaller business and others who want a short introduction to unfair contract terms law. The Guidance says that it does not state the law, only the view of the CMA about how it is to operate.

D. WHAT CONTRACTS AND NOTICES ARE COVERED BY THIS PART?

6.18 This Part applies to a contract between a trader and a consumer.[10] A contract to which this this Part applies is referred to as a 'consumer contract'.[11] Importantly, this Part applies to a notice, to the extent that it:

• Relates to rights or obligations as between a trader and a consumer; or
• Purports to exclude or restrict a trader's liability to a consumer.

6.19 As the Explanatory Notes[12] explain, this applies to both contractual and non-contractual consumer notices. A consumer notice includes an announcement or other communication which it is reasonable to assume is intended to be read by a consumer:

Non contractual consumer notices (e.g. a sign in a car park) do not include an exchange of something in return for something else of value (known as 'consideration') as a contract does.

6.20 The Guidance explains that the Act's intended effect is to apply in substance the same test for consumer notices and contract terms.[13]

6.21 This does not include a contract of employment or an apprenticeship. It also does not include a notice relating to rights, obligations or liabilities as between an employer and an employee, as they are regulated by specific employment legislation.

---

[8] See e.g. *Gut Springenheid GmbH and Rudolf Tusky v Oberkreisdirektor des Kreises Steinfurt-Amt fur Lebensmitteluberwachung* (C-210/96) [1998] ECR I-4657, as well as reg. 2(2) of the Consumer Protection from Unfair Trading Regulations 2008 ('CPRs').
[9] <https://www.gov.uk/government/system/uploads/attachment_data/file/450440/Unfair_Terms_Main_Guidance.pdf>.
[10] See Ch 1.
[11] s. 61(1) and (2).
[12] para. 295.
[13] para. 2.9.

E. WHAT ARE THE GENERAL RULES ABOUT FAIRNESS OF CONTRACT TERMS AND NOTICES?

1. Section 62: Requirement for Contract Terms and Notices to be Fair

An unfair contract term is not binding on the consumer; nor is an unfair consumer **6.22** notice.[14] This has come from regulation 8 of the UTCCRs. This does not prevent the consumer from relying on the term or notice if the consumer chooses to do so.

The critical two subsections dealing with contractual terms are as follows: **6.23**

Section 62(4)

A term is unfair if, contrary to the requirement of good faith, it causes a significant imbalance in the parties' rights and obligations under the contract to the detriment of the consumer.

This provision reflects regulation 8 of the UTCCRs.[15] **6.24**

Section 62(5)

Whether a term is fair is to be determined—
(a) Taking into account the nature of the subject matter of the contract, and
(b) by reference to all the circumstances existing when the term was agreed and to all of the other terms of the contract or of any other contract on which it depends.

The critical two subsections dealing with notices are as follows. There are subtle **6.25** differences:

Section 62(6)

A notice is unfair if, contrary to the requirement of good faith, it causes a significant imbalance in the parties' rights and obligations to the detriment of the consumer.

Section 62(7)

Whether a notice is fair is to be determined—
(a) taking into account the nature of the subject matter of the notice, and
(b) by reference to all the circumstances existing when the rights or obligations to which it relates arose and to the terms of any contract on which it depends.

These four subsections do not affect the operation of the other provisions of the **6.26** Act that deal with the exclusion of liability for goods, digital content contracts, and service contracts, and the exclusion of negligence liability from the provisions of the Act.[16] The effect is that terms that are void will still be void regardless of the fairness test explained in this section.

This Part brings together sections 4 and 11 UCTA, and implements articles 3, **6.27** 4, and 6 UTD.

The Guidance explains that the fairness test contains three elements: 'signifi- **6.28** cant imbalance', 'consumer detriment', and 'good faith'. The overall requirement is a

---

[14] s. 62(1) and (2).
[15] See art. 3 UTD.
[16] See ss 31, 47, 57, and 65.

unitary one—the question is whether a term is unfair. A rigid approach, the Guidance suggests, is not appropriate.[17]

2. Significant Imbalance and Good Faith

6.29 Assistance with regard to these terms is to be found in the *First National Bank* case:[18]

> The requirement of significant imbalance is met if a term is so weighted in favour of the supplier as to tilt the parties' rights and obligations under the contract significantly in his favour. This may be by the granting to the supplier of a beneficial option or discretion or power, or by the imposing on the consumer of a disadvantageous burden or risk or duty...But the imbalance must be to the detriment of the consumer; a significant imbalance to the detriment of the supplier, assumed to be the stronger party, is not a mischief that the Regulations seek to address. The requirement of good faith in this context is one of fair and open dealing. Openness requires that the terms should be expressed fully, clearly and legibly, containing no concealed pitfalls or traps. Appropriate prominence should be given to terms that might operate disadvantageously to the customer. Fair dealing requires that a supplier should not, whether deliberately or unconsciously, take advantage of the consumer's necessity, indigence, lack of experience, unfamiliarity with the subject matter of the contract, weak bargaining position or any other factor listed in or analogous to those listed in [...] the Regulations.

6.30 A further example of how this provision might work in practice is set out in the Explanatory Notes:[19]

> For example, a contract to subscribe to a magazine could contain a term allowing the publisher to cancel the subscription at short notice. In deciding whether this is fair or not, the court could consider issues such as whether the subscriber can also cancel at short notice or obtain a refund if the publisher cancels the contract.

6.31 The Guidance also refers to the fact that the focus of the fairness test, particularly as regards imbalance, is upon the consumer's broad legal rights. It gives the example of a term which allowed the trader to pass on information which is contrary to the Data Protection Act. That may not involve cost, but would take away a consumer's rights under other legislation. Recital (16) in the preamble to the UTD explains that the fairness assessment must include an 'overall evaluation of the different interests involved'.

6.32 The CMA also considers that the Act seeks to address the fact that most consumers do not read standard written contracts before making a purchase. The Guidance cites with approval the judgment of Mr Justice Kitchin in *OFT v Ashbourne Management Services Limited*,[20] which concerned contracts for gym clubs. The learned judge had regard to the consumer's own irrationality:[21]

> In this regard, the defendants know that the average consumer overestimates the use he will make of the gym and that frequently unforeseen circumstances make its continued use impossible or

---

[17] Guidance para 2.10.
[18] *Director General of Fair Trading v First National Bank* [2001] UKHL 52 at para. 17.
[19] para. 299.
[20] [2011] EWHC 1237 (Ch).
[21] See discussion in the Introduction regarding behavioural economics.

his continued membership unaffordable. They are also well aware that the average consumer is induced to enter into one of their agreements because of the relatively low monthly subscriptions associated with them but that if he ceases to use the gym after between three and six months he would be better off joining on a pay per month basis. Yet the defendants take no steps to have these matters brought to the attention of consumers. Nor do the defendants ensure that consumers are made clearly aware of their overall liability at the outset which might alert them to the risks associated with early termination and the likely benefits of entering into an agreement for a shorter term.

3. All the Circumstances Existing When the Term was Agreed

In the Guidance, the CMA makes the distinction between what this term means when considering a particular contract, and when considering enforcement action for the CMA:
  6.33

A term must be assessed taking account of all the circumstances existing when it was agreed. This is not inherently difficult in a case involving a single transaction. An example of a relevant circumstance would be whether the consumer was given a genuine opportunity to understand and consider the term. For the purpose of an enforcement case, however, the position is less straightforward, because enforcement action focuses on consumer transactions generally. The CMA considers that the assessment of fairness in such cases cannot appropriately be based on all the circumstances existing at the time any particular term was agreed. Rather the enforcer should apply the above requirement as best it can, by reference to a correctly defined hypothetical consumer for that case. In order for the provision to work effectively in such cases, account needs to be taken of the effects of contemplated or typical relationships between the contracting parties.[22]

They cite with approval the exhortation of Lord Steyn in *Director of First Trading v First National Bank*[23] that:
  6.34

The Directive and the Regulations must be made to work sensibly and effectively and this can only be done by taking into account the effects of contemplated and or typical relationships between the contracting parties.

4. Section 63: Contract Terms which May or Must be Regarded as Unfair

Section 63 cross-refers to Part 1 of Schedule 2. It contains an indicative and non-exhaustive list of terms on consumer contracts that may be regarded as unfair for the purposes of this Part. It comes from the 'Grey List' of the UTCCRs.[24] This list should be construed restrictively.[25] The Secretary of State may add, modify or remove an entry in the list.[26] The regulations used letters, to which the authorities make reference. Schedule 2 uses numbering. Both are included in the table below for ease of reference.
  6.35

---

[22] Guidance para. 2.34.

[23] [2002] 1 AC 481 para. 33.

[24] This kind of list creation is quite popular in EU consumer law. The CPRs contains a 'black list' of banned practices.

[25] per Lord Steyn in *First National Bank* at para. 34 and per Lord Walker in *OFT v Abbey National* para. 43.

[26] s. 63(3).

6.36   Part 2 of Schedule II qualifies the scope of the Grey List. Three new paragraphs have been added to the Grey List as result of the recommendations of the Law Commissions in their report of March 2013. There are also some subtle changes to the language from the UTCCRs.

6.37   The three new ones are as follows:

- Terms of a contact which have the object or effect of requiring that a consumer pay a disproportionate amount if he or she decided not to continue the contract; for example, termination fees.[27]

- Terms which have the object or effect of allowing the trade to determine the subject matter of the contract after the contract has been agreed with the consumer.[28] In certain circumstances, this does not apply to contracts which last indefinitely.

- Terms which have the object or effect of allowing the trader to set for the first time the price under a contract *after* the contact has been agreed with the consumer.[29] Table 6.1 sets out the contracts to which this does not apply. Terms on the Grey List are assessable for fairness even if they would otherwise qualify for an exemption under section 64 below, and even if they are 'transparent' and 'prominent'.

6.38   A useful summary of the type of terms in the Grey List Schedule is found in the Guidance.[30] It is said that the Grey List terms cause or allow one or more of the following common problems:

(1) Consumers being denied full redress if things go wrong;

(2) Consumers being tied into the contract unfairly;

(3) The trader not having to perform his or her obligations;

(4) Consumers unfairly losing prepayments if the contract is cancelled;

(5) The trader unfairly varying the terms after they have been agreed, for instance, so as to supply a different product, raise the price or reduce consumer rights;

(6) The trader determining the price or subject matter of the contract after the consumer is bound by it;

(7) Consumers being subject to unfair financial penalties.

6.39   The role of the list was described in *Commission v Sweden*,[31] which was a case brought by the Commission about how the Grey List had appeared in the Swedish legislation incorporating the UTD:

It is not disputed that a term appearing in the list need not necessarily be considered unfair and, conversely, a term that does not appear in the list may none the less be regarded as unfair...In so far as it does not limit the discretion of the national authorities to determine the unfairness

---

[27] See no. 5 in Table 6.1.
[28] See no. 12 in Table 6.1.
[29] See no. 15 in Table 6.1.
[30] Guidance para. 2.39.
[31] (C-478/99) [2002] ECR I-4147.

of a term, the list contained in the annex to the Directive does not seek to give consumers rights going beyond those that result from Articles 3 to 7 of the Directive...Inasmuch as the list contained in the annex to the Directive is of indicative and illustrative value, it constitutes a source of information both for the national authorities responsible for applying the implementing measures and for individuals affected by those measures. (paras 20–22)

The content of the annex should be regarded as an essential element on which the court may base its assessment as to the unfair nature of the term.[32] However, as the Guidance sets out, there are some consumer contract terms which fail the test of fairness without obviously corresponding to any of the types of potential unfairness set out in the Grey List (see Table 6.1).[33] They give examples of allowing a trader to impose unfair financial burdens, transferring inappropriate risks to consumers, unfair enforcement powers, excluding a consumer's right to assign, and others. The table below contains the relevant terms, and then the paragraphs that qualify them.

6.40

F. THE GREY LIST

Table 6.1 The Grey List

1 (a)	A term which has the object or effect of excluding or limiting the trader's liability in the event of the death of or personal injury to the consumer resulting from an act or omission of the trader. This does not include a term which is of no effect by virtue of section 66 (exclusion for negligence liability).
2(b)	A term which has the object or effect of inappropriately excluding or limiting the legal rights of the consumer in relation to the trader or another party in the event of total or partial non-performance or inadequate performance by the trader of any of the contractual obligations, including the option of offsetting a debt owed to the trader against any claim which the consumer may have against the trader.
3 (c)	A term which has the object or effect of making an agreement binding on the consumer in a case where the provision of services by the trader is subject to a condition whose realization depends on the trader's will alone.
4 (d)	A term which has the object or effect of permitting the trader to retain sums paid by the consumer where the consumer decides not to conclude or perform the contract, without providing for the consumer to receive compensation of an equivalent amount from the trader where the trader is the party cancelling the contract.
5 (New)	A term which has the object or effect of requiring that, where the consumer decides not to conclude or perform the contract, the consumer must pay the trader a disproportionately high sum in compensation, or for services which have not been supplied.
6 (e)	A term which has the object or effect of requiring a consumer who fails to fulfil his obligations under the contract to pay a disproportionately high sum in compensation.
7 (f)	A term which has the object or effect of authorising the trader to dissolve the contract on a discretionary basis where the same facility is not granted to the consumer, or permitting the trader to retain the sums paid for services not yet supplied by the trader where it is the trader who dissolves the contract.

(Continued)

---

[32] *See Nemzeti Fogyasztovedelmi Hatosag v Invitel Tavkozlesi Zrt* (C-472/10) [2012] 3 CMLR 1 and *Matei and another v SC Volksbank România SA* [2015] 1 WLR 2385.

[33] Guidance para. 5A.1.

Table 6.1 (*Continued*)

8 (g)	A term which has the object or effect of enabling the trader to terminate a contract of indeterminate duration without reasonable notice except where there are serious grounds for doing so. This is subject to paragraphs 22, 23, and 24. See below.
9 (h)	A term which has the object or effect of automatically extending a contract of fixed duration where the consumer does not indicate otherwise, when the deadline fixed for the consumer to express a desire not to extend the contract is unreasonably early.
10 (i)	A term which has the object or effect of irrevocably binding the consumer to terms with which the consumer has had no real opportunity of becoming acquainted before the conclusion of the contract.
11 (j)	A term which has the object or effect of enabling the trader to alter the terms of the contract unilaterally without a valid reason which is specified in the contract. This is subject to paragraphs 22, 23, and 24.
12 (new)	A term which has the object or effect of permitting the trader to determine the characteristics of the subject matter of the contract after the consumer has become bound by it. This is subject to paragraph 23.
13(k)	A term which has the object or effect of enabling the trader to alter unilaterally without a valid reason any characteristics of the goods, digital content, or services to be provided.
14 (New)	A term which has the object or effect of giving the trader the discretion to decide the price payable under the contract after the consumer has become bound by it, where no price or method of determining the price is agreed when the consumer becomes bound. This is subject to paragraphs 23, 24, and 25.
15(l)	A term which has the object or effect of permitting a trader to increase the price of goods, digital content, or services without giving the consumer the right to cancel the contract if the final price is too high in relation to the price agreed when the contract was concluded. This is subject to paragraphs 24 and 25.
16 (m)	A term which has the object or effect of giving the trader the right to determine whether the goods, digital content, or services supplied are in conformity with the contract, or giving the trader the exclusive right to interpret any term of the contract.
17 (n)	A term which has the object or effect of limiting the trader's obligation to respect commitments undertaken by the trader's agents or making the trader's commitments subject to compliance with a particular formality.
18 (o)	A term which has the object or effect of obliging the consumer to fulfil all of the consumer's obligations where the trader does not perform the trader's obligations.
19 (p)	A term which has the object or effect of allowing the trader to transfer the trader's rights and obligations under the contract, where this may reduce the guarantees for the consumer, without the consumer's agreement.
20 (q)	A term which has the object or effect of excluding or hindering the consumer's right to take legal action or exercise any other legal remedy, in particular by— (a) requiring the consumer to take disputes exclusively to arbitration not covered by legal provisions, (b) unduly restricting the evidence available to the consumer, or (c) imposing on the consumer a burden of proof which, according to the applicable law, should lie with another party to the contract.

QUALIFYING PARAGRAPHS

21	Paragraph 8 (cancellation without reasonable notice) does not include a term by which a supplier of financial services reserves the right to terminate unilaterally a contract of indeterminate duration without notice where there is a valid reason, if the supplier is required to inform the consumer of the cancellation immediately.

22   Paragraph 11 (variation of contract without valid reason) does not include a term by which
      a supplier of financial services reserves the right to alter the rate of interest payable by or due
      to the consumer, or the amount of other charges for financial services without notice where
      there is a valid reason, if—
           (a) the supplier is required to inform the consumer of the alteration at the earliest
                opportunity, and
           (b) the consumer is free to dissolve the contract immediately.

23   Paragraphs 11 (variation of contract without valid reason), 12 (determination of
      characteristics of goods etc after consumer bound) and 14 (determination of price after
      consumer bound) do not include a term under which a trader reserves the right to alter
      unilaterally the conditions of a contract of indeterminate duration if—
           (a) the trader is required to inform the consumer with reasonable notice, and
           (b) the consumer is free to dissolve the contract.

24   Paragraphs 8 (cancellation without reasonable notice), 11 (variation of contract without
      valid reason), 14 (determination of price after consumer bound) and 15 (increase in price) do
      not apply to—
           (a) transactions in transferable securities, financial instruments and other products or
                services where the price is linked to fluctuations in a stock exchange quotation or
                index or a financial market rate that the trader does not control, and
           (b) contracts for the purchase or sale of foreign currency, traveller's cheques or
                international money orders denominated in foreign currency.

25   Paragraphs 14 (determination of price after consumer bound) and 15 (increase in price) do
      not include a term which is a price-indexation clause (where otherwise lawful), if the method
      by which prices vary is explicitly described.

1. The Distance Marketing Directive

The Distance Marketing Directive was implemented in the UK in the Financial   6.41
Services (Distance Marketing Regulations) 2004.[34] It applies to distance contracts
made on or after 31 October 2004. It sets common minimum standards for the
information that must be given to cancellation rights. It has provisions to protect
consumers in relation to the misuse of payment cards in connection with distance
contracts for financial services, unsolicited supplies of financial services, and unsolicited communications about such services.

Section 63(6) explains that a term of a consumer contract must be regarded as   6.42
unfair if it has the effect of the consumer having to bear the burden of proof to
show non-compliance with the Directive.

2. Section 64: Exclusion from Assessment of Fairness

Section 64 concerns the limitations to sections 62 and 63. If a term is in the Grey   6.43
List it can be assessed for fairness. All other terms in a consumer contract can be
assessed for fairness except for those governed by section 64.

Before looking at the specific provisions, it is important to consider the background.   6.44

---

[34] The Directive is complex and outside the scope of this book.

3. *Office of Fair Trading v Abbey National Plc* [2009] UKSC 6

6.45   This was a test case brought by the Office of Fair Trading ('OFT') against seven banks and a building society. The issue to be determined was whether charged-for unauthorized overdrafts were exempt from an assessment for fairness because they were price terms within the meaning of regulation 6(2).

6.46   However, the limited nature of what the Supreme Court was determining is emphasized in the speech of Lord Walker in the Supreme Court:

> The members of the court are well aware of the limited nature of the issue which we have to decide in this appeal. But many of the general public (who are understandably taking a close interest in the matter) are not so well aware of its limited scope. It is therefore appropriate to spell out at the outset that the court does not have the task of deciding whether the system of charging personal current account customers adopted by United Kingdom banks is fair [...] The question for the court is much more limited, and more technical. It is whether as a matter of law the fairness of bank charges levied on personal current account customers in respect of unauthorized overdrafts (including unpaid item charges and other related charges as described below) can be challenged by the respondent, the Office of Fair Trading ('OFT'), as excessive in relation to the services supplied to the customers.

6.47   The case is concerned with regulation 6(2) of the 1999 Regulations:

> Assessment of the unfair nature of the terms shall relate neither to the definition of the main subject matter of the contract nor to the adequacy of the price and remuneration, on the one hand, as against the services or goods supplied in exchange, on the other, in so far as these terms are in plain intelligible language.

6.48   The OFT advanced the argument that the fairness of payment obligations falling within regulation 6(2)(b) were exempt from assessment in point of adequacy (appropriateness) only if they formed part of the essential bargain between the parties. The essential bargain constituted only so much of the contract as the consumer can be said to have consented to freely. The relevant charges were *ancillary* payment obligations and were not incurred in the normal performance of the contract. The typical consumer would not clearly recognize them as the price of services supplied by the banks in exchange.

6.49   The Supreme Court did not agree. Banking overdraft charges were monetary consideration for the package of banking services supplied. They were an important part of the bank's charging structure. Provided the terms were in plain and intelligible language, any assessment under the UTCCRs was excluded by regulation 6(2).

6.50   The decision made by the Supreme Court has led to fundamental uncertainty. That, at least, was the view of the Law Commission in their Consultation Paper.[35] Their view was that the Supreme Court decision can be interpreted in several ways, and the courts could use it to justify a variety of approaches:

- Some judicial statements in the case say that price terms in plain, intelligible language are exempt from review—and suggest that any term requiring the

---

[35] Law Commission, 'Unfair Terms on Contracts Issues', July 2012, para. 5.84.

consumer to pay money may constitute the price if it forms part of the trader's revenue stream.

- Other statements suggest that not all payments constitute the 'price or remuneration' of goods or services supplied in exchange. In particular, terms on the Grey List, including default payments and price escalation charges, are not exempt from review.
- Some statements say that even price terms can be challenged as unfair, provided the challenge is on grounds which do not relate to the appropriateness of their amount.

Reaction to the decision was 'strong and predictable', to quote the Law Commission.[36] **6.51** The banks thought the decision was a good one. Consumer groups were disappointed and shocked. An empathetic commentary to the position the Supreme Court found itself in was provided by Philip Morgan:[37]

The Supreme Court was in a very difficult position. If the OFT had been successful, the Banks would be facing an Armageddon claim...This could expose the Banks to vast claims covering the time period from the introduction of such charges. Following the demise of Equitable Life, the Supreme Court must be well aware that one appellate decision can be the deathblow to a financial institution. Given the economic climate and the state support for the banking sector, the taxpayer would be left to pick up the bill. One cannot but wonder if this is the hidden theme behind the judgment.

The Law Commission summarized the four main arguments against the Supreme **6.52** Court's reasoning:

- The court focused too much on the money the banks made from the charges.
- The court had failed to take a purposive approach.
- It should have referred the case to the CJEU.
- The court had failed to protect consumers against unfair surprise.

However, *Abbey National* is cited with approval in the Explanatory Notes: **6.53**

The Supreme Court concluded that the concepts of main subject matter and price are to be narrowly construed as "*the two sides of the* quid pro quo *inherent in any consumer contract*", that is, the goods or service that the trader agrees to provide, and the price that the consumer agrees to pay.[38]

The author of the note also points out the narrow nature of the interpretation of **6.54** the decision in *Abbey National*.

---

[36] 'Unfair Terms in Consumer Contracts Issues' para. 6.1.
[37] P. Morgan, 'Bank charges and the Unfair Terms in Consumer Contracts Regulations 1999: the end of the road for consumers' (2010) *Lloyds Maritime and Commercial Law Quarterly* 208 p. 214, cited by the Law Commission, 'Unfair Terms in Consumer Contracts Issues,' para. 6.5.
[38] Explanatory Notes para. 315.

4. Section 64: The Core Exemption[39]

6.55 Section 64 is therefore the critical section:

(1) A term of a consumer contract may not be assessed for fairness under section 62 to the extent that—
   (a) it specifies the main subject matter of the contract, or
   (b) the assessment is of the appropriateness of the price payable under the contract by comparison with the goods, digital content or services supplied under it.
(2) Subsection (1) excludes a term from an assessment under section 62 only if it is transparent and prominent.
(3) A term is transparent for the purposes of this Part if it is expressed in plain and intelligible language and (in the case of a written term) is legible.
(4) A term is prominent for the purposes of this section if it is brought to the consumer's attention in such a way that an average consumer would be aware of the term.

6.56   In order for a contract to be excluded from assessment, it must be transparent *and* prominent.

6.57   The Law Commission had, in 2005, included a clause to state that the price exemption did not include payments that would be 'incidental or ancillary to the main purpose of the contract'.

6.58   In *Abbey National*, this approach was criticized on the basis that in many contracts it was impossible to distinguish between main and ancillary charges. As Lord Walker explained at paragraph 46, whilst terms such as 'ancillary', 'subordinate', 'incidental', 'non-core', and 'collateral' may be of some assistance, they should be treated with caution.

6.59   During the course of the debates in the Public Bill Committee there was a discussion about whether or not this clause needed to cover future fees or charges, and an amendment to that effect was proposed by the Opposition. The relevant Minster said the following:

The amendment covers an issue that the Government have looked at in great detail. We asked the Law Commission to look at it twice, in 2005 and 2012. It was also widely debated when we published the draft Bill and during the pre-legislative scrutiny. We all agree that it is important to get this right. The breadth of the exemption and how to access it has been unclear for far too long. It should not have taken several high-profile cases to interpret the law. Consumers should know what to expect and traders should know what they have to do . . . . The advice from the Law Commission was that the word prominent would tease out a lot of the issues that have been raised.[40]

5. Prominence and Transparency

6.60 In order for a trader to be able to rely on section 64, the term must be transparent and prominent. A term is transparent if it is expressed in plain and intelligible

---

[39] The Guidance at s. 5 sets down the CMA's views as to the scope of the exemptions from the fairness assessment in Part 2 of the Act.

[40] Hansard House of Commons Public Bill Committee: 6 March 2014 at Col 493.

language and (in the case of a written term) is legible. A term is prominent for the purposes of this section if it is brought to the consumer's attention in such a way that an average consumer would be aware of the term. Section 69(1) makes it clear that if a term in a consumer contract or notice could have different meanings, the meaning that is most favourable to the consumer is to prevail.

Section 68 requires that the contract terms must be transparent, but that is not 6.61 enough. If a company produces clear terms, a consumer might not read them if they are at the bottom of a long and rather tedious document. The Law Commission opined that this means that a reasonable consumer must be aware of the terms even if he did not read the full contractual document.

The Minister gave the following assistance during the Public Bill Committee: 6.62

The point is that this matter has been considered at length by the Supreme Court, which gave a clear judgment on what could and could not be considered as part of the price. Clearly, hidden charges that people do not know about or that are suddenly included in a contract at a later date could not be considered to have been prominent at the beginning. The costs associated with a particular contract are protected if they are transparent and prominent. If they are not transparent or prominent, they are not protected or exempt from being assessed for fairness. If an organisation hides price terms in the small print or they are not clear to consumers, those price terms would not be considered prominent and transparent and so would be assessable for fairness. The protection is only for price terms that are prominent and transparent.[41]

Furthermore, the more unusual or onerous the term, the more prominent it will 6.63 need to be. This is not explicit in the Act, but is plain from the Explanatory Notes, which in turn cross-refer to the common law position. If a party seeks to rely on such a term, that party must take the necessary steps to bring it to the attention of the other contracting party.

The leading UK case on this issue remains *Interfoto Picture Library Ltd v Stiletto* 6.64 *Visual Programmes Ltd*.[42] The court cited with approval an earlier judgment of Lord Denning in *J. Spurling v Bradshaw*[43] that some terms 'would need to be printed in red ink on the face of the document with a red hand pointing to it before the notice could be held to be sufficient'.

They held that, where clauses incorporated into a contract contained a particu- 6.65 larly onerous or unusual condition, the party seeking to enforce that condition had to show that it had been brought fairly and reasonably to the attention of the other party.

Lord Bingham's judgment in *Interfoto* contains a rather dry summary of the 6.66 English law's approach to the whole issue of fair trading:

In many civil law systems, and perhaps in most legal systems outside the common law world, the law of obligations recognizes and enforces an overriding principle that in making and carrying out contracts parties should act in good faith. This does not simply mean that they

---

[41] Hansard House of Commons Public Bill Committee: 6 March 2014 at Col 493.
[42] [1989] 1 QB 433.
[43] [1956] 1 WLR 461.

should not deceive each other, a principle which any legal system must recognise; its effect is perhaps most aptly conveyed by such metaphorical colloquialisms as "playing fair," "coming clean" or "putting one's cards face upwards on the table." It is in essence a principle of fair and open dealing. [...] English law has, characteristically, committed itself to no such overriding principle but has developed piecemeal solutions in response to demonstrated problems of unfairness.

6.67   The importance of the Guidance was highlighted during the passage of the Bill through the House of Lords:

The noble Baroness, Lady Drake, said that prominence is not sufficient to ensure that consumers understand the terms. We agree that terms should be written in language that consumers understand and that is why all terms must be written in plain and intelligible language. We will be giving guidance on what prominence requires and how it is defined. Business prefers this guidance to detail on the face of the Bill.[44]

6.68   Transparency is a specific requirement in its own right as well as being fundamental to fairness in a general sense.[45] The UTD requires (in recital (20)) that the consumer should actually be given an opportunity to examine all the terms. The Guidance also gives the following important drafting tip:

Terms should not only be comprehensible but drafted to ensure that consumers are put in a position where they can make an informed choice about whether or not to enter the contract, on the basis of a proper understanding of the terms for sensible and practical purposes. Contracts should be structured clearly, and explained in accompanying literature as necessary. Consumers need to be able to see and understand terms that could disadvantage them. However, in relation to 'the core exemption', the requirement of transparency is supplemented by an additional condition of prominence.[46]

6. The Average Consumer

6.69   Who is the average consumer? He is a consumer who is reasonably well-informed, observant, and circumspect.[47] This is an objective test, which is not based on the understanding or expectations of a particular consumer.[48] The European Commission Guidance has emphasized that the average consumer is a 'critical person, conscious and circumspect in his or her market behaviour'. However the average consumer's level of attention is likely to vary according to the category of goods and services in question.[49] The view of the Law Commission was that the average consumer cannot be expected to read every term in a standard contract presented

---

[44] Lords Hansard 1 July 2014 at Col 1693 per Viscount Younger.

[45] Guidance para. 2.44.

[46] Guidance para. 3.19.

[47] s. 66(5).

[48] See reg. 2(2) Consumer Protection from Unfair Trading Regulations 2008 *and Gut Springenheide GmbH and Rudolf Tusky v Oberkreisdirektor des Kreises Steinfurt-Amt für Lebensmittelüberwachung* (C-210/96) [1998] ECR I-4657.

[49] *Office of Fair Trading v Ashbourne Management Services Ltd* [2001] EWHC 1237 (Ch) at para. 55.

Table 6.2 Chart for core exemption

Q1	Does the term have the object or effect of a term on the Grey List?	Yes	The term is fully assessable for fairness	No	Go to Q2
Q2	Is the fairness assessment of the main subject matter of the contract?	Yes	Go to Q4	No	Go to Q3
Q3	Is the fairness assessment of the appropriateness of the price in comparison with the services, goods or digital content supplied in exchange?	Yes	Go to Q4	No (i.e. answers to Q2 and A3 are no)	The 'core exemption' does not apply
Q4	Is the term transparent and prominent?	Yes	The term benefits from 'the core exemption'	No	The term is fully assessable for fairness

to them.[50] Table 6.2 sets out the core exemptions included in the Guidance at   **6.70**
paragraph 3.16.

7. Section 65: Bar on Exclusion or Restriction of Negligence Liability

Section 2 UCTA has been re-written and transposed into this section as it applies   **6.70**
to business-to-consumer contracts.

A trader cannot by a term of a consumer contract or by a consumer notice exclude   **6.71**
or restrict liability for death or personal injury resulting from negligence.

Where a term of a consumer contract, or a consumer notice, purports to exclude or   **6.72**
restrict a trader's liability for negligence, a person is not to be taken to have voluntarily
accepted any risk merely because the person agreed to or knew about the term or notice.

In this section, 'personal injury' includes any disease and any impairment of   **6.73**
physical or mental condition.

In this section, 'negligence' means: **6.74**

(1) the breach of any obligation to take reasonable care or exercise reasonable skill
in the performance of a contract where the obligation arises from an express or
implied term of the contract;

(2) a common law duty to take reasonable care or exercise reasonable skill;

(3) the common duty of care imposed by the Occupiers' Liability Act 1957 or the
Occupiers' Liability Act (Northern Ireland) 1957.

It is immaterial for the purposes of subsection (4):   **6.75**

(1) whether a breach of duty or obligation was inadvertent or intentional; or

(2) whether liability for it arises directly or vicariously.

---

[50] See Law Commission, 'Unfair Terms in Consumer Contracts Issues,' para. 7.42 which includes a helpful discussion of the European case law.

6.76   As the Explanatory Notes set out with regard to other loss or damage, the trader can only limit his or her liability if the clause is 'fair', as defined in paragraph 6.22. They give the following example:

> For example, if an individual contracts with a catering company to provide a buffet lunch, and a term in that contract states that the catering company accepts no responsibility for death by food poisoning caused by their negligence, that term is not binding. The catering company can, however, and providing the clause is fair, limit liability if it breaks kitchen equipment.[51]

6.77   Section 66 limits the scope of section 65 to a limited extent. It does not apply to insurance contracts, or contracts involving interests in land.

6.78   Section 67 deals with the rest of the non-infringing part of the contract. The rest continues to have effect in every other respect. The rationale is that it may not be in the interests of the consumer or the business for the entire contract not to be binding any more.[52]

8. The Black List

6.79   The Guidance provides the following very useful compendious table regarding when terms are 'blacklisted' under the Act.[53] We have set it out in Appendix 5. The Act makes certain contract terms and notices legally ineffective. They are neither binding on, nor enforceable against, consumers. They are automatically unenforceable without having regarding to any general fairness test in Part 2 of the Act.

G. HOW ARE THE GENERAL RULES TO BE ENFORCED?

1. Section 70: Enforcement of the Law on Unfair Contract Terms

6.80   Schedule 3 sets out the rules regarding enforcement. It makes it plain that the Schedule applies to the same material as this section of the Act (i.e. terms and notices).

6.81   A regulator[54] may consider a complaint about a term or notice.[55] If that is to be done by someone other than the CMA, they must notify the CMA. If they decide not to act, they must notify the complainant with reasons.

6.82   An injunction may be sought under Schedule 3 paragraph 3 if the regulator thinks that the following grounds are made out:

- The person is using, or proposing or recommending the use of, a term or notice to which the Schedule applies;
- The notice purports to exclude liability for the lists of requirements in sections 31, 47, 57 and 65(1); in other words, any purported exclusion from the fundamental

---

[51] Explanatory Notes para. 317.
[52] Reflecting reg. 6 of the UTCCRs, which in turn implemented art. 4(2) of the UTD.
[53] At para 4.28.
[54] Defined as including the following: the CMA, a weights and measures authority, the Financial Conduct Authority, the Office of Communications, the Office of Rail and Road, the Consumers Association, and the water, gas, and electricity regulators.
[55] Sch. 3 para. 2.

requirements within the Act for goods contracts, digital content contracts, and services contracts, as well as the provisions within this section regarding business liability for death or personal injury;

- The term or notice is unfair to any extent;
- The term breaches the section 68 requirement for transparency.

A regulator may apply for an injunction under this section whether or not there **6.83** has been a complaint. There is obviously scope for the CMA to continue to regulate by exploring parts of the market about which it is concerned, even in the absence of a complaint. If any application is to be made by a regulator other than the CMA, it must notify the CMA that it intends to do so. The regulator may make the application only if fourteen days have passed since the CMA was notified, or the CMA has waived that requirement. It must notify the CMA afterwards of the outcome and the conditions of any application.

The court may grant an injunction on such conditions as it thinks fit, not surpris- **6.84** ingly. The scope of any such injunction could be very wide, since the court is given power to include provisions about any term of any consumer contract of a similar kind with similar effect. Furthermore, it is not a defence to show that because of a rule of law the term would not be enforceable in any event.

The regulator may accept undertakings from a person against whom it has **6.85** applied or thinks it is entitled to apply. These provisions echo the amendments to the Enterprise Act set out in Schedule 7 of the Act.

There are various provisions dealing with the publication of such applications. **6.86**

H. SUPPLEMENTARY PROVISIONS

1. Section 71: Duty of Court to Consider Fairness of Terms

The court is obliged to consider the fairness of a term even if none of the parties to **6.87** the proceedings has raised the issue.[56] However, the court must consider whether it has sufficient legal and factual material to enable it to consider the fairness of the term.

This is an obligation made plain in the EU jurisprudence. *Mostaza Claro v Centro* **6.88** *Movil Millennium* SL[57] made it plain that there was an obligation on the court to consider whether a term was unfair, whether or not that had been pleaded by consumer:

The nature and importance of the public interest underlying the protection which the Directive confers on consumers justify, moreover, the national court being required to assess of its own motion whether a contractual term is unfair, compensating in that way for the imbalance which exists between the consumer and the seller or supplier.

---

[56] s. 71.
[57] [2007] Bus LR 60 para. 38.

6.89   There is an obligation on the national court as a result of the UTD to consider the unfairness of a contractual term where it had available to it the legal and factual elements necessary for that task.[58] The court should focus on the term or terms in question, rather than the entire contract.

6.90   If a term of a secondary contract reduces the rights or remedies, or for that matter increases the obligations of a person under another contract, then it is governed by section 72. In those circumstances, the term is subject to the provisions of this part of the Act. It does not matter whether or not the parties are the same, or for that matter whether the secondary contract is a consumer contract. The rationale is that consumers are protected from other agreements made after, before, or in addition to the contract they have signed.[59]

6.91   This Part[60] does not apply to a term of a contract which reflects mandatory statutory or regulatory provisions, or principles of an international convention to which the UK or the EU is a signatory. This reflects article 1(2) of the UTD:

> The contractual terms which reflect mandatory statutory or regulatory provisions and the provisions or principles of international conventions to which the Member States or the Community are party, particularly in the transport area, shall not be subject to the provisions of this Directive.

6.92   If the law of a country or territory other than an European Economic Area ('EEA') state is chosen by the parties to govern the contract, but the consumer contract has a close connection with the UK, the Part still applies.

6.93   The Rome I Regulation[61] governs which law applies to a consumer contract. It confirms that it is open to a consumer and trader to choose the law of any country to govern their contract. However, if the trader pursues or directs his or her activities to the UK, and the consumer is habitually resident in the UK, the protections in the Act will apply.

6.94   If there is no choice as to jurisdiction and the trader pursues activities in the UK, the contract is also governed by UK law.[62] A trader who claims that an individual is not a consumer must prove it. That applies in relation to Part 2 of the Act as well as Part 1.[63]

I. OTHER RELEVANT LEGISLATION

6.95   As the Guidance makes plain, the Act should not be looked at in a vacuum. The interaction with other Regulations is important, in particular the Consumer Protection from Unfair Trading Regulations 2008 (as amended) and the Consumer Contracts

---

[58] *Pannon GSM Zrt v Sustikne Gyorfi* [2010] 1 All ER (Comm) 640 and see the Explanatory Notes at para. 335.
[59] See Explanatory Notes para. 336.
[60] s. 73.
[61] EC Regulation 593/2008.
[62] s. 74.
[63] s. 2(4).

(Information, Cancellation, and Additional Charges) Regulations 2013.[64] The former are described as the CPRs in the Guidance.

1. The Consumer Protection from Unfair Trading Regulations 2008

It is suggested in the Guidance that the CPRs create a general duty not to trade unfairly.[65] That is to describe the Regulations in rather inflated language. The CPRs suggest that unfair commercial practices are prohibited, but then go on to set out the circumstances in which a commercial practice is unfair. The CPRs cover commercial practices, and are concerned with acts (etc.) by a trader directly connected with the promotion, sale, or supply of a product to or from consumers, and whether before, after, or during the commercial transaction. 'Product' means any goods or service, and so covers both goods within the Act and no doubt digital content as well.   **6.96**

An example of the overlap is given in the Guidance regarding misleading actions and omissions.[66] The Guidance suggests that a term which is potentially onerous, but hidden away, or buried in the small print, may be open to challenge in three ways: as an unfair term; as a breach of the transparency provisions in the Act; or as a breach of the CPRs.[67]   **6.97**

Another example is given which demonstrates how potentially wide ranging the Act and CPRs are in tandem: **6.98**

The CPRs' misleading practices provisions are particularly relevant to the requirement that written terms or notice are transparent. There may also be overlaps between the use of unfair terms and the other provisions in the CPRs. For instance, the CPRs prohibit commercial practices which fail to meet a standard defined particularly by reference to honest market practice, where there is likely to be an appreciable impact on consumers' ability to make an informed decision. Using, recommending or enforcing a contract term that is unfair under the Act, and therefore unenforceable, is inherently likely to be considered an unfair practice under the CPRs, and subject to enforcement action, having regard to this standard.[68]

2. The Consumer Contracts (Information, Cancellation and Additional Charges Regulations 2013)

The CCRs require pre-contract information to be provided to consumers. The information should be provided in a clear and comprehensible manner. The information includes: **6.99**

- The main characteristics of the goods, services or digital content;

- Arrangements for carrying out the contract (for example, performing the service or delivering the goods);

---

[64] The Guidance cites the CPUT guidance issued by the OFT in 2008 (OFT 1008).
[65] reg. 3(1).
[66] regs 5 and 6 of the CPUTs.
[67] Guidance para. 1.50.
[68] Guidance para. 6.24.

- The total price;
- In the case of digital content, its functionality and compatibility.

6.100   This pre-contractual information is legal binding as much as the contract itself. Businesses cannot contract out of this obligation. Any term which purports to do so is blacklisted in the Act. The Guidance points out that any variation provision in the pre-contractual information (for example, a price change over time) must be subject to the requirements of fairness under the Act, including transparency. As a result, the consumer must be able to foresee the incidence, nature, and extent of any changes.[69]

---

[69] Guidance para. 6.28.

7

CONSUMER LAW
ENFORCEMENT POWERS

A. OVERVIEW

In March 2012, the government launched a consultation on the modernization and consolidation of enforcement powers in the field of consumer law.[1] Schedule 5 of the Act 2015 is the end product of that consultation.

The policy of the government was clear:

7.01

7.02

I accept that local authority budgets are squeezed, and sometimes trading standards are squeezed relatively severely. We can help with that by helping to rationalize their operations, training and cross-border co-operation. A further set of measures in the Bill relates to consumer law enforcement. We will consolidate and simplify the investigatory powers of consumer law enforcers—this takes us back to the discussion we have just had on local trading standards officers—into one generic set to make it easier for enforcers and businesses to understand what powers can be used and in what circumstances. We estimate that that measure alone will save businesses around £40 million during the next 10 years. We will also make it easier for trading standards to collaborate across local authority boundaries to tackle the kind of rogues we saw in a recent scam drawing people throughout the country into costly and unnecessary driveway repairs.[2]

The Act consolidates the plethora of investigatory and enforcement powers that govern the diverse areas covered by existing consumer protection legislation. Prior to the Act, investigatory and enforcement powers were spread over sixty different pieces of legislation. Over and above the fact that many pieces of legislation overlapped each other, the dispersal of these provisions over so many pieces of legislation made for an enforcement regime that was said to be unclear and inconsistent.[3]

7.03

---

[1] 'Enhancing consumer confidence through effective enforcement, a consultation on consolidating and modernising consumer law enforcement powers', Department for Business, Innovations and Skills, March 2012 <http://www.bis.gov.uk/Consultations/consultation-on-consumer-law-enforcement-powers>.

[2] Hansard House of Commons 28 January 2014 Col. 772, per Vince Cable Secretary of State for BIS.

[3] See para. 343 of the Explanatory Notes <http://www.publications.parliament.uk/pa/bills/lbill/2014-2015/0029/en/15029en.pdf>.

7.04   Additionally, the powers to be found in the various pieces of legislation were often subtly different in application even where similar in form. Respondents to the Department for Business, Enterprise and Regulatory Reform Consumer Law Review Call for Evidence in 2008 felt that this variation in investigatory powers was confusing to businesses and enforcers, making it difficult for them to know what these powers were in every circumstance. In their response to the Consumer Law Review, the Confederation of British Industries said:

> For instance at the moment the powers of entry and investigation vary considerably according to the legislation under which they are exercised; there is significant variation between the powers to enter premises, to inspect and seize goods or documents with or without a warrant under the Consumer Protection from Unfair Trading Regulations The Act consolidates the plethora of Investigatory and Enforcement Powers that govern the diverse areas covered by existing Consumer Protection legislation. Prior to the Act; Investigatory and Enforcement Powers were spread over 60 different pieces of legislation, over and above the fact that many pieces of legislation overlapped each other, the dispersal of these provisions over so many pieces of legislation made for an enforcement regime that was said to be unclear and inconsistent.[4]

7.05   The focus of the Act has therefore been to ensure a consistency of approach by simplifying and streamlining the legislation, thus reducing the scope for conflict between enforcers, business, and the consumer about what powers are applicable and in what circumstances they can be used. It should, however, be noted that the Act only consolidates those powers under Department for Business, Innovation and Skills ('BIS') led pieces of legislation. Therefore the enforcement powers in relation to other areas, such as food or animals, will be unaffected.

7.06   The Act now contains a generic set of powers which are based on those currently found in Part 4 of the Consumer Protection from Unfair Trading Regulations 2008 ('CPUTR'); these are therefore said to be relatively modern and reflective of current business practices.[5] As such, these consolidated powers will be largely familiar to enforcers, businesses, and consumers alike. Alongside the generic powers, specific powers emanating from weights and measures legislation and general product safety legislation have been retained.

7.07   Broadly speaking, the powers can be viewed as having been split into two categories: those powers which can be exercised without entry into premises having to be gained; and those that are reliant on entry to premises.

7.08   Over and above consolidation, the Act adds certain safeguards to the way powers can be used by enforcers, the rationale behind this being that it will reduce the burden on businesses in complying with their obligations. Whether this concession to businesses will become a hindrance to effective enforcement remains to be seen.

7.09   Furthermore, the powers contained within the Act are still subject to the provisions found in the Regulation of Investigatory Powers Act 2000, and the limitations on the use of those powers as set out in the Protection of Freedoms Act 2012.

---

[4] See para. 351 of the Explanatory Notes.
[5] See para. 353 of the Explanatory Notes.

As such, enforcers will still need to be mindful of those provisions, including seeking judicial approval for use of certain investigatory techniques where appropriate.

The generic set of powers applies to all enforcers detailed in Schedule 5 except 7.10 where access to powers is specifically limited for particular enforcers. For example, the powers of unfair contract terms enforcers and public designated enforcers are restricted to the power to require production of information. Equally, some powers have specific limitations placed upon their application; for example, the new power to require the production of information can only be used if the enforcer has a reasonable belief that a breach of the legislation has taken place.

In addition, the Bill implements some provisions (in respect of enforcement) of EC 7.11 Regulation 2006/2004 of the European Parliament and Council on co-operation between national authorities responsible for the enforcement of consumer protection laws; EC Regulation 765/2008 of the European Parliament and Council on the requirements for accreditation and market surveillance relating to the marketing of products; Directive 2001/95/EC of the European Parliament and Council on general product safety; and Directive 98/27/EC of the European Parliament and Council on injunctions for the protection of consumers' interests.

To those who are area enforcers, the thorny issue of jurisdiction has now been clari- 7.12 fied once and for all. The spectre of section 222 of the Local Government Act 1972 has been forever banished with the conformation that proceedings for infringements of the enforcers' legislation may be brought outside the boundaries of the area enforcer.

Given that enforcement is key to effective regulation, it is perhaps surprising that 7.13 the provisions are tucked away in the Schedules to the Act, specifically Schedules 5 and 6. Section 77 of the Act gives effect to these Schedules. In respect of Chapter 3 Part 3 (Duties of Letting Agents to Publicize Fees etc.), section 77 and Schedule 5 are in force as of the 27 May 2015 in England only.[6] Otherwise, the provisions will come into force on a day to be appointed.[7]

B. WHO CAN ENFORCE?

The type of enforcer has to be determined by reference to what is being investigated 7.14 and enforced. This also determines what investigatory powers are available. An examination of who is able to enforce will be the first step in most investigations. The Act sets out four broad categories of enforcer: a domestic enforcer;[8] an EU enforcer;[9] a public designated enforcer;[10] and an unfair contract terms enforcer.[11]

---

[6] See The Consumer Rights Act 2015 (Commencement) (England) Order 2015 (SI 2015/965 (C. 62)).
[7] See The Consumer Rights Act 2015 (Commencement No. 3, Transitional Provisions, Savings and Consequential Amendments) Order 2015 (SI 2015/1630).
[8] Sch. 5 para. 2(1)(a).
[9] Sch. 5 para. 2(1)(b).
[10] Sch. 5 para. 2(1)(c).
[11] Sch. 5 para. 2(1)(d).

These are further defined in paragraphs 3 to 6 of Schedule 5. As will be seen below, a number of different bodies fall into more than one category.

7.15   Paragraph 3 of Schedule 5 lists those enforcers who are domestic enforcers, namely:

(a) the Competition and Markets Authority;
(b) a local weights and measures authority in Great Britain;
(c) a district council in England;
(d) the Department of Enterprise, Trade and Investment in Northern Ireland;
(e) a district council in Northern Ireland;
(f) the Secretary of State;
(g) the Gas and Electricity Markets Authority;[12]
(h) the British Hallmarking Council;
(i) an assay office within the meaning of the Hallmarking Act 1973; or
(j) any other person to whom the duty in subsection (1) of section 27 of the Consumer Protection Act 1987 (duty to enforce safety provisions) applies by virtue of regulations under subsection (2) of that section.

7.16   Domestic enforcers are those who have specific powers or duties to enforce consumer protection legislation or notices within the United Kingdom.[13] If a piece of legislation is not contained within either paragraph 10 or 11 of Schedule 5, then there is no specific duty to enforce and the generic powers contained within the Act will not be applicable. Paragraph 10 thus provides a consolidated list of those pieces of legislation where there is a duty to enforce. For everyone dealing with the area of consumer protection, paragraph 10 is to be welcomed, as it provides a handy ready reckoner of those pieces of domestic legislation to which the powers will apply.[14]

7.17   The table contained in paragraph 11 of Schedule 5 of the Act is reproduced in Table 7.1:

Table 7.1 Schedule 5 paragraph 11

Enforcer	Legislation
A local weights and measures authority in Great Britain or the Department of Enterprise, Trade and Investment in Northern Ireland.	Section 35ZA of the Registered Designs Act 1949.
A local weights and measures authority in Great Britain or the Department of Enterprise, Trade and Investment in Northern Ireland.	The Measuring Container Bottles (EEC Requirements) Regulations 1977 (SI 1977/932).
The Secretary of State.	The Alcoholometers and Alcohol Hydrometers (EEC Requirements) Regulations 1977 (SI 1977/1753).

---

[12] But is not a domestic enforcer for the purposes of Part 4 of the Schedule, Sch. 5 para. 3(2).

[13] Sch. 5 para. 9(1)(a) and (b).

[14] See the Appendices to this work.

A local weights and measures authority in Great Britain.	The Weights and Measures Act 1985 and regulations and orders made under that Act.
A local weights and measures authority in Great Britain or the Department of Enterprise, Trade and Investment in Northern Ireland.	The Measuring Instruments (EEC Requirements) Regulations 1988 (SI 1988/186).
A local weights and measures authority in Great Britain or the Department of Enterprise, Trade and Investment in Northern Ireland.	The Financial Services and Markets Act 2000 so far as it relates to a relevant regulated activity within the meaning of section 107(4)(a) of the Financial Services Act 2012.
A local weights and measures authority in Great Britain or the Department of Enterprise, Trade and Investment in Northern Ireland.	The Non-Automatic Weighing Instruments Regulations 2000 (SI 2000/3236).

Domestic enforcers have over recent years brought proceedings under more   7.18
diverse legislation than that which is contained in paragraphs 10 and 11, using the
wide discretion conferred by section 222 of the Local Government Act 1972, the
Fraud Act 2006 being one such example. By limiting the list of applicable legislation to those where there is a pre-existing statutory duty to enforce and investigate,
the drafters may have inadvertently set the scene for further confusion and conflict
between enforcers and businesses over what powers are applicable when utilizing
these provisions.

An EU enforcer is a UK enforcement body that has been designated for   7.19
the purpose of Regulation 2006/2004 on consumer protection cooperation.
This Regulation sets out the framework for the designated authorities in EU
Member States to co-operate with each other on the enforcement of consumer
protection laws.

Paragraph 4 sets out those enforcers who are EU enforcers, namely: 7.20

(a) the Competition and Markets Authority;

(b) a local weights and measures authority in Great Britain;

(c) the Department of Enterprise, Trade and Investment in Northern Ireland;

(d) the Financial Conduct Authority;

(e) the Civil Aviation Authority;

(f) the Secretary of State;

(g) the Department of Health, Social Services and Public Safety in Northern Ireland;

(h) the Office of Communications;

(i) an enforcement authority within the meaning of section 120(15) of the Communications Act 2003 (regulation of premium rate services);

(j) the Information Commissioner.

Paragraph 5 of Schedule 5 defines public designated enforcers. At the time of   7.21
writing, these include: the Financial Conduct Authority ('FCA'); the Information
Commissioner ('ICO'); the Consumers' Association (Which?); Ofcom; Ofgem; the

Office of Rail Regulation; the Water Services Regulation Authority; the Director General of Electricity Supply for Northern Ireland; and the Director General of Gas for Northern Ireland; all of whom have been designated by the Secretary for State under section 213 of the Enterprise Act 2002. These are in addition to the Competition and Markets Authority, every weights and measures agency in Great Britain, and the Department of Enterprise, Trade and Investment in Northern Ireland.

7.22   In order to be an unfair contract terms enforcer, a body needs to be both a public authority, as defined in section 6 of the Human Rights Act 1998, and also be listed in paragraph 8 of Schedule 3 to the Act.[15]

C. THE POWERS

7.23   As stated above, the Act contains a set of generic powers that are applicable to all pieces of consumer legislation listed in Schedule 5, paragraphs 10 and 11 to the Act, in addition to the power to compel the provision of information. The generic powers are only available to domestic and EU enforcers, and then can only be used in certain circumstances.

7.24   Whilst each broad category of generic power will be looked at in more depth, the table at Appendix 6 sets out the powers, where to find them and pre-conditions as to their use for both domestic and EU enforcers.

D. POWERS NOT RELIANT ON ENTRY INTO PREMISES

1. Test Purchase

7.25   The test purchase has proved over the years to be a powerful tool in the enforcer's armoury; however, it has hitherto not been a power conferred by all consumer legislation. This has now been rectified.[16] Modelled on regulation 20 of the CPUTR, paragraph 21 of Schedule 5 to the Act confers the power on any officer of an enforcer to purchase any product[17] or enter into an agreement for the provision of any product.[18]

7.26   The definition of 'officer' in Schedule 5 paragraph 7(1)(d) extends this power to authorized persons, which will include volunteers. This is clearly an important extension, as without it enforcers would be unable effectively to monitor compliance with a range of legislation, including those where the age of the purchaser is of prime importance.

---

[15] Sch. 5 paras 6(a) and (b).
[16] Subject to the legislative provision being one listed in either para. 10 or 11.
[17] Sch. 5 para. 21(1)(a).
[18] Sch. 5 para. 21(1)(b).

If an enforcer needs to enter premises to exercise the power to test purchase, it 7.27
need not either give notice or obtain a warrant.[19] The power to enter to purchase
a product is confined to those areas where the public have access, irrespective of
whether the public have access at the time when the power is being exercised.[20]
Likewise, the power to inspect any product is limited to those on site which the
public can also inspect.[21]

Paragraph 35 of Schedule 5 contains an interpretation section which makes it 7.28
clear that premises includes stalls, vehicles, vessels, and aircraft,[22] and that products includes goods, services, digital content, immovable property, and rights and
obligations.[23]

A test purchase does not require any suspicion or belief that an offence has been 7.29
committed, and is often therefore the first stage in an investigation. Depending
upon the outcome, the test purchase may give rise to a reasonable belief or suspicion
that a breach of the enforcer's legislation is taking place, and may thus be a precur-
sor to the utilizing of other powers.

Allied to the power to make test purchases is a power to allow an officer of an 7.30
enforcer to enter premises (again without a warrant or giving notice) in order to
observe the carrying out of a business.[24] As no notice needs to be given (as it is likely
that this would defeat any purpose in carrying out such observations), this provision allows for surveillance to be carried out in business premises. It will therefore
be necessary to read this provision alongside those contained in the Regulation of
Investigatory Powers Act 2000 and the Protection of Freedoms Act 2012.

E. PRODUCTION OF INFORMATION

Paragraph 14 provides a generic power to an enforcer, by way of a written notice 7.31
to require a person to provide the enforcer with specific information. This also
includes a requirement that certain documents are created for the enforcer if they
so request.[25] All documents must be presented in a legible form.[26] This is a provision
that has been modelled on sections 224 to 227 of the Enterprise Act 2002 and has
now extended the requirements to criminal investigations.

Given the sanctions that are made available when it is thought that there has 7.32
been a failure to comply, there are certain statutory safeguards and limitations
placed on the exercise of this power.

---

[19] Sch. 5 para. 21(3).
[20] Sch. 5 para. 21(2)(a).
[21] Sch. 5 para. 21(2)(b).
[22] Sch. 5 para. 35.
[23] Sch. 5 para. 35.
[24] Sch. 5 para. 22.
[25] Sch. 5 para. 15(4)(a).
[26] Sch. 5 para. 15(5).

7.33   The first limitation on how the power can be used is dependent upon the status of the enforcer. Table 7.2 sets out when and in what circumstances each enforcer can utilize these powers. These are the only circumstances where this power can be used.

Table 7.2 Production of information

Enforcer	*Exercisable Purpose*
Competitions and Markets Authority	(a) to enable the authority to exercise or to consider whether to exercise any function it has under Part 8 of the Enterprise Act 2002; (b) to enable a private designated enforcer[27] to consider whether to exercise any function it has under that Part; (c) to enable a Community enforcer to consider whether to exercise any function it has under that Part; (d) to ascertain whether a person has complied with or is complying with an enforcement order or an interim enforcement order; (e) to ascertain whether a person has complied with or is complying with an undertaking given under section 217(9), 218(10), or 219 of the Enterprise Act 2002.[28]
Public designated enforcer	(a) to enable that enforcer to exercise or to consider whether to exercise any function it has under Part 8 of the Enterprise Act 2002; (b) to ascertain whether a person has complied with or is complying with an enforcement order or an interim enforcement order made on the application of that enforcer; (c) to ascertain whether a person has complied with or is complying with an undertaking given under section 217(9) or 218(10) of the Enterprise Act 2002 following such an application; (d) to ascertain whether a person has complied with or is complying with an undertaking given to that enforcer under section 219 of that Act.[29]
Local weights and measures authority in Great Britain	(a) to enable that enforcer to exercise or to consider whether to exercise any function it has under Part 8 of the Enterprise Act 2002; (b) to ascertain whether a person has complied with or is complying with an enforcement order or an interim enforcement order made on the application of that enforcer; (c) to ascertain whether a person has complied with or is complying with an undertaking given under section 217(9) or 218(10) of the Enterprise Act 2002 following such an application; (d) to ascertain whether a person has complied with or is complying with an undertaking given to that enforcer under section 219 of that Act;[30] (e) to enable it to determine whether to make an order under section 3 or 4 of the Estate Agents Act 1979; (f) to enable it to exercise any of its functions under section 5, 6, 8, 13, or 17 of that Act.[31]

---

[27] See Sch. 5 para. 13(10) for definition of a private designated enforcer.
[28] Sch. 5 para. 13(2).
[29] Sch. 5 para. 13(3).
[30] Sch. 5 para. 13(3).
[31] Sch. 5 para. 13(9).

Department of Enterprise, Trade and Investments in Northern Ireland	(a) to enable that enforcer to exercise or to consider whether to exercise any function it has under Part 8 of the Enterprise Act 2002; (b) to ascertain whether a person has complied with or is complying with an enforcement order or an interim enforcement order made on the application of that enforcer; (c) to ascertain whether a person has complied with or is complying with an undertaking given under section 217(9) or 218(10) of the Enterprise Act 2002 following such an application; (d) to ascertain whether a person has complied with or is complying with an undertaking given to that enforcer under section 219 of that Act.[32]
EU enforcer[33]	(a) to enable that enforcer to exercise or to consider whether to exercise any function it has under Part 8 of the Enterprise Act 2002; (b) to ascertain whether a person has complied with or is complying with an enforcement order or an interim enforcement order made on the application of that enforcer; (c) to ascertain whether a person has complied with or is complying with an undertaking given under section 217(9) or 218(10) of the Enterprise Act 2002 following such an application; (d) to ascertain whether a person has complied with or is complying with an undertaking given to that enforcer under section 219 of that Act.[34]
Domestic enforcer	(a) Where an officer of the enforcer has a reasonable suspicion that there has been a breach of the enforcer's legislation.[35]
Unfair contract terms provider	(a) to enable the enforcer to exercise or to consider whether to exercise any function it has under Schedule 3 (enforcement of the law on unfair contract terms and notices), but only if an officer reasonably suspects that a person is using or proposing or recommending the use of a contractual term or notice within paragraph 3 of Schedule 3;[36] (b) to ascertain whether a person has complied with or is complying with an injunction or interdict (within the meaning of that Schedule) granted under paragraph 5 of that Schedule or an undertaking given under paragraph 6 of that Schedule.[37]

7.34 Schedule 5 is also prescriptive about the form that the notice must take, in that it must be written and must specify the purpose for which the information sought is required. Where the reason behind the notice is to exercise a function or consider the exercising of a function, the notice must also specify what that function is said to be.[38]

7.35 Given that one of the government's stated aims is to ease the burden of compliance on businesses, it is perhaps unfortunate that the next provisions in Schedule 5 paragraph 15, insofar as they are applicable to the enforcer, are not mandatory

---

[32] Sch. 5 para. 13(3).
[33] Other than the Competitions and Markets Authority (Sch. 5 para. 13(3)).
[34] Sch. 5 para. 13(3).
[35] Sch. 5 para. 13(4).
[36] Sch. 5 para. 13(8).
[37] Sch. 5 para. 13(7).
[38] Sch. 5 para. 15(1) and (2).

clauses. As such, the enforcer *may* specify the time, manner, and form in which the information sought is to be provided.[39] As currently drafted, there is still scope for delay and misunderstandings to arise over how, when, and in what form information is to be provided. Much will therefore depend on the individual policies of the individual enforcers, thus leaving businesses open to inconsistent and varied approaches.

7.36   Further limitations are provided by Schedule 5 paragraphs 15(6) and 17. These provide that, firstly, there is no requirement to produce information or create documents which would be subject to legal professional privilege in High Court or Court of Sessions proceedings.[40] Secondly, where an individual has complied with a paragraph 14 notice in criminal proceedings, the material cannot be used in criminal proceedings by the prosecution.[41] The only caveat is that the material may become admissible where the defendant or his representative adduces it. In short, the rules against self-incrimination where material is compelled is maintained and extended to all consumer protection legislation within Schedule 5 paragraphs 10 and 11 of the Act.

7.37   Where an officer of an enforcer or enforcer believes that there has been a failure to comply with a properly issued notice under Schedule 5 paragraph 14 of the Act, he may apply to the court[42] for an order of enforcement. Where such an order is granted, there may be costs attached.[43] The court can order that anything a person can reasonably do to ensure compliance be done.[44]

F. POWERS RELIANT ON ENTRY INTO PREMISES

1. Powers of Entry

7.38   The powers to seize goods and documents are found in Schedule 5 paragraphs 28 (goods) and 29 (documents), and only apply once an enforcer has entered premises either under a warrant[45] or using powers in Schedule 5 paragraph 23(1). Likewise, there are provisions allowing for the inspection and testing of certain products and procedures.[46] Where entry into premises has been gained using the latter provision, these premises must not be used either wholly or mainly as a dwelling. This is a

---

[39] Sch. 5 para. 15(3)(a) and (b).

[40] Sch. 5 para. 15(6) and (7).

[41] Unless the prosecution is for obstruction of an officer, an offence under s. 5 of the Perjury Act 1911, an offence under s. 44(2) of the Criminal Law (Consolidation) (Scotland) Act 1995, or an offence under art. 10 of the Perjury (Northern Ireland) Order 1979: Sch. 5 para. 17(5).

[42] That being either the High Court, in relation to England and Wales, the county court, in relation to Northern Ireland, a county court, the Court of Session, or the sheriff: Sch. 5 para. 16(6).

[43] Sch. 5 para. 16(4).

[44] Sch. 5 para. 16(3).

[45] Sch. 5 para. 32.

[46] Sch. 5 paras 25(1) and 25(3).

strengthening of the protection afforded to the individual, as the corresponding provisions in regulation 21(1)(a) CPUTR only prohibited entry into premises that were used only as a dwelling.

When planning to enter without a warrant, the enforcer must give written notice   7.39 to the occupier of the premises prior to any entry. Not only that, the Schedule makes clear that the two days required are from receipt of the notice by the occupier. In practice, this may mean that enforcers will have to call and check that the occupier has received the notice before embarking on what would otherwise be a fruitless visit to the premises concerned, albeit the Guidance as issued by BIS ('Investigatory Powers of Consumer Law Enforcers') envisages that the business will be the one doing the calling.[47] Again, the Guidance makes clear, whereas the Schedule does not, that written notice can also be in the form of an e-mail.

A notice must also provide a warning as to the offence of obstruction of an officer   7.40 under Schedule 5 paragraph 36, as well as saying why entry into the premises is deemed necessary.

It is possible for the occupier of premises to waive the need for notice to be   7.41 given.[48] Furthermore, there are four separate caveats to the need to give notice, which are found in Schedule 5 paragraph 23(6):

(6) In this paragraph "routine inspection" means an exercise of the power in sub-paragraph (1) other than where—
   (a) the power is exercised by an officer of a domestic enforcer who reasonably suspects a breach of the enforcer's legislation;
   (b) the officer reasonably considers that to give notice in accordance with sub-paragraph (3) would defeat the purpose of the entry;
   (c) it is not reasonably practicable in all the circumstances to give notice in accordance with that sub-paragraph, in particular because the officer reasonably suspects that there is an imminent risk to public health or safety; or
   (d) the enforcer is a market surveillance authority within the meaning of Article 2(18) of the Regulation on Accreditation and Market Surveillance and the entry is for the purpose of market surveillance within the meaning of Article 2(17) of that Regulation.

Should any of the exceptions be used and the premises be occupied, the officer of   7.42 the enforcer must provide a document setting out why entry is necessary and provide the occupier with the details of the offence of obstruction.[49] The officer should also provide the occupier with evidence of his or her identity and authority. [50] However, this need not happen if it is not reasonably practicable to do so.[51] Even where it is reasonably practicable to do so, and there is a failure to provide the information as required by paragraphs 23(7) and (8), any proceedings resulting from the exercise of the power of entry are not invalidated because of such a failure.

---

[47] See case study one in BIS 'Guidance on Investigatory Powers of Consumer Law Enforcers'.
[48] Sch. 5 para. 23(5).
[49] Sch. 5 para. 23(7).
[50] Sch. 5 para. 23(8).
[51] Sch. 5 para. 23(9).

7.43 Schedule 5 paragraph 32 governs what is required when enforcers are seeking entry with a warrant. The Schedule merely states that it is entry into premises that is permitted. Under the corresponding enforcement provisions in the CPUTR, regulation 22 included the words 'any premises', and this has been confirmed to include private dwellings.[52] When drafting Schedule 5 paragraph 32, the word 'any' has been omitted. When defining premises, the interpretation section for Part 4 of Schedule 5 makes no mention of domestic premises at all. Given the increase in protection afforded to dwellings where no warrant is required, and the omission of the word 'any', there may now be scope for re-arguing this point. However, it should be noted that the Guidance does not envisage this being an issue and specifically mentions entry into domestic premises:

Can enforcers enter wholly or mainly private dwellings?

42. To protect civil liberties of people in their own homes, enforcers cannot use a power to enter premises which are wholly or mainly used as private dwellings without a warrant. This includes where a business is run from home. Instead, enforcers must either seek consent from the occupier or obtain a court warrant to enter these premises.[53]

7.44 There are a number of conditions precedent before a warrant can be obtained. These are safeguards against unnecessary intrusions by enforcers. All such applications should be subject to proper scrutiny before being granted. The conditions required are set out in Table 7.2 above and Appendix 6.

7.45 Schedule 5 paragraph 33 allows an officer of the enforcer to enter premises at reasonable times and using reasonable force once a warrant has been obtained.[54] It further provides that a warrant is time limited, in that it is only valid for a period of one month from the date of issue.[55]

7.46 Provisions found in the CPUTR to allow officers of enforcers to take with them such equipment and persons as they see fit have been maintained.[56]

G. SEARCH AND SEIZURE

7.47 Once entry has been gained, there are a number of powers provided by the Schedule that an enforcer has recourse to. One of the key provisions is that of search and seizure.

7.48 Where the premises from which the goods are being seized are occupied, unless it is not reasonably practicable to do so an officer seizing goods must produce evidence of his or her identity and authority prior to the seizing of any goods.[57] Furthermore,

---

[52] See *R (on the application of Vuciterni) v Brent Magistrates Court* [2012] EWHC 2140 (Admin).
[53] BIS guidance on investigatory powers of consumer law enforcers.
[54] Sch. 5 para. 33(1).
[55] Sch. 5 para. 33(2).
[56] Sch. 5 para. 33(3).
[57] Sch. 5 para. 28(2) and (3).

an officer must take reasonable steps to inform the person from whom the goods are seized that they have been so seized, and also provide that person with a record of what has been seized.[58]

When determining what reasonable steps to take to inform the individual from whom the goods are seized and to provide them with a written record of what was seized, there is a mandatory requirement for officers to have regard to those codes of practice relevant to the seizure of property issued pursuant to section 66 of the Police and Criminal Evidence Act 1984 (in England and Wales) or article 65 of the Police and Criminal Evidence (Northern Ireland) Order 1989. 7.49

These requirements are repeated in Schedule 5 paragraph 29 in an identical form when dealing with the seizure of documents that may be required as evidence. 7.50

Schedule 5 paragraph 31 provides a power to request an individual to open a container for the purposes of the powers in paragraphs 28 to 30. Should the request not be complied with, officers of enforcers are empowered to break into containers themselves.[59] As a container includes any electronic device, it is suggested that this will give powers to seize documents on USB sticks, external hard drives, and in the Cloud or other remote electronic storage device. 7.51

Where any goods are seized from a vending machine, there are additional requirements placed on the seizing officer also to take reasonable steps to inform and provide a written record of what was seized to the person whose name and address appear on the side of the machine. Where no such name is apparent, then the reasonable steps taken to provide the information must be exercised in favour of the occupier of the premises on which the machine is fixed.[60] 7.52

Where documents are being seized, there is a prohibition on seizing anything that would be subject to legal professional privilege. Equally, an individual cannot be asked to create a document that would offend against legal professional privilege.[61] Enforcers will need to be mindful of this when exercising their powers. 7.53

An interesting provision is found at Schedule 5 paragraph 28(7) of the Act, and a near identical provision in relation to documents at Schedule 5 paragraph 29(8): 7.54

Goods seized under this paragraph (except goods seized for a purpose mentioned in paragraph 19(5)(b)) may not be detained—

(a) for a period of more than 3 months beginning with the day on which they were seized; or
(b) where the goods are reasonably required to be detained for a longer period by the enforcer for a purpose for which they were seized, for longer than they are required for that purpose.

In essence, unless goods are being retained for the purposes of seizure, the primary position under the Schedule is that both seized goods and documents should 7.55

---

[58] Sch. 5 para. 28(4)(a) and (b).
[59] Sch. 5 para. 31(1)and (2).
[60] Sch. 5 para. 28(5).
[61] Sch. 5 para. 29(6) and (7).

not be held any longer than three months beginning with the day on which they were seized.[62] These mirror the existing provisions contained in regulation 21(7) of the CPUTR. If the aim of these and previously existing provisions was to speed up investigations by enforcers, then the following provisions in Schedule 5 paragraphs 28(7)(b) and 29(8)(b) effectively remove the need for urgency and make the preceding provisions largely obsolete. As the purpose for which the items will have been seized will be to ascertain whether there has been a breach of the enforcer's legislation, whilst that is being ascertained by the enforcer (in however long a period that takes), that purpose will be ongoing; as such, the three-month period is effectively able to be ignored.

7.56 Where goods and documents have been seized and detained by an enforcer under Part 4 of Schedule 5, there is now a right for the individual from whom the item was seized to have access to that item if they so request.[63] However, an enforcer need not grant access if he or she has a reasonable ground for believing that allowing access to the items would prejudice the investigation.[64]

7.57 The request must come from the individual or his or her representative who had custody or control of the item or document immediately before it was seized.[65] He or she may request access to the item, which must (subject to the caveat in paragraph 38(5)) be granted. Where access is granted, it is to be supervised by an officer of the enforcer.[66] There is also provision made for an individual or his or her representative to be able to request that either he or she (or his or her representative) be granted access in order to make a copy or photograph of the item, or that the enforcer provide them with the same.[67] Again, unless the caveat in paragraph 38(5) applies, access must be granted. If the enforcer provides copies rather than allows access, the Schedule allows for reasonable costs for copying to be charged.

7.58 These are provisions that are separate to the disclosure regime under the Criminal Procedure and Investigations Act 1996. Offences that are triable summarily only, which many consumer legislative offences are, often have an abbreviated disclosure process. Where an enforcer believes the disclosure test is not met, those provisions may provide an alternative route to that material so long as it originally came from the person who is making the request.

7.59 Where items are being retained, Schedule 5 paragraph 40 provides that, in certain circumstances, any person with an interest in the item can bring the matter before a magistrates' court in England, Wales, and Northern Ireland (in Scotland the matter can be raised before the Sheriff), in order to have the items released.

---

[62] Sch. 5 paras 28(7) and 29(8).
[63] Sch. 5 para. 38(2).
[64] Sch. 5 para. 38(5).
[65] Sch. 5 para. 38(2) and (7).
[66] Sch. 5 para. 38(2).
[67] Sch. 5 para. 38(3)(a) and (b).

The pre-conditions that need to exist before such an application can be made are as follows: 7.60

Schedule 5 paragraph 40(6) Condition A is that: 7.61

(a) no proceedings have been brought—
  (i) for an offence as the result of the investigation in the course of which the goods or documents were seized; or
  (ii) for the forfeiture of the goods or documents or (in the case of seized documents) any goods to which the documents relate; and
(b) the period of 6 months beginning with the date the goods or documents were seized has expired

Condition B is that: 7.62

(a) proceedings of a kind mentioned in sub-paragraph (6)(a) have been brought; and
(b) those proceedings have been concluded without the goods or documents being forfeited

Clearly, the six-month time limit above may create a tension between the person with an interest in the items seized and the enforcer, as for many criminal offences the time limit for bringing proceedings is longer than six months. 7.63

Both the enforcer and the individual asking for return and release of the goods have a right of appeal to the Crown Court (in England and Wales) and to a county court (in Northern Ireland) against any decision of the magistrates in relation to this provision.[68] 7.64

Where goods have been seized by either a domestic enforcer or an EU enforcer under Schedule 5 paragraphs 19(5)(a) and 20(5)(a), and no infringements have been disclosed, as long as there was no neglect or default on the part of the person from whom the goods were seized there is a right to compensation for any loss or damage arising out of the seizure.[69] Where there is a dispute about the amount to be paid in compensation, this will be determined by arbitration.[70] 7.65

H. POWER TO INSPECT

Once inside premises, either with or without a warrant, officers of enforcers have a general power to inspect any product that is on the premises[71] and also to 'examine any procedure (including any arrangements for carrying out a test) connected with the production of a product.'[72] These are the generic powers. 7.66

Specific powers in relation to the Consumer Protection Act 1987, General Product Safety Regulations 2005, Weights and Measures (Packaged Goods) Regulations 2006 and Weights and Measures (Packaged Goods) Regulations (Northern Ireland) 7.67

---

[68] Sch. 5 para. 40(8).
[69] Sch. 5 para. 41(2) and (3)(a) and (b).
[70] Sch. 5 para. 41(5).
[71] Sch. 5 para. 25(1).
[72] Sch. 5 para. 25(3).

2011 have also been retained.[73] However, these are only in respect of domestic, rather than EU, enforcers.

7.68   Equally, the powers retained in Schedule 5 paragraph 26 to the Act are only applicable to domestic enforcers. This allows for the testing of equipment used for weighing, measuring, or marking up packets. Given that these are specific weights and measures powers, it is not surprising that the interpretation of any expressions used in the paragraph are to have the same meaning as identical expressions found in the Weights and Measures Act 1985 for all domestic enforcers in Great Britain, and for Northern Ireland those found in the Weights and Measures (Northern Ireland) Order 1981.[74]

7.69   Where an officer of an enforcer is testing any equipment used for marking up packages, then they must be acting pursuant to either the Weights and Measures (Packaged Goods) Regulations 2006 in Great Britain or the Weights and Measures (Packaged Goods) Regulations (Northern Ireland) 2011.[75] Once again, these powers have been based on pre-existing powers found in the CPUTR and as such they will be familiar to both enforcers and businesses alike.

7.70   Modelled on provisions found in weights and measures legislation, Schedule 5 paragraph 34 extends the requirement for individuals found on premises to provide such assistance or information to an officer of an enforcement authority as that officer reasonably considers necessary. This power exists regardless of whether entry has been achieved via a warrant or otherwise.

7.71   It is of note that the requirement to provide information and assistance is widely drawn and relates to any person on the premises, not just the owner or occupier. The failure to comply and provide information or assistance may lead to prosecution for the offence of obstruction.

I. OFFENCES

7.72   Part 5 of Schedule 5 contains two offences, both of which are summary only offences. The first offence is that of obstruction of an officer and the second is that of purporting to act as an officer.

7.73   Paragraph 36 of Schedule 5 creates the offence of obstruction. It can be committed in the following three ways by anyone who:

(a)   intentionally obstructs an enforcer or an officer of an enforcer who is exercising or seeking to exercise a power under Part 4 of this Schedule in accordance with that Part;

(b)   intentionally fails to comply with a requirement properly imposed by an enforcer or an officer of an enforcer under Part 4 of this Schedule; or

(c)   without reasonable cause fails to give an enforcer or an officer of an enforcer any other assistance or information which the enforcer or officer reasonably requires of the person for a purpose for which the enforcer or officer may exercise a power under Part 4 of this Schedule.

---

[73] Sch. 5 para. 25(2) and (4).
[74] Sch. 5 para. 26(2).
[75] Sch. 5 para. 23(4).

The offence covered in paragraph 36(1)(c) can, in and of itself, be committed in   7.74
two ways: either by knowingly giving a false or misleading statement, or by recklessly making the same. The statement given must be false or misleading in a material respect.[76] The penalty for committing an offence under this paragraph is found
in paragraph 36(3) and is a fine that is limited to level 3 on the standard scale.[77] As
there is no separate timescale for bringing prosecutions, the time limit will be the
standard six months applicable to summary offences.

The offence cannot be committed where an individual is refusing to give infor-   7.75
mation or answer any question that might serve to incriminate that person.[78] In
essence, there is retention of the right against self-incrimination. What there is
not is a power to prevent the answering of questions or provision of information
that might incriminate another. Where the individual from whom information is
sought is an employee of a business, it is questionable as to whether he would be
aware of his rights against self-incrimination. It would therefore be wise for any
officers of enforcers to remind individuals of this right before asking for any information or assistance.

A further offence is created by Schedule 5 paragraph 37. This is an offence of   7.76
'purporting to act as an officer'. The offence is committed should someone who
is not an officer of an enforcer purport to act as such under either Part 3 or 4 of
Schedule 5. In other words, for the actus reas to be committed, an individual needs
to be attempting to exercise the powers contained in the Schedule; simply pretend-
ing to be an officer of an enforcer will be insufficient.

At the time of drafting the Schedule, section 85(1) of the Legal Aid, Sentencing   7.77
and Punishment of Offenders Act 2012 was not in force and the offence of purporting to act as an officer was subject to a maximum fine of level 5 on the standard
scale i.e. £5000. However, as of 12 March 2015, the section has been brought into
force[79] with the effect that the £5000 cap has been removed and the punishment is
now an unlimited fine.

Once again, there is no specific time limit placed on commencing proceedings   7.78
for this offence and it will therefore be subject to the standard six months from
commission of offence.

J. EXERCISE OF ENFORCEMENT BY AREA ENFORCERS

Part 6 of Schedule 5 will be a welcome sight to all those who are deemed to be area   7.79
enforcers, as it finally removes the argument about whether an enforcer has jurisdiction to bring proceedings outside of his boundaries. No more will area enforcers

---

[76] Sch. 5 para. 36(2)(a) and (b).
[77] Which at the time of writing is £1000.
[78] Sch. 5 para. 36(4).
[79] The Legal Aid, Sentencing and Punishment of Offenders Act 2012 (Commencement No. 11) Order
2015 (SI 2005/504).

have to ask themselves whether they 'consider it expedient for the promotion or protection of the interests of the inhabitants of their area…'[80] before deciding whether they will institute civil proceedings or defend or prosecute any other legal proceedings'.

7.80   An area enforcer is either a local weights and measures authority in Great Britain or a District Council in England or Northern Ireland.[81]

7.81   Part 6 has three primary paragraphs dealing with investigatory powers, civil proceedings and criminal proceedings. Paragraph 44 deals with investigatory powers and confirms that 'a local weights and measures authority in England or Wales may exercise the power in a part of England or Wales which is outside that authority's area'.[82]

7.82   The investigatory powers that are available on a cross-border basis are those that are contained in Parts 3 and 4 of Schedule 5. Additionally, where a piece of consumer legislation is contained within paragraphs 10 and 11 and contains separate and distinct investigatory powers, these are also available on a cross-border basis.[83]

7.83   When considering whether to bring civil proceedings, an area enforcer is now entitled to bring proceedings outside its area by virtue of Schedule 5 paragraph 45(1) in respect of the following provisions only:

(a) Part 8 of the Enterprise Act 2002;
(b) Schedule 3 to this Act;
(c) legislation which, by virtue of a provision listed in paragraph 10 of this Schedule, the area enforcer has a duty or power to enforce;
(d) legislation under which legislation mentioned in paragraph (c) is made; or
(e) legislation listed in the second column of the table in paragraph 11 of this Schedule.

7.84   The power to bring forfeiture proceedings under section 35ZC of the Registered Designs Act 1949, section 16 of the Consumer Protection Act 1987, section 97 of the Trade Marks Act 1994 (including as applied by the Olympic Symbols etc. (Protection) Act 1995), and under legislation in Schedule 5 paragraph 10 of the Act where there have been no related criminal proceedings, is likewise extended.[84]

7.85   Some criminal proceedings have also had the same treatment when it comes to effective border removal in the bringing of proceedings. In England and Wales, local weights and measures authorities may bring proceedings for a consumer offence allegedly committed outside their immediate geographic area. For a local weights and measures authority, a consumer offence is defined by Schedule 5 paragraph 46(2) as follows:

(a) an offence under legislation which, by virtue of a provision listed in paragraph 10 of this Schedule, a local weights and measures authority in England or Wales has a duty or power to enforce,

---

[80] s. 222 of the Local Government Act 1972.

[81] Sch. 5 para. 43(1)(a), (b), and (c).

[82] The same applies for District Councils in England and Northern Ireland, and weights and measures authorities in Scotland.

[83] Sch. 5 para. 44(2)(a) and (b).

[84] Sch. 5 para. 45(2).

(b) an offence under legislation under which legislation within paragraph (a) is made,

(c) an offence under legislation listed in the second column of the table in paragraph 11 of this Schedule in relation to which a local weights and measures authority is listed in the corresponding entry in the first column of the table as an enforcer,

(d) an offence originating from an investigation into a breach of legislation mentioned in paragraph (a), (b) or (c), or

(e) an offence described in paragraph 36 or 37 of this Schedule

7.86 District Councils in England, Wales, and Northern Ireland have the same powers to bring proceedings for alleged commissions of consumer offences outside their boundaries save that the definition of a consumer offence omits subparagraph (c) as set out at para 7.85 above.

7.87 It is noticeable that the widening of the powers to bring criminal proceedings are limited to only those areas listed at paragraph 7.85 above. Unless paragraph 10 is amended (as there is power to do) to include legislation such as the Fraud Act 2006, then it is suggested that great care will be needed when deciding what offences to lay before the court where proceedings are outside the boundaries of those bringing proceedings. This is because, in those circumstances, section 222 of the Local Government Act 1972 will still have a role to play and area enforcers may still find themselves on the wrong end of an argument about the misuse of their powers.

8
ENHANCED CONSUMER MEASURES

A. BACKGROUND

The stated aim for this part of the Act[1] was to amend the existing civil enforce- **8.01**
ment regime found in Part 8 of the Enterprise Act 2002 ('EA 2002'), in order to
expand the remedies available to both courts and enforcers when seeking enforcement orders and undertakings, thereby providing a regime with greater flexibility.
It is hoped that the greater flexibility will lead to 'better outcomes for consumers
who have been the victims of a breach of the law'.[2]

In the relevant consultation document 'Extending the Range of Remedies **8.02**
Available to Public Enforcers of Consumer Law',[3] it is made plain that a series
of steps are supposed to take place in circumstances where traders fail to comply
with consumer law and fail to meet consumer expectations with regard to remedies. Enforcers are supposed to work informally with the trader to secure remedial
actions to amend their behaviour before more formal action is taken. The formal
action follows two well-established routes: criminal prosecution and civil action.

The difficulty with both of the above routes is that they do not include rem- **8.03**
edies that benefit individual consumers; instead they punish in some way the rogue
trader. It is these deficiencies that the enhanced consumer measures are aimed at
addressing.

One key problem with the pre-existing provisions was their general inability to **8.04**
cause a positive change in the behaviour of a trader. They had the power to stop
breaches of consumer legislation, but were lacking any power to make the trader
change his or her trading behaviours and practices for the good of consumers.

---

[1] This being s. 79 and Sch. 7.

[2] See para. 5 of the draft guidance on enhanced consumer measures, <https://bisgovuk.citizenspace.com/
consumer-rights-bill/guidance-2014/supporting_documents/Enhanced%20Consumer%20Measures%20
%20Draft%20Guidance%20For%20Testing.pdf>.

[3] <https://www.gov.uk/government/uploads/system/uploads/attachment_data/file/32713/12-1193-civil
-enforcement-remedies-consultation-on-extending.pdf>.

8.05   As such, the consultation set out as clear policy that the new remedies should
be aimed at achieving one or more of the following outcomes. Over and above any
measure being just, reasonable, and proportionate they should:

- Increase business compliance with the law;
- Improve redress for consumers affected by the breach; and
- Provide for more confident consumers who are empowered to exercise greater consumer choice.[4]

8.06   The consultation acknowledged that there will be cases where there is plainly a
wider public interest in criminal prosecution. This is a stance that is maintained in
the guidance published by BIS ('Investigatory Powers of Consumer Law Enforcers'),
where it specifically envisages not only scenarios whereby criminal prosecution is
the appropriate route for enforcement, but also those cases where civil enforcement
action is taken post criminal proceedings.

B. ENTERPRISE ACT 2002

1. Overview—the Old Law

8.07   It is important to note that the Act merely amends and broadens the pre-existing
EA 2002 regimes; as such, the procedures, interpretations, and definitions to be
followed will already be largely familiar to both enforcers and businesses alike.

8.08   Previously, the EA 2002 allowed enforcers only to seek either a form of civil injunctive relief or accept undertakings under Part 8 for infringements of a number of pieces
of consumer protection legislation, including those deriving their authority both from
Acts of Parliament and those emanating from the European Union ('EU').

8.09   Broadly speaking, before any enforcement order could be applied for, there were
three general criteria that needed to be met. These remain largely unaltered; therefore, enforcers should still have regard to them. The criteria are:

(1) The trader has or is engaging in conduct which constitutes domestic or community infringement, or alternatively is likely to engage in conduct which constitutes a Community infringement;

(2) There is, has, or is likely to be harm to the collective interests of consumers
based in the UK;

(3) There has been a period of consultation between the infringer and the enforcer
which has failed to remedy the conduct over which complaint is made, or the
need for consultation has been waived.

---

[4] <https://www.gov.uk/government/uploads/system/uploads/attachment_data/file/32713/12-1193-civil
-enforcement-remedies-consultation-on-extending.pdf>.

The enforcement orders available previously were limited in that they could 8.10
demand that the relevant infringer stop engaging in the conduct in question and
little else. There was an ability to order that the court's order be published, and also
that a corrective statement be published.

The enforcer (typically the trading standards department of a local authority) 8.11
can require undertakings, which may on occasion be rather more flexible than the
enforcement order. Both of the above measures have been perceived as having a lack
of teeth. Additionally, they were not very consumer-centric in their focus.

C. LEGISLATIVE SCOPE

1. The Infringements

The enforcement procedure is set out at sections 210 to 223 of the EA 2002, and 8.12
has in certain areas undergone some significant redrafting. Section 211 set out at
8.13 below appears as amended and as such will be in force from 1 October 2015.

The EA 2002 provides for two types of infringement. One is a domestic infringe- 8.13
ment and the other is a Community infringement. A domestic infringement is
defined by section 211 EA 2002. The new subsection is at (1A):

Section 211: Domestic infringements

(1)   In this Part a domestic infringement is an act or omission which—
    (a) is done or made by a person in the course of a business,
    (b) falls within subsection (2), and
    (c) harms the collective interests of consumers

(1A) But an act or omission which satisfies the conditions in subsection (1) is a domestic
    infringement only if at least one of the following is satisfied—
    (a) the person supplying (or seeking to supply) goods or services has a place of business in
       the United Kingdom, or
    (b) the goods or services are supplied (or sought to be supplied) to or for a person in the
       United Kingdom (see section 232).

(2)   An act or omission falls within this subsection if it is of a description specified by the
    Secretary of State by order and consists of any of the following—
    (a) a contravention of an enactment which imposes a duty, prohibition or restriction
       enforceable by criminal proceedings;
    (b) an act done or omission made in breach of contract;
    (c) an act done or omission made in breach of a non-contractual duty owed to a person by
       virtue of an enactment or rule of law and enforceable by civil proceedings;
    (d) an act or omission in respect of which an enactment provides for a remedy or sanction
       enforceable by civil proceedings;
    (e) an act done or omission made by a person supplying or seeking to supply goods or
       services as a result of which an agreement or security relating to the supply is void or
       unenforceable to any extent;
    (f) an act or omission by which a person supplying or seeking to supply goods or ser-
       vices purports or attempts to exercise a right or remedy relating to the supply in

circumstances where the exercise of the right or remedy is restricted or excluded under or by virtue of an enactment;

(g) an act or omission by which a person supplying or seeking to supply goods or services purports or attempts to avoid (to any extent) liability relating to the supply in circumstances where such avoidance is restricted or prevented under an enactment.

(3) But an order under this section may provide that any description of act or omission falling within subsection (2) is not a domestic infringement.

(4) For the purposes of subsection (2) it is immaterial—

(a) whether or not any duty, prohibition or restriction exists in relation to consumers as such;

(b) whether or not any remedy or sanction is provided for the benefit of consumers as such;

(c) whether or not any proceedings have been brought in relation to the act or omission;

(d) whether or not any person has been convicted of an offence in respect of the contravention mentioned in subsection (2)(a);

(e) whether or not there is a waiver in respect of the breach of contract mentioned in subsection (2)(b).

8.14   As can be seen, the amendment to this section is consumer-focused. Whereas, previously, action could only be taken where an infringement harmed the collective interests of consumers based in the UK, the addition of section 211(1A) allows for action to be taken where either the consumer receiving the goods or services is based in the UK or, alternatively, the supplier to the consumer is based in the UK. In practice, this will now allow action to be taken against those who operate from outside the UK, or indeed harm the collective interests of those consumers abroad. The Act has therefore caught up with the modern global markets.

8.15   However, before any action can be taken for a domestic infringement, the Secretary of State must have specified the legislation (see Table 8.1). The Enterprise Act 2002 (Part 8 Domestic Infringements) Order 2003,[5] as amended by the Consumer Protection from Unfair Trading Regulations 2008,[6] provides for the following:[7]

Table 8.1 Legislation pertaining to domestic infringement

Legislation	Extent
Accommodation Agencies Act 1953	The whole Act
Administration of Justice Act 1970	Section 40 (unlawful harassment of debtors)
Cancer Act 1939	Sections 4, 5, and 7 (prohibition of certain advertisements relating to cancer)
Charities Act 1992	Sections 60, 61, and 63 (information requirements, cancellation rights and false statements in respect of fundraising)
Children and Young Persons Act 1933	Section 7(1) to (2) (prohibition on sale of tobacco to persons under 16)

[5] SI 2003/1593.
[6] SI 2008/1277.
[7] Table as of 31 Janaury 2015.

Legislation	Extent
Children and Young Persons (Protection from Tobacco) Act 1991	Section 4 (display of warning statements)
Children and Young Persons (Scotland) Act 1937	Section 18(1) and (2) (prohibition on sale of tobacco to persons under 16)
Companies Act 2006	Part 41 (business names)
Company, Limited Liability Partnership and Business (Names and Trading Disclosures) Regulations 2015	Part 6 of the Company, Limited Liability Partnership and Business (Names and Trading Disclosures) Regulations 2015 and any other provision of those Regulations having effect for the purpose of Part 6
Consumer Credit Act 1974	The whole Act
Copyright, Designs and Patents Act 1988	Sections 107 (making or dealing with infringing articles etc), 198 (making, dealing with or using illicit recordings), 297A (making and dealing with unauthorised decoders)
Estate Agents Act 1979	The whole Act
Hallmarking Act 1973	The whole Act
Intoxicating Substances (Supply) Act 1985	The whole Act
Lotteries and Amusements Act 1976	Part I (legal and illegal lotteries) and section 14 (prize competitions)
Malicious Communications Act 1988	The whole Act
Misrepresentation Act 1967	The whole Act
National Lottery etc Act 1993	Sections 13 (contravention of regulations) and 16 (false representations)
Prices Act 1974	Section 4 (price marking)
Protection from Harassment Act 1997	The whole Act
Pyrotechnic Articles (Safety) Regulations 2010	Regulation 15 (prohibition on supply of category 1 fireworks to persons under 16 years and category 2 or 3 fireworks to persons under 18 years)
Road Traffic Act 1988	Sections 75 (vehicles not to be sold in unroadworthy condition etc) and 76 (fitting and supplying defective or unsuitable vehicle parts)
Sale of Goods Act 1979	The whole Act
Supply of Goods (Implied Terms) Act 1973	The whole Act
Supply of Goods and Services Act 1982	The whole Act
Tobacco Advertising and Promotion Act 2002	The whole Act
Tobacco Products (Manufacture, Presentation and Sale) (Safety) Regulations 2002	The whole Regulations
Torts (Interference with Goods) Act 1977	Section 12 (power of sale of uncollected goods)
Trade Descriptions Act 1968	The whole Act
Trade Marks Act 1994	Section 92 (unauthorised use of trade marks etc in relation to goods)
Unfair Contract Terms Act 1977	The whole Act

(Continued)

Table 8.1 (*Continued*)

Legislation	Extent
Weights and Measures Act 1985	Sections 21 to 23, 25 (requirements to sell goods by particular quantities etc), 28 (short weight etc), [...] 30 (quantity less than stated), 31 (incorrect statements), 32 (offences due to default of third person), 50(5) and (6) (possession for sale, etc of inadequate regulated package)

8.16   Additionally, in Northern Ireland the following legislation is also included:

Legislation	Extent
Betting, Gaming, Lotteries and Amusements (Northern Ireland) Order 1985	Articles 131 to 135 (illegal lotteries etc) and 168 (prize competitions)
Business Names (Northern Ireland) Order 1986	The whole Order
Children and Young Persons (Protection from Tobacco) (Northern Ireland) Order 1991	Article 5 (display of warning statements)
Companies (Northern Ireland) Order 1986	Articles 356, 357, and 359 (company name to appear outside place of business and name and other particulars to appear in its correspondence)
Explosives (Fireworks) Regulations (Northern Ireland) 1999	Regulation 11(1) (requirement for notice as to underage sales)
Health and Personal Social Services (Northern Ireland) Order 1978	Articles 3 and 4 (prohibition on sale of tobacco to persons apparently under 16)
Misrepresentation Act (Northern Ireland) 1967	The whole Act
Malicious Communications (Northern Ireland) Order 1988	The whole Order
Protection from Harassment (Northern Ireland) Order 1997	The whole Order
Road Traffic (Northern Ireland) Order 1995	Articles 83 (vehicles not to be sold in unroadworthy condition etc) and 84 (fitting and supplying defective or unsuitable vehicle parts)
Weights and Measures (Northern Ireland) Order 1981	Articles 19(1) to (6), 20, 22 (requirements to sell goods by particular quantities, short weight, misrepresentation, quantity less than stated, incorrect statements, etc), 25(2) (offences due to default of third person), and 32(5) (possession for sale etc, of inadequate regulated package)

8.17   Finally, there are two applicable rules of law listed in the Enterprise Act 2002 (Part 8 Domestic Infringements) Order 2003 Schedule 1 Part 3. Those are: (i) an act done or omission made in breach of contract for the supply of goods or services to a consumer, and (ii) an act done or omission made in breach of a duty of care owed to a consumer under the law of tort or delict of negligence.

Community infringements are covered by section 212 of the EA 2002 and there   8.18
has been no amendment to this section. The relevant part is as set out below:

Section 212 Community infringements

(1) In this Part a Community infringement is an act or omission which harms the collective
interests of consumers and which—

(a) contravenes a listed Directive as given effect by the laws, regulations or administrative
provisions of an EEA State,

(b) contravenes such laws, regulations or administrative provisions which provide additional permitted protections,

(c) contravenes a listed Regulation, or

(d) contravenes any laws, regulations or administrative provisions of an EEA State which
give effect to a listed Regulation.

Listed Directives and Regulations can be found in Schedule 13 to the EA 2002.   8.19
Additionally, the Secretary of State has made orders under section 212(3) specifying
the UK law which gives effect to the listed Regulations and Directives. These are set
out in the snappily titled Schedule to the Enterprise Act 2002 (Part 8 Community
Infringements UK Laws) Order,[8] as amended, and are set out in Table 8.2. For
reasons of space, the full titles of the Directives have not been included since they
are to be found in the relevant statutory instrument.

Table 8.2 Directives and their implementing provisions of UK law

Directive	*Specified UK law*
Directive 85/577/EEC	Cancellation of Contracts made in a Consumer's Home or Place of Work etc. Regulations 2008
Directive 90/314/EEC	Package Travel, Package Holidays and Package Tours Regulations 1992
Directive 93/13/EEC	Unfair Terms in Consumer Contracts Regulations 1999
Directive 90/314/ EEC	Package Travel, Package Holidays and Package Tours Regulations 1992
Directive 93/13/EEC	Unfair Terms in Consumer Contracts Regulations 1999
Directive 97/7/EC	Consumer Protection (Distance Selling) Regulations 2000
Article 10 of the above Directive	Regulations 19 to 24 of the Privacy and Electronic Communications (EC Directive) Regulations 2003 in their application to consumers (use of telecommunications services for direct marketing purposes)
Directive 1999/44/EC	(i) Sections 9 to 11 of the Supply of Goods (Implied Terms) Act 1973, sections 13 to 15 and 15B of the Sale of Goods Act 1979, sections 3 to 5, 11C to 11E, and 13 of the Supply of Goods and Services Act 1982, and any rule of law in Scotland which provides comparable protection to section 13 of the Supply of Goods and Services Act 1982 (implied terms as to quality and fitness)

(Continued)

---

[8] SI 2003/1374.

Table 8.2 (*Continued*)

Directive	Specified UK law
	(ii) Sections 20 and 32 of the Sale of Goods Act 1979 11 (passing of risk and delivery of goods)
	(iii) Sections 48A to 48F of the Sale of Goods Act 1979, and sections 11M, 11N, and 11P to 11S of the Supply of Goods and Services Act 1982 (additional remedies for consumers)
	(iv) Regulation 15 of the Sale and Supply of Goods to Consumers Regulations 2002 [...]
	(v) Sections 6(2), 7(1), 7(2), 20(2), 21, and 27(2) of the Unfair Contract Terms Act 1977 and article 3 of the Consumer Transactions (Restrictions on Statements) Order 1976 (anti-avoidance measures)
	Regulations 6, 7, 8, 9, and 11 of the Electronic Commerce (EC Directive) Regulations 2002 (requirements as to information and orders)
Directive 2000/31/EC	Regulations 6, 7, 8, 9, and 11 of the Electronic Commerce (EC Directive) Regulations 2002 (requirements as to information and orders)
Directive 2002/65/EC	Financial Services (Distance Marketing) Regulations 2004; rules corresponding to any provisions of those Regulations made by the [Financial Conduct Authority] or a designated professional body within the meaning of section 326(2) of the Financial Services and Markets Act 2000
Directive 2005/29/EC	Consumer Protection from Unfair Trading Regulations 2008
Directive 2008/48/EC	Consumer Credit Act 1974 and secondary legislation made thereunder (not including consumer hire agreements)
Directive 2008/122/EC	Timeshare, Holiday Products, Resale and Exchange Contracts Regulations 2010
Articles 10 to 21 of Directive 89/552/EEC	The provisions of the Broadcasting Acts 1990 and 1996, and codes and rules made by the Independent Television Commission thereunder, in particular sections 6(1) (in relation to advertising), 8, 9, 60, and 79(4) of the Broadcasting Act 1990 (regulations as to advertising) and sections 18(5), 25(5), and 30(5) of the Broadcasting Act 1996, in so far as they apply sections 6 to 12 of the Broadcasting Act 1990 to digital programme services, digital additional services, and qualifying teletext services
Articles 86 to 100 of Directive 2001/83/EC	Chapters 1 and 2 of Part 14 (advertising) of the Human Medicines Regulations 2012
Article 13 of Directive 2002/58/EC	Regulations 19 to 26, 30 and 32 of the Privacy and Electronic Communications (EC Directive) Regulations 2003

8.20   The critical difference between Community infringements and domestic infringements is that an application may be made for an order regarding conduct that may take place in the *future* which is likely to constitute a Community infringement.

8.21   Once it has been ascertained what consumer legislation is covered, the next issue is who can enforce it.

D. THE ENFORCERS

8.22   Section 213 EA 2002 sets out the distinctions between the various enforcers. The Competition and Markets Authority ('CMA') and every local weights and measures authority in Great Britain, and the Department of Enterprise, Trade and Investment in Northern Ireland, are all 'general enforcers'.[9]

The Secretary of State may, by an order, designate a body as an enforcer. These are therefore known as 'designated enforcers'. The conditions precedent before the Secretary of State can so designate are that the Secretary thinks that the body has, as one of its purposes, the collective interest of consumers,[10] and that the body is independent (in the case of a public body).[11] The Secretary of State may also designate a non-public body or entity. The criteria to be fulfilled in that case are set by a separate order.[12] The current list of enforcers includes the Office of Communications, the Financial Conduct Authority ('FCA'), and the Consumers Association. 8.23

There are two further categories of enforcers: Community enforcers and Consumer Protection Co-operation ('CPC') enforcers. 8.24

Community enforcers are qualified entities for the purposes of Directive 98/27/EC ('the Injunctions Directive').[13] This allows enforcers from other EU Member States to make applications for enforcement orders before the UK courts so long as they are listed in the Official Journal of the European Communities. The proviso for making an application is that the infringement has originated in the UK but the effects of the infringement are felt in the Member State of the particular enforcer. 8.25

The Injunctions Directive also permits an enforcer[14] from the UK to seek injunctive relief for cessation or prohibition of a breach in the courts of an EEA Member State.[15] This is clearly a necessary power in an increasing global market where, with the rise of internet purchasing, consumers may be buying products, goods, or services from other EU Member States. 8.26

Section 221(4) provides for co-operation between community enforcers and designated, general, and CPC enforcers where there is a need to assist a UK enforcer taking proceedings in an EEA State or a Community enforcer taking action in the UK. 8.27

CPC enforcers are governed by section 213(5A) EA 2002. These are bodies that are specifically designated by the Secretary of State pursuant to article 4(1) or (2) of the CPC Regulation.[16] Currently, this includes: the CMA; the Civil Aviation Authority; the FCA; the Secretary of State for Health; weights and measures authorities in Great Britain; the Information Commissioner; the Department of Enterprise, Trade and Investment in Northern Ireland; and the Department of Health, Social Services and Public Safety in Northern Ireland, amongst others. 8.28

---

[9] s. 213(1) EA 2002.
[10] s.213(2)(a) EA 2002.
[11] s.213(3) EA 2002.
[12] s.213(4) EA 2002.
[13] s.213(5) EA 2002.
[14] Either designated public body or general enforcer.
[15] An EEA State is defined by s. 221(5) EA 2002 and is a State which is a contracting party to the Agreement on the European Economic Area signed at Oporto on 2 May 1992 as adjusted by the Protocol signed at Brussels on 17 March 1993.
[16] EC Regulation 2006/2004 of the European Parliament and of the Council passed on 27 October 2004.

E. CONSUMERS

8.29 Consumers are defined by section 210, as set out below. As can be seen, the definition is near identical to that found in section 2(2) of the Act.

(1) In this Part references to consumers must be construed in accordance with this section.

(2) In relation to a domestic infringement a consumer is an individual in respect of whom the first and second conditions are satisfied.

(3) The first condition is that—

  (a) goods are or are sought to be supplied to the individual (whether by way of sale or otherwise) in the course of a business carried on by the person supplying or seeking to supply them, or

  (b) services are or are sought to be supplied to the individual in the course of a business carried on by the person supplying or seeking to supply them.

(4) The second condition is that—

  (a) the individual receives or seeks to receive the goods or services otherwise than in the course of a business carried on by him, or

  (b) the individual receives or seeks to receive the goods or services with a view to carrying on a business but not in the course of a business carried on by him.

(5) [Repealed].

(6) [...]

(7) [...]

(8) A business includes—

  (a) a professional practice;

  (b) any other undertaking carried on for gain or reward;

  (c) any undertaking in the course of which goods or services are supplied otherwise than free of charge.

8.30 In short, a consumer, whether for the purposes of domestic or Community infringements, must not be acting in either a professional or trading capacity in order to meet the definition.

F. INVESTIGATORY POWERS

8.31 The investigatory powers that were contained within the EA 2002 have now been removed. New section 223A EA 2002 reads as follows:

223A Investigatory powers

For the investigatory powers available to enforcers for the purposes of enforcers' functions under this Part, see Schedule 5 to the Consumer Rights Act 2015.

8.32 Those seeking information as to the investigatory powers available to enforcers under the EA 2002 are directed to Chapter 7 of this work.

G. PROCEDURE

Before any enforcement action can be taken, there is, by and large, an obligation to   8.33
enter into a period of consultation with the individual who the enforcement action
is being considered against. In practice, this has been the cause of difficulties for
both enforcers and businesses. One of the main problems caused by consultation is
that what consultation is and means has not been defined by the EA 2002. The only
assistance provided by the EA 2002 is that consultation must be 'appropriate'.[17].
Clearly, what is appropriate will vary from case to case.

It should also be born in mind that the primary purpose of consultation is to   8.34
seek a cessation of the infringement without having to seek recourse to the courts
if at all possible.

The time for consultation runs from the moment the request for such a consultation   8.35
is received by the trader. In most cases, the time limit for consultation will still be a
minimum of fourteen days. However, there are now circumstances where this has been
extended to a minimum of twenty-eight days by the amendments made in the Act.
However, it is suggested that because the purpose of the Act is to cause a cessation of
the behaviour that is harming consumers, the consultation period should in reality not
be any longer than the period stipulated. If there is a protracted period of consultation,
the risk of harm to consumers continuing must be high. In practice, therefore, enforcers would be wise to have completed sufficient amounts of their investigations into the
alleged infringements to be able to make sensible decisions and move the process along
with all due expediency. Subsections (4)(A) and (4)(B) of section 214 are new:

Section 214 Consultation

(1) An enforcer must not make an application for an enforcement order unless—
    (a) the enforcer has engaged in appropriate consultation with the person against whom
the enforcement order would be made, and
    (b) if the enforcer is not the CMA, the enforcer has given notice to the CMA of the
enforcer's intention to apply for the enforcement order, and the appropriate minimum
period has elapsed.

(1A) The appropriate minimum period is—
    (a) in the case of an enforcement order, 14 days beginning with the day on which notice
under subsection (1)(b) is given;
    (b) in the case of an interim enforcement order, seven days beginning with the day on
which notice under subsection (1)(b) is given.

(2) Appropriate consultation is consultation for the purpose of—
    (a) achieving the cessation of the infringement in a case where an infringement is occurring;
    (b) ensuring that there will be no repetition of the infringement in a case where the
infringement has occurred;
    (c) ensuring that there will be no repetition of the infringement in a case where the cessa-
tion of the infringement is achieved under paragraph (a);

---

[17] See s. 214(1) EA 2002.

    (d) ensuring that the infringement does not take place in the case of a Community infringement which the enforcer believes is likely to take place.

(3) Subsection (1) does not apply if the CMA thinks that an application for an enforcement order should be made without delay.

(4) Subsection (1)(a) ceases to apply—

    (a) for the purposes of an application for an enforcement order at the end of the period of 14 days or, where subsection (4A) applies, 28 days beginning with the day after the person against whom the enforcement order would be made receives a request for consultation from the enforcer;

    (b) for the purposes of an application for an interim enforcement order at the end of the period of seven days beginning with the day after the person against whom the interim enforcement order would be made receives a request for consultation from the enforcer.

(4A) This subsection applies where the person against whom the enforcement order would be made is a member of, or is represented by, a representative body, and that body operates a consumer code which has been approved by

    (a) an enforcer, other than a designated enforcer which is not a public body,

    (b) a body which is representative of an enforcer mentioned in paragraph (a); or

    (c) a group of enforcers mentioned in paragraph (a).

(4B) In subsection (4A) "consumer code" means a code of practice or other document(however described) intended, with a view to safeguarding or promoting the interests of consumers, to regulate by any means the conduct of persons engaged in the supply of goods or services to consumers (or the conduct of their employees or representatives), and "representative body" means an organization established to represent the interests of two or more businesses in a particular sector or area, and for this purpose "business" has the meaning it bears in section 210.

(5) [...]

(6) [...]

8.36   As can be seen from the section reproduced above, where the consultation is with a trader who is a member of a representative body or is represented by such a body, and they have a consumer code, the consultation period is now twenty-eight days.

8.37   The guidance issued by BIS, at paragraph 44, states as follows:

The extended consultation period may be used, for example, by the person that may be subject to the enforcement order or undertaking to propose their own measures to address the detriment caused and be based on the requirements of the relevant consumer code. Depending on the circumstances of the case, this may be an indicator that the infringement will not be repeated. At the end of the 28 day period, the enforcer may take further action if they consider it appropriate. They can either commence court action to seek an enforcement order and/or seek to work with the person to agree undertakings.[18]

8.38   It can therefore be seen that the intention is to give further time to come to appropriate agreements in cases where it is likely that the trader is engaging with the process, thus signaling an intention that the breach will not be repeated. This

---

[18] Draft guidance on enhanced consumer measures, <https://bisgovuk.citizenspace.com/consumer-rights-bill/guidance-2014/supporting_documents/Enhanced%20Consumer%20Measures%20%20Draft%20Guidance%20For%20Testing.pdf>.

was also the indication given in the Explanatory Notes for the section as the Bill made its way through the House of Lords.[19]

The Enterprise Act 2002 (Part 8 Request for Consultation) Order 2003[20] lays down the rules in respect of the making and receipt of an enforcer's initial request for consultation to the person concerned. It is prescriptive and must therefore include the method of communication, address for service, the person to whom the request for consultation should be addressed, and the deemed date of receipt of the request.

8.39

It is suggested that, for the consultation to be effective, the notice should set out in clear terms the substance of the alleged breaches and the legislation that is said to be being infringed. It is also suggested that the notice should specify the suggested amendments to the trader's practices that the enforcer is seeking, alongside setting out a clear timescale for when the consultation period will end. In this way, the trader will have the maximum amount of information available to him to undertake a meaningful consultation should he choose to engage. This, then, has the added bonus of demonstrating to a court that the enforcer has given the trader all reasonable and proportionate avenues to pursue and respond to should the consultation fail and an application for an enforcement order need to be made.

8.40

The need for consultation can be dispensed with where there is a real degree of urgency about the situation and/or it is thought that engaging in consultation with the trader would be futile. Where this situation arises, a waiver must be sought from the CMA and the application to the court should be made without any further delay.

8.41

It is suggested that this procedure should only be used where there is a real sense of immediate danger of serious harm to consumers. Where at all possible, it will be preferable to attempt to engage in consultation, as it is likely that this will secure the best outcome, either because formal court proceedings can be avoided or because a court will be more likely to grant an order.

8.42

At the end of the consultation period, the enforcer will either be in a position to make an application to a court for an enforcement order or to accept an undertaking under section 219 EA 2002. As both undertakings and enforcement orders have been amended to include enhanced consumer measures, they will be looked at together in section H below.

8.43

H. ENHANCED CONSUMER MEASURES

The EA 2002 has hitherto only been able to obtain relief aimed at bringing about the cessation of the breach by the trader through prohibition. The new powers provided by the amendments in the Act have given a greater degree of flexibility

8.44

---

[19] See para. 382 of the Explanatory Notes to the Consumer Rights Bill as brought from the House of Commons on 17 June 2014 [HL Bill 29].

[20] SI 2003/1375.

to both the enforcer and the courts when seeking to address the breaches that are alleged. There are three new provisions that can be added to the existing powers. Those are redress; compliance; and choice; the definitions of which are set out in section 219A EA 2002. Each will be looked at in turn below:

Section 219A Definition of enhanced consumer measures

(1) In this Part, enhanced consumer measures are measures (not excluded by subsection (5)) falling within—
    (a) the redress category described in subsection (2),
    (b) the compliance category described in subsection (3), or
    (c) the choice category described in subsection (4).

8.45   The new measures are not retrospective in nature and as such cannot be added to existing orders. They will only be applicable to those orders or undertakings made or entered into after 1 October 2015.

8.46   As the aim of the legislation is to be as flexible as possible, the types of measures that can be sought under the new categories have not been defined. This is thought to be for the benefit of both businesses and enforcers alike, as it leaves both free to put forward measures that can adapt to the individual situation before them. However, whilst this is likely to be welcomed by both enforcers and businesses, it does nothing for the consumer, as he will not know what type of actions might be available to the enforcer where he has lodged his complaint.

8.47   The consultation 'Extending the Range of Remedies Available to Public Enforcers of Consumer Law'[21] document, under the heading of increased business compliance with the law, did set out a list of potential measures. It was suggested that the relevant company could: sign up to a primary authority scheme;[22] appoint a compliance officer; provide additional training; use spot checks; improve record-keeping and the collection of customer feedback; and, importantly, sign up to an alternative dispute resolution scheme.

8.48   The above illustrates the types of measures that may now be sought when seeking either undertakings or enforcement orders. They have also been reproduced in the draft guidance issued by BIS.

8.49   However, although the measures themselves were not explicitly spelt out, those measures that are not to be considered as enhanced consumer measures were set out in section 219A(5), which reads as follows:

(5) The following are not enhanced consumer measures—
    (a) a publication requirement included in an enforcement order as described in section 217(8),
    (b) a publication requirement included in an undertaking accepted by the court as described in section 217(10), or

---

[21] <https://www.gov.uk/government/uploads/system/uploads/attachment_data/file/32713/12-1193-civil-enforcement-remedies-consultation-on-extending.pdf>.
[22] Pursuant to s. 25 of the Regulatory Enforcement and Sanctions Act 2008.

(c) a publication requirement included in an undertaking accepted by a CPC enforcer as described in section 219(5A)(a).

As stated above, the enhanced consumer measures are able to be added to both undertakings (whether given to the court or to the enforcer) and to enforcement orders. 8.50

Whether attached to an order or undertaking given to the court or to the enforcer, before any enhanced consumer measure can be added it must be just, reasonable, and proportionate. It is submitted that, when deciding whether the measures sought meet this test, regard should be had to the Regulators Code.[23] 8.51

Section 219B sets out the details of what needs to be considered when looking at attaching an enhanced consumer measure. 8.52

Section 219B Inclusion of enhanced consumer measures etc.

(1) An enforcement order or undertaking may include only such enhanced consumer measures as the court or enforcer (as the case may be) considers to be just and reasonable.
(2) For the purposes of subsection (1) the court or enforcer must in particular consider whether any proposed enhanced consumer measures are proportionate, taking into account—
    (a) the likely benefit of the measures to consumers,
    (b) the costs likely to be incurred by the subject of the enforcement order or undertaking, and
    (c) the likely cost to consumers of obtaining the benefit of the measures.
(3) The costs referred to in subsection (2)(b) are—
    (a) the cost of the measures, and
    (b) the reasonable administrative costs associated with taking the measures.

It is therefore clear that, when determining whether a measure is proportionate, both courts and enforcers will need to undertake some form of cost benefit analysis. Where an enhanced consumer measure is being suggested by the enforcer as part of the consultation process, it may in practice be difficult to achieve the analysis without the input of the trader in question, unless as part of the investigation process financial documentation has either been seized or information about the financial position of the company and any potential measures has been requested. Given that the powers for enforcers are now generic (see Chapter 7), it would be wise for enforcers to have the EA 2002 provisions in mind when entering premises, asking for information, or searching under a warrant. 8.53

Whilst one of the measures can include paying money to a consumer, and there will be associated costs that go alongside the implementation of an enhanced consumer measure, the draft guidance issued by BIS ('Draft Guidance on Enhanced Consumer Measures') in FAQ 6[24] is at pains to point out that, because the Treasury does not see any of the money, these are not financial penalties. Whilst this is strictly true, it is unlikely that those who are the subject of an order or undertaking that requires money to be spent, whether directly to consumers or otherwise, will view it in this way! 8.54

---

[23] <https://www.gov.uk/government/publications/regulators-code>.
[24] BIS, 'Draft Guidance on Enhanced Consumer Measures' at p. 13.

1. Redress Category

8.55   As one of the main reasons for adding enhanced consumer measures to the EA 2002 was to provide greater powers to enforcers and courts to 'give back' to consumers that which a rogue trader had taken, this often being money, the redress category is the most important of the three when considering enhanced consumer measures and should, it is suggested, be considered before either of the other two available measures. Equally, where it would be disproportionate to use all three enhanced consumer measures in an order or undertaking, then redress should take priority.

8.56   Given that redress will cost the trader money, it may be that this is a category which proves to be costly to enforcers in the long run. It may be that it is in the minority of cases where a trader accepts a redress-enhanced consumer measure as part of an undertaking directly following consultation; therefore, litigation is likely when redress is part of the enhanced consumer measures sought, especially where the number of consumers seeking redress is high.

8.57   Section 219A(2) sets out the detail of what is meant by redress:

(2) The measures in the redress category are—
   (a) measures offering compensation or other redress to consumers who have suffered loss as a result of the conduct which has given rise to the enforcement order or undertaking,
   (b) where the conduct referred to in paragraph (a) relates to a contract, measures offering such consumers the option to terminate (but not vary) that contract,
   (c) where such consumers cannot be identified, or cannot be identified without disproportionate cost to the subject of the enforcement order or undertaking, measures intended to be in the collective interests of consumers.

8.58   Redress is only available where there has been a loss to the consumers. Section 219B(4) is explicit on that, and further goes on to define what is meant by the term 'loss case':

(4) An enforcement order or undertaking may include enhanced consumer measures in the redress category—
   (a) only in a loss case, and
   (b) only if the court or enforcer (as the case may be) is satisfied that the cost of such measures to the subject of the enforcement order or undertaking is unlikely to be more than the sum of the losses suffered by consumers as a result of the conduct which has given rise to the enforcement order or undertaking.
(5) The cost referred to in subsection (4)(b) does not include the administrative costs associated with taking the measures.
(6) Subsection (7) applies if an enforcement order or undertaking includes enhanced consumer measures offering compensation and a settlement agreement is entered into in connection with the payment of compensation.
(7) A waiver of a person's rights in the settlement agreement is not valid if it is a waiver of the right to bring civil proceedings in respect of conduct other than the conduct which has given rise to the enforcement order or undertaking.
(8) The following definitions apply for the purposes of subsection (4)(a).

(9) In the case of an enforcement order or undertaking under section 217, "a loss case" means a case in which—

    (a) subsection (1) of that section applies (a finding that a person has engaged in conduct which constitutes an infringement), and

    (b) consumers have suffered loss as a result of that conduct.

(10) In the case of an undertaking under section 219, "a loss case" means a case in which—

    (a) subsection (3)(a) or (b) of that section applies (a belief that a person has engaged or is engaging in conduct which constitutes an infringement), and

    (b) consumers have suffered loss as a result of that conduct

It remains to be seen how the need for an actual loss to consumers fits with undertakings under section 219(3)(c) where the enforcer need only believe that the trader is engaging in conduct that is a community infringement. **8.59**

It is acknowledged that every case will be different and that in not every case will 100 per cent of fiscal redress be appropriate. Enforcers should consider the factors in Table 8.3 before deciding whether redress will be just, reasonable, and proportionate in an individual case. **8.60**

It is suggested that in most cases it will be the responsibility of the trader to contact the consumer or group thereof with the offer of compensation, thus reducing the burden placed upon the enforcer. However, there will obviously be some cases where this is inappropriate, for example where elderly or otherwise vulnerable consumers have been targeted, or where the order or undertaking is sought whilst there are ongoing or recently concluded criminal proceedings. **8.61**

As can be seen from section 219B(7), it is possible to seek a waiver as part of any settlement where redress is being utilized. Consumers are able to waive their **8.62**

Table 8.3 Factors to be considered[25]

Consideration	Explanation
The likely benefit to consumers if the measures are used	• Have consumers suffered loss? • How much loss have they suffered? • Are they likely to receive any money back?
The cost likely to be incurred by the business of putting the measures in place	• The reasonable administrative costs of putting the redress scheme in place i.e. if a large number of consumers have lost a small amount of money, a full redress scheme may not be proportionate. • Will the cost of the redress scheme be more than the loss caused to consumers?
The likely cost to consumers of obtaining the benefits of the measures being used	• Will it cost consumers more to collect redress. Is the business being clear about what it is offering as part of a redress scheme?

[25] Draft guidance on enhanced consumer measures, <https://bisgovuk.citizenspace.com/consumer-rights-bill/guidance-2014/supporting_documents/Enhanced%20Consumer%20Measures%20%20Draft%20Guidance%20For%20Testing.pdf>.

rights to take civil action for further damages over and above the redress scheme in respect of the particular breach/loss covered by the scheme. It is not open to have a condition that waives a consumer's rights to take action for other damages caused by other breaches not covered by the scheme.

8.63   Furthermore, there is no power to make an individual consumer accept compensation as part of redress or redress at all. In the (hopefully) rare cases where the consumer declines redress, he or she can still pursue civil action.

8.64   Given that redress is going to involve a payment of money, the question as to what happens in the case of bankruptcy must be considered. The draft guidance at FAQ 15 addresses this issue:[26]

FAQ 15 – Can a business declare themselves bankrupt to avoid paying redress?

If the redress order was against the company director then the order to pay redress remains in place, regardless of whether the company is in liquidation.

If the order is obtained against a sole trader who declares bankruptcy, the redress order becomes a debt in the bankruptcy.

If the order is against the company and it goes into liquidation, the redress order becomes a debt in the liquidation

8.65   It would therefore be prudent always to make (where possible) the order against both the company director and the company. This is especially so where there are fears that the rogue trader in question may 'do a phoenix'. It is noticeable that the FAQ does not address the situation of an undertaking. It is suggested that where the undertaking is a formal undertaking to the court, the above will apply.

2. Compliance

8.66   What is meant by compliance is set out at section 219(B)(3) EA 2002:

(3) The measures in the compliance category are measures intended to prevent or reduce the risk of the occurrence or repetition of the conduct to which the enforcement order or undertaking relates (including measures with that purpose which may have the effect of improving compliance with consumer law more generally).

8.67   It is therefore clear that any proposed measure must have at its heart the aim of preventing or reducing the risk of reccurrence of the specific breach or breaches that have brought the trader under the investigation of the enforcer, alongside any measures the enforcer believes will increase compliance with the law generally.

8.68   As can be seen from the above, the powers are very wide in that they are only limited by the need to be reasonable, just, and proportionate. The types of measures envisaged are: making a trader join the primary authority scheme; increasing and improving

---

[26] Draft guidance on enhanced consumer measures, <https://bisgovuk.citizenspace.com/consumer-rights-bill/guidance-2014/supporting_documents/Enhanced%20Consumer%20Measures%20%20 Draft%20Guidance%20For%20Testing.pdf>.

employee training to prevent further breaches; and appointing a dedicated member of staff to be responsible for ensuring compliance.

When determining whether suggested measures are reasonable, just, and propor- 8.69
tionate, it is suggested that the enforcer should have in mind the nature of the behaviour that is the cause for concern, the cost of implementing the measures, and the size of the business. For example, in the setting of a small shop employing one or two people, where there might be issues with pricing (for example, the shelf label gives a price which is not honoured at the till point as the price reduction had not been reflected on the electronic till), increasing training and the types of documents kept in order to monitor compliance might be more just, reasonable, and proportionate than insisting that the shop join the primary authority scheme or take on extra staff.

It is easy to see how this type of measure can be combined with the redress measure. 8.70
In the above example where the price differential between what the consumer paid for the goods and the actual price of a product can be determined, redress can be provided for the difference. This can be combined with increased training to ensure that the tills are updated to reflect the price labels and that checks are made on a daily basis to make sure that has happened. Records should be kept to illustrate that this is being done.

3. Choice

Although called the 'choice' category, from the trader's point of view the section 8.71
is really about information. What information needs to be supplied to consumers to enable the consumer to make an informed choice in his or her purchasing decisions? The thought behind this section is that the greater the degree of information provided to consumers, the greater will be their ability to exercise their choice. It is thought that this will lead to increased competition.

Section 219B(4) provides the broad definition of the types of measures intended 8.72
to fall within the choice category: '(4) The measures in the choice category are measures intended to enable consumers to choose more effectively between persons supplying or seeking to supply goods or services'.

Once again, there is no assistance given by the Act as to how this is to be 8.73
achieved. It is suggested in the guidance that, if consumers know about a business's past performance as to breaches and how it has dealt with them, this will have a great degree of impact on the consumer's decision whether or not to contract with the trader.[27]

To an extent this is true. For example, when a consumer is considering buying 8.74
something from an online trader who is hosted within another platform (such as Ebay or Amazon Market Place) he may look at reviews, not just for the product he wishes to purchase, but also about the individual he is contracting with, and use this information when deciding whether to buy or to move on. The same may

---

[27] See para. 60 of the draft guidance on enhanced consumer measures, <https://bisgovuk.citizens pace.com/consumer-rights-bill/guidance-2014/supporting_documents/Enhanced%20Consumer%20 Measures%20%20Draft%20Guidance%20For%20Testing.pdf>.

apply to small traders operating outside a digital platform. For small businesses, it is submitted that the choice provision may have a real, and in some cases detrimental, effect on their business.

8.75 However, it is submitted that the same consumer considerations are unlikely to apply to multi-site or multi-national companies to an extent that matters to the trader. In recent years, although there has been a proliferation of negative news stories about these types of companies on a range of issues, they are still here with no appreciable difference in their profit margins.

8.76 It is for this reason that there needs to be careful consideration about whether a measure is just, reasonable, and proportionate to the aims sought, and why there cannot be a one-size-fits-all policy.

I. LIMITATIONS

8.77 The Act inserts section 219C into the EA 2002. This acts as a limitation on using the enhanced consumer measures by designated enforcers:

Section 219C Availability of enhanced consumer measures to private enforcers

(1) An enforcement order made on the application of a designated enforcer which is not a public body may require a person to take enhanced consumer measures only if the following conditions are satisfied.

(2) An undertaking given under section 217(9) following an application for an enforcement order made by a designated enforcer which is not a public body, or an undertaking given to such an enforcer under section 219, may include a further undertaking by a person to take enhanced consumer measures only if the following conditions are satisfied.

(3) The first condition is that the enforcer is specified for the purposes of this section by order made by the Secretary of State.

(4) The second condition is that the enhanced consumer measures do not directly benefit the enforcer or an associated undertaking.

8.78 Subsection (5) makes it plain that the kind of measures that are envisaged as benefitting the enforcer would include requiring a person to pay money to the enforcer, or requiring a person to participate in a scheme administered by the enforcer or one in which the enforcer might obtain a commercial advantage.

8.79 Subsection (7) provides that the Secretary of State can only use the power in subsection (3) if the private enforcer is subject to the principles of good regulation in the Regulators Code and section 21 of the Legislative and Regulatory Reform Act 2006 (transparency, accountability, proportionality, consistency, and targeting cases that need action). Subsections (9) and (10) set out a requirement on private enforcers that, when using enhanced consumer measures, they must act consistently with advice or guidance given to the enforcer or to the person subject to the measures by a primary authority.

8.80 In this way, businesses are protected from having enforcer action taken by a private designated enforcer where they are following advice given by their primary authority. It will therefore be necessary for any private designated enforcer to ascertain what advice has been given before seeking any orders.

J. APPLICATIONS

The application to the court is still governed by section 215 EA 2002. No amend- **8.81** ments to this provision have been made. Applications will still be made to the High Court or county court in England, Wales, or Northern Ireland[28] where the person against whom an order is sought has their place of business in those jurisdictions. In all but the most serious of cases, it is suggested that proceedings will ordinarily be commenced in the local county court.

As with every pleading, the application must still name the person against whom **8.82** the order is sought as the person engaging in conduct which is an infringement of Community or domestic provisions.[29]

Section 216 EA 2002 is likewise unaffected by any amendments. The CMA can **8.83** still order that only they bring proceedings,[30] or specify another enforcer who can only bring proceedings.[31] Section 216 will still allow undertakings under section 219 EA 2002 to be accepted by either the CMA or another enforcer.[32] Section 216 cannot prevent an application for an enforcement order being made by a Community enforcer.[33]

Section 222 EA 2002 is also left untouched, so that the provisions on accessories **8.84** remains as was. Therefore, if the conduct that is infringing takes place with the consent or connivance of a person who has a special relationshop with the body corporate, the very consent or connivance is also an infringement in and of itself. As has been stated above, rogue traders have in the past been known to 'do a phoenix'; therefore, any order or undertaking will be worthless if they do so where only the corporate entity has been named in the order.

Given that the corporate entity (in whatever guise) cannot operate without indi- **8.85** viduals who will almost always have had a part to play in the infringement that is alleged, it makes clear good sense and practical policy to name the accessories in the pleadings and seek orders or undertakings from them too.

---

[28] s. 15(5)(a) EA 2002.
[29] s. 215(1)(a) and (b) EA 2002.
[30] s. 216(2)(a) EA 2002.
[31] s. 216(2)(b) EA 2002.
[32] s. 216(3)(a) EA 2002.
[33] s. 216(6) EA 2002.

9

PRIVATE ACTIONS
IN COMPETITION LAW

A. OVERVIEW

The intention of this part of the Act is to make it easier for consumers and busi-   9.01
nesses to gain access to redress where there has been an infringement of antitrust
provisions: competition law. The history of competition law is far outside the scope
of this work. A well-known quotation from Adam Smith[1] suffices to illustrate the
potential danger for consumers:

People of the same trade seldom meet together, even for merriment and diversion, but the con-
versation ends in a conspiracy against the public, or in some contrivance to raise prices. It is
impossible indeed to prevent such meetings, by any law which could be executed, or would be
consistent with liberty and justice. But though the law cannot hinder people of the same trade
from sometimes assembling together, it ought to do nothing to facilitate such assemblies; much
less to render them necessary.

The merits of vigorous competition have been the policy of successive govern-   9.02
ments of differing parties. In 2001, the Labour government described the merits of
competition as follows:

The importance of competition in an increasingly innovative and globalised economy is
clear. Vigorous competition between firms is the lifeblood of strong and effective markets.
Competition helps consumers get a good deal. It encourages firms to innovate by reducing
slack, putting downward pressure on costs and providing incentives for the efficient organisation
of production. As such, competition is a central driver for productivity growth in the economy,
and hence the UK's international competitiveness.[2]

Since accession to the EU, UK competition law has been largely aligned to that   9.03
of the EU.[3] Article 3 of the Treaty on the Functioning of the European Union

---

[1] A. Smith, *Wealth of Nations* (London: T. Nelson & Sons, 1776) Book 1 p. 54.
[2] See House of Commons Library, *The UK Competition Regime* Antony Seely, 16 January 2015.
[3] This was certainly the policy behind the Competition Act 1998. See Lord Haskel, Hansard House of
Lords 17 November 1997 at Col 417.

('TFEU') makes it plain that the Union shall have exclusive competence in establishing the competition rules necessary for the function of the internal market.

9.04   The Competition Act 1998 ('CA') prohibits anti-competitive agreements between businesses. The Chapter One prohibition is contained in section 2 CA:

2.— Agreements etc. preventing, restricting or distorting competition.

(1) Subject to section 3, agreements between undertakings, decisions by associations of undertakings or concerted practices which—
   (a) may affect trade within the United Kingdom, and
   (b) have as their object or effect the prevention, restriction or distortion of competition within the United Kingdom,
   are prohibited unless they are exempt in accordance with the provisions of this Part.

(2) Subsection (1) applies, in particular, to agreements, decisions or practices which—
   (a) directly or indirectly fix purchase or selling prices or any other trading conditions;
   (b) limit or control production, markets, technical development or investment;
   (c) share markets or sources of supply;
   (d) apply dissimilar conditions to equivalent transactions with other trading parties, thereby placing them at a competitive disadvantage;
   (e) make the conclusion of contracts subject to acceptance by the other parties of supplementary obligations which, by their nature or according to commercial usage, have no connection with the subject of such contracts.

(3) Subsection (1) applies only if the agreement, decision or practice is, or is intended to be, implemented in the United Kingdom.

(4) Any agreement or decision which is prohibited by subsection (1) is void.

9.05   Article 101 TFEU is the old article 81 EC. It is in very similar terms to the Chapter One prohibition:

1. The following shall be prohibited as incompatible with the internal market: all agreements between undertakings, decisions by associations of undertakings and concerted practices which may affect trade between Member States and which have as their object or effect the prevention, restriction or distortion of competition within the internal market, and in particular those which:
   (a) directly or indirectly fix purchase or selling prices or any other trading conditions;
   (b) limit or control production, markets, technical development, or investment;
   (c) share markets or sources of supply;
   (d) apply dissimilar conditions to equivalent transactions with other trading parties, thereby placing them at a competitive disadvantage;
   (e) make the conclusion of contracts subject to acceptance by the other parties of supplementary obligations which, by their nature or according to commercial usage, have no connection with the subject of such contracts.

2. Any agreements or decisions prohibited pursuant to this Article shall be automatically void.

3. The provisions of paragraph 1 may, however, be declared inapplicable in the case of:
   – any agreement or category of agreements between undertakings,
   – any decision or category of decisions by associations of undertakings,
   – any concerted practice or category of concerted practices,which contributes to improving the production or distribution of goods or to promoting technical or economic progress, while allowing consumers a fair share of the resulting benefit, and which does not:

(a) impose on the undertakings concerned restrictions which are not indispensable to the attainment of these objectives;

(b) afford such undertakings the possibility of eliminating competition in respect of a substantial part of the products in question.

Chapter One prohibitions are primarily concerned with horizontal agreements, which are agreements to collude between firms on the same level of the supply chain. The Competition and Markets Authority ('CMA') can bring proceedings against undertakings who engage in such activities and are able to levy fines as a result. Exemptions from prohibition are available if the firm can demonstrate that these practices are in the interest of the consumer through increasing market efficiencies or advancing technical progress. **9.06**

The Chapter Two prohibition is contained in section 18 CA: **9.07**

18.— Abuse of dominant position.

(1) Subject to section 19, any conduct on the part of one or more undertakings which amounts to the abuse of a dominant position in a market is prohibited if it may affect trade within the United Kingdom.

(2) Conduct may, in particular, constitute such an abuse if it consists in—

(a) directly, or indirectly imposing unfair purchase or selling prices or other unfair trading conditions;

(b) limiting production, markets or technical development to the prejudice of consumers;

(c) applying dissimilar conditions to equivalent transactions with other trading parties, thereby placing them at a competitive disadvantage;

(d) making the conclusion of contracts subject to acceptance by the other parties of supplementary obligations which, by their nature or according to commercial usage, have no connection with the subject of the contracts.

(3) In this section—

"dominant position" means a dominant position within the United Kingdom; and *"the United Kingdom"* means the United Kingdom or any part of it.

Article 102 TFEU is the old article 82 EC and is in similar terms to the Chapter Two prohibition: **9.08**

Any abuse by one or more undertakings of a dominant position within the internal market or in a substantial part of it shall be prohibited as incompatible with the internal market in so far as it may affect trade between Member States.

Such abuse may, in particular, consist in:

(a) directly or indirectly imposing unfair purchase or selling prices or other unfair trading conditions;

(b) limiting production, markets or technical development to the prejudice of consumers;

(c) applying dissimilar conditions to equivalent transactions with other trading parties, thereby placing them at a competitive disadvantage;

(d) making the conclusion of contracts subject to acceptance by the other parties of supplementary obligations which, by their nature or according to commercial usage, have no connection with the subject of such contracts.

In investigating a breach of a Chapter Two prohibition, there is a two stage process. The first is that the firm possesses a dominant market position (section 18(1)). **9.09**

This is done through various indices, including the Herfudahl-Hirchman Index. The next is to establish one of the matters in subsection (2).

9.10   There are broadly two types of proceedings before the UK courts: claims against individuals for breaches of the rules, and appeals against decisions of the competition authorities. The latter are a species of public law proceedings; the former a type of private action. Private actions are often (but not exclusively) pleaded as a breach of statutory duty.[4] Before these reforms, such **stand-alone** claims could only be brought in the High Court. The Competition Appeal Tribunal ('CAT') had jurisdiction under section 47A of the Competition Act 1998 following a prior finding of a competition infringement. These actions are described as **follow-on** actions.[5] Section 47B of the same Act provided a mechanism for **collective actions** made by a specified body on behalf of consumers, the best example of such a body being the Consumer Association (Which?).

9.11   There are three main practical changes to the way in which proceedings can be brought in the UK. The substantive law has not changed, but the procedural changes are about as far-reaching as procedural changes can be.

B. THE THREE OBJECTIVES

9.12   The Act has three objectives:

- To widen the types of competition cases that the CAT hears and to make other changes to the procedure of bringing a private action before the CAT;[6]
- To provide for opt-out collective actions and opt-out collective settlements;[7]
- To provide for voluntary redress schemes.[8]

C. BACKGROUND: THE PERCEIVED PROBLEMS

9.13   These reforms are part of a package that included the creation of the CMA and removed the element of dishonesty from the cartel offence in section 188 of the Enterprise Act 2002 ('EA 2002').

9.14   The government explained in the Consultation[9] that the Office of Fair Trading ('OFT') had calculated that the competition regime had benefited consumers by almost £689 million in 2010/2011. It is hoped that the reforms to the CMA will

---

[4] See *Garden Cottage Foods Ltd v Milk Marketing Board* [1984] AC 130.
[5] See *BCL v BASF* [2008] CAT 24.
[6] See Explanatory Notes paras 420–33.
[7] See Explanatory Notes paras 434–5.
[8] See Explanatory Notes paras 446–50.
[9] 'Private Actions in Competition Law: A Consultation on Options for Reform'. Department for Business Innovation and Skills ('BIS'), January 2013.

result in more high impact cases to be taken forward. However, it was said that private sector challenges could complement public enforcement.

The proposals are designed to increase growth by empowering small businesses 9.15 to tackle anti-competitive behaviour that is stifling their business, and to promote fairness by enabling consumers and businesses who have suffered loss due to anti-competitive behaviour to obtain redress.

The government made a distinction between the rationales for public and private 9.16 actions. The function of a public competition authority is to detect, enforce, and deter competition infringements. The purpose of such an authority is to prevent the costs to society as a whole of productive and allocative inefficiency: reduced choice for consumers, sub-optimal allocation of resources, and reduced innovation. The role that private actions could play was explained as follows:

However, consumers and businesses also have a fundamental right to seek redress for themselves for damages that they have suffered. In some circumstances, private actors may be better placed to know where anticompetitive behaviour is causing them harm and are best placed to weigh up the relative costs and rewards to them of pursuing an action. SMEs in particular may be vulnerable to being harmed by cases which would not be significant on the scale of the entire economy, but which are harmful or fatal to them as individual businesses.

The primary need from government is to create a framework whereby individuals and businesses can represent their own interests, rather than to extend its own involvement in competition law. Empowering and enabling businesses and consumers to take direct action against anticompetitive behaviour will be essential to establishing a private actions regime that complements public enforcement.[10]

The government took the view that some of the existing legal mechanisms were 9.17 not adequate to meet the problem for three reasons.

Firstly, the right for consumers to bring collective actions under the previous sec- 9.18 tion 47B CA had been used once by Which? in their action against JJB for replica football shirts. Only 130 consumers signed up for the collective action, which was less than 0.1 per cent of those affected.

The representative action rule in the Civil Procedure Rules 1988 rule 19.6 could 9.19 not be easily used as a result of the decision in *Emerald Supplies v British Airways* [2011] 2 WLR 203.[11] That case involved a claim that BA had been party to agreements with other competitors who supplied air freight services contrary to article 101 and section 2 CA. In that case, the Court of Appeal upheld a decision of the Chancery Division to strike out the assertion by the claimants that they were representative of all other direct or indirect purchasers of airflight services, the prices for which had been inflated as a result of the alleged agreements or concerted practices.

The CAT had been restricted as to which competition law cases it could hear. It 9.20 could hear follow-on actions where an infringement had been found by a relevant

---

[10] 'Private Actions in Competition Law', para. 3.9.
[11] See, in particular, paras 27, 28, 31.

competition authority. In *Enron v EWS,* the Court of Appeal ruled that the scope for the CAT to go beyond the findings of those bodies is extremely limited:[12]

The jurisdiction of the tribunal is therefore limited to determining what are commonly referred to as follow-on claims for damages based on a finding of infringement of the Chapter II prohibition or article 82 which has been made by the Office of Fair Trading [...]. The existence of such a finding is not only a precondition to the making of a claim under section 47A(1). It also operates to determine and define the limits of that claim and the tribunal's jurisdiction in respect of it.[13]

9.21   By way of contrast a stand-alone action requires the party which brings the proceedings to prove the infringement. Such actions can and have been brought in the High Court.

9.22   The Consultation suggests that there are many cases where it would be inappropriate for the OFT, or sectoral regulators or the European Commission, to take action. There were said to be meritorious cases where it would be an inefficient use of public resources to bring the full force of an investigation to bear. And even in cases brought by the various state authorities, there was no specific provision to made redress to those who had suffered loss.

D. OBJECTIVE ONE: WIDEN THE TYPES OF CASES WHICH THE CAT CAN HEAR

1. Changes to the Competition Act 1998

9.23   There have been substantial amendments to the CA.[14] Existing sections have been amended, and new sections inserted as per Table 9.1.

Table 9.1 Amendments to Competition Act 1998

New section	Title
47A	Proceedings before the Tribunal: Claims for damages etc.
47B	Collective proceedings before the Tribunal
47C	Collective proceedings: Damages and costs
47D	Proceedings under section 47A or collective proceedings: Injunctions etc.
47E	Limitation or prescriptive periods for proceedings under section 47A and collective proceedings
49A	Collective settlements: Where a collective proceedings order has been made
49B	Collective settlements: Where a collective proceedings order has not been made

---

[12] *English Welsh & Scottish Railway Limited v Enron Coal Service Limited* [2009] EWCA Civ 647.

[13] Op. cit. para. 30 per Patten LJ.

[14] This chapter follows the Explanatory Notes, rather than the paras of Sch. 8, since it has a more cohesive structure.

49C	Approval of redress schemes by the CMA
49D	Redress schemes: recovery of costs
49E	Enforcement of approved schemes
58A	Infringement decisions

2. Section 47A Competition Act 1998

Section 47A CA is replaced by a new section. The old provision only allowed 9.24
follow-on cases to be heard before the CAT. The section applies to a person who
has suffered loss or damage as a result of an infringement decision or an alleged
infringement of the four prohibitions.

The relevant claims are those for damages, other claims for a sum of money, or a 9.25
claim for an injunction.[15] For the purpose of identifying claims which may be made
in civil proceedings, any limitation rules or rules relating to prescription that would
apply in such proceedings are to be disregarded.

The new section 47A enables the CAT to hear a *stand-alone claim* as well as a 9.26
follow-on claim and also have the power to grant injunctions. It is made plain that
the right to make a claim in the CAT does not affect the right to bring other proceedings for competition infringements.

Section 47 A(2) makes it plain that it applies to follow-on as well as stand alone 9.27
claims since it describes 'infringement decisions or alleged infringement decisions'.
Infringement decisions are defined within the section.[16] The rationale for this is to
prevent clashes between the applicable limitation periods in the High Court and
those in the CAT.

Importantly, paragraph 4(2) makes it plain that this applies to claims arising 9.28
before the commencement of the paragraph. By way of example, if there has already
been a decision of the CMA that there has been a competition infringement before
the commencement of this provision, a claim could be brought before the CAT.

3. Certification of Claims

The manner of commencing proceedings under section 47A is governed by CAT 9.29
rule 30. The claimant is required to provide a statement about whether or not the
claim is about a final infringement decision as defined by section 58A CA. Section
58A prescribes that the court (and therefore now the CAT) is bound by competition decisions of the CMA or CAT once appeal procedures have been exhausted.
The claimant must make it plain where in the UK action is taking place. A concise statement of the relevant facts and contentions of law must be provided. The
claimant must indicate what relief is sought, including an estimate of the amount

---

[15] New s. 47A(1–3).
[16] See s. 47A(6).

claimed in damages or, if applicable, a statement that the claimant would like an injunction.

9.30   Where the claim form is to be served on foreign defendants, there must be a statement of the legal basis and relevant facts by which it is said that the Tribunal has jurisdiction.

9.31   The form must include reasons (if applicable) why the application should be subjected to the fast track procedure. The form may only be amended with the written consent of the parties or with the permission of the Tribunal.

9.32   Once the claim form has been received, CAT rule 33 applies. Where a defendant is domiciled within the UK, receipt must be acknowledged within seven days. If the defendant is outside the UK, the CAT registrar shall determine the time limit for service. A defendant may then dispute the CAT's jurisdiction to hear the claim[17] within fourteen days.

9.33   A defence must be provided within twenty-eight days.[18] It must contain sufficient detail to indicate which of the facts and contentions of law in the claim form it admits or denies; and on what grounds, and on what other facts or contentions of law it relies. A claimant may then file a reply in response within twenty-one days of the defence.[19] No further pleadings may be filed without the permission of the Tribunal.[20]

4. Fast Track Rules

9.34   Paragraph 15A is inserted into the EA 2002 which provides for fast track rules. Rule 57 of the CAT Rules 2015 covers the fast track procedure ('FTP'). 'Fast track' means a set of proceedings in which the final hearing will be fixed to commence as soon as possible, and in any event within six months of the order that the particular proceedings are within the fast track. If a hearing is within the fast track, the amount of recoverable costs will be capped.

9.35   The policy behind this change was plain from the second reading of the Bill. Vince Cable said: 'We will try to discourage parties from engaging in costly court cases by encouraging alternative dispute resolution. We propose reforming the Competition Appeal Tribunal by introducing a fast-track regime so that small and medium-sized companies can get quicker and cheaper access'.[21]

9.36   In order to determine whether proceedings should be subjected to the FTP, the Tribunal will take into account all matters which shall include: (this list is not exhaustive) the complexity and novelty of the issues; whether the time estimate for the final hearing is three days or less; whether there are to be additional claims;

---

[17] CAT rule 34.
[18] CAT rule 35.
[19] CAT rule 36.
[20] CAT rule 37.
[21] Hansard House of Commons 28 January 2014, second reading, at Col 776.

the scale of the papers and number of witnesses; the extent of disclosure; and the amount of damages.

The CAT also has to consider whether one or more of the parties is an individual 9.37 or a micro-, small- or medium-sized enterprise:[22]

- A 'micro-enterprise' employs fewer than ten persons with an annual turnover and/or balance sheet not exceeding €2 million;

- A 'small enterprise' employs fewer than fifty persons with an annual turnover and/or balance sheet not exceeding €10 million; and

- A 'medium enterprise' employs fewer than 250 persons with an annual turnover and/or balance sheet not exceeding €43 million.

5. Injunctions

Paragraph 7 introduces a new section 47D CA. An injunction granted under sec- 9.38 tion 47A and for collective proceedings is enforceable as though it were granted by the High Court.

The new section makes it plain that the Tribunal must apply the same rules as 9.39 would apply under section 37(1) of the Senior Courts Act 1981. Rules 67 to 70 apply. The CAT may grant an injunction in all cases in which it appears just and convenient to do so, and unconditionally, or on such terms and conditions as the Tribunal thinks just.[23] The application may be made before proceedings at any time, including before proceedings are started and after judgment has been given. The former may only be granted if the matter is urgent or it is otherwise necessary to do so in the interests of justice.

Importantly, in proceedings subject to the FTP, the CAT may grant an interim 9.40 injunction without requiring the applicant to provide an undertaking as to damages or, in the alternative, subject to a cap on the amount of the undertaking as to damages.[24] This is important since one of the disincentives in bringing actions in competition proceedings on behalf of consumers is the litigation risk.

Rule 69 explains how to apply for an injunction. It must be supported by evidence 9.41 unless the CAT orders otherwise. It must include all material information regarding the applicant's ability to pay under any undertaking for damages. If the application is without notice, reasons must be given.

Rule 70 governs the enforcement of the injunction. If a party contends that the 9.42 party subject to the injunction has failed to comply, then the matter can be transferred to the High Court.[25] The relevant part of Schedule 4 EA 2002 has been amended to facilitate this.[26] The parties must be given an opportunity to be heard in the CAT

---

[22] Commission Recommendation of 6 May 2003 [2003] OJ L124/36.
[23] CAT rule 67.
[24] CAT rule 68(5).
[25] Pursuant to para. 1A of Sch. 4, EA 2002.
[26] By para. 24.

first.[27] If the High Court, on enquiry, finds that an individual would have been in contempt in High Court proceedings, then the court may deal with them as though they had been.[28]

6. Time Limits/Prescription Periods

9.43 The limitation periods for claims under section 47A or collective proceedings are extended to be consistent with normal civil litigation. The Limitation Act 1980 applies. The relevant period is therefore six years.[29] Hitherto, there had been a difference between the limitation periods in the CAT and the High Court.

7. Other Procedural Provisions

9.44 The CAT is bound (as a result of amendments to section 58 CA) by a finding of fact of the CMA unless it directs otherwise. This puts the CAT in the same position as the High Court. A new section 58A CA deals with when a court or the CAT is bound by a decision that there has been a competition infringement. As one might expect, that is when appellate proceedings have stopped. Once an infringement decision is final, the court or CAT is bound by it.

9.45 Section 49 CA is amended to allow a right of appeal from the CAT.[30] Appeals are available for a decision about an award of damages, or the grant of injunction. Appeals are available regarding the amount of an award of damages or other sum (including costs). An appeal which arises from a decision in respect of a stand-alone claim may include consideration of a point of law arising from a finding of the CAT.

9.46 A party that has been acting pro bono may receive payments. The CAT may also stay or sist proceedings.[31]

E. OBJECTIVE TWO: COLLECTIVE ACTIONS AND OPT-OUT COLLECTIVE SETTLEMENTS

1. Government's Aims

9.47 The Explanatory Notes set out the aim of the Act regarding these types of proceedings:

The second aim is to introduce an opt-out collective actions regime and an opt-out collective settlement regime (both of which involve the case being brought forward on behalf of a group of clients to obtain compensation for their losses). Cases will be able to be brought by representatives on behalf of individuals and/or businesses. The CAT can already hear opt-in collective actions under the existing section 47B of the CA. An opt-in regime requires claimants to 'opt-in' to the

---

[27] CAT rule 70(3).
[28] para. 1A of Sch. 4 EA 2002.
[29] There are particular rules in the case of collective actions.
[30] s. 49(1A)-(1D) CA.
[31] See, e.g. CAT rule 82(4).

legal action to be able to obtain any damages. However the CAT does not currently have the power to hear opt-out collective actions. The purpose of introducing 'opt-out' collective actions is to allow consumers and businesses to easily achieve redress for losses they have suffered as a result of breaches of competition law.

The function of a collective settlement regime is to introduce a procedure for infringements of competition law, where those who have suffered a loss and the alleged infringer may jointly apply to the CAT to improve the settlement of a dispute on an opt-out basis. The collective settlement regime will operate on the same opt-out principles as the opt-out collective proceedings.[32]

9.48 The reason for these changes was set out in the response to the initial consultation in April 2012, which was released in January 2013.[33] The Secretary of State for Business Innovation and Skills ('BIS') summarized the responses in this way:

The responses to the consultation confirmed that the existing private actions regime is not working. Whilst some large businesses are able to successfully bring cases, for the vast majority of consumers and small businesses justice is out of reach. This means that even if the perpetrators of a price fixing scandal are caught, consumers and business still lose out.[34]

9.49 The same document dealt with the proposal in summary form:

Breaches of competition law, such as price-fixing, often involve very large numbers of people each losing a small amount, meaning it is not cost-effective for any individual to bring a case to court. Allowing actions to be brought collectively would overcome this problem, allowing consumers and business to get back the money that is rightfully theirs – as well as acting as a further deterrent to anyone thinking of breaking the law.

Recognising the concerns raised that this could lead to frivolous or unmeritorious litigation, the Government is introducing a set of strong safeguards, including:

- Strict judicial certification of cases so that only meritorious cases are taken forward.
- No treble damages
- No contingency fees for lawyers.
- Maintaining the 'loser-pays' rule so that those who bring unsuccessful cases pay the full price.

Claims will only be allowed to be brought by claimants or by genuine representatives of the claimants, such as trade associations or consumer associations, not by law firms, third party funders or special purpose vehicles. Any unclaimed sums would be allocated to the Access to Justice Foundation.

2. Section 47B Proceedings

9.50 Section 47B has been inserted into the EA 2002. It provides for opt-out proceedings whilst continuing to provide for opt-in proceedings. The two are defined as follows:

"Opt-in collective proceedings" are collective proceedings, which are brought on behalf of each class member who opts in by notifying the representative, in a manner and by a time specified, that the claim should be included in the collective proceedings.[35]

---

[32] Explanatory Notes para. 424.
[33] 'Private Actions in Competition Law. A consultation on options for reform—government response' (January 2013).
[34] Op. cit. p. 3. Per Rt. Hon. Dr Vince Cable.
[35] s. 47B(10) EA 2002.

"Opt-out collective proceedings" are collective proceedings which are brought on behalf of each class member except—

(a) any class member who opts out by notifying the representative, in a manner and by a time specified, that the claim should not be included in the collective proceedings, and
(b) Any class member who—
   (i) is not domiciled in the United Kingdom at a time specified, and
   (ii) does not, in a manner and by a time specified, opt in by notifying the representative that the claim should be included in the collective proceedings.[36]

9.51   The latter subsections are important since they mean that a person who is not domiciled in the UK must opt in to become part of the proceedings.

3. Relevant CAT Rules

9.52   The relevant section of the CAT rules is Part V. Rule 72 includes the various definitions of the concepts involved in collective proceedings and collective settlements. The CAT rules set out the manner of commencing proceedings under section 47B.[37] The form must have a full name and address of the proposed class representative. The applicant must make it plain whether he is making an application for opt-in or opt-out proceedings. He must indicate whether he has used an alternative dispute resolution procedure. He must indicate that he believes the claims have a real prospect of success. The application must include a statement of truth (no doubt designed to focus minds).

9.53   It must also describe: the class of claimants; the description of any possible sub-classes and how their interests might be represented; the numbers in the class; whether the proceedings relate to an infringement decision which has become final; a concise statement of the facts; a concise statement of the law; and details of the relief sought in the proceedings. The details of the relief should include any calculations which have been undertaken to arrive at the claimed amount.

9.54   Collective proceedings may be continued only if the Tribunal makes a collective proceedings order.[38] Such an order may only be made if the CAT thinks that the person who brings the proceedings could be authorized to act as the representative in the proceedings.[39] Claims are eligible for inclusion in collective proceedings only if the CAT considers that they raise the same, similar, or related issues of fact or law and are suitable to be brought in collective proceedings.[40] Additional details are added by the CAT rules, as will be seen in paragraphs 9.55 and 9.56 below.

9.55   Once the collective proceedings form has been served, the Registrar shall publish the details of the application on the CAT website.[41] He shall send an acknowledgement of receipt to the proposed class representative and send a copy of the claim form to each

---

[36] s. 47B(11) EA 2002.
[37] CAT rule 75.
[38] s. 47B(4) CA.
[39] s. 47B(5) CA.
[40] s. 47B(6) CA.
[41] CAT rule 76, which governs the responses to a collective proceedings claim form.

defendant, or else direct that the proposed class representative do so. The Tribunal will have a case management conference and give various directions. The rules anticipate that the CAT might consider a stay of proceedings whilst the parties attempt to compromise the proceedings by alternative dispute resolution or other means.

However, the effect of rule 76(11) of the CAT rules is that, subject to any directions of the Tribunal, the defendant need not, before the hearing of the application for a collective proceedings order, file a defence to the collective proceedings claim form. This emphasizes that the consideration by the CAT of the following preliminary steps is absolutely critical. Those steps are that the class representative is authorized, and that the claims have been certified as being eligible for inclusion in collective proceedings. It is anticipated that there would be a hearing to deal with this important first step.[42]

9.56

4. Authorization of the Class Representative

The CAT may authorize a person to act as the class representative,[43] whether or not the person is a class member. The previous section 47B CA only allowed for named representative bodies to bring opt-in collective actions, and the consumer organization Which? was the only one so named.

9.57

The CAT must consider that it is just and reasonable for the person to act as a class representative in the collective proceedings. In order to determine that, the CAT must consider whether the person:

9.58

• Would fairly and adequately act in the interests of the class members;

• Does not have, in relation to the common issues for the class members, a material interest that is in conflict with the interests of class members;

• (If there is more than one person seeking approval to act as the class representative in respect of the same claims) would be the most suitable to act as such;

• Will be able to pay the defendant's recoverable costs if ordered to do so; and

• Where an interim injunction is sought, will be able to satisfy any undertaking as to damages required by the Tribunal.

In considering whether the proposed representative would act fairly, the court shall take into account all of the circumstances, which also include the following:

9.59

• Whether the proposed class representative is a member of the class, and if so, his suitability to manage the proceedings;

• If the proposed representative is not a member of the class, whether it is a pre-existing body and the nature and functions of that body;

- Whether the proposed class representative has prepared a plan for the collective proceedings that satisfactorily includes:
  - o A method for bringing the proceedings on behalf of the represented persons and for notifying represented persons of the progress of the proceedings;
  - o A procedure for governance and consultation which takes into account the size and nature of the class; and
  - o Any estimate and/or details of arrangements as to costs, fees, or disbursements which the Tribunal orders that the proposed class representatives must provide.

5. Certification of the Claims

9.60   The CAT may certify claims as being eligible for inclusion in collective proceedings if the following three elements are all present:[44]

- The collective proceedings are brought on behalf of an identifiable class of persons;
- The claims raise common issues; and
- The claims are suitable to be brought in collective proceedings.

9.61   In determining whether the claims are suitable to be brought in collective proceedings, the CAT can have regard to any matters it thinks fit, which include but are not limited to the following:

- Whether collective proceedings are an appropriate means for the fair and efficient resolution of the common issues;
- The costs and benefits of continuing the collective proceedings;
- Whether any separate proceedings making claims of the same or a similar nature have already been commenced by members of the same class;
- The size and nature of the class;
- Whether it is possible to determine for any person whether he is or is not a member of the class;
- Whether the claims are suitable for an aggregate award of damages;
- The availability of alternative dispute resolution and any other means of resolving the dispute.

9.62   It is plain from rule 79(3) that the decision about whether the proceedings are to be opt-in or opt-out is a matter for the CAT. It can have regard to the strength of the claims and whether it is practical for the proceedings to be brought as opt-in collective proceedings, particularly bearing in mind the estimated amount of damages that individual class members may recover.

---

[44] CAT rule 79.

At the hearing of the application for a collective proceedings order ('CPO'), the 9.63
CAT may hear any application to strike out the claims or ask for summary judgment.[45]

Once the CAT has determined that there shall be a CPO, the class representative 9.64
is authorized. He must provide the details of the defendants, the classes, the claims,
the type of action and, importantly, the relevant domicile date. In the case of opt-in
proceedings, he must indicate the time and manner in which a class member may
opt in, and in the case of opt-out proceedings, the date by which those in the UK
may opt out and those not in the UK opt in.[46] There shall then be a notice to the
members of the class.[47] That notice must identify the parties. It must contain a summary in plain and easily understood language of the collective proceedings claim
form and the common issues. It should include a statement explaining that any
judgment on the common issues will bind the represented persons. It must draw
attention to the provisions of the CPO setting out what a class member is required
to do and by what date. Once the CPO has been made, the class representative
must establish a register of the various class members and their status within the
proceedings.[48]

The following other points apply to collective proceedings: 9.65

• It is not a requirement that all of the claims should be against all of the defendants
  in the proceedings;
• The proceedings may combine claims which have been made in proceedings
  under section 47A and claims which have not;
• A claim which has been made in proceedings under section 47A may be continued in collective proceedings only with the consent of the person who made that
  claim.[49]

The CAT rules[50] govern the extent to which individuals may opt in and out 9.66
of collective proceedings. The timings are governed by the collective proceedings
order. If an individual does not opt in or opt out (in the way governed by the proceeding provisions) within the relevant time limit set by that order, the CAT may
vary it, depending on whether the delay was caused by the particular class member
and whether the defendant would suffer substantial prejudice.

The proceedings are then managed pursuant to CAT rule 88. The CAT may (for 9.67
example) order that common issues for the classes or sub-classes are determined
together. Disclosure is dealt with (in very broad terms) in rule 89.

---

[45] Pursuant to CAT rules 41(1) and 43(1).
[46] CAT rule 80.
[47] It must comply with rule 81.
[48] CAT rule 83.
[49] s. 47B(3) CA.
[50] CAT rule 82(4).

6. Collective Proceedings: Damages, Costs, and Limitation Periods

9.68   Paragraph 6 introduces a new section 47C into the CA. The CAT may not award exemplary damages in collective proceedings. The CAT may make an award of damages without undertaking an assessment of the amount of damages recoverable in respect of the claim of each represented person. When there are opt-out collective proceedings, the damages *shall* be paid to an individual (either the representative or such person as the CAT thinks is appropriate). If there are opt-in proceedings, they *may* be paid to a representative person. Paragraph 26 amends Schedule 4 EA to ensure that where damages, costs, or expenses are granted to someone who is *not* the representative or other authorized person *before* it became part of the collective proceedings, it may only be enforced if the High Court grants permission.

9.69   Rule 91 governs the judgments and orders in collective proceedings. Once there has been notice of judgment or order by the CAT, the class representative must give notice to all of the represented persons. That notice must explain in clear language the fact that represented persons may be entitled to individual remedies, stating the steps that must be taken to claim the remedy, and stating the consequences of failing to take those steps.

9.70   Where the CAT makes an aggregate award of damages, it shall give directions for assessment of the amount that may be claimed by individual represented persons out of that award.[51] Directions may include a method or formula whereby such amounts shall be quantified and provision for interim payments. It is open to the CAT to appoint an independent third party to determine a claim or dispute by any represented person regarding the quantification of the amount which he will receive.

9.71   Where the CAT makes an award of damages in opt-out collective proceedings, it must make an order providing for the damages to be paid on behalf of the represented persons to the class representative or such other person as they see fit.[52] Any order made in collective proceedings shall specify the date by which represented persons must claim their entitlement to a share of the aggregate award, and the date by which the CAT shall be notified of any undistributed damages.

9.72   In opt-out collective proceedings, any damages not claimed by the represented persons must be paid to a charity prescribed by order.[53] The CAT may also order that all or part of the damages can be paid to the representative as part of the costs or expenses incurred by the representatives in connection with the proceedings. However, a damages–based agreement is unenforceable if it relates to opt-out collective proceedings. A damages-based agreement is where some of the damages are paid to the legal representative.

9.73   Paragraph 27 amends Schedule 4 EA so that, if any award of costs is made against a representative, the legal costs cannot be passed on from the representative to the person who is being represented.

---

[51] CAT rule 92.
[52] CAT rule 93.
[53] Currently the Access to Justice Foundation.

Paragraph 8 introduces a new section 47E to the CA. Where a claim is made 9.74 under section 47B CA, the limitation period is suspended.[54] The effect is that parties are discouraged from commencing separate section 47A proceedings before the CAT to protect their position because of the time limits. As the Explanatory Notes explain: 'the suspension of the limitation/prescription period offers protection to those claimants who might otherwise be time-barred in bringing a single claim if the collective proceedings fail'.[55] Subsection 5 sets out when the limitation period will start to run again.

7. Settlement of Disputes: Where a CPO has been Made

Paragraph 10 inserts section 49A into the CA. The CAT may make an order 9.75 approving the settlement of claims in collective proceedings where a CPO has been made and the CAT has specified that the proceedings are opt-out collective proceedings. The application must be made by both parties to the proceedings.[56] They must provide agreed details of the claims to be settled by the proposed collective settlement and the proposed terms of the settlement.[57] The CAT may only make an order approving a proposed collective settlement if the terms are just and reasonable.[58] If a subsection applies, a collective settlement approved by the CAT is binding on all persons falling within the class of persons described in the CPO.[59] A collective settlement is not binding on a person who opts out by notifying the representative that the claim should not be included in the collective settlement, or if the individual does not live in the UK or has not opted in.[60]

CAT rule 94 deals with the relevant procedure. It adds flesh to the bones 9.76 of section 49A. In particular, it appears to anticipate that the application is a joint application by both class representative and defendant (although it does not say so explicitly). The application must contain a statement that the applicants believe the terms of the proposed settlement are just and reasonable, supported by evidence which may include a report by an independent expert. It must include information about how the settlement is to be apportioned.

Once the application has been received, the CAT may give additional directions, 9.77 which may include the confidential treatment of any part of the application for a collective approval order, and for further evidence to be filed if necessary.[61]

---

[54] s. 47E(4) CA.
[55] Explanatory Notes para. 432.
[56] s. 49A(2) CA.
[57] s. 49A(3) CA.
[58] s. 49A(5) CA.
[59] s. 49A(9) CA.
[60] s. 49A(10) CA.
[61] CAT rule 94.

9.78   It is not anticipated that this procedure will be a rubber-stamping exercise. There are detailed provisions about how the CAT will ensure that the decision is a just and reasonable one. The CAT should consider the following factors:

- The amount and terms of the settlement, including any related provisions as to the payment of costs, fees, and disbursements;
- The number, or estimated number, of persons likely to be entitled to a share in the settlement;
- The likelihood of judgment being obtained in the collective proceedings for an amount significantly in excess of the amount of the settlement;
- The likely duration and costs of any trial;
- The opinion of any independent expert;
- The views of any represented person.

9.79   The final subsection is important. This section applies to claims arising before the commencement of the paragraph as well as claims after that time.

8. Settlement of Disputes: Where a CPO has Not been Made

9.80   Paragraph 11 introduces a new section 49B into the CA which may be of assistance if the proceedings are at an early stage. A collective settlement may be made where a CPO has not been made, but if collective proceedings had not been brought, the claims could still be made at the commencement of the proceedings. The application for approval of a proposed collective settlement must be made to the Tribunal by the person who proposes to be the settlement representative in relation to the settlement, and the person who would be the defendant.[62]

9.81   Again, the details of the claim and the proposed terms of the settlement must be available to the CAT. The CAT can only make a collective settlement if it first makes a collective settlement order. It may only make such an order if it considers that there is a suitable person to act as the settlement representative, and that the claim is a suitable one.[63]

9.82   These orders must include the authorization of the settlement representative, and the description of the class of person within the settlement.[64] The order cannot be made unless its terms are just and reasonable.[65] It is binding on all the persons described in the collective settlement order. It is not, however, binding on an individual who indicates (within time) that he does not wish to be bound, nor a person who does not live within the UK and does not explicitly opt in.[66]

---

[62] s. 49B(2) CA.
[63] For the same reasons as in s. 47B(6) CA.
[64] s. 49B(6) CA.
[65] s. 49B(8) CA.
[66] s. 49B(10) CA.

9. Reaction to Extension of Powers of the CAT

The proposals regarding objectives one and two have been somewhat controversial. 9.83
Many respondents supported all of these proposals, although their implementation
was subject to suggestions. As the Competition Law Association said:

In principle, we agree that a fast-track mechanism of some kind may encourage SMEs to bring more
stand-alone claims…The difficulty, however, will lie in striking the right balance between facilitat-
ing access to court and ensuring that defendants are not unjustly burdened in the process of doing
so. We are not convinced, at this stage, that the proposed model strikes the right balance (point 2.9).

Some respondents to the consultation process were entirely against the proposed 9.84
fast track and the power to grant injunctions: 'competition matters often involve
complex issues and important points of principle that may be ill suited to a fast track
process'.[67] It was also pointed out that making the CAT effectively a superior court
of record would be incompatible with the original purpose of the CAT 'to provide
a flexible jurisdiction to hear competition cases of all sizes, and to be able to offer
a "light touch" alternative to the Senior Courts, in this complex area of the law.'[68]

Some were in favour of the grant of new, yet flexible, powers to the CAT: 9.85

SMEs are particularly vulnerable to anti-competitive behaviour due to the difficulties with the
current system of obtaining redress…By comparison to the current system the proposed "light
touch" procedure would without doubt considerably reduce the costs and risk exposure to a
SME, particularly if the case is settled after the grant of a swift interim injunction.[69]

A note of caution was sounded in terms of the CAT's ability to deal with an 9.86
influx of claims in the fast track process, and its ability to deal with standalone
cases in a fast track at all: 'The additional work required to certify collective actions,
and to resolve appropriate SME cases within six months, could damage the CAT's
currently effective and flexible case management procedures'.[70]

It was said that standalone cases are slow and expensive because it is often hard 9.87
to prove an infringement of competition law:

Such difficulties arise both from the lack of evidence of an infringement…and from the complexity of distinguishing anticompetitive from benign conduct. The latter issue is particularly
evident in abuse of dominance claims, which is the category of infringement that BIS appears
to be most concerned about, as far as the impact on SMEs is concerned…By attempting to
use procedural (rather than substantive) rules to tilt the playing field decisively in favour of
SME claimants against defendant businesses, these proposals are bound to lead to at least some
unmeritorious claims and, through the granting of injunctions on limited evidence, to the prohibition of behaviour that may well be lawful.[71]

It is obvious that the CAT is going to need considerable additional resources. 9.88

---

[67] Response to the BIS Consultation paper from British Bankers Association p. 2.
[68] Response to the BIS Consultation paper from Rachael Mulheron and Vincent Smith p. 5.
[69] Response to BIS Consultation paper from British Chamber of Commerce p. 2.
[70] Response to BIS Consultation paper from Eversheds p. 4.
[71] Response to BIS Consultation paper from Joint Working Party of the Bars and Law Societies of the
United Kingdom on Competition Law, paras 13–14.

F. OBJECTIVE THREE: VOLUNTARY REDRESS

1. New Competition Act 1988 Sections 49C, 49D, and 49E

9.89   The third objective was to define a voluntary redress scheme. The idea is that the parties who are found to be in breach of competition law are to settle before the matter gets anywhere near a court. What is proposed is that the CMA can certify a voluntary redress scheme entered into by businesses found to have infringed competition law:

> We have improved provision for private actions in competition law. First, we are allowing the Competition and Markets Authority—the CMA—to approve an outline of a voluntary redress scheme, and for the business to create a full scheme afterwards. That is part of a wider Government initiative to promote alternative dispute resolution, and it allows responsible businesses who wish to make redress to those they have wronged an avenue to do so. The amendment allows the CMA to impose conditions necessary to set up a full scheme. If those conditions are not complied with when the full scheme is set up, the CMA can withdraw approval or consider a revised scheme.[72]

9.90   The incentive for the breaching organization is obvious from the Explanatory Notes: 'The intention would be that the CMA could take into account whether a business had bound themselves to provide redress when assessing the level of fine for the competition law breach'.[73]

9.91   As a result, there is now a new section 49C CA. What is interesting is that the scheme has to wait for the infringement decision to have been made. There is no option to create a scheme if the relevant company knows that it has been in breach. The CMA can put conditions on the redress scheme in the sense that it can ask that further information is provided about the operation of the scheme, which includes the value of the compensation. If the level of compensation is inadequate, the CAT can reject it. The CMA then has a supervisory role over the scheme. It can approve it, subject to other conditions. It can withdraw approval if any conditions have not been met. It can approve a replacement scheme.

9.92   The section provides that the Secretary of State may make regulations about these kinds of schemes, and can publish guidance. It was published in September 2015.[74]

2. Guidance

9.93   The scheme only works for competition decisions made by the CMA. It does not apply to infringement decisions of other regulators or the European Commission. The compensating party is under a duty to comply with the scheme; a breach

---

[72] Hansard House of Commons 12 January 2015 at Col 672, per Jo Swinson.
[73] Explanatory Notes para. 448.
[74] Guidance on Voluntary Redress: CMA. There is a particularly helpful diagram at p. 9 of the Guidance.

resulting in loss or damage can result in an action in civil proceedings,[75] and the CMA can itself bring proceedings for breach of the duty.

The Guidance included some helpful steers as to how the CMA is likely to approach matters. The Guidance envisages pre-application discussions with the CMA, which it will not consider as an admission of the suspected infringement being considered by it.   9.94

It sets out the advantages from the perspective of the consumer: 9.95

Consumers and businesses can gain access to compensation more quickly, easily, and without the costs of litigation.[76]

The scheme must have worked out which potential beneficiaries there might be, and how they might apply for compensation, together with a reasonable timetable. The applicant must set up a board responsible for determining compensation.   9.96

In the draft Guidance[77] the CMA envisaged that it may approve a scheme in one of the following three scenarios: 9.97

- Where the compensating party is under CMA investigation for a suspected infringement and wishes to submit a scheme outline for approval;

- Where the compensating party is under CMA investigation for a suspected infringement and wishes to submit a full redress scheme for approval; and

- Where an infringement decision has already been made by the CMA, the European Commission, or a sector regulator against the compensating party and the latter wishes to submit a full redress scheme for approval.

The final Guidance also sets out the inter-relationship between the redress scheme and whether or not it would be appropriate to make a penalty reduction. There is no right to any such reduction and any penalty discount is likely to be up to a maximum of 20 per cent of the penalty the Authority would have otherwise imposed.   9.98

If it is considering approving a scheme in relation to a potential CMA infringement decision, the CMA will consider whether – were it to decide to approve the scheme – it would be appropriate to make a penalty reduction in light of the infringing party's voluntary provision of redress. Where possible, the intention to grant a penalty discount in light of a redress scheme will be noted in the draft penalty statement that the CMA issues in accordance with its procedures in CA cases.[78]

---

[75] s. 49E CA.

[76] Guidance on Voluntary Redress: CMA para. 1.29.

[77] Draft Guidance on Voluntary Redress: CMA para. 2.16

[78] There are interesting disclosure issues raised here which are outside the scope of this work. See the Guidance on Voluntary Redress: CMA para 3.26.

10

SECONDARY TICKETING
AND OTHER TOPICS

A. DUTY OF LETTING AGENTS TO PUBLICIZE FEES

The Explanatory Notes set out the purpose of Chapter 3: 10.01

This Chapter imposes a duty on letting agents to publicise their fees, whether or not they are a member of a client money protection scheme and which redress scheme they have joined... Currently, although consumer rights legislation and guidance recommend that traders are clear and upfront about the fees which they charge, there is no specific duty for letting agents to display or publish their fees.

This duty applies to a person who engages in letting agency work whether or not 10.02 he or she engages in other work.[1] A salaried employee is not the person responsible for publishing the fees.[2]

There is now a requirement for letting agents to publicize their fees. They must 10.03 be shown at each of the agent's premises where there is face-to-face dealing with consumers,[3] and at a place where the list is likely to be seen by such persons. The list of fees also has to be published on the agent's website.

The list of fees must include the following: 10.04

- A description of each fee to enable the consumer to understand the service or cost covered by the fee;[4]

- An indication of whether the fee relates to each dwelling-house or each tenant under the tenancy of the dwelling-house;[5]

- The amount of each fee inclusive of tax, or a description of how that fee is calculated.[6]

---

[1] s. 84(1).
[2] s. 84(2).
[3] s. 83(2).
[4] s. 83(4)(a).
[5] s. 83(4)(b).
[6] s. 83(4)(c).

10.05   The fees to which the duty applies are those payable to the agent by a landlord or tenant in respect of letting agency work or property management work. 'Fees' are not the same as rent, fees which an agent gets from a landlord under a tenancy or behalf of another person, a tenancy deposit, or fees or charges specified by the appropriate national authority.[7] The appropriate authority is the Secretary of State in England, and in Wales the Welsh Ministers.[8]

10.06   Section 86 defines what 'letting agency work' and 'property management work' mean. The former definition applies to prospective landlords and tenants who are wishing to rent or rent out an assured tenancy. This work does not include advertising or disseminating information, or providing means by which advertisement can be responded to, or means by which other forms of communication can take place. The latter kind of work is also concerned with an assured tenancy and it applies to fees for services, repairs, insurance, improvement, or insurance in respect of the management of premises on the person's behalf.

10.07   If the agent holds money, then information must be provided as to whether the agent is a member of a client money protection scheme. If an agent has to be a member of a complaint redress scheme, then that scheme must be identified with the list of fees. The redress schemes specified are those under section 83 or 84 of the Enterprise and Regulatory Reform Act 2013. The schemes for letting agency work are governed by statutory instruments under this provision.[9]

10.08   The provisions of this chapter duty are to be enforced by every local weights and measures authority in England and Wales. If an authority is satisfied on the balance of probabilities that a letting agent has breached a duty within section 83, there may be a financial penalty. It must not exceed £5,000.

10.09   Schedule 9 explains how such financial penalties are to be imposed. There must be a notice which has to be served six months before the first day on which the local authority has sufficient evidence of the breach.[10]

10.10   This section therefore creates a time limit similar to that within section 127 of the Magistrates Court Act 1980, and no doubt the authorities on that section will apply to resolve disputes about whether the proceedings have been brought in time.

10.11   The provisions are also similar to regulation 14 of the Consumer Protection (Amendment) Regulations 2014, and there is a number of authorities dealing with similar provisions in various regulatory authorities.[11]

10.12   The document to be served is described as a 'notice of intent' and it must set out the amount of the proposed financial penalty, the reasons why, and the right to make representations.[12] That right is continued in Schedule 9(2). A person may

[7] s. 83(2).
[8] s. 88(1).
[9] See SI 2014/2359.
[10] Sch. 9 para. 1.
[11] See, inter alia, *Burwell v DPP* [2009] EWHC 1069, *R v Haringey Magistrates Court, ex parte Amvrosiou* [1996] EWHC Admin 14, *Tesco Stores Limited v The London Borough of Harrow* [2011] EWHC 2919 Admin, *R v Carmello Gale* [2005] EWCA Crim 286.
[12] Sch.9. para. 2.

make such representations within twenty-eight days. The local authority must then decide if it is going to impose a financial penalty, and then send a notice containing the amount of the penalty, the reasons for its imposition, and the consequences of not complying with the notice.

An aggrieved agent has a remedy to the First-tier Tribunal, but only if the deci-   10.13
sion made by the local authority was based on an error of law, was wrong in law, the amount of the penalty was unreasonable, or the decision was unreasonable for any other reason.[13] If the agent does not pay the penalty, it can be covered as though it were an order of the county court.[14]

B. STUDENT COMPLAINTS SCHEME

The Office of the Independent Adjudicator for Higher Education operates a scheme   10.14
to deal with complaints under the Higher Education Act 2004. The website sets out the various rules. From 1 September 2015, the scheme will have to include higher education providers and section 89 achieves that.

C. SECONDARY TICKETING

1. Duty to Provide Information about Tickets

The Explanatory Notes explain that this chapter deals with the online secondary   10.15
ticketing market. That is the market where tickets for sporting, recreational, and cultural events are re-sold, having been first bought or otherwise acquired on the primary market from an event organiser.[15]

The All Party Parliamentary Group of Ticket Abuse was established in December   10.16
2013, among other reasons to push on a cross-party basis for government action to reform the secondary ticketing market in the interests of consumers and rights holders, particularly by increasing the transparency of ticket supply. This group was very influential when this part of the Act was debated. In the debates in the House of Lords, it was stressed that there had been a DCMS Select Committee report in 2007 (following an Office of Fair Trading report in 2005) which demonstrated that the secondary ticket market was not operating satisfactorily. In 2013, there was a Metropolitan Police Report which made it plain that the lack of legislation in this area enabled fraud and placed the public at risk of economic crime.[16] Various estimates have suggested that millions of pounds worth of criminal fraud are made from secondary ticketing scams. Furthermore, there was concern that the use of

---

[13] Sch. 9 para. 5.
[14] Sch. 9 para. 2.
[15] Explanatory Notes para. 486.
[16] Hansard House of Lords 15 October 2014 at GC139 and following.

computerized programmes to block the purchase of tickets was preventing genuine fans from attending popular events.

10.17   It should be borne in mind that there is quite a lot of other legislation which covers the online ticketing market:

- The Consumer Contracts (Information, Cancellation and Additional Charges) Regulations 2013 (SI 2013/3134) provide that certain information must be provided when goods, a service, or digital content are sold by a trader to a consumer, including sales concluded at a distance (for example, online);

- Section 166 of the Criminal Justice and Public Order Act 1994 regulates the re-selling of tickets for certain football matches;

- The Fraud Act 2006 and the Consumer Protection from Unfair Trading Regulations 2008 (SI 2008/1277) aim to protect buyers from misleading or fraudulent sales; and

- The Unfair Terms in Consumer Contracts Regulations 1999 (SI 1999/2083) (which are to be replaced by Part 2 of the Act once Part 2 comes into force) provide that terms in a consumer contract must be fair.

10.18   When a person re-sells a ticket for a recreational, sporting, or cultural event in the UK through a secondary ticketing facility, there is a duty to provide information. The definition of a secondary ticketing facility is an internet-based facility for the re-sale of tickets for recreational, sporting, or cultural events.[17] This might be a website, but could be a web-based application or some other kind of online facility. The duty to provide information rests on both the seller of the ticket and the person who is *operating* the online facility. The latter term is defined by section 95.

10.19   An 'operator' is a person who exercises control over the operation of the facility and receives revenue from the facility.[18] An 'organiser' of an event is a person who is responsible for organizing or managing the event, or receives some or all of the revenue from the event.

2. Information that Must be Provided

10.20   The following information must be given:[19]

- Where the ticket is for a particular seat or standing area at the venue for the event, the information necessary to enable the buyer to identify that seat or standing area;

- Information about any restriction which limits use of the ticket to persons of a particular description;

---

[17] s. 95(1).
[18] Subject to any regulations made by the Secretary of State.
[19] s. 90(3).

- The face value of the ticket, which means for the avoidance of doubt the amount stated on the ticket as its price;[20]
- The information about where the ticket is in the premises must include, so far as it is applicable, the name of the area in the venue ('The Kop', 'The Johnny Haynes Stand', etc.), the block, and the number or letter, or other distinguishing feature.[21]

3. Who Must Provide the Information

This information must be provided by the following people: 10.21

- An operator of the secondary ticketing facility;
- A person who is a parent undertaking or a subsidiary undertaking in relation to an operator of the secondary ticketing facility;
- A person who is employed or engaged by an operator of the secondary ticketing market, or a person acting on its behalf;
- An organizer of the event or a person acting on behalf of an organiser of the event.

The definitions above regarding 'undertakings' come from sections 1161 and   10.22
1162 of the Companies Act 2006 and Schedule 7 of that Act. An undertaking is a body corporate, partnership, or an unincorporated association carrying on a trade or business with or without a view to profit. And, in essence, a parent undertaking is one which does one of the following things:

- Holds a majority of the voting rights;
- Is a member of the undertaking and has the right to appoint or remove a majority of its board of directors;
- Has the right to exercise a dominant influence of the undertaking (in various ways); or
- Is a member of the undertaking and controls alone a majority of the voting rights in the undertaking.

The information in section 90(3) must be provided in a clear and comprehensible   10.23
manner and before the buyer is bound by the contract for the sale of the ticket.[22]

4. Prohibition on Cancellation or Blacklisting

Information under section 90 above could be used in theory by an event organiser   10.24
to cancel a ticket or blacklist a seller. Section 91 means that a ticket cannot be cancelled or a seller blacklisted unless two conditions are met.

It has to have been a term of the original contract that the ticket could not be   10.25
re-sold or offered for re-sale, and that clause could not be unfair as defined by

---

[20] s. 90(5).
[21] s. 90(4).
[22] s. 90(8).

Part 2 of the Act.[23] A ticket being cancelled is defined in section 91(5). Cancellation takes place if the organiser takes steps that result in the holder for the time being no longer being entitled to attend the event.[24] A person is blacklisted if an organiser takes steps to prevent the person from acquiring a ticket or restricts a person's opportunity to acquire a ticket.[25]

5. Duty to Report Criminal Activity

10.26   There is a duty on the operator of a secondary ticketing facility in circumstances where he knows that a person has used, or is using, the facility in such a way that an offence is being committed.[26] The offence must be related to the re-sale of a recreational, sporting, or cultural event in the UK.

10.27   This disclosure must include the identity of the person who has used or is using the facility in a criminal way, and the fact that the operator knows that an offence has been or is being committed. The disclosure must be made to a police constable or the organiser of the appropriate event. The section does not require the disclosure to be made to the organiser of the event if the operator has reasonable grounds for believing that to do so will prejudice the investigation of any offence. For reasons set out in section 6 below, it is rather odd that the disclosure cannot be made to a trading standards officer since they are the ones who are responsible for enforcement.

10.28   This section only applies in relation to offences committed after commencement.

6. Enforcement

10.29   This Part of the Act[27] is to be enforced by all local weights and measures authorities in the UK (Trading Standards). When such an authority is satisfied on the balance of probabilities that a duty or prohibition has been breached, a financial penalty may be imposed.

10.30   There is a due diligence defence available, which is in similar terms to that within regulation 17 of the Consumer Protection from Unfair Trading Regulations 2008. However, since the tribunal of fact is the local authority, the section is drafted differently from a case where a jury or magistrates' court would have to make the determination.

10.31   But in the case of the breach of a duty in section 90 or a prohibition in section 91, an enforcement authority may not impose a financial penalty on a person ('P') if the authority is satisfied on the balance of probabilities that:

- the breach was due to:
  - a mistake;
  - reliance on information supplied to P by another person;

---

[23] See Ch 6.
[24] s. 91(5).
[25] s. 91(6).
[26] s. 92.
[27] s. 93.

- the act or default of another person;
- an accident; or
- another cause beyond P's control; and

- P took all reasonable precautions and exercised all due diligence to avoid the breach.

10.32 It is therefore for the potential defendant to establish to the local authority that there is a defence on the balance of probabilities, either in correspondence or in written representations.

10.33 There is an important extension to the normal provisions about jurisdiction. A local weights and measures authority in England and Wales may impose a penalty under this section in respect of a breach which occurs in England and Wales but outside that authority's area. The maximum penalty is £5,000 and only one penalty under this section may be imposed on the same person in respect of the same breach.

10.34 Schedule 10 has effect regarding the procedures for financial penalties. The terms are very similar to those for the requirements for the duties of letting agents under Schedule 9 (see above).

10.35 Because this section was relatively controversial when it was passed (and was the subject matter of quite a lot of parliamentary ping-pong) there is due to be a report by the Secretary of State twelve months after the section comes into force. It will be interesting to see whether (for example) the lack of a sanction against using harvesting software ('botnets') will be demonstrated to have been an opportunity missed.

D. UNWRAPPED BREAD

10.36 Within Part III, section 78 amends the Weights and Measures (Packaged Goods) Regulations 2006 (SI 2006/659), as it affects unwrapped bread. Those Regulations are outside the scope of this work. As the Explanatory Notes explain, this provides an automatic exemption from keeping records of checks for packers of bread which is sold in unwrapped or open packs.

10.37 A press release from the National Measurement Office[28] said the following about these provisions:

This change will relieve bakers of the burden of keeping records of their weight checks, benefiting small and large businesses, from independent bakers to supermarket in-store bakeries. It will also remove the bureaucracy from bakers applying and Trading Standards issuing exemption certificates and remove any inconsistency in their use. Bakers may choose to continue to keep records of their checks for due diligence purposes, but they will no longer be required to do so. This is estimated to save business in the region of £600,000 a year. However, consumer

---

[28] 5 February 2014.

protection will be maintained as bakers will still have to ensure that the quantity of their bread is accurate, and Trading Standards may still choose to carry out inspections of the business, in accordance with the Weights and Measures (Packaged Goods) Regulations 2006.

10.38   It is likely that this section will have more benefit to consumers than the amendments to the CA set out in the previous chapter.

Consumer Rights Act 2015
Chapter 15

An Act to amend the law relating to the rights of consumers and protection of their interests; to make provision about investigatory powers for enforcing the regulation of traders; to make provision about private actions in competition law and the Competition Appeal Tribunal; and for connected purposes.

[26th March 2015]

Be it enacted by the Queen's most Excellent Majesty, by and with the advice and consent of the Lords Spiritual and Temporal, and Commons, in this present Parliament assembled, and by the authority of the same, as follows:—

PART 1
CONSUMER CONTRACTS FOR GOODS, DIGITAL CONTENT AND SERVICES

CHAPTER 1
Introduction

1 Where Part 1 applies

(1) This Part applies where there is an agreement between a trader and a consumer for the trader to supply goods, digital content or services, if the agreement is a contract.

(2) It applies whether the contract is written or oral or implied from the parties' conduct, or more than one of these combined.

(3) Any of Chapters 2, 3 and 4 may apply to a contract—
   (a) if it is a contract for the trader to supply goods, see Chapter 2;
   (b) if it is a contract for the trader to supply digital content, see Chapter 3 (also, subsection (6));
   (c) if it is a contract for the trader to supply a service, see Chapter 4 (also, subsection (6)).

(4) In each case the Chapter applies even if the contract also covers something covered by another Chapter (a mixed contract).

(5) Two or all three of those Chapters may apply to a mixed contract.

(6) For provisions about particular mixed contracts, see—
   (a) section 15 (goods and installation);
   (b) section 16 (goods and digital content).

(7) For other provision applying to contracts to which this Part applies, see Part 2 (unfair terms).

2 Key definitions

(1) These definitions apply in this Part (as well as the definitions in section 59).

(2) 'Trader' means a person acting for purposes relating to that person's trade, business, craft or profession, whether acting personally or through another person acting in the trader's name or on the trader's behalf.

(3) 'Consumer' means an individual acting for purposes that are wholly or mainly outside that individual's trade, business, craft or profession.

(4) A trader claiming that an individual was not acting for purposes wholly or mainly outside the individual's trade, business, craft or profession must prove it.

(5) For the purposes of Chapter 2, except to the extent mentioned in subsection (6), a person is not a consumer in relation to a sales contract if—

    (a) the goods are second hand goods sold at public auction, and

    (b) individuals have the opportunity of attending the sale in person.

(6) A person is a consumer in relation to such a contract for the purposes of—

    (a) sections 11(4) and (5), 12, 28 and 29, and

    (b) the other provisions of Chapter 2 as they apply in relation to those sections.

(7) 'Business' includes the activities of any government department or local or public authority.

(8) 'Goods' means any tangible moveable items, but that includes water, gas and electricity if and only if they are put up for supply in a limited volume or set quantity.

(9) 'Digital content' means data which are produced and supplied in digital form.

CHAPTER 2

Goods

What goods contracts are covered?

3 Contracts covered by this Chapter

(1) This Chapter applies to a contract for a trader to supply goods to a consumer.

(2) It applies only if the contract is one of these (defined for the purposes of this Part in sections 5 to 8)—

    (a) a sales contract;

    (b) a contract for the hire of goods;

    (c) a hire-purchase agreement;

    (d) a contract for transfer of goods.

(3) It does not apply—

    (a) to a contract for a trader to supply coins or notes to a consumer for use as currency;

    (b) to a contract for goods to be sold by way of execution or otherwise by authority of law;

    (c) to a contract intended to operate as a mortgage, pledge, charge or other security;

    (d) in relation to England and Wales or Northern Ireland, to a contract made by deed and for which the only consideration is the presumed consideration imported by the deed;

    (e) in relation to Scotland, to a gratuitous contract.

(4) A contract to which this Chapter applies is referred to in this Part as a 'contract to supply goods'.

(5) Contracts to supply goods include—

    (a) contracts entered into between one part owner and another;

    (b) contracts for the transfer of an undivided share in goods;

    (c) contracts that are absolute and contracts that are conditional.

(6) Subsection (1) is subject to any provision of this Chapter that applies a section or part of a section to only some of the kinds of contracts listed in subsection (2).

(7) A mixed contract (see section 1(4)) may be a contract of any of those kinds.

4 Ownership of goods

(1) In this Chapter ownership of goods means the general property in goods, not merely a special property.

(2) For the time when ownership of goods is transferred, see in particular the following provisions of the Sale of Goods Act 1979 (which relate to contracts of sale)—

section 16:	goods must be ascertained
section 17:	property passes when intended to pass
section 18:	rules for ascertaining intention
section 19:	reservation of right of disposal
section 20A:	undivided shares in goods forming part of a bulk
section 20B:	deemed consent by co-owner to dealings in bulk goods

5 Sales contracts

(1) A contract is a sales contract if under it—
   (a) the trader transfers or agrees to transfer ownership of goods to the consumer, and
   (b) the consumer pays or agrees to pay the price.

(2) A contract is a sales contract (whether or not it would be one under subsection (1)) if under the contract—
   (a) goods are to be manufactured or produced and the trader agrees to supply them to the consumer,
   (b) on being supplied, the goods will be owned by the consumer, and
   (c) the consumer pays or agrees to pay the price.

(3) A sales contract may be conditional (see section 3(5)), but in this Part 'conditional sales contract' means a sales contract under which—
   (a) the price for the goods or part of it is payable by instalments, and
   (b) the trader retains ownership of the goods until the conditions specified in the contract (for the payment of instalments or otherwise) are met;
   and it makes no difference whether or not the consumer possesses the goods.

6 Contracts for the hire of goods

(1) A contract is for the hire of goods if under it the trader gives or agrees to give the consumer possession of the goods with the right to use them, subject to the terms of the contract, for a period determined in accordance with the contract.

(2) But a contract is not for the hire of goods if it is a hire-purchase agreement.

7 Hire-purchase agreements

(1) A contract is a hire-purchase agreement if it meets the two conditions set out below.

(2) The first condition is that under the contract goods are hired by the trader in return for periodical payments by the consumer (and 'hired' is to be read in accordance with section 6(1)).

(3) The second condition is that under the contract ownership of the goods will transfer to the consumer if the terms of the contract are complied with and—
   (a) the consumer exercises an option to buy the goods,
   (b) any party to the contract does an act specified in it, or
   (c) an event specified in the contract occurs.

(4) But a contract is not a hire-purchase agreement if it is a conditional sales contract.

8 Contracts for transfer of goods

A contract to supply goods is a contract for transfer of goods if under it the trader transfers or agrees to transfer ownership of the goods to the consumer and—

(a) the consumer provides or agrees to provide consideration otherwise than by paying a price, or
(b) the contract is, for any other reason, not a sales contract or a hire-purchase agreement.

What statutory rights are there under a goods contract?

9 Goods to be of satisfactory quality

(1) Every contract to supply goods is to be treated as including a term that the quality of the goods is satisfactory.
(2) The quality of goods is satisfactory if they meet the standard that a reasonable person would consider satisfactory, taking account of—
  (a) any description of the goods,
  (b) the price or other consideration for the goods (if relevant), and
  (c) all the other relevant circumstances (see subsection (5)).
(3) The quality of goods includes their state and condition; and the following aspects (among others) are in appropriate cases aspects of the quality of goods—
  (a) fitness for all the purposes for which goods of that kind are usually supplied;
  (b) appearance and finish;
  (c) freedom from minor defects;
  (d) safety;
  (e) durability.
(4) The term mentioned in subsection (1) does not cover anything which makes the quality of the goods unsatisfactory—
  (a) which is specifically drawn to the consumer's attention before the contract is made,
  (b) where the consumer examines the goods before the contract is made, which that examination ought to reveal, or
  (c) in the case of a contract to supply goods by sample, which would have been apparent on a reasonable examination of the sample.
(5) The relevant circumstances mentioned in subsection (2)(c) include any public statement about the specific characteristics of the goods made by the trader, the producer or any representative of the trader or the producer.
(6) That includes, in particular, any public statement made in advertising or labelling.
(7) But a public statement is not a relevant circumstance for the purposes of subsection (2)(c) if the trader shows that—
  (a) when the contract was made, the trader was not, and could not reasonably have been, aware of the statement,
  (b) before the contract was made, the statement had been publicly withdrawn or, to the extent that it contained anything which was incorrect or misleading, it had been publicly corrected, or
  (c) the consumer's decision to contract for the goods could not have been influenced by the statement.
(8) In a contract to supply goods a term about the quality of the goods may be treated as included as a matter of custom.
(9) See section 19 for a consumer's rights if the trader is in breach of a term that this section requires to be treated as included in a contract.

10 Goods to be fit for particular purpose

(1) Subsection (3) applies to a contract to supply goods if before the contract is made the consumer makes known to the trader (expressly or by implication) any particular purpose for which the consumer is contracting for the goods.

(2) Subsection (3) also applies to a contract to supply goods if—

    (a) the goods were previously sold by a credit-broker to the trader,

    (b) in the case of a sales contract or contract for transfer of goods, the consideration or part of it is a sum payable by instalments, and

    (c) before the contract is made, the consumer makes known to the credit-broker (expressly or by implication) any particular purpose for which the consumer is contracting for the goods.

(3) The contract is to be treated as including a term that the goods are reasonably fit for that purpose, whether or not that is a purpose for which goods of that kind are usually supplied.

(4) Subsection (3) does not apply if the circumstances show that the consumer does not rely, or it is unreasonable for the consumer to rely, on the skill or judgment of the trader or credit-broker.

(5) In a contract to supply goods a term about the fitness of the goods for a particular purpose may be treated as included as a matter of custom.

(6) See section 19 for a consumer's rights if the trader is in breach of a term that this section requires to be treated as included in a contract.

11 Goods to be as described

(1) Every contract to supply goods by description is to be treated as including a term that the goods will match the description.

(2) If the supply is by sample as well as by description, it is not sufficient that the bulk of the goods matches the sample if the goods do not also match the description.

(3) A supply of goods is not prevented from being a supply by description just because—

    (a) the goods are exposed for supply, and

    (b) they are selected by the consumer.

(4) Any information that is provided by the trader about the goods and is information mentioned in paragraph (a) of Schedule 1 or 2 to the Consumer Contracts (Information, Cancellation and Additional Charges) Regulations 2013 (SI 2013/3134) (main characteristics of goods) is to be treated as included as a term of the contract.

(5) A change to any of that information, made before entering into the contract or later, is not effective unless expressly agreed between the consumer and the trader.

(6) See section 2(5) and (6) for the application of subsections (4) and (5) where goods are sold at public auction.

(7) See section 19 for a consumer's rights if the trader is in breach of a term that this section requires to be treated as included in a contract.

12 Other pre-contract information included in contract

(1) This section applies to any contract to supply goods.

(2) Where regulation 9, 10 or 13 of the Consumer Contracts (Information, Cancellation and Additional Charges) Regulations 2013 (SI 2013/3134) required the trader to provide information to the consumer before the contract became binding, any of that information that was provided by the trader other than information about the goods and mentioned in paragraph (a) of Schedule 1 or 2 to the Regulations (main characteristics of goods) is to be treated as included as a term of the contract.

(3) A change to any of that information, made before entering into the contract or later, is not effective unless expressly agreed between the consumer and the trader.

(4) See section 2(5) and (6) for the application of this section where goods are sold at public auction.

(5) See section 19 for a consumer's rights if the trader is in breach of a term that this section requires to be treated as included in the contract.

13 Goods to match a sample

(1) This section applies to a contract to supply goods by reference to a sample of the goods that is seen or examined by the consumer before the contract is made.

(2) Every contract to which this section applies is to be treated as including a term that—
    (a) the goods will match the sample except to the extent that any differences between the sample and the goods are brought to the consumer's attention before the contract is made, and
    (b) the goods will be free from any defect that makes their quality unsatisfactory and that would not be apparent on a reasonable examination of the sample.

(3) See section 19 for a consumer's rights if the trader is in breach of a term that this section requires to be treated as included in a contract.

14 Goods to match a model seen or examined

(1) This section applies to a contract to supply goods by reference to a model of the goods that is seen or examined by the consumer before entering into the contract.

(2) Every contract to which this section applies is to be treated as including a term that the goods will match the model except to the extent that any differences between the model and the goods are brought to the consumer's attention before the consumer enters into the contract.

(3) See section 19 for a consumer's rights if the trader is in breach of a term that this section requires to be treated as included in a contract.

15 Installation as part of conformity of the goods with the contract

(1) Goods do not conform to a contract to supply goods if—
    (a) installation of the goods forms part of the contract,
    (b) the goods are installed by the trader or under the trader's responsibility, and
    (c) the goods are installed incorrectly.

(2) See section 19 for the effect of goods not conforming to the contract.

16 Goods not conforming to contract if digital content does not conform

(1) Goods (whether or not they conform otherwise to a contract to supply goods) do not conform to it if—
    (a) the goods are an item that includes digital content, and
    (b) the digital content does not conform to the contract to supply that content (for which see section 42(1)).

(2) See section 19 for the effect of goods not conforming to the contract.

17 Trader to have right to supply the goods etc

(1) Every contract to supply goods, except one within subsection (4), is to be treated as including a term—

(a) in the case of a contract for the hire of goods, that at the beginning of the period of hire the trader must have the right to transfer possession of the goods by way of hire for that period,

(b) in any other case, that the trader must have the right to sell or transfer the goods at the time when ownership of the goods is to be transferred.

(2) Every contract to supply goods, except a contract for the hire of goods or a contract within subsection (4), is to be treated as including a term that—

(a) the goods are free from any charge or encumbrance not disclosed or known to the consumer before entering into the contract,

(b) the goods will remain free from any such charge or encumbrance until ownership of them is to be transferred, and

(c) the consumer will enjoy quiet possession of the goods except so far as it may be disturbed by the owner or other person entitled to the benefit of any charge or encumbrance so disclosed or known.

(3) Every contract for the hire of goods is to be treated as including a term that the consumer will enjoy quiet possession of the goods for the period of the hire except so far as the possession may be disturbed by the owner or other person entitled to the benefit of any charge or encumbrance disclosed or known to the consumer before entering into the contract.

(4) This subsection applies to a contract if the contract shows, or the circumstances when they enter into the contract imply, that the trader and the consumer intend the trader to transfer only—

(a) whatever title the trader has, even if it is limited, or

(b) whatever title a third person has, even if it is limited.

(5) Every contract within subsection (4) is to be treated as including a term that all charges or encumbrances known to the trader and not known to the consumer were disclosed to the consumer before entering into the contract.

(6) Every contract within subsection (4) is to be treated as including a term that the consumer's quiet possession of the goods—

(a) will not be disturbed by the trader, and

(b) will not be disturbed by a person claiming through or under the trader, unless that person is claiming under a charge or encumbrance that was disclosed or known to the consumer before entering into the contract.

(7) If subsection (4)(b) applies (transfer of title that a third person has), the contract is also to be treated as including a term that the consumer's quiet possession of the goods—

(a) will not be disturbed by the third person, and

(b) will not be disturbed by a person claiming through or under the third person, unless the claim is under a charge or encumbrance that was disclosed or known to the consumer before entering into the contract.

(8) In the case of a contract for the hire of goods, this section does not affect the right of the trader to repossess the goods where the contract provides or is to be treated as providing for this.

(9) See section 19 for a consumer's rights if the trader is in breach of a term that this section requires to be treated as included in a contract.

18 No other requirement to treat term about quality or fitness as included

(1) Except as provided by sections 9, 10, 13 and 16, a contract to supply goods is not to be treated as including any term about the quality of the goods or their fitness for any particular purpose, unless the term is expressly included in the contract.

(2) Subsection (1) is subject to provision made by any other enactment (whenever passed or made).

What remedies are there if statutory rights under a goods contract are not met?

19 Consumer's rights to enforce terms about goods

(1) In this section and sections 22 to 24 references to goods conforming to a contract are references to—
   (a) the goods conforming to the terms described in sections 9, 10, 11, 13 and 14,
   (b) the goods not failing to conform to the contract under section 15 or 16, and
   (c) the goods conforming to requirements that are stated in the contract.

(2) But, for the purposes of this section and sections 22 to 24, a failure to conform as mentioned in subsection (1)(a) to (c) is not a failure to conform to the contract if it has its origin in materials supplied by the consumer.

(3) If the goods do not conform to the contract because of a breach of any of the terms described in sections 9, 10, 11, 13 and 14, or if they do not conform to the contract under section 16, the consumer's rights (and the provisions about them and when they are available) are—
   (a) the short-term right to reject (sections 20 and 22);
   (b) the right to repair or replacement (section 23); and
   (c) the right to a price reduction or the final right to reject (sections 20 and 24).

(4) If the goods do not conform to the contract under section 15 or because of a breach of requirements that are stated in the contract, the consumer's rights (and the provisions about them and when they are available) are—
   (a) the right to repair or replacement (section 23); and
   (b) the right to a price reduction or the final right to reject (sections 20 and 24).

(5) If the trader is in breach of a term that section 12 requires to be treated as included in the contract, the consumer has the right to recover from the trader the amount of any costs incurred by the consumer as a result of the breach, up to the amount of the price paid or the value of other consideration given for the goods.

(6) If the trader is in breach of the term that section 17(1) (right to supply etc) requires to be treated as included in the contract, the consumer has a right to reject (see section 20 for provisions about that right and when it is available).

(7) Subsections (3) to (6) are subject to section 25 and subsections (3)(a) and (6) are subject to section 26.

(8) Section 28 makes provision about remedies for breach of a term about the time for delivery of goods.

(9) This Chapter does not prevent the consumer seeking other remedies—
   (a) for a breach of a term that this Chapter requires to be treated as included in the contract,
   (b) on the grounds that, under section 15 or 16, goods do not conform to the contract, or
   (c) for a breach of a requirement stated in the contract.

(10) Those other remedies may be ones—
   (a) in addition to a remedy referred to in subsections (3) to (6) (but not so as to recover twice for the same loss), or
   (b) instead of such a remedy, or
   (c) where no such remedy is provided for.

(11) Those other remedies include any of the following that is open to the consumer in the circumstances—
   (a) claiming damages;
   (b) seeking specific performance;
   (c) seeking an order for specific implement;
   (d) relying on the breach against a claim by the trader for the price;
   (e) for breach of an express term, exercising a right to treat the contract as at an end.

(12) It is not open to the consumer to treat the contract as at an end for breach of a term that this Chapter requires to be treated as included in the contract, or on the grounds that, under section 15 or 16, goods do not conform to the contract, except as provided by subsections (3), (4) and (6).

(13) In this Part, treating a contract as at an end means treating it as repudiated.

(14) For the purposes of subsections (3)(b) and (c) and (4), goods which do not conform to the contract at any time within the period of six months beginning with the day on which the goods were delivered to the consumer must be taken not to have conformed to it on that day.

(15) Subsection (14) does not apply if—
(a) it is established that the goods did conform to the contract on that day, or
(b) its application is incompatible with the nature of the goods or with how they fail to conform to the contract.

20 Right to reject

(1) The short-term right to reject is subject to section 22.

(2) The final right to reject is subject to section 24.

(3) The right to reject under section 19(6) is not limited by those sections.

(4) Each of these rights entitles the consumer to reject the goods and treat the contract as at an end, subject to subsections (20) and (21).

(5) The right is exercised if the consumer indicates to the trader that the consumer is rejecting the goods and treating the contract as at an end.

(6) The indication may be something the consumer says or does, but it must be clear enough to be understood by the trader.

(7) From the time when the right is exercised—
(a) the trader has a duty to give the consumer a refund, subject to subsection (18), and
(b) the consumer has a duty to make the goods available for collection by the trader or (if there is an agreement for the consumer to return rejected goods) to return them as agreed.

(8) Whether or not the consumer has a duty to return the rejected goods, the trader must bear any reasonable costs of returning them, other than any costs incurred by the consumer in returning the goods in person to the place where the consumer took physical possession of them.

(9) The consumer's entitlement to receive a refund works as follows.

(10) To the extent that the consumer paid money under the contract, the consumer is entitled to receive back the same amount of money.

(11) To the extent that the consumer transferred anything else under the contract, the consumer is entitled to receive back the same amount of what the consumer transferred, unless subsection (12)applies.

(12) To the extent that the consumer transferred under the contract something for which the same amount of the same thing cannot be substituted, the consumer is entitled to receive back in its original state whatever the consumer transferred.

(13) If the contract is for the hire of goods, the entitlement to a refund extends only to anything paid or otherwise transferred for a period of hire that the consumer does not get because the contract is treated as at an end.

(14) If the contract is a hire-purchase agreement or a conditional sales contract and the contract is treated as at an end before the whole of the price has been paid, the entitlement to a refund extends only to the part of the price paid.

(15) A refund under this section must be given without undue delay, and in any event within 14 days beginning with the day on which the trader agrees that the consumer is entitled to a refund.

(16) If the consumer paid money under the contract, the trader must give the refund using the same means of payment as the consumer used, unless the consumer expressly agrees otherwise.

(17) The trader must not impose any fee on the consumer in respect of the refund.

(18) There is no entitlement to receive a refund—
  (a) if none of subsections (10) to (12) applies,
  (b) to the extent that anything to which subsection (12) applies cannot be given back in its original state, or
  (c) where subsection (13) applies, to the extent that anything the consumer transferred under the contract cannot be divided so as to give back only the amount, or part of the amount, to which the consumer is entitled.

(19) It may be open to a consumer to claim damages where there is no entitlement to receive a refund, or because of the limits of the entitlement, or instead of a refund.

(20) Subsection (21) qualifies the application in relation to England and Wales and Northern Ireland of the rights mentioned in subsections (1) to (3) where—
  (a) the contract is a severable contract,
  (b) in relation to the final right to reject, the contract is a contract for the hire of goods, a hire-purchase agreement or a contract for transfer of goods, and
  (c) section 26(3) does not apply.

(21) The consumer is entitled, depending on the terms of the contract and the circumstances of the case—
  (a) to reject the goods to which a severable obligation relates and treat that obligation as at an end (so that the entitlement to a refund relates only to what the consumer paid or transferred in relation to that obligation), or
  (b) to exercise any of the rights mentioned in subsections (1) to (3) in respect of the whole contract.

21 Partial rejection of goods

(1) If the consumer has any of the rights mentioned in section 20(1) to (3), but does not reject all of the goods and treat the contract as at an end, the consumer—
  (a) may reject some or all of the goods that do not conform to the contract, but
  (b) may not reject any goods that do conform to the contract.

(2) If the consumer is entitled to reject the goods in an instalment, but does not reject all of those goods, the consumer—
  (a) may reject some or all of the goods in the instalment that do not conform to the contract, but
  (b) may not reject any goods in the instalment that do conform to the contract.

(3) If any of the goods form a commercial unit, the consumer cannot reject some of those goods without also rejecting the rest of them.

(4) A unit is a 'commercial unit' if division of the unit would materially impair the value of the goods or the character of the unit.

(5) The consumer rejects goods under this section by indicating to the trader that the consumer is rejecting the goods.

(6) The indication may be something the consumer says or does, but it must be clear enough to be understood by the trader.

(7) From the time when a consumer rejects goods under this section—
  (a) the trader has a duty to give the consumer a refund in respect of those goods (subject to subsection (10)), and
  (b) the consumer has a duty to make those goods available for collection by the trader or (if there is an agreement for the consumer to return rejected goods) to return them as agreed.

(8) Whether or not the consumer has a duty to return the rejected goods, the trader must bear any reasonable costs of returning them, other than any costs incurred by the consumer in returning those goods in person to the place where the consumer took physical possession of them.

(9) Section 20(10) to (17) apply to a consumer's right to receive a refund under this section (and in section 20(13) and (14) references to the contract being treated as at an end are to be read as references to goods being rejected).

(10) That right does not apply—

    (a) if none of section 20(10) to (12) applies,

    (b) to the extent that anything to which section 20(12) applies cannot be given back in its original state, or

    (c) to the extent that anything the consumer transferred under the contract cannot be divided so as to give back only the amount, or part of the amount, to which the consumer is entitled.

(11) It may be open to a consumer to claim damages where there is no right to receive a refund, or because of the limits of the right, or instead of a refund.

(12) References in this section to goods conforming to a contract are to be read in accordance with section 19(1) and (2), but they also include the goods conforming to the terms described in section 17.

(13) Where section 20(21)(a) applies the reference in subsection (1) to the consumer treating the contract as at an end is to be read as a reference to the consumer treating the severable obligation as at an end.

22 Time limit for short-term right to reject

(1) A consumer who has the short-term right to reject loses it if the time limit for exercising it passes without the consumer exercising it, unless the trader and the consumer agree that it may be exercised later.

(2) An agreement under which the short-term right to reject would be lost before the time limit passes is not binding on the consumer.

(3) The time limit for exercising the short-term right to reject (unless subsection (4) applies) is the end of 30 days beginning with the first day after these have all happened—

    (a) ownership or (in the case of a contract for the hire of goods, a hire-purchase agreement or a conditional sales contract) possession of the goods has been transferred to the consumer,

    (b) the goods have been delivered, and

    (c) where the contract requires the trader to install the goods or take other action to enable the consumer to use them, the trader has notified the consumer that the action has been taken.

(4) If any of the goods are of a kind that can reasonably be expected to perish after a shorter period, the time limit for exercising the short-term right to reject in relation to those goods is the end of that shorter period (but without affecting the time limit in relation to goods that are not of that kind).

(5) Subsections (3) and (4) do not prevent the consumer exercising the short-term right to reject before something mentioned in subsection (3)(a), (b) or (c) has happened.

(6) If the consumer requests or agrees to the repair or replacement of goods, the period mentioned in subsection (3) or (4) stops running for the length of the waiting period.

(7) If goods supplied by the trader in response to that request or agreement do not conform to the contract, the time limit for exercising the short-term right to reject is then either—

    (a) 7 days after the waiting period ends, or

    (b) if later, the original time limit for exercising that right, extended by the waiting period.

(8) The waiting period—
  (a) begins with the day the consumer requests or agrees to the repair or replacement of the goods, and
  (b) ends with the day on which the consumer receives goods supplied by the trader in response to the request or agreement.

23 Right to repair or replacement

(1) This section applies if the consumer has the right to repair or replacement (see section 19(3) and (4)).
(2) If the consumer requires the trader to repair or replace the goods, the trader must—
  (a) do so within a reasonable time and without significant inconvenience to the consumer, and
  (b) bear any necessary costs incurred in doing so (including in particular the cost of any labour, materials or postage).
(3) The consumer cannot require the trader to repair or replace the goods if that remedy (the repair or the replacement)—
  (a) is impossible, or
  (b) is disproportionate compared to the other of those remedies.
(4) Either of those remedies is disproportionate compared to the other if it imposes costs on the trader which, compared to those imposed by the other, are unreasonable, taking into account—
  (a) the value which the goods would have if they conformed to the contract,
  (b) the significance of the lack of conformity, and
  (c) whether the other remedy could be effected without significant inconvenience to the consumer.
(5) Any question as to what is a reasonable time or significant inconvenience is to be determined taking account of—
  (a) the nature of the goods, and
  (b) the purpose for which the goods were acquired.
(6) A consumer who requires or agrees to the repair of goods cannot require the trader to replace them, or exercise the short-term right to reject, without giving the trader a reasonable time to repair them (unless giving the trader that time would cause significant inconvenience to the consumer).
(7) A consumer who requires or agrees to the replacement of goods cannot require the trader to repair them, or exercise the short-term right to reject, without giving the trader a reasonable time to replace them (unless giving the trader that time would cause significant inconvenience to the consumer).
(8) In this Chapter, 'repair' in relation to goods that do not conform to a contract, means making them conform.

24 Right to price reduction or final right to reject

(1) The right to a price reduction is the right—
  (a) to require the trader to reduce by an appropriate amount the price the consumer is required to pay under the contract, or anything else the consumer is required to transfer under the contract, and
  (b) to receive a refund from the trader for anything already paid or otherwise transferred by the consumer above the reduced amount.
(2) The amount of the reduction may, where appropriate, be the full amount of the price or whatever the consumer is required to transfer.

(3) Section 20(10) to (17) applies to a consumer's right to receive a refund under subsection (1)(b).

(4) The right to a price reduction does not apply—

(a) if what the consumer is (before the reduction) required to transfer under the contract, whether or not already transferred, cannot be divided up so as to enable the trader to receive or retain only the reduced amount, or

(b) if anything to which section 20(12) applies cannot be given back in its original state.

(5) A consumer who has the right to a price reduction and the final right to reject may only exercise one (not both), and may only do so in one of these situations—

(a) after one repair or one replacement, the goods do not conform to the contract;

(b) because of section 23(3) the consumer can require neither repair nor replacement of the goods; or

(c) the consumer has required the trader to repair or replace the goods, but the trader is in breach of the requirement of section 23(2)(a) to do so within a reasonable time and without significant inconvenience to the consumer.

(6) There has been a repair or replacement for the purposes of subsection (5)(a) if—

(a) the consumer has requested or agreed to repair or replacement of the goods (whether in relation to one fault or more than one), and

(b) the trader has delivered goods to the consumer, or made goods available to the consumer, in response to the request or agreement.

(7) For the purposes of subsection (6) goods that the trader arranges to repair at the consumer's premises are made available when the trader indicates that the repairs are finished.

(8) If the consumer exercises the final right to reject, any refund to the consumer may be reduced by a deduction for use, to take account of the use the consumer has had of the goods in the period since they were delivered, but this is subject to subsections (9) and (10).

(9) No deduction may be made to take account of use in any period when the consumer had the goods only because the trader failed to collect them at an agreed time.

(10) No deduction may be made if the final right to reject is exercised in the first 6 months (see subsection (11)), unless—

(a) the goods consist of a motor vehicle, or

(b) the goods are of a description specified by order made by the Secretary of State by statutory instrument.

(11) In subsection (10) the first 6 months means 6 months beginning with the first day after these have all happened—

(a) ownership or (in the case of a contract for the hire of goods, a hire-purchase agreement or a conditional sales contract) possession of the goods has been transferred to the consumer,

(b) the goods have been delivered, and

(c) where the contract requires the trader to install the goods or take other action to enable the consumer to use them, the trader has notified the consumer that the action has been taken.

(12) In subsection (10)(a) 'motor vehicle'—

(a) in relation to Great Britain, has the same meaning as in the Road Traffic Act 1988 (see sections 185 to 194 of that Act);

(b) in relation to Northern Ireland, has the same meaning as in the Road Traffic (Northern Ireland) Order 1995 (SI 1995/2994 (NI 18)) (see Parts I and V of that Order).

(13) But a vehicle is not a motor vehicle for the purposes of subsection (10)(a) if it is constructed or adapted—

(a) for the use of a person suffering from some physical defect or disability, and

(b) so that it may only be used by one such person at any one time.

(14) An order under subsection (10)(b)—
(a) may be made only if the Secretary of State is satisfied that it is appropriate to do so because of significant detriment caused to traders as a result of the application of subsection (10)in relation to goods of the description specified by the order;
(b) may contain transitional or transitory provision or savings.
(15) No order may be made under subsection (10)(b) unless a draft of the statutory instrument containing it has been laid before, and approved by a resolution of, each House of Parliament.

Other rules about remedies under goods contracts

25 Delivery of wrong quantity

(1) Where the trader delivers to the consumer a quantity of goods less than the trader contracted to supply, the consumer may reject them, but if the consumer accepts them the consumer must pay for them at the contract rate.
(2) Where the trader delivers to the consumer a quantity of goods larger than the trader contracted to supply, the consumer may accept the goods included in the contract and reject the rest, or may reject all of the goods.
(3) Where the trader delivers to the consumer a quantity of goods larger than the trader contracted to supply and the consumer accepts all of the goods delivered, the consumer must pay for them at the contract rate.
(4) Where the consumer is entitled to reject goods under this section, any entitlement for the consumer to treat the contract as at an end depends on the terms of the contract and the circumstances of the case.
(5) The consumer rejects goods under this section by indicating to the trader that the consumer is rejecting the goods.
(6) The indication may be something the consumer says or does, but it must be clear enough to be understood by the trader.
(7) Subsections (1) to (3) do not prevent the consumer claiming damages, where it is open to the consumer to do so.
(8) This section is subject to any usage of trade, special agreement, or course of dealing between the parties.

26 Instalment deliveries

(1) Under a contract to supply goods, the consumer is not bound to accept delivery of the goods by instalments, unless that has been agreed between the consumer and the trader.
(2) The following provisions apply if the contract provides for the goods to be delivered by stated instalments, which are to be separately paid for.
(3) If the trader makes defective deliveries in respect of one or more instalments, the consumer, apart from any entitlement to claim damages, may be (but is not necessarily) entitled—
(a) to exercise the short-term right to reject or the right to reject under section 19(6) (as applicable) in respect of the whole contract, or
(b) to reject the goods in an instalment.
(4) Whether paragraph (a) or (b) of subsection (3) (or neither) applies to a consumer depends on the terms of the contract and the circumstances of the case.
(5) In subsection (3), making defective deliveries does not include failing to make a delivery in accordance with section 28.
(6) If the consumer neglects or refuses to take delivery of or pay for one or more instalments, the trader may—

(a) be entitled to treat the whole contract as at an end, or

(b) if it is a severable breach, have a claim for damages but not a right to treat the whole contract as at an end.

(7) Whether paragraph (a) or (b) of subsection (6) (or neither) applies to a trader depends on the terms of the contract and the circumstances of the case.

27 Consignation, or payment into court, in Scotland

(1) Subsection (2) applies where—

(a) a consumer has not rejected goods which the consumer could have rejected for breach of a term mentioned in section 19(3) or (6),

(b) the consumer has chosen to treat the breach as giving rise only to a claim for damages or to a right to rely on the breach against a claim by the trader for the price of the goods, and

(c) the trader has begun proceedings in court to recover the price or has brought a counter-claim for the price.

(2) The court may require the consumer—

(a) to consign, or pay into court, the price of the goods, or part of the price, or

(b) to provide some other reasonable security for payment of the price.

Other rules about goods contracts

28 Delivery of goods

(1) This section applies to any sales contract.

(2) Unless the trader and the consumer have agreed otherwise, the contract is to be treated as including a term that the trader must deliver the goods to the consumer.

(3) Unless there is an agreed time or period, the contract is to be treated as including a term that the trader must deliver the goods—

(a) without undue delay, and

(b) in any event, not more than 30 days after the day on which the contract is entered into.

(4) In this section—

(a) an 'agreed' time or period means a time or period agreed by the trader and the consumer for delivery of the goods;

(b) if there is an obligation to deliver the goods at the time the contract is entered into, that time counts as the 'agreed' time.

(5) Subsections (6) and (7) apply if the trader does not deliver the goods in accordance with subsection (3) or at the agreed time or within the agreed period.

(6) If the circumstances are that—

(a) the trader has refused to deliver the goods,

(b) delivery of the goods at the agreed time or within the agreed period is essential taking into account all the relevant circumstances at the time the contract was entered into, or

(c) the consumer told the trader before the contract was entered into that delivery in accordance with subsection (3), or at the agreed time or within the agreed period, was essential, then the consumer may treat the contract as at an end.

(7) In any other circumstances, the consumer may specify a period that is appropriate in the circumstances and require the trader to deliver the goods before the end of that period.

(8) If the consumer specifies a period under subsection (7) but the goods are not delivered within that period, then the consumer may treat the contract as at an end.

(9) If the consumer treats the contract as at an end under subsection (6) or (8), the trader must without undue delay reimburse all payments made under the contract.

(10) If subsection (6) or (8) applies but the consumer does not treat the contract as at an end—

(a) that does not prevent the consumer from cancelling the order for any of the goods or rejecting goods that have been delivered, and

(b) the trader must without undue delay reimburse all payments made under the contract in respect of any goods for which the consumer cancels the order or which the consumer rejects.

(11) If any of the goods form a commercial unit, the consumer cannot reject or cancel the order for some of those goods without also rejecting or cancelling the order for the rest of them.

(12) A unit is a 'commercial unit' if division of the unit would materially impair the value of the goods or the character of the unit.

(13) This section does not prevent the consumer seeking other remedies where it is open to the consumer to do so.

(14) See section 2(5) and (6) for the application of this section where goods are sold at public auction.

29 Passing of risk

(1) A sales contract is to be treated as including the following provisions as terms.

(2) The goods remain at the trader's risk until they come into the physical possession of—
   (a) the consumer, or
   (b) a person identified by the consumer to take possession of the goods.

(3) Subsection (2) does not apply if the goods are delivered to a carrier who—
   (a) is commissioned by the consumer to deliver the goods, and
   (b) is not a carrier the trader named as an option for the consumer.

(4) In that case the goods are at the consumer's risk on and after delivery to the carrier.

(5) Subsection (4) does not affect any liability of the carrier to the consumer in respect of the goods.

(6) See section 2(5) and (6) for the application of this section where goods are sold at public auction.

30 Goods under guarantee

(1) This section applies where—
   (a) there is a contract to supply goods, and
   (b) there is a guarantee in relation to the goods.

(2) 'Guarantee' here means an undertaking to the consumer given without extra charge by a person acting in the course of the person's business (the 'guarantor') that, if the goods do not meet the specifications set out in the guarantee statement or in any associated advertising—
   (a) the consumer will be reimbursed for the price paid for the goods, or
   (b) the goods will be repaired, replaced or handled in any way.

(3) The guarantee takes effect, at the time the goods are delivered, as a contractual obligation owed by the guarantor under the conditions set out in the guarantee statement and in any associated advertising.

(4) The guarantor must ensure that—
   (a) the guarantee sets out in plain and intelligible language the contents of the guarantee and the essential particulars for making claims under the guarantee,
   (b) the guarantee states that the consumer has statutory rights in relation to the goods and that those rights are not affected by the guarantee, and
   (c) where the goods are offered within the territory of the United Kingdom, the guarantee is written in English.

(5) The contents of the guarantee to be set out in it include, in particular—

(a) the name and address of the guarantor, and

(b) the duration and territorial scope of the guarantee.

(6) The guarantor and any other person who offers to supply to consumers the goods which are the subject of the guarantee must, on request by the consumer, make the guarantee available to the consumer within a reasonable time, in writing and in a form accessible to the consumer.

(7) What is a reasonable time is a question of fact.

(8) If a person fails to comply with a requirement of this section, the enforcement authority may apply to the court for an injunction or (in Scotland) an order of specific implement against that person requiring that person to comply.

(9) On an application the court may grant an injunction or (in Scotland) an order of specific implement on such terms as it thinks appropriate.

(10) In this section—

- 'court' means—

    (a) in relation to England and Wales, the High Court or the county court,

    (b) in relation to Northern Ireland, the High Court or a county court, and

    (c) in relation to Scotland, the Court of Session or the sheriff;

- 'enforcement authority' means—

    (a) the Competition and Markets Authority,

    (b) a local weights and measures authority in Great Britain, and

    (c) the Department of Enterprise, Trade and Investment in Northern Ireland.

Can a trader contract out of statutory rights and remedies under a goods contract?

31 Liability that cannot be excluded or restricted

(1) A term of a contract to supply goods is not binding on the consumer to the extent that it would exclude or restrict the trader's liability arising under any of these provisions—

(a) section 9 (goods to be of satisfactory quality);

(b) section 10 (goods to be fit for particular purpose);

(c) section 11 (goods to be as described);

(d) section 12 (other pre-contract information included in contract);

(e) section 13 (goods to match a sample);

(f) section 14 (goods to match a model seen or examined);

(g) section 15 (installation as part of conformity of the goods with the contract);

(h) section 16 (goods not conforming to contract if digital content does not conform);

(i) section 17 (trader to have right to supply the goods etc);

(j) section 28 (delivery of goods);

(k) section 29 (passing of risk).

(2) That also means that a term of a contract to supply goods is not binding on the consumer to the extent that it would—

(a) exclude or restrict a right or remedy in respect of a liability under a provision listed in subsection (1),

(b) make such a right or remedy or its enforcement subject to a restrictive or onerous condition,

(c) allow a trader to put a person at a disadvantage as a result of pursuing such a right or remedy, or

(d) exclude or restrict rules of evidence or procedure.

(3) The reference in subsection (1) to excluding or restricting a liability also includes preventing an obligation or duty arising or limiting its extent.

(4) An agreement in writing to submit present or future differences to arbitration is not to be regarded as excluding or restricting any liability for the purposes of this section.

(5) Subsection (1)(i), and subsection (2) so far as it relates to liability under section 17, do not apply to a term of a contract for the hire of goods.

(6) But an express term of a contract for the hire of goods is not binding on the consumer to the extent that it would exclude or restrict a term that section 17 requires to be treated as included in the contract, unless it is inconsistent with that term (and see also section 62 (requirement for terms to be fair)).

(7) See Schedule 3 for provision about the enforcement of this section.

32 Contracts applying law of non-EEA State

(1) If—
  (a) the law of a country or territory other than an EEA State is chosen by the parties to be applicable to a sales contract, but
  (b) the sales contract has a close connection with the United Kingdom,
  this Chapter, except the provisions in subsection (2), applies despite that choice.

(2) The exceptions are—
  (a) sections 11(4) and (5) and 12;
  (b) sections 28 and 29;
  (c) section 31(1)(d), (j) and (k).

(3) For cases where those provisions apply, or where the law applicable has not been chosen or the law of an EEA State is chosen, see Regulation (EC) No. 593/2008 of the European Parliament and of the Council of 17 June 2008 on the law applicable to contractual obligations.

CHAPTER 3

Digital content

What digital content contracts are covered?

33 Contracts covered by this Chapter

(1) This Chapter applies to a contract for a trader to supply digital content to a consumer, if it is supplied or to be supplied for a price paid by the consumer.

(2) This Chapter also applies to a contract for a trader to supply digital content to a consumer, if—
  (a) it is supplied free with goods or services or other digital content for which the consumer pays a price, and
  (b) it is not generally available to consumers unless they have paid a price for it or for goods or services or other digital content.

(3) The references in subsections (1) and (2) to the consumer paying a price include references to the consumer using, by way of payment, any facility for which money has been paid.

(4) A trader does not supply digital content to a consumer for the purposes of this Part merely because the trader supplies a service by which digital content reaches the consumer.

(5) The Secretary of State may by order provide for this Chapter to apply to other contracts for a trader to supply digital content to a consumer, if the Secretary of State is satisfied that it is appropriate to do so because of significant detriment caused to consumers under contracts of the kind to which the order relates.

(6) An order under subsection (5)—
  (a) may, in particular, amend this Act;
  (b) may contain transitional or transitory provision or savings.

(7) A contract to which this Chapter applies is referred to in this Part as a 'contract to supply digital content'.

(8) This section, other than subsection (4), does not limit the application of section 46.

(9) The power to make an order under subsection (5) is exercisable by statutory instrument.

(10) No order may be made under subsection (5) unless a draft of the statutory instrument containing it has been laid before, and approved by a resolution of, each House of Parliament.

What statutory rights are there under a digital content contract?

34 Digital content to be of satisfactory quality

(1) Every contract to supply digital content is to be treated as including a term that the quality of the digital content is satisfactory.

(2) The quality of digital content is satisfactory if it meets the standard that a reasonable person would consider satisfactory, taking account of—
   (a) any description of the digital content,
   (b) the price mentioned in section 33(1) or (2)(b) (if relevant), and
   (c) all the other relevant circumstances (see subsection (5)).

(3) The quality of digital content includes its state and condition; and the following aspects (among others) are in appropriate cases aspects of the quality of digital content—
   (a) fitness for all the purposes for which digital content of that kind is usually supplied;
   (b) freedom from minor defects;
   (c) safety;
   (d) durability.

(4) The term mentioned in subsection (1) does not cover anything which makes the quality of the digital content unsatisfactory—
   (a) which is specifically drawn to the consumer's attention before the contract is made,
   (b) where the consumer examines the digital content before the contract is made, which that examination ought to reveal, or
   (c) where the consumer examines a trial version before the contract is made, which would have been apparent on a reasonable examination of the trial version.

(5) The relevant circumstances mentioned in subsection (2)(c) include any public statement about the specific characteristics of the digital content made by the trader, the producer or any representative of the trader or the producer.

(6) That includes, in particular, any public statement made in advertising or labelling.

(7) But a public statement is not a relevant circumstance for the purposes of subsection (2)(c) if the trader shows that—
   (a) when the contract was made, the trader was not, and could not reasonably have been, aware of the statement,
   (b) before the contract was made, the statement had been publicly withdrawn or, to the extent that it contained anything which was incorrect or misleading, it had been publicly corrected, or
   (c) the consumer's decision to contract for the digital content could not have been influenced by the statement.

(8) In a contract to supply digital content a term about the quality of the digital content may be treated as included as a matter of custom.

(9) See section 42 for a consumer's rights if the trader is in breach of a term that this section requires to be treated as included in a contract.

35 Digital content to be fit for particular purpose

(1) Subsection (3) applies to a contract to supply digital content if before the contract is made the consumer makes known to the trader (expressly or by implication) any particular purpose for which the consumer is contracting for the digital content.

(2) Subsection (3) also applies to a contract to supply digital content if—
- (a) the digital content was previously sold by a credit-broker to the trader,
- (b) the consideration or part of it is a sum payable by instalments, and
- (c) before the contract is made, the consumer makes known to the credit-broker (expressly or by implication) any particular purpose for which the consumer is contracting for the digital content.

(3) The contract is to be treated as including a term that the digital content is reasonably fit for that purpose, whether or not that is a purpose for which digital content of that kind is usually supplied.

(4) Subsection (3) does not apply if the circumstances show that the consumer does not rely, or it is unreasonable for the consumer to rely, on the skill or judgment of the trader or credit-broker.

(5) A contract to supply digital content may be treated as making provision about the fitness of the digital content for a particular purpose as a matter of custom.

(6) See section 42 for a consumer's rights if the trader is in breach of a term that this section requires to be treated as included in a contract.

36 Digital content to be as described

(1) Every contract to supply digital content is to be treated as including a term that the digital content will match any description of it given by the trader to the consumer.

(2) Where the consumer examines a trial version before the contract is made, it is not sufficient that the digital content matches (or is better than) the trial version if the digital content does not also match any description of it given by the trader to the consumer.

(3) Any information that is provided by the trader about the digital content that is information mentioned in paragraph (a), (j) or (k) of Schedule 1 or paragraph (a), (v) or (w) of Schedule 2 (main characteristics, functionality and compatibility) to the Consumer Contracts (Information, Cancellation and Additional Charges) Regulations 2013 (SI 2013/3134) is to be treated as included as a term of the contract.

(4) A change to any of that information, made before entering into the contract or later, is not effective unless expressly agreed between the consumer and the trader.

(5) See section 42 for a consumer's rights if the trader is in breach of a term that this section requires to be treated as included in a contract.

37 Other pre-contract information included in contract

(1) This section applies to any contract to supply digital content.

(2) Where regulation 9, 10 or 13 of the Consumer Contracts (Information, Cancellation and Additional Charges) Regulations 2013 (SI 2013/3134) required the trader to provide information to the consumer before the contract became binding, any of that information that was provided by the trader other than information about the digital content and mentioned in paragraph (a), (j) or (k) of Schedule 1 or paragraph (a), (v) or (w) of Schedule 2 to the Regulations (main characteristics, functionality and compatibility) is to be treated as included as a term of the contract.

(3) A change to any of that information, made before entering into the contract or later, is not effective unless expressly agreed between the consumer and the trader.

(4) See section 42 for a consumer's rights if the trader is in breach of a term that this section requires to be treated as included in a contract.

38 No other requirement to treat term about quality or fitness as included

(1) Except as provided by sections 34 and 35, a contract to supply digital content is not to be treated as including any term about the quality of the digital content or its fitness for any particular purpose, unless the term is expressly included in the contract.

(2) Subsection (1) is subject to provision made by any other enactment, whenever passed or made.

39 Supply by transmission and facilities for continued transmission

(1) Subsection (2) applies where there is a contract to supply digital content and the consumer's access to the content on a device requires its transmission to the device under arrangements initiated by the trader.

(2) For the purposes of this Chapter, the digital content is supplied—

    (a) when the content reaches the device, or

    (b) if earlier, when the content reaches another trader chosen by the consumer to supply, under a contract with the consumer, a service by which digital content reaches the device.

(3) Subsections (5) to (7) apply where—

    (a) there is a contract to supply digital content, and

    (b) after the trader (T) has supplied the digital content, the consumer is to have access under the contract to a processing facility under arrangements made by T.

(4) A processing facility is a facility by which T or another trader will receive digital content from the consumer and transmit digital content to the consumer (whether or not other features are to be included under the contract).

(5) The contract is to be treated as including a term that the processing facility (with any feature that the facility is to include under the contract) must be available to the consumer for a reasonable time, unless a time is specified in the contract.

(6) The following provisions apply to all digital content transmitted to the consumer on each occasion under the facility, while it is provided under the contract, as they apply to the digital content first supplied—

    (a) section 34 (quality);

    (b) section 35 (fitness for a particular purpose);

    (c) section 36 (description).

(7) Breach of a term treated as included under subsection (5) has the same effect as breach of a term treated as included under those sections (see section 42).

40 Quality, fitness and description of content supplied subject to modifications

(1) Where under a contract a trader supplies digital content to a consumer subject to the right of the trader or a third party to modify the digital content, the following provisions apply in relation to the digital content as modified as they apply in relation to the digital content as supplied under the contract—

    (a) section 34 (quality);

    (b) section 35 (fitness for a particular purpose);

    (c) section 36 (description).

(2) Subsection (1)(c) does not prevent the trader from improving the features of, or adding new features to, the digital content, as long as—

    (a) the digital content continues to match the description of it given by the trader to the consumer, and

    (b) the digital content continues to conform to the information provided by the trader as mentioned in subsection (3) of section 36, subject to any change to that information that has been agreed in accordance with subsection (4) of that section.

(3) A claim on the grounds that digital content does not conform to a term described in any of the sections listed in subsection (1) as applied by that subsection is to be treated as arising at the time when the digital content was supplied under the contract and not the time when it is modified.

41 Trader's right to supply digital content

(1) Every contract to supply digital content is to be treated as including a term—
  (a) in relation to any digital content which is supplied under the contract and which the consumer has paid for, that the trader has the right to supply that content to the consumer;
  (b) in relation to any digital content which the trader agrees to supply under the contract and which the consumer has paid for, that the trader will have the right to supply it to the consumer at the time when it is to be supplied.
(2) See section 42 for a consumer's rights if the trader is in breach of a term that this section requires to be treated as included in a contract.

What remedies are there if statutory rights under a digital content contract are not met?

42 Consumer's rights to enforce terms about digital content

(1) In this section and section 43 references to digital content conforming to a contract are references to the digital content conforming to the terms described in sections 34, 35 and 36.
(2) If the digital content does not conform to the contract, the consumer's rights (and the provisions about them and when they are available) are—
  (a) the right to repair or replacement (see section 43);
  (b) the right to a price reduction (see section 44).
(3) Section 16 also applies if an item including the digital content is supplied.
(4) If the trader is in breach of a term that section 37 requires to be treated as included in the contract, the consumer has the right to recover from the trader the amount of any costs incurred by the consumer as a result of the breach, up to the amount of the price paid for the digital content or for any facility within section 33(3) used by the consumer.
(5) If the trader is in breach of the term that section 41(1) (right to supply the content) requires to be treated as included in the contract, the consumer has the right to a refund (see section 45 for provisions about that right and when it is available).
(6) This Chapter does not prevent the consumer seeking other remedies for a breach of a term to which any of subsections (2), (4) or (5) applies, instead of or in addition to a remedy referred to there (but not so as to recover twice for the same loss).
(7) Those other remedies include any of the following that is open to the consumer in the circumstances—
  (a) claiming damages;
  (b) seeking to recover money paid where the consideration for payment of the money has failed;
  (c) seeking specific performance;
  (d) seeking an order for specific implement;
  (e) relying on the breach against a claim by the trader for the price.
(8) It is not open to the consumer to treat the contract as at an end for breach of a term to which any of subsections (2), (4) or (5) applies.
(9) For the purposes of subsection (2), digital content which does not conform to the contract at any time within the period of six months beginning with the day on which it was supplied must be taken not to have conformed to the contract when it was supplied.
(10) Subsection (9) does not apply if—

(a) it is established that the digital content did conform to the contract when it was supplied, or

(b) its application is incompatible with the nature of the digital content or with how it fails to conform to the contract.

43 Right to repair or replacement

(1) This section applies if the consumer has the right to repair or replacement.

(2) If the consumer requires the trader to repair or replace the digital content, the trader must—

(a) do so within a reasonable time and without significant inconvenience to the consumer; and

(b) bear any necessary costs incurred in doing so (including in particular the cost of any labour, materials or postage).

(3) The consumer cannot require the trader to repair or replace the digital content if that remedy (the repair or the replacement)—

(a) is impossible, or

(b) is disproportionate compared to the other of those remedies.

(4) Either of those remedies is disproportionate compared to the other if it imposes costs on the trader which, compared to those imposed by the other, are unreasonable, taking into account—

(a) the value which the digital content would have if it conformed to the contract,

(b) the significance of the lack of conformity, and

(c) whether the other remedy could be effected without significant inconvenience to the consumer.

(5) Any question as to what is a reasonable time or significant inconvenience is to be determined taking account of—

(a) the nature of the digital content, and

(b) the purpose for which the digital content was obtained or accessed.

(6) A consumer who requires or agrees to the repair of digital content cannot require the trader to replace it without giving the trader a reasonable time to repair it (unless giving the trader that time would cause significant inconvenience to the consumer).

(7) A consumer who requires or agrees to the replacement of digital content cannot require the trader to repair it without giving the trader a reasonable time to replace it (unless giving the trader that time would cause significant inconvenience to the consumer).

(8) In this Chapter, 'repair' in relation to digital content that does not conform to a contract, means making it conform.

44 Right to price reduction

(1) The right to a price reduction is the right to require the trader to reduce the price to the consumer by an appropriate amount (including the right to receive a refund for anything already paid above the reduced amount).

(2) The amount of the reduction may, where appropriate, be the full amount of the price.

(3) A consumer who has that right may only exercise it in one of these situations—

(a) because of section 43(3)(a) the consumer can require neither repair nor replacement of the digital content, or

(b) the consumer has required the trader to repair or replace the digital content, but the trader is in breach of the requirement of section 43(2)(a) to do so within a reasonable time and without significant inconvenience to the consumer.

(4) A refund under this section must be given without undue delay, and in any event within 14 days beginning with the day on which the trader agrees that the consumer is entitled to a refund.

(5) The trader must give the refund using the same means of payment as the consumer used to pay for the digital content, unless the consumer expressly agrees otherwise.

(6) The trader must not impose any fee on the consumer in respect of the refund.

45 Right to a refund

(1) The right to a refund gives the consumer the right to receive a refund from the trader of all money paid by the consumer for the digital content (subject to subsection (2)).

(2) If the breach giving the consumer the right to a refund affects only some of the digital content supplied under the contract, the right to a refund does not extend to any part of the price attributable to digital content that is not affected by the breach.

(3) A refund must be given without undue delay, and in any event within 14 days beginning with the day on which the trader agrees that the consumer is entitled to a refund.

(4) The trader must give the refund using the same means of payment as the consumer used to pay for the digital content, unless the consumer expressly agrees otherwise.

(5) The trader must not impose any fee on the consumer in respect of the refund.

Compensation for damage to device or to other digital content

46 Remedy for damage to device or to other digital content

(1) This section applies if—
  (a) a trader supplies digital content to a consumer under a contract,
  (b) the digital content causes damage to a device or to other digital content,
  (c) the device or digital content that is damaged belongs to the consumer, and
  (d) the damage is of a kind that would not have occurred if the trader had exercised reasonable care and skill.

(2) If the consumer requires the trader to provide a remedy under this section, the trader must either—
  (a) repair the damage in accordance with subsection (3), or
  (b) compensate the consumer for the damage with an appropriate payment.

(3) To repair the damage in accordance with this subsection, the trader must—
  (a) repair the damage within a reasonable time and without significant inconvenience to the consumer, and
  (b) bear any necessary costs incurred in repairing the damage (including in particular the cost of any labour, materials or postage).

(4) Any question as to what is a reasonable time or significant inconvenience is to be determined taking account of—
  (a) the nature of the device or digital content that is damaged, and
  (b) the purpose for which it is used by the consumer.

(5) A compensation payment under this section must be made without undue delay, and in any event within 14 days beginning with the day on which the trader agrees that the consumer is entitled to the payment.

(6) The trader must not impose any fee on the consumer in respect of the payment.

(7) A consumer with a right to a remedy under this section may bring a claim in civil proceedings to enforce that right.

(8) The Limitation Act 1980 and the Limitation (Northern Ireland) Order 1989 (SI 1989/1339 (NI 11)) apply to a claim under this section as if it were an action founded on simple contract.

(9) The Prescription and Limitation (Scotland) Act 1973 applies to a right to a remedy under this section as if it were an obligation to which section 6 of that Act applies.

Can a trader contract out of statutory rights and remedies under a digital content contract?

47 Liability that cannot be excluded or restricted

(1) A term of a contract to supply digital content is not binding on the consumer to the extent that it would exclude or restrict the trader's liability arising under any of these provisions—

(a) section 34 (digital content to be of satisfactory quality),

(b) section 35 (digital content to be fit for particular purpose),

(c) section 36 (digital content to be as described),

(d) section 37 (other pre-contract information included in contract), or

(e) section 41 (trader's right to supply digital content).

(2) That also means that a term of a contract to supply digital content is not binding on the consumer to the extent that it would—

(a) exclude or restrict a right or remedy in respect of a liability under a provision listed in subsection (1),

(b) make such a right or remedy or its enforcement subject to a restrictive or onerous condition,

(c) allow a trader to put a person at a disadvantage as a result of pursuing such a right or remedy, or

(d) exclude or restrict rules of evidence or procedure.

(3) The reference in subsection (1) to excluding or restricting a liability also includes preventing an obligation or duty arising or limiting its extent.

(4) An agreement in writing to submit present or future differences to arbitration is not to be regarded as excluding or restricting any liability for the purposes of this section.

(5) See Schedule 3 for provision about the enforcement of this section.

(6) For provision limiting the ability of a trader under a contract within section 46 to exclude or restrict the trader's liability under that section, see section 62.

CHAPTER 4
Services
What services contracts are covered?

48 Contracts covered by this Chapter

(1) This Chapter applies to a contract for a trader to supply a service to a consumer.

(2) That does not include a contract of employment or apprenticeship.

(3) In relation to Scotland, this Chapter does not apply to a gratuitous contract.

(4) A contract to which this Chapter applies is referred to in this Part as a 'contract to supply a service'.

(5) The Secretary of State may by order made by statutory instrument provide that a provision of this Chapter does not apply in relation to a service of a description specified in the order.

(6) The power in subsection (5) includes power to provide that a provision of this Chapter does not apply in relation to a service of a description specified in the order in the circumstances so specified.

(7) An order under subsection (5) may contain transitional or transitory provision or savings.

(8) No order may be made under subsection (5) unless a draft of the statutory instrument containing it has been laid before, and approved by a resolution of, each House of Parliament.

What statutory rights are there under a services contract?

49 Service to be performed with reasonable care and skill

(1) Every contract to supply a service is to be treated as including a term that the trader must perform the service with reasonable care and skill.

(2) See section 54 for a consumer's rights if the trader is in breach of a term that this section requires to be treated as included in a contract.

50 Information about the trader or service to be binding

(1) Every contract to supply a service is to be treated as including as a term of the contract anything that is said or written to the consumer, by or on behalf of the trader, about the trader or the service, if—

    (a) it is taken into account by the consumer when deciding to enter into the contract, or

    (b) it is taken into account by the consumer when making any decision about the service after entering into the contract.

(2) Anything taken into account by the consumer as mentioned in subsection (1)(a) or (b) is subject to—

    (a) anything that qualified it and was said or written to the consumer by the trader on the same occasion, and

    (b) any change to it that has been expressly agreed between the consumer and the trader (before entering into the contract or later).

(3) Without prejudice to subsection (1), any information provided by the trader in accordance with regulation 9, 10 or 13 of the Consumer Contracts (Information, Cancellation and Additional Charges) Regulations 2013 (SI 2013/3134) is to be treated as included as a term of the contract.

(4) A change to any of the information mentioned in subsection (3), made before entering into the contract or later, is not effective unless expressly agreed between the consumer and the trader.

(5) See section 54 for a consumer's rights if the trader is in breach of a term that this section requires to be treated as included in a contract.

51 Reasonable price to be paid for a service

(1) This section applies to a contract to supply a service if—

    (a) the consumer has not paid a price or other consideration for the service,

    (b) the contract does not expressly fix a price or other consideration, and does not say how it is to be fixed, and

    (c) anything that is to be treated under section 50 as included in the contract does not fix a price or other consideration either.

(2) In that case the contract is to be treated as including a term that the consumer must pay a reasonable price for the service, and no more.

(3) What is a reasonable price is a question of fact.

52 Service to be performed within a reasonable time

(1) This section applies to a contract to supply a service, if—

    (a) the contract does not expressly fix the time for the service to be performed, and does not say how it is to be fixed, and

    (b) information that is to be treated under section 50 as included in the contract does not fix the time either.

(2) In that case the contract is to be treated as including a term that the trader must perform the service within a reasonable time.

(3) What is a reasonable time is a question of fact.

(4) See section 54 for a consumer's rights if the trader is in breach of a term that this section requires to be treated as included in a contract.

53 Relation to other law on contract terms

(1) Nothing in this Chapter affects any enactment or rule of law that imposes a stricter duty on the trader.

(2) This Chapter is subject to any other enactment which defines or restricts the rights, duties or liabilities arising in connection with a service of any description.

What remedies are there if statutory rights under a services contract are not met?

54 Consumer's rights to enforce terms about services

(1) The consumer's rights under this section and sections 55 and 56 do not affect any rights that the contract provides for, if those are not inconsistent.

(2) In this section and section 55 a reference to a service conforming to a contract is a reference to—

   (a) the service being performed in accordance with section 49, or

   (b) the service conforming to a term that section 50 requires to be treated as included in the contract and that relates to the performance of the service.

(3) If the service does not conform to the contract, the consumer's rights (and the provisions about them and when they are available) are—

   (a) the right to require repeat performance (see section 55);

   (b) the right to a price reduction (see section 56).

(4) If the trader is in breach of a term that section 50 requires to be treated as included in the contract but that does not relate to the service, the consumer has the right to a price reduction (see section 56 for provisions about that right and when it is available).

(5) If the trader is in breach of what the contract requires under section 52 (performance within a reasonable time), the consumer has the right to a price reduction (see section 56 for provisions about that right and when it is available).

(6) This section and sections 55 and 56 do not prevent the consumer seeking other remedies for a breach of a term to which any of subsections (3) to (5) applies, instead of or in addition to a remedy referred to there (but not so as to recover twice for the same loss).

(7) Those other remedies include any of the following that is open to the consumer in the circumstances—

   (a) claiming damages;

   (b) seeking to recover money paid where the consideration for payment of the money has failed;

   (c) seeking specific performance;

   (d) seeking an order for specific implement;

   (e) relying on the breach against a claim by the trader under the contract;

   (f) exercising a right to treat the contract as at an end.

55 Right to repeat performance

(1) The right to require repeat performance is a right to require the trader to perform the service again, to the extent necessary to complete its performance in conformity with the contract.

(2) If the consumer requires such repeat performance, the trader—

   (a) must provide it within a reasonable time and without significant inconvenience to the consumer; and

   (b) must bear any necessary costs incurred in doing so (including in particular the cost of any labour or materials).

(3) The consumer cannot require repeat performance if completing performance of the service in conformity with the contract is impossible.

(4) Any question as to what is a reasonable time or significant inconvenience is to be determined taking account of—

   (a) the nature of the service, and

   (b) the purpose for which the service was to be performed.

56 Right to price reduction

(1) The right to a price reduction is the right to require the trader to reduce the price to the consumer by an appropriate amount (including the right to receive a refund for anything already paid above the reduced amount).

(2) The amount of the reduction may, where appropriate, be the full amount of the price.

(3) A consumer who has that right and the right to require repeat performance is only entitled to a price reduction in one of these situations—

(a) because of section 55(3) the consumer cannot require repeat performance; or

(b) the consumer has required repeat performance, but the trader is in breach of the requirement of section 55(2)(a) to do it within a reasonable time and without significant inconvenience to the consumer.

(4) A refund under this section must be given without undue delay, and in any event within 14 days beginning with the day on which the trader agrees that the consumer is entitled to a refund.

(5) The trader must give the refund using the same means of payment as the consumer used to pay for the service, unless the consumer expressly agrees otherwise.

(6) The trader must not impose any fee on the consumer in respect of the refund.

Can a trader contract out of statutory rights and remedies under a services contract?

57 Liability that cannot be excluded or restricted

(1) A term of a contract to supply services is not binding on the consumer to the extent that it would exclude the trader's liability arising under section 49 (service to be performed with reasonable care and skill).

(2) Subject to section 50(2), a term of a contract to supply services is not binding on the consumer to the extent that it would exclude the trader's liability arising under section 50 (information about trader or service to be binding).

(3) A term of a contract to supply services is not binding on the consumer to the extent that it would restrict the trader's liability arising under any of sections 49 and 50 and, where they apply, sections 51 and 52 (reasonable price and reasonable time), if it would prevent the consumer in an appropriate case from recovering the price paid or the value of any other consideration. (If it would not prevent the consumer from doing so, Part 2 (unfair terms) may apply.)

(4) That also means that a term of a contract to supply services is not binding on the consumer to the extent that it would—

(a) exclude or restrict a right or remedy in respect of a liability under any of sections 49 to 52,

(b) make such a right or remedy or its enforcement subject to a restrictive or onerous condition,

(c) allow a trader to put a person at a disadvantage as a result of pursuing such a right or remedy, or

(d) exclude or restrict rules of evidence or procedure.

(5) The references in subsections (1) to (3) to excluding or restricting a liability also include preventing an obligation or duty arising or limiting its extent.

(6) An agreement in writing to submit present or future differences to arbitration is not to be regarded as excluding or restricting any liability for the purposes of this section.

(7) See Schedule 3 for provision about the enforcement of this section.

CHAPTER 5

General and supplementary provisions

58 Powers of the court

(1) In any proceedings in which a remedy is sought by virtue of section 19(3) or (4), 42(2) or 54(3), the court, in addition to any other power it has, may act under this section.

(2) On the application of the consumer the court may make an order requiring specific performance or, in Scotland, specific implement by the trader of any obligation imposed on the trader by virtue of section 23, 43 or 55.

(3) Subsection (4) applies if—

   (a) the consumer claims to exercise a right under the relevant remedies provisions, but

   (b) the court decides that those provisions have the effect that exercise of another right is appropriate.

(4) The court may proceed as if the consumer had exercised that other right.

(5) If the consumer has claimed to exercise the final right to reject, the court may order that any reimbursement to the consumer is reduced by a deduction for use, to take account of the use the consumer has had of the goods in the period since they were delivered.

(6) Any deduction for use is limited as set out in section 24(9) and (10).

(7) The court may make an order under this section unconditionally or on such terms and conditions as to damages, payment of the price and otherwise as it thinks just.

(8) The 'relevant remedies provisions' are—

   (a) where Chapter 2 applies, sections 23 and 24;

   (b) where Chapter 3 applies, sections 43 and 44;

   (c) where Chapter 4 applies, sections 55 and 56.

59 Interpretation

(1) These definitions apply in this Part (as well as the key definitions in section 2)—

   • 'conditional sales contract' has the meaning given in section 5(3);

   • 'Consumer Rights Directive' means Directive 2011/83/EU of the European Parliament and of the Council of 25 October 2011 on consumer rights, amending Council Directive93/13/EEC and Directive 1999/44/EC of the European Parliament and of the Council and repealing Council Directive 85/577/EEC and Directive 97/7/EC of the European Parliament and of the Council;

   • 'credit-broker' means a person acting in the course of a business of credit brokerage carried on by that person;

   • 'credit brokerage' means—

      (a) introducing individuals who want to obtain credit to persons carrying on any business so far as it relates to the provision of credit,

      (b) introducing individuals who want to obtain goods on hire to persons carrying on a business which comprises or relates to supplying goods under a contract for the hire of goods, or

      (c) introducing individuals who want to obtain credit, or to obtain goods on hire, to other persons engaged in credit brokerage;

   • 'delivery' means voluntary transfer of possession from one person to another;

   • 'enactment' includes—

      (a) an enactment contained in subordinate legislation within the meaning of the Interpretation Act 1978,

      (b) an enactment contained in, or in an instrument made under, a Measure or Act of the National Assembly for Wales,

      (c) an enactment contained in, or in an instrument made under, an Act of the Scottish Parliament, and

      (d) an enactment contained in, or in an instrument made under, Northern Ireland legislation;

   • 'producer', in relation to goods or digital content, means—

      (a) the manufacturer,

      (b) the importer into the European Economic Area, or

  (c) any person who purports to be a producer by placing the person's name, trade mark or other distinctive sign on the goods or using it in connection with the digital content.

(2) References in this Part to treating a contract as at an end are to be read in accordance with section 19(13).

60 Changes to other legislation

Schedule 1 (amendments consequential on this Part) has effect.

PART 2

UNFAIR TERMS

What contracts and notices are covered by this Part?

61 Contracts and notices covered by this Part

(1) This Part applies to a contract between a trader and a consumer.
(2) This does not include a contract of employment or apprenticeship.
(3) A contract to which this Part applies is referred to in this Part as a 'consumer contract'.
(4) This Part applies to a notice to the extent that it—
  (a) relates to rights or obligations as between a trader and a consumer, or
  (b) purports to exclude or restrict a trader's liability to a consumer.
(5) This does not include a notice relating to rights, obligations or liabilities as between an employer and an employee.
(6) It does not matter for the purposes of subsection (4) whether the notice is expressed to apply to a consumer, as long as it is reasonable to assume it is intended to be seen or heard by a consumer.
(7) A notice to which this Part applies is referred to in this Part as a 'consumer notice'.
(8) In this section 'notice' includes an announcement, whether or not in writing, and any other communication or purported communication.

What are the general rules about fairness of contract terms and notices?

62 Requirement for contract terms and notices to be fair

(1) An unfair term of a consumer contract is not binding on the consumer.
(2) An unfair consumer notice is not binding on the consumer.
(3) This does not prevent the consumer from relying on the term or notice if the consumer chooses to do so.
(4) A term is unfair if, contrary to the requirement of good faith, it causes a significant imbalance in the parties' rights and obligations under the contract to the detriment of the consumer.
(5) Whether a term is fair is to be determined—
  (a) taking into account the nature of the subject matter of the contract, and
  (b) by reference to all the circumstances existing when the term was agreed and to all of the other terms of the contract or of any other contract on which it depends.
(6) A notice is unfair if, contrary to the requirement of good faith, it causes a significant imbalance in the parties' rights and obligations to the detriment of the consumer.
(7) Whether a notice is fair is to be determined—
  (a) taking into account the nature of the subject matter of the notice, and

(b) by reference to all the circumstances existing when the rights or obligations to which it relates arose and to the terms of any contract on which it depends.

(8) This section does not affect the operation of—

(a) section 31 (exclusion of liability: goods contracts),

(b) section 47 (exclusion of liability: digital content contracts),

(c) section 57 (exclusion of liability: services contracts), or

(d) section 65 (exclusion of negligence liability).

63 Contract terms which may or must be regarded as unfair

(1) Part 1 of Schedule 2 contains an indicative and non-exhaustive list of terms of consumer contracts that may be regarded as unfair for the purposes of this Part.

(2) Part 1 of Schedule 2 is subject to Part 2 of that Schedule; but a term listed in Part 2 of that Schedule may nevertheless be assessed for fairness under section 62 unless section 64 or 73 applies to it.

(3) The Secretary of State may by order made by statutory instrument amend Schedule 2 so as to add, modify or remove an entry in Part 1 or Part 2 of that Schedule.

(4) An order under subsection (3) may contain transitional or transitory provision or savings.

(5) No order may be made under subsection (3) unless a draft of the statutory instrument containing it has been laid before, and approved by a resolution of, each House of Parliament.

(6) A term of a consumer contract must be regarded as unfair if it has the effect that the consumer bears the burden of proof with respect to compliance by a distance supplier or an intermediary with an obligation under any enactment or rule implementing the Distance Marketing Directive.

(7) In subsection (6)—

- 'the Distance Marketing Directive' means Directive 2002/65/EC of the European Parliament and of the Council of 23 September 2002 concerning the distance marketing of consumer financial services and amending Council Directive 90/619/EEC and Directives 97/7/EC and 98/27/EC;

- 'distance supplier' means—

  (a) a supplier under a distance contract within the meaning of the Financial Services (Distance Marketing) Regulations 2004 (SI 2004/2095), or

  (b) a supplier of unsolicited financial services within the meaning of regulation 15 of those regulations;

- 'enactment' includes an enactment contained in subordinate legislation within the meaning of the Interpretation Act 1978;

- 'intermediary' has the same meaning as in the Financial Services (Distance Marketing) Regulations 2004;

- 'rule' means a rule made by the Financial Conduct Authority or the Prudential Regulation Authority under the Financial Services and Markets Act 2000 or by a designated professional body within the meaning of section 326(2) of that Act.

64 Exclusion from assessment of fairness

(1) A term of a consumer contract may not be assessed for fairness under section 62 to the extent that—

(a) it specifies the main subject matter of the contract, or

(b) the assessment is of the appropriateness of the price payable under the contract by comparison with the goods, digital content or services supplied under it.

(2) Subsection (1) excludes a term from an assessment under section 62 only if it is transparent and prominent.

(3) A term is transparent for the purposes of this Part if it is expressed in plain and intelligible language and (in the case of a written term) is legible.

(4) A term is prominent for the purposes of this section if it is brought to the consumer's attention in such a way that an average consumer would be aware of the term.

(5) In subsection (4) 'average consumer' means a consumer who is reasonably well-informed, observant and circumspect.

(6) This section does not apply to a term of a contract listed in Part 1 of Schedule 2.

65 Bar on exclusion or restriction of negligence liability

(1) A trader cannot by a term of a consumer contract or by a consumer notice exclude or restrict liability for death or personal injury resulting from negligence.

(2) Where a term of a consumer contract, or a consumer notice, purports to exclude or restrict a trader's liability for negligence, a person is not to be taken to have voluntarily accepted any risk merely because the person agreed to or knew about the term or notice.

(3) In this section 'personal injury' includes any disease and any impairment of physical or mental condition.

(4) In this section 'negligence' means the breach of—
   (a) any obligation to take reasonable care or exercise reasonable skill in the performance of a contract where the obligation arises from an express or implied term of the contract,
   (b) a common law duty to take reasonable care or exercise reasonable skill,
   (c) the common duty of care imposed by the Occupiers' Liability Act 1957 or the Occupiers' Liability Act (Northern Ireland) 1957, or
   (d) the duty of reasonable care imposed by section 2(1) of the Occupiers' Liability (Scotland) Act 1960.

(5) It is immaterial for the purposes of subsection (4)—
   (a) whether a breach of duty or obligation was inadvertent or intentional, or
   (b) whether liability for it arises directly or vicariously.

(6) This section is subject to section 66 (which makes provision about the scope of this section).

66 Scope of section 65

(1) Section 65 does not apply to—
   (a) any contract so far as it is a contract of insurance, including a contract to pay an annuity on human life, or
   (b) any contract so far as it relates to the creation or transfer of an interest in land.

(2) Section 65 does not affect the validity of any discharge or indemnity given by a person in consideration of the receipt by that person of compensation in settlement of any claim the person has.

(3) Section 65 does not—
   (a) apply to liability which is excluded or discharged as mentioned in section 4(2)(a) (exception to liability to pay damages to relatives) of the Damages (Scotland) Act 2011, or
   (b) affect the operation of section 5 (discharge of liability to pay damages: exception for mesothelioma) of that Act.

(4) Section 65 does not apply to the liability of an occupier of premises to a person who obtains access to the premises for recreational purposes if—
   (a) the person suffers loss or damage because of the dangerous state of the premises, and
   (b) allowing the person access for those purposes is not within the purposes of the occupier's trade, business, craft or profession.

67 Effect of an unfair term on the rest of a contract

Where a term of a consumer contract is not binding on the consumer as a result of this Part, the contract continues, so far as practicable, to have effect in every other respect.

68 Requirement for transparency

(1) A trader must ensure that a written term of a consumer contract, or a consumer notice in writing, is transparent.
(2) A consumer notice is transparent for the purposes of subsection (1) if it is expressed in plain and intelligible language and it is legible.

69 Contract terms that may have different meanings

(1) If a term in a consumer contract, or a consumer notice, could have different meanings, the meaning that is most favourable to the consumer is to prevail.
(2) Subsection (1) does not apply to the construction of a term or a notice in proceedings on an application for an injunction or interdict under paragraph 3 of Schedule 3.

How are the general rules enforced?

70 Enforcement of the law on unfair contract terms

(1) Schedule 3 confers functions on the Competition and Markets Authority and other regulators in relation to the enforcement of this Part.
(2) For provision about the investigatory powers that are available to those regulators for the purposes of that Schedule, see Schedule 5.

Supplementary provisions

71 Duty of court to consider fairness of term

(1) Subsection (2) applies to proceedings before a court which relate to a term of a consumer contract.
(2) The court must consider whether the term is fair even if none of the parties to the proceedings has raised that issue or indicated that it intends to raise it.
(3) But subsection (2) does not apply unless the court considers that it has before it sufficient legal and factual material to enable it to consider the fairness of the term.

72 Application of rules to secondary contracts

(1) This section applies if a term of a contract ('the secondary contract') reduces the rights or remedies or increases the obligations of a person under another contract ('the main contract').
(2) The term is subject to the provisions of this Part that would apply to the term if it were in the main contract.
(3) It does not matter for the purposes of this section—
    (a) whether the parties to the secondary contract are the same as the parties to the main contract, or
    (b) whether the secondary contract is a consumer contract.
(4) This section does not apply if the secondary contract is a settlement of a claim arising under the main contract.

223

73 Disapplication of rules to mandatory terms and notices

(1) This Part does not apply to a term of a contract, or to a notice, to the extent that it reflects—
  (a) mandatory statutory or regulatory provisions, or
  (b) the provisions or principles of an international convention to which the United Kingdom or the EU is a party.

(2) In subsection (1) 'mandatory statutory or regulatory provisions' includes rules which, according to law, apply between the parties on the basis that no other arrangements have been established.

74 Contracts applying law of non-EEA State

(1) If—
  (a) the law of a country or territory other than an EEA State is chosen by the parties to be applicable to a consumer contract, but
  (b) the consumer contract has a close connection with the United Kingdom,
  this Part applies despite that choice.

(2) For cases where the law applicable has not been chosen or the law of an EEA State is chosen, see Regulation (EC) No. 593/2008 of the European Parliament and of the Council of 17 June 2008 on the law applicable to contractual obligations.

75 Changes to other legislation

Schedule 4 (amendments consequential on this Part) has effect.

76 Interpretation of Part 2

(1) In this Part—
  • 'consumer contract' has the meaning given by section 61(3);
  • 'consumer notice' has the meaning given by section 61(7);
  • 'transparent' is to be construed in accordance with sections 64(3) and 68(2).

(2) The following have the same meanings in this Part as they have in Part 1—
  • 'trader' (see section 2(2));
  • 'consumer' (see section 2(3));
  • 'goods' (see section 2(8));
  • 'digital content' (see section 2(9)).

(3) Section 2(4) (trader who claims an individual is not a consumer must prove it) applies in relation to this Part as it applies in relation to Part 1.

PART 3
MISCELLANEOUS AND GENERAL

CHAPTER 1
Enforcement etc.

77 Investigatory powers etc

(1) Schedule 5 (investigatory powers etc) has effect.

(2) Schedule 6 (investigatory powers: consequential amendments) has effect.

78 Amendment of weights and measures legislation regarding unwrapped bread

(1) In the Weights and Measures (Packaged Goods) Regulations 2006 (S.I. 2006/659), Schedule 5 (application to bread) is amended in accordance with subsections (2) and (3).

(2) For paragraph 9 substitute—

"9 Regulation 9(1)(b)(ii) (duty to keep records) does not apply to bread which is sold unwrapped or in open packs."

(3) After paragraph 13 insert—

'Transitional provision

14(1) Regulation 9(1)(b)(ii) (duty to keep records) does not apply to a packer who holds a notice of exemption which is in force.

(2) A "notice of exemption" means a notice issued under paragraph 9 as it stood before section 78 of the Consumer Rights Act 2015 came into force.'

(4) The use of this Act to make amendments to the Weights and Measures (Packaged Goods) Regulations 2006 has no effect on the availability of any power in the Weights and Measures Act 1985 to amend or revoke those Regulations, including the provision substituted by subsection (2) and that inserted by subsection (3).

(5) In the Weights and Measures (Packaged Goods) Regulations (Northern Ireland) 2011 (SR 2011/331), Schedule 5 (application to bread) is amended in accordance with subsections (6) and (7).

(6) For paragraph 9 substitute—

'9 Regulation 9(1)(b)(ii) (duty to keep records) does not apply to bread which is sold unwrapped or in open packets.'

(7) After paragraph 13 insert—

'Transitional provision

14(1) Regulation 9(1)(b)(ii) (duty to keep records) does not apply to a packer who holds a notice of exemption which is in force.

(2) A "notice of exemption" means a notice issued under paragraph 9 as it stood before section 78 of the Consumer Rights Act 2015 came into force.'

(8) The use of this Act to make amendments to the Weights and Measures (Packaged Goods) Regulations (Northern Ireland) 2011 has no effect on the availability of any power in the Weights and Measures (Northern Ireland) Order 1981 (SI 1981/231 (NI 10)) to amend or revoke those Regulations, including the provision substituted by subsection (6) and that inserted by subsection (7).

79 Enterprise Act 2002: enhanced consumer measures and other enforcement

(1) Schedule 7 contains amendments of Part 8 of the Enterprise Act 2002 (enforcement of certain consumer legislation).

(2) The amendments have effect only in relation to conduct which occurs, or which is likely to occur, after the commencement of this section.

80 Contravention of code regulating premium rate services

(1) In section 120(3) of the Communications Act 2003 (conditions under section 120 must require compliance with directions given in accordance with an approved code or with an order under section 122) before paragraph (a) insert—

'(za)the provisions of an approved code;'

(2) In section 121(5) of that Act (provision about enforcement that may be made by approved code) after paragraph (a) insert—

  '(aa) provision that applies where there is or has been more than one contravention of the code or directions given in accordance with it by a person and which enables—

    (i) a single penalty (which does not exceed that maximum penalty) to be imposed on the person in respect of all of those contraventions, or

    (ii) separate penalties (each of which does not exceed that maximum penalty) to be imposed on the person in respect of each of those contraventions,

    according to whether the person imposing the penalty determines that a single penalty or separate penalties are appropriate and proportionate to those contraventions;'.

(3) Section 123 of that Act (enforcement by OFCOM of conditions under section 120) is amended as follows.

(4) After subsection (1) insert—

  '(1A) Subsection (1B) applies where a notification under section 94 as applied by this section relates to more than one contravention of—

    (a) a code approved under section 121,

    (b) directions given in accordance with such a code, or

    (c) an order under section 122.

  (1B) Section 96(3) as applied by this section enables OFCOM to impose—

    (a) a single penalty in respect of all of those contraventions, or

    (b) separate penalties in respect of each of those contraventions,

  according to whether OFCOM determine that a single penalty or separate penalties are appropriate and proportionate to those contraventions.'

(5) In subsection (2) (maximum amount of penalty) for 'the penalty' substitute 'each penalty'.

CHAPTER 2
Competition

81 Private actions in competition law

Schedule 8 (private actions in competition law) has effect.

82 Appointment of judges to the Competition Appeal Tribunal

(1) In section 12(2) of the Enterprise Act 2002 (constitution of the Competition Appeal Tribunal) after paragraph (a) insert—

  '(aa) such judges as are nominated from time to time by the Lord Chief Justice of England and Wales from the High Court of England and Wales;

  (ab) such judges as are nominated from time to time by the Lord President of the Court of Session from the judges of the Court of Session;

  (ac) such judges as are nominated from time to time by the Lord Chief Justice of Northern Ireland from the High Court in Northern Ireland;'.

(2) In section 14 of that Act (constitution of the Competition Appeal Tribunal for particular proceedings and its decisions)—

  (a) in subsection (2) after 'the President' insert ', a judge within any of paragraphs (aa) to (ac) of section 12(2)', and

  (b) in subsection (3) for 'either' substitute 'the judges within paragraphs (aa) to (ac) of section 12(2),'.

(3) In Schedule 4 (Tribunal procedure) to that Act, in paragraph 18(3)(b) (consequences of member of Tribunal being unable to continue) after 'if that person is not' insert 'a judge within any of paragraphs (aa) to (ac) of section 12(2) or'.

CHAPTER 3
Duty of letting agents to publicise fees etc

83 Duty of letting agents to publicise fees etc

(1) A letting agent must, in accordance with this section, publicise details of the agent's relevant fees.

(2) The agent must display a list of the fees—
  (a) at each of the agent's premises at which the agent deals face-to-face with persons using or proposing to use services to which the fees relate, and
  (b) at a place in each of those premises at which the list is likely to be seen by such persons.

(3) The agent must publish a list of the fees on the agent's website (if it has a website).

(4) A list of fees displayed or published in accordance with subsection (2) or (3) must include—
  (a) a description of each fee that is sufficient to enable a person who is liable to pay it to understand the service or cost that is covered by the fee or the purpose for which it is imposed (as the case may be),
  (b) in the case of a fee which tenants are liable to pay, an indication of whether the fee relates to each dwelling-house or each tenant under a tenancy of the dwelling-house, and
  (c) the amount of each fee inclusive of any applicable tax or, where the amount of a fee cannot reasonably be determined in advance, a description of how that fee is calculated.

(5) Subsections (6) and (7) apply to a letting agent engaging in letting agency or property management work in relation to dwelling-houses in England.

(6) If the agent holds money on behalf of persons to whom the agent provides services as part of that work, the duty imposed on the agent by subsection (2) or (3) includes a duty to display or publish, with the list of fees, a statement of whether the agent is a member of a client money protection scheme.

(7) If the agent is required to be a member of a redress scheme for dealing with complaints in connection with that work, the duty imposed on the agent by subsection (2) or (3) includes a duty to display or publish, with the list of fees, a statement—
  (a) that indicates that the agent is a member of a redress scheme, and
  (b) that gives the name of the scheme.

(8) The appropriate national authority may by regulations specify—
  (a) other ways in which a letting agent must publicise details of the relevant fees charged by the agent or (where applicable) a statement within subsection (6) or (7);
  (b) the details that must be given of fees publicised in that way.

(9) In this section—
  • 'client money protection scheme' means a scheme which enables a person on whose behalf a letting agent holds money to be compensated if all or part of that money is not repaid to that person in circumstances where the scheme applies;
  • 'redress scheme' means a redress scheme for which provision is made by order under section 83 or 84 of the Enterprise and Regulatory Reform Act 2013.

84 Letting agents to which the duty applies

(1) In this Chapter 'letting agent' means a person who engages in letting agency work (whether or not that person engages in other work).

(2) A person is not a letting agent for the purposes of this Chapter if the person engages in letting agency work in the course of that person's employment under a contract of employment.

(3) A person is not a letting agent for the purposes of this Chapter if—
    (a) the person is of a description specified in regulations made by the appropriate national authority;
    (b) the person engages in work of a description specified in regulations made by the appropriate national authority.

85 Fees to which the duty applies

(1) In this Chapter 'relevant fees', in relation to a letting agent, means the fees, charges or penalties (however expressed) payable to the agent by a landlord or tenant—
    (a) in respect of letting agency work carried on by the agent,
    (b) in respect of property management work carried on by the agent, or
    (c) otherwise in connection with—
        (i) an assured tenancy of a dwelling-house, or
        (ii) a dwelling-house that is, has been or is proposed to be let under an assured tenancy.
(2) Subsection (1) does not apply to—
    (a) the rent payable to a landlord under a tenancy,
    (b) any fees, charges or penalties which the letting agent receives from a landlord under a tenancy on behalf of another person,
    (c) a tenancy deposit within the meaning of section 212(8) of the Housing Act 2004, or
    (d) any fees, charges or penalties of a description specified in regulations made by the appropriate national authority.

86 Letting agency work and property management work

(1) In this Chapter 'letting agency work' means things done by a person in the course of a business in response to instructions received from—
    (a) a person ('a prospective landlord') seeking to find another person wishing to rent a dwelling-house under an assured tenancy and, having found such a person, to grant such a tenancy, or
    (b) a person ('a prospective tenant') seeking to find a dwelling-house to rent under an assured tenancy and, having found such a dwelling-house, to obtain such a tenancy of it.
(2) But 'letting agency work' does not include any of the following things when done by a person who does nothing else within subsection (1)—
    (a) publishing advertisements or disseminating information;
    (b) providing a means by which a prospective landlord or a prospective tenant can, in response to an advertisement or dissemination of information, make direct contact with a prospective tenant or a prospective landlord;
    (c) providing a means by which a prospective landlord and a prospective tenant can communicate directly with each other.
(3) 'Letting agency work' also does not include things done by a local authority.
(4) In this Chapter 'property management work', in relation to a letting agent, means things done by the agent in the course of a business in response to instructions received from another person where—
    (a) that person wishes the agent to arrange services, repairs, maintenance, improvements or insurance in respect of, or to deal with any other aspect of the management of, premises on the person's behalf, and
    (b) the premises consist of a dwelling-house let under an assured tenancy.

87 Enforcement of the duty

(1) It is the duty of every local weights and measures authority in England and Wales to enforce the provisions of this Chapter in its area.

(2) If a letting agent breaches the duty in section 83(3) (duty to publish list of fees etc on agent's website), that breach is taken to have occurred in each area of a local weights and measures authority in England and Wales in which a dwelling-house to which the fees relate is located.

(3) Where a local weights and measures authority in England and Wales is satisfied on the balance of probabilities that a letting agent has breached a duty imposed by or under section 83, the authority may impose a financial penalty on the agent in respect of that breach.

(4) A local weights and measures authority in England and Wales may impose a penalty under this section in respect of a breach which occurs in England and Wales but outside that authority's area (as well as in respect of a breach which occurs within that area).

(5) But a local weights and measures authority in England and Wales may impose a penalty in respect of a breach which occurs outside its area and in the area of a local weights and measures authority in Wales only if it has obtained the consent of that authority.

(6) Only one penalty under this section may be imposed on the same letting agent in respect of the same breach.

(7) The amount of a financial penalty imposed under this section—
   (a) may be such as the authority imposing it determines, but
   (b) must not exceed £5,000.

(8) Schedule 9 (procedure for and appeals against financial penalties) has effect.

(9) A local weights and measures authority in England must have regard to any guidance issued by the Secretary of State about—
   (a) compliance by letting agents with duties imposed by or under section 83;
   (b) the exercise of its functions under this section or Schedule 9.

(10) A local weights and measures authority in Wales must have regard to any guidance issued by the Welsh Ministers about—
   (a) compliance by letting agents with duties imposed by or under section 83;
   (b) the exercise of its functions under this section or Schedule 9.

(11) The Secretary of State may by regulations made by statutory instrument—
   (a) amend any of the provisions of this section or Schedule 9 in their application in relation to local weights and measures authorities in England;
   (b) make consequential amendments to Schedule 5 in its application in relation to such authorities.

(12) The Welsh Ministers may by regulations made by statutory instrument—
   (a) amend any of the provisions of this section or Schedule 9 in their application in relation to local weights and measures authorities in Wales;
   (b) make consequential amendments to Schedule 5 in its application in relation to such authorities.

88 Supplementary provisions

(1) In this Chapter—
   • 'the appropriate national authority' means—
      (a) in relation to England, the Secretary of State, and
      (b) in relation to Wales, the Welsh Ministers;
   • 'assured tenancy' means a tenancy which is an assured tenancy for the purposes of the Housing Act 1988 except where—
      (a) the landlord is—
         (i) a private registered provider of social housing,
         (ii) a registered social landlord, or
         (iii) a fully mutual housing association, or
      (b) the tenancy is a long lease;

- 'dwelling-house' may be a house or part of a house;
- 'fully mutual housing association' has the same meaning as in Part 1 of the Housing Associations Act 1985 (see section 1(1) and (2) of that Act);
- 'landlord' includes a person who proposes to be a landlord under a tenancy and a person who has ceased to be a landlord under a tenancy because the tenancy has come to an end;
- 'long lease' means a lease which—
  (a) is a long lease for the purposes of Chapter 1 of Part 1 of the Leasehold Reform, Housing and Urban Development Act 1993, or
  (b) in the case of a shared ownership lease (within the meaning given by section 7(7) of that Act), would be a lease within paragraph (a) of this definition if the tenant's total share (within the meaning given by that section) were 100%;
- 'registered social landlord' means a body registered as a social landlord under Chapter 1 of Part 1 of the Housing Act 1996;
- 'tenant' includes a person who proposes to be a tenant under a tenancy and a person who has ceased to be a tenant under a tenancy because the tenancy has come to an end.

(2) In this Chapter 'local authority' means—
  (a) a county council,
  (b) a county borough council,
  (c) a district council,
  (d) a London borough council,
  (e) the Common Council of the City of London in its capacity as local authority, or
  (f) the Council of the Isles of Scilly.

(3) References in this Chapter to a tenancy include a proposed tenancy and a tenancy that has come to an end.

(4) References in this Chapter to anything which is payable, or which a person is liable to pay, to a letting agent include anything that the letting agent claims a person is liable to pay, regardless of whether the person is in fact liable to pay it.

(5) Regulations under this Chapter are to be made by statutory instrument.

(6) A statutory instrument containing (whether alone or with other provision) regulations made by the Secretary of State under section 87(11) is not to be made unless a draft of the instrument has been laid before, and approved by a resolution of, each House of Parliament.

(7) A statutory instrument containing (whether alone or with other provision) regulations made by the Welsh Ministers under section 87(12) is not to be made unless a draft of the instrument has been laid before, and approved by a resolution of, the National Assembly for Wales.

(8) A statutory instrument containing regulations made by the Secretary of State under this Chapter other than one to which subsection (6) applies is subject to annulment in pursuance of a resolution of either House of Parliament.

(9) A statutory instrument containing regulations made by the Welsh Ministers under this Chapter other than one to which subsection (7) applies is subject to annulment in pursuance of a resolution of the National Assembly for Wales.

(10) Regulations under this Chapter—
  (a) may make different provision for different purposes;
  (b) may make provision generally or in relation to specific cases.

(11) Regulations under this Chapter may include incidental, supplementary, consequential, transitional, transitory or saving provision.

CHAPTER 4

Student complaints scheme

89 Qualifying institutions for the purposes of the student complaints scheme

(1) The Higher Education Act 2004 is amended as follows.

(2) In section 11 (qualifying institutions for the purposes of the student complaints scheme) after paragraph (d) insert—

'(e) an institution (other than one within another paragraph of this section) which provides higher education courses which are designated for the purposes of section 22 of the 1998 Act by or under regulations under that section;

(f) an institution (other than one within another paragraph of this section) whose entitlement to grant awards is conferred by an order under section 76(1) of the 1992 Act.'

(3) In section 12 (qualifying complaints for the purposes of the student complaints scheme)—

(a) in subsection (1) for 'subsection (2)' substitute 'subsections (2) and (3)', and

(b) after subsection (2) insert—

'(3) The designated operator may determine that a complaint within subsection (1) about an act or omission of a qualifying institution within paragraph (e) or (f) of section 11 is a qualifying complaint only if it is made by a person who is undertaking or has undertaken a particular course or a course of a particular description.'

CHAPTER 5

Secondary ticketing

90 Duty to provide information about tickets

(1) This section applies where a person ('the seller') re-sells a ticket for a recreational, sporting or cultural event in the United Kingdom through a secondary ticketing facility.

(2) The seller and each operator of the facility must ensure that the person who buys the ticket ('the buyer') is given the information specified in subsection (3), where this is applicable to the ticket.

(3) That information is—

(a) where the ticket is for a particular seat or standing area at the venue for the event, the information necessary to enable the buyer to identify that seat or standing area,

(b) information about any restriction which limits use of the ticket to persons of a particular description, and

(c) the face value of the ticket.

(4) The reference in subsection (3)(a) to information necessary to enable the buyer to identify a seat or standing area at a venue includes, so far as applicable—

(a) the name of the area in the venue in which the seat or standing area is located (for example the name of the stand in which it is located),

(b) information necessary to enable the buyer to identify the part of the area in the venue in which the seat or standing area is located (for example the block of seats in which the seat is located),

(c) the number, letter or other distinguishing mark of the row in which the seat is located, and

(d) the number, letter or other distinguishing mark of the seat.

(5) The reference in subsection (3)(c) to the face value of the ticket is to the amount stated on the ticket as its price.

(6) The seller and each operator of the facility must ensure that the buyer is given the information specified in subsection (7), where the seller is—

(a) an operator of the secondary ticketing facility,

(b) a person who is a parent undertaking or a subsidiary undertaking in relation to an operator of the secondary ticketing facility,

(c) a person who is employed or engaged by an operator of the secondary ticketing facility,

(d) a person who is acting on behalf of a person within paragraph (c), or

(e) an organiser of the event or a person acting on behalf of an organiser of the event.

(7) That information is a statement that the seller of the ticket is a person within subsection (6) which specifies the ground on which the seller falls within that subsection.

(8) Information required by this section to be given to the buyer must be given—

(a) in a clear and comprehensible manner, and

(b) before the buyer is bound by the contract for the sale of the ticket.

(9) This section applies in relation to the re-sale of a ticket through a secondary ticketing facility only if the ticket is first offered for re-sale through the facility after the coming into force of this section.

91 Prohibition on cancellation or blacklisting

(1) This section applies where a person ('the seller') re-sells, or offers for re-sale, a ticket for a recreational, sporting or cultural event in the United Kingdom through a secondary ticketing facility.

(2) An organiser of the event must not cancel the ticket merely because the seller has re-sold the ticket or offered it for re-sale unless—

(a) a term of the original contract for the sale of the ticket—

(i) provided for its cancellation if it was re-sold by the buyer under that contract,

(ii) provided for its cancellation if it was offered for re-sale by that buyer, or

(iii) provided as mentioned in sub-paragraph (i) and (ii), and

(b) that term was not unfair for the purposes of Part 2 (unfair terms).

(3) An organiser of the event must not blacklist the seller merely because the seller has re-sold the ticket or offered it for re-sale unless—

(a) a term of the original contract for the sale of the ticket—

(i) provided for the blacklisting of the buyer under that contract if it was re-sold by that buyer,

(ii) provided for the blacklisting of that buyer if it was offered for re-sale by that buyer, or

(iii) provided as mentioned in sub-paragraph (i) and (ii), and

(b) that term was not unfair for the purposes of Part 2 (unfair terms).

(4) In subsections (2) and (3) 'the original contract' means the contract for the sale of the ticket by an organiser of the event to a person other than an organiser of the event.

(5) For the purposes of this section an organiser of an event cancels a ticket if the organiser takes steps which result in the holder for the time being of the ticket no longer being entitled to attend that event.

(6) For the purposes of this section an organiser of an event blacklists a person if the organiser takes steps—

(a) to prevent the person from acquiring a ticket for a recreational, sporting or cultural event in the United Kingdom, or

(b) to restrict the person's opportunity to acquire such a ticket.

(7) Part 2 (unfair terms) may apply to a term of a contract which, apart from that Part, would permit the cancellation of a ticket for a recreational, sporting or cultural event in the United

Kingdom, or the blacklisting of the seller of such a ticket, in circumstances other than those mentioned in subsection (2) or (3).

(8) Before the coming into force of Part 2, references to that Part in this section are to be read as references to the Unfair Terms in Consumer Contracts Regulations 1999 (SI 1999/2083).

(9) This section applies in relation to a ticket that is re-sold or offered for re-sale before or after the coming into force of this section; but the prohibition in this section applies only to things done after its coming into force.

92 Duty to report criminal activity

(1) This section applies where—
   (a) an operator of a secondary ticketing facility knows that a person has used or is using the facility in such a way that an offence has been or is being committed, and
   (b) the offence relates to the re-sale of a ticket for a recreational, sporting or cultural event in the United Kingdom.

(2) The operator must, as soon as the operator becomes aware that a person has used or is using the facility as mentioned in subsection (1), disclose the matters specified in subsection (3) to—
   (a) an appropriate person, and
   (b) an organiser of the event (subject to subsection (5)).

(3) Those matters are—
   (a) the identity of the person mentioned in subsection (1), if this is known to the operator, and
   (b) the fact that the operator knows that an offence has been or is being committed as mentioned in that subsection.

(4) The following are appropriate persons for the purposes of this section—
   (a) a constable of a police force in England and Wales,
   (b) a constable of the police service of Scotland, and
   (c) a police officer within the meaning of the Police (Northern Ireland) Act 2000.

(5) This section does not require an operator to make a disclosure to an organiser of an event if the operator has reasonable grounds for believing that to do so will prejudice the investigation of any offence.

(6) References in this section to an offence are to an offence under the law of any part of the United Kingdom.

(7) This section applies only in relation to an offence of which an operator becomes aware after the coming into force of this section.

93 Enforcement of this Chapter

(1) A local weights and measures authority in Great Britain may enforce the provisions of this Chapter in its area.

(2) The Department of Enterprise, Trade and Investment may enforce the provisions of this Chapter in Northern Ireland.

(3) Each of the bodies referred to in subsections (1) and (2) is an 'enforcement authority' for the purposes of this Chapter.

(4) Where an enforcement authority is satisfied on the balance of probabilities that a person has breached a duty or prohibition imposed by this Chapter, the authority may impose a financial penalty on the person in respect of that breach.

(5) But in the case of a breach of a duty in section 90 or a prohibition in section 91 an enforcement authority may not impose a financial penalty on a person ('P') if the authority is satisfied on the balance of probabilities that—

    (a) the breach was due to—
       (i) a mistake,
       (ii) reliance on information supplied to P by another person,
       (iii) the act or default of another person,
       (iv) an accident, or
       (v) another cause beyond P's control, and
    (b) P took all reasonable precautions and exercised all due diligence to avoid the breach.

(6) A local weights and measures authority in England and Wales may impose a penalty under this section in respect of a breach which occurs in England and Wales but outside that authority's area (as well as in respect of a breach which occurs within that area).

(7) A local weights and measures authority in Scotland may impose a penalty under this section in respect of a breach which occurs in Scotland but outside that authority's area (as well as in respect of a breach which occurs within that area).

(8) Only one penalty under this section may be imposed on the same person in respect of the same breach.

(9) The amount of a financial penalty imposed under this section—
    (a) may be such as the enforcement authority imposing it determines, but
    (b) must not exceed £5,000.

(10) Schedule 10 (procedure for and appeals against financial penalties) has effect.

(11) References in this section to this Chapter do not include section 94.

94 Duty to review measures relating to secondary ticketing

(1) The Secretary of State must—
    (a) review, or arrange for a review of, consumer protection measures applying to the re-sale of tickets for recreational, sporting or cultural events in the United Kingdom through secondary ticketing facilities,
    (b) prepare a report on the outcome of the review or arrange for such a report to be prepared, and
    (c) publish that report.

(2) The report must be published before the end of the period of 12 months beginning with the day on which this section comes into force.

(3) The Secretary of State must lay the report before Parliament.

(4) In this section 'consumer protection measures' includes such legislation, rules of law, codes of practice and guidance as the Secretary of State considers relate to the rights of consumers or the protection of their interests.

95 Interpretation of this Chapter

(1) In this Chapter—
- 'enforcement authority' has the meaning given by section 93(3);
- 'operator', in relation to a secondary ticketing facility, means a person who—
    (a) exercises control over the operation of the facility, and
    (b) receives revenue from the facility,
    but this is subject to regulations under subsection (2);
- 'organiser', in relation to an event, means a person who—
    (a) is responsible for organising or managing the event, or
    (b) receives some or all of the revenue from the event;
- 'parent undertaking' has the meaning given by section 1162 of the Companies Act 2006;
- 'secondary ticketing facility' means an internet-based facility for the re-sale of tickets for recreational, sporting or cultural events;

- 'subsidiary undertaking' has the meaning given by section 1162 of the Companies Act 2006;
- 'undertaking' has the meaning given by section 1161(1) of the Companies Act 2006.

(2) The Secretary of State may by regulations provide that a person of a description specified in the regulations is or is not to be treated for the purposes of this Chapter as an operator in relation to a secondary ticketing facility.

(3) Regulations under subsection (2)—
   (a) are to be made by statutory instrument;
   (b) may make different provision for different purposes;
   (c) may include incidental, supplementary, consequential, transitional, transitory or saving provision.

(4) A statutory instrument containing regulations under subsection (2) is not to be made unless a draft of the instrument has been laid before, and approved by a resolution of, each House of Parliament.

CHAPTER 6
General

96 Power to make consequential provision

(1) The Secretary of State may by order made by statutory instrument make provision in consequence of this Act.

(2) The power conferred by subsection (1) includes power—
   (a) to amend, repeal, revoke or otherwise modify any provision made by an enactment or an instrument made under an enactment (including an enactment passed or instrument made in the same Session as this Act);
   (b) to make transitional, transitory or saving provision.

(3) A statutory instrument containing (whether alone or with other provision) an order under this section which amends, repeals, revokes or otherwise modifies any provision of primary legislation is not to be made unless a draft of the instrument has been laid before, and approved by a resolution of, each House of Parliament.

(4) A statutory instrument containing an order under this section which does not amend, repeal, revoke or otherwise modify any provision of primary legislation is subject to annulment in pursuance of a resolution of either House of Parliament.

(5) In this section—
- 'enactment' includes an Act of the Scottish Parliament, a Measure or Act of the National Assembly for Wales and Northern Ireland legislation;
- 'primary legislation' means—
   (a) an Act of Parliament,
   (b) an Act of the Scottish Parliament,
   (c) a Measure or Act of the National Assembly for Wales, and
   (d) Northern Ireland legislation.

97 Power to make transitional, transitory and saving provision

(1) The Secretary of State may by order made by statutory instrument make transitional, transitory or saving provision in connection with the coming into force of any provision of this Act other than the coming into force of Chapter 3 or 4 of this Part in relation to Wales.

(2) The Welsh Ministers may by order made by statutory instrument make transitional, transitory or saving provision in connection with the coming into force of Chapter 3 or 4 of this Part in relation to Wales.

98 Financial provision

There is to be paid out of money provided by Parliament—

(a) any expenses incurred by a Minister of the Crown or a government department under this Act, and

(b) any increase attributable to this Act in the sums payable under any other Act out of money so provided.

99 Extent

(1) The amendment, repeal or revocation of any provision by this Act has the same extent as the provision concerned.

(2) Section 27 extends only to Scotland.

(3) Chapter 3 of this Part extends only to England and Wales.

(4) Subject to that, this Act extends to England and Wales, Scotland and Northern Ireland.

100 Commencement

(1) The provisions of this Act listed in subsection (2) come into force on the day on which this Act is passed.

(2) Those provisions are—

   (a) section 48(5) to (8),

   (b) Chapter 3 of this Part in so far as it confer powers to make regulations,

   (c) section 88(5) to (11),

   (d) this Chapter, and

   (e) paragraph 12 of Schedule 5.

(3) Chapters 3 and 4 of this Part come into force—

   (a) in relation to England, on such day as the Secretary of State may appoint by order made by statutory instrument;

   (b) in relation to Wales, on such day as the Welsh Ministers may appoint by order made by statutory instrument.

(4) Chapter 5 of this Part comes into force at the end of the period of two months beginning with the day on which this Act is passed.

(5) The other provisions of this Act come into force on such day as the Secretary of State may appoint by order made by statutory instrument.

(6) An order under this section may appoint different days for different purposes.

101 Short title

This Act may be cited as the Consumer Rights Act 2015.

APPENDIX 2

Explanatory Notes
Consumer Rights Act 2015
Chapter 15

26 March 2015

INTRODUCTION

1. These explanatory notes relate to the Consumer Rights Act 2015 which received Royal Assent on 26 March 2015. They have been prepared by the Department for Business, Innovation and Skills in order to assist the reader in understanding the Act. They do not form part of the Act and have not been endorsed by Parliament.

2. The notes need to be read in conjunction with the Act. They are not, and are not meant to be, a comprehensive description of the Act. So where a section or part of a section does not seem to require any explanation or comments, none is given.

SUMMARY AND BACKGROUND

3. The Consumer Rights Act 2015 sets out a framework that consolidates in one place key consumer rights covering contracts for goods, services, digital content and the law relating to unfair terms in consumer contracts. In addition, the Act introduces easier routes for consumers and small and medium sized enterprises ('SMEs') to challenge anti-competitive behaviour through the Competition Appeal Tribunal ('CAT'). The Act clarifies the maximum penalties that the regulator of premium rate services can impose on non-compliant and rogue operators. It also consolidates enforcers' powers as listed in Schedule 5 to investigate potential breaches of consumer law and clarifies that certain enforcers (Trading Standards) can operate across local authority boundaries. It will also give the civil courts and public enforcers greater flexibility to take the most appropriate action for consumers when dealing with breaches or potential breaches of consumer law. Additionally, it changes the way in which judges are able to sit as chairs in the CAT; and imposes a duty on letting agents to publish their fees and other information. Further, the Act expands the list of higher education providers which are required to join the higher education complaints handling scheme, and includes certain requirements relating to resale of tickets for recreational, sporting and cultural events.

4. The Act is in three Parts:

- Consumer contracts for goods, digital content and services;
- Unfair terms; and
- Miscellaneous and general, including investigatory powers; amendment of the Weights and Measures (Packaged Goods) Regulations 2006; enhanced consumer measures and other enforcement under the Enterprise Act 2002; clarification of the maximum penalties that the

regulator of premium rate services can impose on non-compliant and rogue operators; private actions in competition law; a change in the way in which judges are able to sit as chairs in the CAT; a duty on letting agents to publicise fees and other information; expansion of the list of higher education providers which are required to join the higher education complaints handling scheme; and certain requirements relating to resale of tickets for recreational, sporting and cultural events.

Background

5. There is general agreement across business and consumer groups that the existing UK consumer law is unnecessarily complex. It is fragmented and, in places, unclear, for example where the law has not kept up with technological change or lacks precision or where it is couched in legalistic language. There are also overlaps and inconsistencies between changes made by virtue of implementing European Union ('EU') legislation alongside unamended pre-existing UK legislation.

6. The law that protects consumers when they enter into contracts has developed piecemeal over time. Initially it was the courts that recognised that a person buying goods has certain clear and justified, but sometimes unspoken, expectations. The courts developed a body of case law which gave buyers rights when these expectations were not met. This case law was then made into legislation that protected buyers when buying goods, originally in the Sale of Goods Act 1893, updated by the Sale of Goods Act 1979 ('SGA'). These rights were then extended by the introduction of the Supply of Goods and Services Act 1982 ('SGSA') to cover the situations when goods were provided other than by sale (for example when someone hires goods). The SGSA also covers (in relation to England, Wales and Northern Ireland) certain protections for the recipients of services supplied by traders. Legislation setting out rules on unfairness in contract terms was established domestically in the Unfair Contract Terms Act 1977 ('UCTA'). These pieces of legislation currently cover more than just consumer contracts but certain of their provisions offer extra protection to consumers (as opposed to other types of buyers).

7. The EU has also legislated to protect consumers and so the UK legislation has been amended to incorporate this European legislation; sometimes this has been implemented in domestic law without resolving inconsistencies or overlaps.

8. The relevant domestic law is currently mainly contained in the following legislation:

- Supply of Goods (Implied Terms) Act 1973
- Sale of Goods Act 1979
- Supply of Goods and Services Act 1982
- Sale and Supply of Goods Act 1994
- Sale and Supply of Goods to Consumers Regulations 2002
- Unfair Contract Terms Act 1977
- Unfair Terms in Consumer Contracts Regulations 1999
- Unfair Terms in Consumer Contracts (Amendment) Regulations 2001
- Competition Act 1998
- Enterprise Act 2002

9. The European Directives implemented in the Act are:

- Directive 99/44/EC of the European Parliament and of the Council on certain aspects of the sale of consumer goods and associated guarantees;
- Directive 93/13/EEC of the Council on unfair terms in consumer contracts;
- Some provisions of Directive 2011/83/EU of the European Parliament and of the Council on consumer rights. See sections 11, 12, 36, 37 and 50 in relation to the enforcement of

information requirements and also see paragraph 11 below. See also section 28 in relation to default rules for the delivery of goods, and section 29 regarding the passing of risk in goods.

10. In addition, the Act implements some provisions (in respect of enforcement) of:

- Regulation (EC) No. 2006/2004 of the European Parliament and of the Council on cooperation between national authorities responsible for the enforcement of consumer protection laws;
- Regulation (EC) No. 765/2008 of the European Parliament and of the Council setting out the requirements for accreditation and market surveillance relating to the marketing of products;
- Directive 2001/95/EC of the European Parliament and of the Council on general product safety; and
- Directive 98/27/EC of the European Parliament and of the Council on injunctions for the protection of consumers' interests.

Wider reforms to the consumer legislation framework

11. In addition to the Act, the Consumer Contracts (Information, Cancellation and Additional Charges) Regulations 2013 implement Directive 2011/83/EU of the European Parliament and of the Council on consumer rights (commonly known as the Consumer Rights Directive ('CRD')) in regulations made under the European Communities Act 1972. These regulations came into force on 13 June 2014. However, a small number of the CRD's provisions are implemented in the Act, as indicated above. The CRD:

- for all contracts where a trader supplies goods, services or digital content to a consumer, requires that a trader must provide certain information (for example on the main characteristics of the goods, services and digital content) before the consumer is bound by the contract;
- specifies the consumer's cancellation rights (during so-called 'cooling off periods') for goods, services and digital content contracts concluded at a distance or off premises; and
- introduces various measures aimed at protecting consumers from hidden charges once they have entered into a contract.

12. A consultation by the Department for Business Innovation and Skills ('BIS') in August 2012 sought views on implementing the CRD in particular highlighting those areas where the UK had some flexibility in the way it might be applied. A Government response was published in August 2013. Part of the CRD was implemented early as the Consumer Rights (Payment Surcharges) Regulations 2012, and the remainder was implemented with effect from 13 June 2014 as the Consumer Contracts (Information, Cancellation and Additional Charges) Regulations 2013.

13. In developing proposals for the Consumer Rights Act 2015, the Government has taken into account the definitions and measures contained within the CRD and, as far as appropriate, has made the Act consistent with the CRD, with the intention of achieving overall a simple, coherent framework of consumer legislation.

14. The Government has also implemented the majority of the recommendations made by the Law Commission and Scottish Law Commission ('the Law Commissions') following their findings that the law surrounding consumer rights to redress following misleading or aggressive practices by traders is fragmented, complex and unclear. The Consumer Protection (Amendment) Regulations 2014 amend the Consumer Protection from Unfair Trading Regulations 2008 ('CPRs') and, as such, this reform did not need to be introduced within the Consumer Rights Act 2015. The new rights came into force on 1 October 2014 and give consumers the right to unwind a contract or payment, or receive a discount on the price paid, if they are subjected to misleading or aggressive practices. The Government published its response to its consultation on the draft regulations on 2 April 2014.

Advice and consultations

15. The University of East Anglia concluded in 2008 that the UK consumer protection regime had two key weaknesses—uneven enforcement and excessively complex law. A call for evidence in the Consumer Law Review in 2008 revealed strong support across the board for consolidating consumer legislation, making it clearer and more accessible. Respondents highlighted a number of benefits that a rewrite would bring—removing discrepancies and inconsistencies, greater use of plain English, greater awareness of rights, remedies and obligations, greater flexibility, future proofing and aiding business growth.

16. A number of consultations and academic research papers over several years have examined proposals that form part of this Act. A single Government response to BIS consultations between March and November 2012 and a report by the Law Commissions of March 2013 (detailed below) was published alongside a draft Bill with accompanying explanatory notes. The draft Bill was scrutinised by the House of Commons Business Innovation and Skills Committee. The Committee published a report in December 2013.

PART 1

17. The Davidson report in 2006, which examined the transposition of European Directives into domestic law, concluded that UK law on the sale of goods was unnecessarily complex. The Law Commissions consulted on potential changes to the law on remedies for faulty goods and made recommendations in 2009. Professors G. Howells and C. Twigg-Flesner examined the law on goods and services in 2010 and made recommendations to BIS on how the law could be clarified and simplified. Also in 2010, Professor Bradgate reported to BIS on the uncertainty in current law around consumer rights to quality for digital content products. Following these various reports, BIS consulted from July to October 2012 on proposals to clarify consumer rights in goods, services and digital content.

PART 2

18. Legislation on unfair contract terms is contained in the UCTA, which currently applies to contracts between businesses and between consumers but contains some particular rules about business to consumer contracts. It makes some terms in contracts automatically non-binding and subjects others to a test of reasonableness. The Unfair Terms in Consumer Contract Regulations 1999 ('UTCCRs') enable consumers to challenge most non-negotiated terms of a contract on the grounds that they are unfair. There are certain terms that cannot be assessed for fairness: terms that relate to the definition of the main subject matter of the contract and those that relate to the adequacy of the price or remuneration as against the goods or services supplied in exchange. These are known as 'exempt terms'. In August 2002 the Law Commissions issued a consultation proposing a unified law on unfair contracts terms and, in February 2005, they issued a report setting out detailed recommendations, which was published alongside a draft Bill. These recommendations were not taken forward at the time. However, in May 2012 the Parliamentary Under-Secretary of State for Employment Relations, Consumer and Postal Affairs, Norman Lamb MP, asked the Law Commissions to look again at unifying a regime on unfair terms in consumer contracts, focusing on the exempt terms. From July to October 2012 the Law Commissions sought views on a discussion paper on revised proposals for the exempt terms and made recommendations to BIS in March 2013 concerning terms in consumer contracts.

PART 3

19. There are a number of pieces of legislation that set out rights and duties on traders. To ensure effective enforcement of these rights and duties, enforcers such as local weights and measures authorities (known as 'Trading Standards') and other regulators (such as the Competition and Markets Authority ('CMA')) have powers to investigate compliance. These investigatory powers are usually set out in the individual pieces of legislation creating the rights or duties and whilst largely similar, have some differences between them. In March 2012, BIS published a consultation on consolidating and modernising enforcement officers' investigatory powers into a generic set. It also consulted on removing the barriers to trading standards operating efficiently. Additionally, views were also sought on reducing burdens on business by introducing certain safeguards on the use of these powers, such as requiring officers to give reasonable notice of routine visits, unless there are good reasons for them to be unannounced.

20. In November 2012, BIS published a consultation paper on extending the range of remedies available to courts when public enforcers apply to them for enforcement orders under Part 8 of the Enterprise Act 2002 ('EA').

21. Research by the OFT showed that businesses view the present approach to private actions by consumers and businesses as one of the least effective aspects of the UK competition regime. BIS consulted on measures to make it easier and simpler for businesses and consumers to challenge anti-competitive behaviour in April 2012 and Government published its response in January 2013.

Structure of the Act

22. The Act consists of three parts and ten Schedules. The general arrangement of the Act is as follows:

Part	Summary
Part 1	• Sets out the standards that goods must meet.
	• Consolidates and aligns the currently inconsistent remedies available to consumers for goods supplied under different contract types, such as sale, work and materials, conditional sale or hire purchase.
	• Sets a time period of 30 days in which consumers can reject substandard goods and be entitled to a full refund.
	• Limits the number of repairs or replacements of substandard goods before traders must offer some money back.
	• Sets limits on the extent to which traders may reduce the level of refund (where goods are not rejected initially) to take account of the use of the goods the consumer has had up to that point.
	• Introduces a new category of digital content.
	• Introduces tailored quality rights for digital content.
	• Introduces tailored remedies if the digital content rights are not met.
	• Introduces a new statutory right that if a trader provides information in relation to a service, and the consumer takes this information into account, the service must comply with that information.
	• Introduces new statutory remedies when things go wrong with a service.
	• Makes it clear that consumers can always request these rights and remedies when a trader supplies a service to them.

(Continued)

(*Continued*)

Part	Summary
Part 2 including Schedules 2, 3 and 4	• Consolidates the legislation governing unfair contract terms in relation to consumer contracts, which currently is found in two separate pieces of legislation, into one place, removes anomalies and overlapping provisions in relation to consumer contracts. • Makes clearer the circumstances when the price or subject matter of the contract cannot be considered for fairness and in particular makes clear that to avoid being considered for fairness those terms must be transparent and prominent. • Clarifies the role of and extends the indicative list of terms which may be regarded as unfair (the so-called 'grey list').
Part 3 including Schedules 5, 6, 7, 8, 9 and 10	• Consolidates and simplifies the investigatory powers of consumer law enforcers in relation to the listed legislation and sets them out in one place as a generic set. • Clarifies the law so that trading standards are able to work across local authority boundaries as simply and efficiently as possible. • Introduces new powers for public enforcers to seek, through applying to the civil courts: • Redress for consumers who have been disadvantaged by breaches of consumer law; • Remedies from traders who have breached consumer law to improve their compliance and reduce the likelihood of future breaches, and/or • Remedies to give consumers more information so they can exercise greater choice and help improve the functioning of the market for consumers and other businesses. • Includes a power for the Secretary of State to extend the use of the enhanced consumer measures to private designated enforcers providing certain conditions are met and subject to safeguards on their use. • Clarifies the maximum penalties that the regulator of premium rate services can impose on non-compliant and rogue operators. • Establishes the CAT as a major venue for competition actions in the UK. • Introduces a limited opt-out collective actions regime, with safeguards, for competition law. • Promotes ADR for competition cases. • Changes the way in which judges are able to sit as chairs in the Competition Appeals Tribunal (CAT). • Imposes a duty on letting agents to publicise fees and a statement of whether or not they are a member of a client money protection scheme and which redress scheme they have joined. • Expands the list of higher education providers which are required to join the higher education complaints handling scheme. • Includes certain requirements relating to resale of tickets for recreational, sporting and cultural events.

Impact on existing legislation

23. The Act brings together key consumer rights from all the enactments listed in paragraph 8 above. It will harmonise existing provisions to give a single approach where appropriate.

24. The provisions in the existing legislation listed below which cover trader to consumer contracts only will be repealed. The provisions which relate to other types of contract (for example contracts between businesses) will remain in the existing legislation.

Supply of Goods (Implied Terms) Act 1973	For business to consumer contracts the provisions of the Supply of Goods (Implied Terms) Act 1973 ('SGITA') will be replaced by the Consumer Rights Act 2015. It will be amended so that it covers business to business contracts and consumer to consumer contracts only.

Sale of Goods Act 1979	For business to consumer contracts this will mainly be replaced by the Consumer Rights Act 2015 but some provisions of SGA will still apply, for example, rules which are applicable to all contracts of sale of goods (as defined by that Act – essentially these are sales of goods for money), regarding matters such as when property in goods passes. The SGA will still apply to business to business contracts and to consumer to consumer contracts.
Supply of Goods and Services Act 1982	For business to consumer contracts, this Act's provisions will be replaced by the Consumer Rights Act 2015. The SGSA will be amended so that it covers business to business contracts and consumer to consumer contracts only.
Sale and Supply of Goods Act 1994	This Act amended the SGA and the SGSA and as such will be superseded by provisions in the Consumer Rights Act 2015 for business to consumer contracts.
Sale and Supply of Goods to Consumers Regulations 2002	These will be replaced by provisions in the Consumer Rights Act 2015.
Unfair Contract Terms Act 1977	In respect of business to consumer contracts the Act's provisions will be replaced by the Consumer Rights Act 2015. The UCTA will be amended so that it covers business to business and consumer to consumer contracts only.
Unfair Terms in Consumer Contracts Regulations 1999	These will be replaced by the Consumer Rights Act 2015.

Territorial extent and application

25. The Act extends to England and Wales, Scotland and Northern Ireland as described below.

26. Parts 1 to 3 largely extend to the whole of the UK. Some of Part 3 does not apply to Scotland or Northern Ireland because of the differences in the law. For example, the provision relating to the Competition Appeal Tribunal issuing injunctions in private actions does not apply to Scotland, and some of the legislation which Part 3 proposes to amend does not extend to Scotland or Northern Ireland, e.g. the Sunday Trading Act 1994. Chapter 3 of Part 3 (duty on letting agents to publicise fees) extends only to England and Wales, and applies in relation to the fees charged by agents in the course of the letting and management of privately rented property in England and Wales. However, the requirement for letting agents to publicise whether or not they are a member of a client money protection scheme and which redress scheme they have joined applies only to England. The obligation to expand the requirement to join the complaints handling scheme in higher education applies to England and Wales on the basis that the original legislation extends to England and Wales only.

Which country's law governs the contract?

27. European Regulation EC 593/2008 on the law applicable to contractual obligations sets out the rules as to which country's law applies to consumer contracts. It is known as the 'Rome I Regulation'. It confirms that it is open to a consumer and a trader to choose the law of any country to govern their contract. Where they do not choose, if a trader pursues its activities in or directs its activities to the UK, (whether the trader is in the UK or not) and the contract covers those activities, the Rome I Regulation provides that a contract with a consumer habitually living

in the UK will be governed by UK law. Even if the consumer and trader do choose another country's law to govern their contract, the Rome I Regulation provides that where the trader pursues or directs its activities to the UK and the consumer is habitually resident in the UK, any UK protections that parties cannot contract out of under UK law (such as the key protections covered by this Act) will still apply. Depending on the circumstances, pursuing or directing activities might, for example, include having a website translated into English or with a '.uk' web address from which consumers in the UK can purchase goods, services or digital content in sterling.

28. Some of the provisions regarding goods and unfair terms will also apply in other circumstances, due to protections in the Directives from which these derive. See the notes on sections 32 and 74 below.

Transposition of EU Directives

29. The Act does not itself implement EU Directives for the first time with the exception of certain parts of Articles 5, 6 18, 20 and 23 of the CRD which are implemented in Part 1 as detailed above in paragraph 9. Other than this, the Act replaces earlier legislation which has implemented EU Directives, most of which is set out in paragraph 9 above.

COMMENTARY ON SECTIONS
PART 1:
CONSUMER CONTRACTS FOR GOODS,
DIGITAL CONTENT AND SERVICES

Section 1: Where Part 1 applies

30. The main purpose behind section 1 is to make clear the scope of Part 1 of the Act. Part 1 is concerned with contracts between a trader and a consumer under which a trader agrees to supply goods, digital content or services (or any combination of these) to a consumer. It does not matter whether the contract is written or oral or implied by the conduct of the trader and consumer, or a combination of these. This means that, for the Part to have effect, there must be a *contract* and the contract must be for a *trader* to supply goods, digital content or services to a *consumer*.

31. At its most basic level, for a contract to be formed under the law of England and Wales or Northern Ireland there needs to be an offer and acceptance (i.e. one party must express a willingness to contract on certain terms and the other party must agree to those terms); and there must be 'consideration,' which is to say that both sides must offer something to the other (e.g. money in return for goods). In Scots law there is no requirement for consideration but the parties' agreement must show an intention to be legally bound. As well as using words, a contract could be implied by conduct of the parties, for example, by jumping into a black cab and stating your destination, this conduct would be taken as an agreement that the taxi driver will take you to your destination and that you will pay a price for it.

32. *Subsections* (4) to (6) set out the position with regard to 'mixed contracts'. There are many examples of mixed contracts, for example contracts involving the supply of both goods and services (e.g. a car service where parts are fitted) or digital content and a service (e.g. supplying and installing anti-virus software). In such contracts, under the Act, the service element of the contract attracts service rights and remedies, the goods elements attract goods rights and remedies and the digital content elements attract the digital content rights and remedies. *Subsection* (3) therefore makes clear that, for such mixed contracts, it will be relevant to look at the rights and remedies for each element of the mixed contract. In most cases it will be relevant to look at the appropriate chapter of the Act (Chapter 2 for goods, 3 for digital content and 4 for services).

Subsection (6) sets out that for particular mixed contracts (goods and installation services, and goods and digital content) it may also be relevant to look at sections 15 and 16.

33. *Subsection* (7) makes clear that consumer contracts are subject to provisions in Part 2 on unfair terms. In addition to the provisions of the Act, some provisions of SGA will continue to apply to trader-to-consumer contracts if they are contracts of sale as defined by SGA (essentially sales of goods for money). The provisions of SGA which continue to cover such contracts are:

- Sections 1-10 (certain provisions regarding formation of the contract)
- Section 11 with the exception of subsection (4) (when condition to be treated as a warranty)
- Sections 16-19, 20A and 20B (certain provisions regarding transfer of property)
- Sections 21-28 (provisions regarding transfer of title, duties of seller and buyer and payment and delivery being concurrent conditions)
- Section 29 with the exception of subsection (3) (rules about delivery)
- Section 34 (buyer's right of examining goods)—the consumer's remedies, if the goods are found to breach the statutory requirements under the Consumer Rights Act 2015, are still as set out in the Consumer Rights Act 2015
- Section 37 (buyer's liability for not taking delivery of goods)
- Part V (rights of unpaid seller against the goods)
- Sections 49-50 (seller's remedies)
- Section 57 (auction sales)
- Sections 60-62 (rights enforceable by action; interpretation and savings)

Section 2: Key definitions

34. One of the policy objectives is to align, as far as possible, the definitions of certain key terms across the Act and other consumer law, such as the Consumer Contracts (Information, Cancellation and Additional Charges) Regulations 2013 which implement the CRD, to facilitate easier interpretation and clearer application of the law. These terms are 'trader,' 'consumer,' 'goods' and 'digital content'. To ensure as much consistency as possible, the definitions of these key terms in the Act are based largely on the definitions within the CRD. This section sets out these key definitions in a section separate from the general interpretation section (section 59, which sets definitions of the other terms used in Part 1 of the Act that need definition) because they are vitally important to understanding the scope of the Act. 'Service' is also a key concept but is not defined by the Act; it was not defined in the SGSA.

35. *Subsection* (2) makes clear that a trader is a person acting for purposes relating to their trade, business, craft or profession. It makes clear that a trader acting through another person acting in the trader's name or on the trader's behalf, for example a trader which subcontracts part of a building contract or a company for which the employees make contracts with customers, is liable for proper performance of the contract. A 'person' is not just a natural person but can also include companies, charities and arms of government (and the reference to a 'person' can also include more than one person). So where these types of body are acting for purposes relating to their trade, business, craft or profession, they are caught by the definition of trader. *Subsection* (7) makes clear that a 'business' includes the activities of government departments and local and public authorities, which means that these bodies may therefore come within the definition of a trader. Not-for-profit organisations, such as charities, mutuals and cooperatives, may also come within the definition of a trader, for example, if a charity shop sells t-shirts or mugs, they would be acting within the meaning of trader.

36. Another key definition is the definition of 'consumer'. Firstly, a consumer must be an 'individual' (that is, a natural person)—the Act's protection for consumers does not apply to small businesses or legally incorporated organisations (e.g. companies formed by groups of residents). If a group of consumers contracts for goods, services or digital content, they are not left without protection. For example if one consumer makes all the arrangements for a group to go to the theatre

or to go on holiday, depending on the circumstances, each member of the group may be able to enforce their rights or the person who made the arrangements may have to enforce the rights on behalf of the group. The other main restriction on who is a consumer is that a consumer must be acting wholly or mainly outside their trade, business, craft or profession. This means, for example, that a person who buys a kettle for their home, works from home one day a week and uses it on the days when working from home would still be a consumer. Conversely a sole trader that operates from a private dwelling who buys a printer of which 95% of the use is for the purposes of the business, is not likely to be held to be a consumer (and therefore the rights in this Part will not protect that sole trader but they would have to look to other legislation. For example, if the sole trader were buying goods, they would have to look to the SGA for protections about the quality of the goods).

37. *Subsection* (5) excludes (for some purposes) from the definition of consumers those acquiring second-hand goods at an auction which they have the opportunity to attend in person. This derives from the CSD (Article 1(3)), and the previous definition of 'dealing as a consumer' under the UCTA. This exclusion applies to the Goods provisions in Chapter 2 only, other than those derived from the CRD (as the scope of the CRD is not subject to this exclusion)—its application is set out in *subsection* (6) and in the relevant sections.

38. *Subsection* (8) sets out another key definition: the meaning of 'goods'. This derives from Article 2(3) of the CRD. Essentially 'goods' means anything physical which you can move ('any tangible moveable item'). Therefore, Chapter 2 of Part 1 of the Act (the goods Chapter) does not apply to purchases of immovable property such as land or a house. However, this subsection makes clear the meaning of goods can include certain utilities (water, gas and electricity) where they are put up for sale in a limited volume or set quantity. Examples of these are a gas cylinder, a bottle of water or a battery. Section 3 contains further provision on the scope of the contracts for goods covered by the Act.

39. The definition of digital content in *subsection* (9) is the same as the definition in the CRD (data produced and supplied in digital form). Digital content may be supplied on a tangible medium (in which case special rules apply) for example a DVD or software, on a computer or not, for example an e-book or music download. The creation of a category of digital content in this Act does not affect the treatment of digital content in any other legislation.

CHAPTER 2:
GOODS

Summary and Background

40. This Chapter concerns contracts where a trader supplies goods to a consumer. It sets out:

- The rights a consumer has when a trader supplies goods under contract (the notes on section 1 explain how a contract may be formed). These are in effect contractual rights and if they are breached it is therefore a breach of contract;
- the statutory remedies to which the consumer is entitled if these rights are breached: namely a right to reject the goods within an initial period, a right to repair or replacement and a subsequent right to a reduction in the price (keeping the goods) or to reject the goods for a refund (subject to deduction for use in some cases);
- that the statutory remedies do not prevent the consumer claiming other remedies from the trader where they are available according to general contract law (e.g. damages); and
- that the trader cannot limit or exclude liability for breaches of the above rights, in most cases.

41. Currently (that is, until Chapter 2 and section 60 of the Act come into force), provisions relating to contracts to supply goods are contained within several different pieces of law. The

SGA, the SGSA and the SGITA each contain provisions which apply, depending on the type of contract. Much of the legislation in place prior to the Act coming into force applies to recipients of goods (whether or not they are consumers), but some protections apply only to consumers.

Contract Type	Description	Current applicable legislation (until Act comes into force)
Sale	Supply of goods in exchange for money.	SGA
Conditional sale	Sale where the consumer pays in instalments and only obtains ownership of the goods when the final payment is made (or other conditions are satisfied), although the consumer may use the goods in the meantime.	SGA
Hire purchase	A contract of hire with an option or condition to buy at the end of the hiring period	SGITA
Barter or exchange	Where goods are exchanged for a consideration other than money	SGSA
Work and materials	Where the contract includes both the provision of a service and the supply of associated goods	SGSA
Hire of goods	A contract of hire where there is no intention that ownership of the goods will be transferred	SGSA

42. The current legislation provides that goods must meet certain standards—such as being of satisfactory quality, fit for purpose, corresponding to descriptions or samples by which they are supplied, and being free from third parties' rights—and provides that the trader must have the right to sell (or hire) the goods. These matters are treated in the current legislation as 'implied terms' of a contract. Implied terms are terms that are not expressly set out in a contract (which are 'express terms') but still form part of the contract.

43. The current legislation categorises these implied terms as 'conditions' of the contract or 'warranties' (save in relation to Scotland as this terminology does not apply in Scots law, but the legislation provides an equivalent effect). Most of the statutory implied terms are categorised as conditions, breach of which enables the consumer to choose either to treat the contract as terminated or to continue with the contract (i.e. keep the goods) but claim damages. The implied terms regarding goods being free from third parties' rights are classified as 'warranties', where a breach is relatively less serious but could give rise to a claim for damages. The current legislation also sets out statutory remedies for consumers, where the implied terms regarding quality, fitness for purpose and corresponding to descriptions or samples are breached in contracts other than for hire or hire purchase. The statutory remedies are repair or replacement of goods, followed in some circumstances by termination of contract or receiving an appropriate reduction from the price.

44. In 2008 the Law Commission and Scottish Law Commission consulted on 'Consumer Remedies for Faulty Goods', and published a report in 2009. Some of the provisions in this Chapter build on the Law Commissions' recommendations.

45. In 2010 the Department for Business, Innovation and Skills ('BIS') commissioned a report, entitled 'Consolidation and Simplification of UK Consumer Law' to examine how existing consumer law might be consolidated and simplified to make it more accessible to consumers, business and their advisers. That report recommended that consumer contract law would be improved if many of the provisions could be brought together into a single consumer contract law that so far as possible subjected all consumer supply contracts to the same rights

and remedies. The report recommended that the remedies for goods would be made clearer and more accessible by incorporating them into a single piece of legislation and aligning the remedies as much as possible.

46. Following these reports, BIS consulted in July 2012 on proposals for reform of the law regarding contractual supplies to consumers of goods, as well as of services and digital content. This consultation included proposals building on the 2009 and 2010 reports.

47. A draft Bill was published in June 2013 and scrutinised by the House of Commons Business Innovation and Skills Committee. The Committee published its report in December 2013.

What goods contracts are covered?

Sections 3-8: Consumer contracts about goods

48. Section 3 sets out what contracts are covered by Chapter 2. The provisions contained in this Chapter apply in most cases where a trader agrees to supply goods to a consumer under a contract—such a contract is referred to in the Act as a 'contract to supply goods'. Chapter 2 applies whether the goods are supplied immediately or the parties agree that the trader will supply them at a future time. (The terms 'trader', 'consumer' and 'goods' are addressed in section 2).

49. *Subsection* (3) provides that the Chapter does not apply to certain contracts. Such contracts therefore do not count as 'contracts to supply goods'.

50. Subsection (3)(a) of section 3 excludes from scope contracts where the goods in question are coins or notes to be used for currency, though coins and notes supplied for another purpose (e.g. bought as a collector's item) are covered.

51. Subsection (3)(b) of section 3 excludes items sold by execution or authority of law. This reflects the CRD and the CSD and excludes from the definition of goods items sold in situations such as a sale by an official under a legal authority to satisfy a debt (e.g. an official authorised to sell off property of a bankrupt).

52. Subsection (3)(d) of section 3 serves to prevent a contract from counting as a contract to supply goods and thus the protections under the Act from applying if the agreement is not supported by consideration other than being executed as a deed (as under the law of England and Wales and of Northern Ireland, a contract lacking consideration will only be enforceable if it is made as a deed, a written document whose signature involves certain limited formalities). The meaning of 'consideration' is set out in paragraph 31. This subsection does not apply to Scotland. Subsection (3)(e) applies in relation to Scotland, as contracts may be gratuitous under Scottish law, which does not require consideration in order to form a contract. The provisions of this Chapter apply only where a contract is not gratuitous; that is, where both parties give something.

53. Under *subsection* (5), contracts to supply goods also fall within the scope of this Chapter if they involve the transfer of a share in the goods, whether between current owners or if one owner transfers their share to a third party.

54. Whilst this Chapter applies to contracts for the supply of goods, there is some variation in how particular provisions apply according to the contract type (for example some of the provisions apply in a different way to hire contracts as the consumer is not paying for ownership of the goods, but for use of them). *Subsection* (6) indicates that more specific provisions for the particular contract types take precedence.

55. *Subsection* (7) provides that with regard to any of the specific types of contracts defined in the following sections, the provisions apply whether goods are supplied alone or alongside a service and/or digital content.

56. Section 4 defines 'ownership of goods' as referred to in Chapter 2 as being the general property in goods, which is the right over goods which an absolute owner has. It can be contrasted with more limited 'special property' in a thing, which means that the person with

special property can only put the item to a particular use rather than having absolute rights of ownership. The general rule is that ownership of the goods transfers to the consumer when the parties intend it to do so. The intention to transfer the ownership of the goods from the trader to the consumer will be dependent on the terms of the contract, what has been decided between the trader and the consumer and the circumstances of the case. The definition of 'ownership of goods' is consistent with the meaning of 'property' in goods under the SGA.

57. Section 18 of the SGA sets out the rules (for contracts of sale, to which the SGA applies) for ascertaining intention as to the time that ownership transfers, unless a different intention appears from the contract or circumstances. Section 4 points to this and other specific provisions in the SGA (sections 16 to 19, 20A and 20B) about the passing of property, which will apply for determining when ownership of goods is transferred under a contract of sale of goods (that is, a contract to which SGA applies).

58. Sections 5 to 8 define the types of contract to supply goods to which particular provisions apply, or apply differently.

- Section 5 defines 'sales contracts'. This is consistent with the category of 'sales contract' under the CRD and certain provisions of this Chapter which derive from the CRD therefore apply to this category of contracts. For a contract to supply goods to be a sales contract, the goods must have a monetary price. The strict legal position may be that a contract where the trader agrees to accept something other than cash, i.e. loyalty points, could be a sales contract but under the Act sales contracts and contracts for the transfer of goods both attract the same rights under sections 9-18 and remedies under sections 19-24. Under section 3(7) the category of 'sales contracts' includes contracts under which services or digital content are provided as well as the contract being for transfer of goods.
- *Subsection* (2) of section 5 clarifies that a contract where the trader agrees to manufacture or produce the goods is a sales contract. For example, where a tailor produces a made-to-measure suit for a consumer, the contract between tailor and consumer would still be a sales contract for the finished suit.
- *Subsection* (3) of section 5 clarifies that the category of sales contract includes conditional sales contracts where goods are paid for in instalments and the trader retains ownership of the goods until the conditions in the contract have been met, whether the consumer has possession of the goods in the meantime or not.
- Section 6 defines contracts for the hire of goods, as they apply between a trader and a consumer. The meaning of this provision is consistent with the definitions under sections 6 and 11G of the SGSA (save that it applies only to trader to consumer contracts, as does all of this Part of the Act), but the opportunity is being taken to simplify the wording. A contract for the hire of goods is covered by the Act irrespective of the consideration given by the consumer i.e. whether the consumer pays cash or exchanges goods in return (provided that the contract falls within section 3).
- Section 7 defines hire-purchase agreements for goods, as they apply between a trader and a consumer. This is consistent with the definitions in section 189 of the Consumer Credit Act 1974 and section 15 of the SGITA, save that it applies only to trader to consumer contracts (as does all of this Part of the Act).
- Section 8 defines contracts for transfer of goods by a trader to a consumer which are not sales contracts or hire-purchase agreements. A contract would be a contract for transfer rather than a sales contract if either (i) there is no monetary value assigned, or (ii) the contract is a mixed contract whether for a monetary price or not and, whilst goods are supplied, the transfer of goods is not sufficiently central to the contract to be a sales contract. If no monetary value is assigned to the goods, this does not preclude money from forming part of the consideration of the contract. For example, if the trader offers goods A in exchange for goods B and a cash fee, no value has been assigned to either goods A or B so the contract would fall under section 8,

despite some money changing hands. The statutory rights under chapter 2 (see sections 9-18) are the same for sales contracts and contracts for transfer.

What statutory rights are there under a goods contract?

59. Sections 9 to 17 set out requirements which the goods supplied, or the trader, must meet. Under sections 9 to 14 and 17, the contracts are to be treated as containing terms that the relevant requirements will be met—or, in the case of section 12, certain details are to be treated as a term of the contract. That is to say that the requirements set by these provisions form part of the contract without either party needing to refer to them.

60. Sections 9 to 11 and 13 to 15 re-transpose Article 2 of the CSD, regarding conformity of goods with the contract. The original transposition was made in the Sale and Supply of Goods to Consumers Regulations 2002 (SI 2002/3045) which amended the SGA and the SGSA. (A transposition note setting out how the main elements of this Directive are transposed in the Act is annexed to these explanatory notes—please see Annex B).

Section 9: Goods to be of satisfactory quality

61. This section provides that goods supplied under a contract to supply goods (as defined in section 3 above) must be of satisfactory quality. It details aspects of quality which may be considered when assessing whether the goods are satisfactory—although the section only gives an indication of such aspects, not an exhaustive list. This section corresponds to section 14 SGA, section 10 SGITA and sections 4, 9, 11D and 11J SGSA in so far as they relate to satisfactory quality. But as with all of this Part it only relates to trader to consumer contracts.

62. *Subsection* (2) provides that the test of whether or not the quality of the goods is satisfactory is determined by what a reasonable person would consider satisfactory for the goods in question, taking into consideration all relevant circumstances including any description, the price and any public statements by the trader or producer or their representatives, such as statements made in advertisements or on the labels of goods. For example, a lower standard might be expected of cheap or disposable goods in comparison to an equivalent item that cost more or was advertised as being particularly durable.

63. *Subsections* (5) and (6) provide that the circumstances to be considered include public statements about the goods, for example, any claims made in advertising or labelling. However, under *subsection* (7) such statements are not to be considered as relevant if the trader was not (and could not reasonably have been expected to be) aware of the statement or if the statement was withdrawn or corrected before the contract was made. The statement is also not to be considered if the consumer's decision could not have been influenced by it.

64. *Subsection* (4) provides that if the consumer is made aware of a particular defect before making the contract then that defect will not be grounds for finding the goods to be unsatisfactory. If the consumer examined the goods before making the contract then a defect which should have been revealed by the examination will not be grounds for finding the goods to be unsatisfactory. If the goods were supplied by sample (even if the consumer did not actually examine the sample) then a defect which should have been revealed by a reasonable examination of the sample will not be grounds for finding the goods to be unsatisfactory.

Section 10: Goods to be fit for particular purpose

65. This section provides that if a consumer acquires goods for a specific purpose, and has made this purpose known to the trader beforehand, the goods must be fit for that purpose unless the consumer does not rely—or it would be unreasonable for the consumer to rely—on the skill or judgement of the trader. This section corresponds to section 14(3) SGA, section 10(3) SGITA

and sections 4(4)-(6), 9(4)-(6), 11D(5)-(7) and 11J(5)-(7) SGSA, but as with all of this Part it only relates to trader to consumer contracts.

66. *Subsection* (2) makes similar provision for transactions in which the consumer makes the purpose known to a credit broker but actually contracts with another party. For example, a consumer buying goods in a store on a payment plan may make a contract with a finance company (which would be the trader) which is introduced by the store (as credit-broker), with the store selling the goods to the finance company in order for it to sell them to the consumer. In this situation, if the consumer makes the specific purpose known to the salesperson in the store (the credit-broker) that is sufficient and the goods must be fit for that purpose—there is no need for the consumer to also have made it known to the credit provider. 'Credit-broker' is defined in section 59.

Section 11: Goods to be as described

67. This section provides that where goods are supplied by description, the goods must be as described. Goods can be supplied by description even if they are available for the consumer to see and select, for example on the shelves of a shop. This section corresponds to section 13 SGA, section 9 SGITA and sections 3, 8, 11C and 11I SGSA, but as with all of this Part it only relates to trader to consumer contracts.

68. This section also, through *subsections* (4) and (5), provides that certain information required by the Consumer Contracts (Information, Cancellation and Additional Charges) Regulations 2013 ('the 2013 Regulations'), which implement the CRD, forms part of the contract. These regulations require traders to provide certain information to consumers before consumers are bound by a contract. The information required by paragraph (a) of Schedule 1 or 2 of these regulations relates to the main characteristics of the goods. The section establishes that any information that is provided by the trader and that is about the main characteristics—so is of a category mentioned in paragraph (a) of Schedule 1 or 2 of the 2013 Regulations—forms part of the contract. If the information regarding the main characteristics is not complied with, the consumer can pursue the protections for breach of section 11, as set out in section 19.

69. Subsection (5) makes clear that any change made to this information before entering into the contract or at a later date will not be effective on the contract unless agreed by both the trader and the consumer (although it may not be necessary to do so where the pre-contract information itself reflects the fact that the particular potential changes envisaged may be made). Nor can the parties agree a change which would deprive the consumer of his or her rights under this Chapter (see section 31).

70. *Subsection* (6) makes clear that the provisions of subsections (4) and (5) apply to a contract for sale of second hand goods which are sold at a public auction, if individuals can attend the auction sale in person. Most of the provisions of Chapter 2 do not apply in these circumstances, as explained further in relation to section 2(5).

Section 12: Other pre-contract information included in contract

71. This section establishes that any other information provided by the trader which is of a category mentioned in Schedule 1 or 2 of the 2013 Regulations, but which does not relate to main characteristics of the goods so does not fall under section 11, also forms part of the contract between the trader and the consumer. If this information is not accurate then the consumer may recover some money—see section 19(5)—but the other remedies (right to reject, repair, replacement etc) are not available.

72. *Subsection* (3) makes clear that the trader will not however be able to change this information without the consumer's agreement (although it may not be necessary to do so where the pre-contract information itself reflects the fact that the particular potential changes envisaged may be made), so there would be a breach of contract if the information provided was not correct

when the contract was made. Nor can the parties agree a change which would deprive the consumer of his or her rights under this Chapter (see section 31).

73. *Subsection* (4) makes clear that the provisions of this section apply to a contract for sale of second hand goods which are sold at a public auction, if individuals can attend the auction sale in person. Most of the provisions of Chapter 2 do not apply in these circumstances, as explained further in relation to section 2(5).

Section 13: Goods to match a sample

74. Under this section, if a consumer enters into a contract for goods on the basis of a sample, the final goods delivered must match the sample, except that any differences brought to the consumer's attention before the contract is made would not breach this requirement. This differs from the following section (Goods to match a model seen or examined) in that a sample is usually only a representative part of the whole goods in question. An example is a consumer buying curtains after having looked at a swatch of the material. This section replaces section 15 SGA, section 11 SGITA and sections 5, 10, 11E and 11K SGSA for trader to consumer contracts.

75. Where goods are held out as a sample then section 13 will be breached if the full goods supplied do not match that sample or they have a defect which makes their quality unsatisfactory (under section 9) and which the consumer would not have discovered by a reasonable examination of the sample goods.

Section 14: Goods to match a model seen or examined

76. This section establishes that if the trader displays or provides a model of the goods in question, then the goods received should match that model, except that any differences brought to the consumer's attention before the contract is made would not breach this protection.

77. An example is a consumer viewing a television on the shop floor but receiving a boxed television from the stockroom. Under this section the delivered model should match the viewed model (unless any differences are brought to the consumer's attention before it is bought).

Section 15: Installation as part of conformity of the goods with the contract

78. Section 15 makes clear that special rules apply where goods are both supplied and installed by a trader (or the installation is done under that same trader's responsibility). In that case, if the installation service is done incorrectly then the goods remedies apply, with the exception of the short-term right to reject.

Section 16: Goods not conforming to contract if digital content does not conform

79. Section 16 makes clear that special rules also apply where goods and digital content are supplied together in one product (e.g. where digital content is supplied on a disk). In that case, section 16 makes clear that if the digital content rights are not met then this will mean the goods are substandard and the consumer has the right to the full suite of goods remedies (including the short-term right to reject).

Section 17: Trader to have right to supply the goods etc

80. This section protects the consumer by making it a term of the contract that the trader has the right to sell or transfer the goods or to transfer possession of them, at the point when the transfer of ownership or possession takes place. In some transactions, the sale, transfer or hire will be immediate so the trader will need to have this right at the time the contract is made. In other cases, the parties may agree that the goods will be sold, transferred or hired at a later stage—the trader must have this right at that later time. This section corresponds to section 12 SGA, section 8 SGITA and sections 2, 7, 11B and 11H SGSA. But as with all of this Part it

only relates to trader to consumer contracts. The general rule is that ownership transfers when the parties intend it to transfer. For contracts of sale (that is, contracts to which SGA applies), rules on establishing the parties' intention as to the time ownership transfers—unless a different intention arises from the contract or the circumstances—are found in SGA, in particular section 18 (note, however, that legislation refers to 'property' as opposed to 'ownership' though the meaning is the same). See the notes on section 4 for further information.

81. The section also guarantees that no other person should have rights over the goods (e.g. a right to use the goods) unless the consumer is made aware of this before making the contract and that the consumer's possession of the goods should not be disturbed by anyone with rights over the goods (except any rights of which the consumer is made aware). These protections do not apply to hire contracts.

82. In the case of hire contracts, there will be other parties with rights over the goods—for example, the goods will be owned by someone other than the consumer, as the consumer is not contracting to own the goods but only to use them. Under *subsection* (3), the consumer's use of the goods may only be interrupted by the owner of the goods or by any third party with rights over the goods if the consumer has been informed of that person's rights over the goods before making the contract.

83. This section does not affect the protection for private purchasers of motor vehicles under section 27 Hire-Purchase Act 1964. Under that provision, where a private purchaser buys a motor vehicle from someone who has it subject to a hire-purchase agreement or conditional sale agreement and does not yet properly own the vehicle (because it is still under the hire-purchase or conditional sale agreement), then, if the private purchaser is a purchaser in good faith and without notice of the hire-purchase agreement or conditional sale agreement, the transaction is treated as if the person selling the vehicle did properly own it.

Section 18: No other requirement to treat term about quality or fitness as included

84. This section corresponds to section 14(1) of the SGA, but for contracts between a trader and consumer. The section serves to state that, unless there is an express term concerning the quality of the goods or the goods' fitness for a particular purpose, or a term implied by another enactment, the contract should not be treated as including any such terms, other than those set out in sections 9, 10, 13 and (where it applies) 16.

What remedies are there if statutory rights under a goods contract are not met?

85. Sections 19 to 24 set out the remedies that apply if the consumer's statutory rights covered in sections 9 to 17 are not met.

86. Sections 19 and 23 to 24 re-transpose Article 3 of the CSD (originally transposed by the Sale and Supply of Goods to Consumers Regulations 2002 which amended the SGA and the SGSA). (A transposition note setting out how the main elements of this Directive are transposed in the Act is annexed to these explanatory notes—please see Annex B).

Section 19: Consumer's rights to enforce terms about goods

87. Depending on the statutory right which is breached, the consumer may have a short-term right to reject, a right to have the goods repaired or replaced and/or (if this is not possible or fails to address the fault) a right to have the purchase price reduced (and keep the goods) or a final right to reject the goods, or a right to recover certain costs. *Subsections* (1) and (3) to (6) outline these rights and also serve to signpost the reader to the relevant sections that detail these remedies and their application.

88. *Subsection* (2) makes clear that if a statutory right is breached due to the goods not conforming to the relevant term (e.g. to be of satisfactory quality), if the non-conformity is due to the materials supplied by the consumer, then this does not count as a failure to conform to the contract.

89. *Subsection* (5) makes clear that if the trader is in breach of any pre-contract information required to be treated as part of the contract by section 12, the consumer has the right to recover any costs which they incurred as a result of the breach. The consumer can recover the amount of these costs up to the full price of the goods (so they could receive a full refund), or the full amount they already paid (if they had only paid in part for the goods). This applies equally where there is other consideration given instead of a price—the cap on the recoverable costs would be the value of that consideration. If the consumer incurs costs or losses above this amount, they may be able to seek damages for breach of contract (see *subsection* (9)).

90. Under subsection (6), if the requirement for the trader to have the right to sell or transfer the goods or possession of them (section 17(1)) is breached, the consumer has a right to reject the goods, as described further in section 20. The right to reject in this instance is not a short-term right to reject nor a final right to reject, therefore section 22 and section 24 respectively do not apply. The other rights provided by section 17—that no other person should have rights over the goods, unless the consumer is made aware of this before making the contract and that the consumer's possession of the goods should not be disturbed by anyone with rights over the goods—are covered by subsections (9) and (10), as breach of these rights does not give rise to a right to reject or the other statutory remedies, but the consumer may seek damages.

91. *Subsection* (7) makes clear that the availability of remedies specified in subsections (3) to (6) is subject to the particular rules for delivery of the wrong quantity and instalment deliveries in sections 25 and 26. If a trader delivers the wrong quantity of goods then the remedies will be determined by section 25. If the parties agree that the goods will be delivered in instalments, any entitlement to exercise the short-term right to reject or the right to reject under section 19(6) will be determined in accordance with section 26.

92. *Subsection* (8) states that the remedies for a breach of a term in the contract about the time or period for the delivery of goods are set out in section 28.

93. Subsections (9) and (10) serve as a reminder that the statutory remedies set out in section 19 do not mean the consumer cannot pursue other remedies, as an alternative or addition to the statutory remedies but the consumer may not recover more than once for the same loss. For example, in some cases the consumer may exercise the short-term right to reject and receive a refund, and also claim damages for additional loss caused by the non-conformity of the goods. In other cases, a consumer may prefer to claim damages instead of pursuing one of the statutory remedies.

94. *Subsection* (11) outlines the other common law remedies that the consumer may be able to seek, such as claiming damages or relying on the breach to relieve the consumer of the obligation to pay the price or some of it (essentially setting the breach off against the price), and that the consumer may pursue equitable remedies. For a breach of an express term (that is a term which the parties expressly agree to) the consumer may be able to treat the contract as at an end, depending on the status of that term. For example, if the consumer and the trader agree an express term in the contract that is so important that a subsequent breach of that term by the trader would leave the consumer deprived of substantially the whole benefit that was intended from the contract, the consumer could treat the contract as at an end.

95. *Subsection* (12) provides that the consumer is only entitled to treat the contract as at an end for breach of one of the statutory rights in sections 9-11, 13-16 or 17(1) by exercising a right to reject under Chapter 2. This overrides any common law right to terminate the contract for breach of the terms which these sections require to be treated as included in the contract.

96. *Subsection* (13) clarifies that references in Part 1 to treating a contract as 'at an end' have the same meaning as treating a contract as 'repudiated'. This means that, where a consumer treats a goods contract as at an end under the Act, the consumer may also be able to recover damages for non-performance of the whole contract by the trader.

97. *Subsections* (14) and (15) provide that, if a breach of the statutory rights—for example a fault—arises in the first 6 months from delivery, it is presumed to have been present at the time of delivery unless the trader proves otherwise or this presumption is incompatible with the nature of the goods or the particular breach or fault. This applies where the consumer exercises their right to a repair or replacement or their right to a price reduction or the final right to reject. This does not apply where the consumer exercises the short-term right to reject. These subsections correspond to section 48A(3) and (4) of the SGA and section 11M(3) and (4) of the SGSA.

98. For goods, sections 19 and 20 provide that in certain situations the consumer has the right to terminate the contract and receive a refund. Where the contract is a mixed contract with a goods element, this means (unless the contract is severable, see paragraph 100 below) that the consumer has the right to terminate the whole contract (both the goods and non-goods elements) and receive a refund of the price of the contract (or for money already paid towards the full price of the contract). If the consumer wishes to continue part of the contract, it is open to the parties to agree to do so.

99. For example, a consumer contracts with a trader to source for them and then install a kitchen. When the trader has finished the work, the granite worktops (the goods) are badly scratched and not fit for purpose. The consumer may ask for their money back, that is any money paid for both the installation service and the kitchen units.

100. As a further example, a consumer purchases a mobile phone handset (goods) with a network service contract. The phone keeps crashing so they return it to the trader. The consumer has the right to ask for a refund for both the phone and service, however in practice they may want to continue with the service to use with another phone, and the consumer and trader could agree to that. The consumer's right to terminate a whole contract (as explained in paragraph 98) is subject to the rules on severable contracts which are explained in paragraphs 119 to 121 below (and in paragraph 124 where partial rejection is concerned).

101. In summary, the statutory remedies that potentially apply for breach of the consumer's statutory rights are as follows:

Statutory right being breached	Statutory remedies that may apply
Goods to be of satisfactory quality (section 9)	• The short-term right to reject (sections 20-22) • The right to repair or replacement (section 23) • The right to a price reduction or the final right to reject (section 24)
Goods to be fit for particular purpose (section 10)	• The short-term right to reject (sections 20-22) • The right to repair or replacement (section 23) • The right to a price reduction or the final right to reject (section 24)
Goods to be as described (section 11), including conforming to information re material characteristics under the CRD	• The short-term right to reject (sections 20-22) • The right to repair or replacement (section 23) • The right to a price reduction or the final right to reject (section 24)
Conformity with contract information provided pursuant to the 2013 Regulations (section 12)	• The right to recover costs incurred, up to the contract price (section 19(5))
Goods to match a sample (section 13)	• The short-term right to reject (sections 20-22) • The right to repair or replacement (section 23) • The right to a price reduction or the final right to reject (section 24)
Goods to match a model seen or examined (section 14)	• The short-term right to reject (sections 20-22) • The right to repair or replacement (section 23) • The right to a price reduction or the final right to reject (section 24)

(*Continued*)

Appendix 2. Explanatory Notes

(*Continued*)

Statutory right being breached	Statutory remedies that may apply
Incorrect installation of goods (by trader or under trader's responsibility) (section 15)	• The right to repair or replacement (section 23) • The right to a price reduction or the final right to reject (section 24)
Goods not conforming to contract if digital content does not conform (section 16)	• The short-term right to reject (sections 20-22) • The right to repair or replacement (section 23) • The right to a price reduction or the final right to reject (section 24)
Trader to have right to sell or transfer the goods or to transfer possession (section 17(1))	• The right to reject (section 20)
Goods to be free from any charge or encumbrance not disclosed or known (section 17 (2) and (5))	• Statutory remedies do not apply but consumers may claim damages (section 19(9) and (10))
Consumer to enjoy quiet possession of the goods (section 17(2), (3), (6) and (7))	• Statutory remedies do not apply but consumers may claim damages (section 19(9) and (10))

102. As set out above, the terms that are to be treated as included in the contract in sections 9-17 are contractual terms and if they are not met it means there is a breach of contract. The common law (that is, law that is set out in cases decided by judges) already provides certain remedies for breach of contract. Subsections (9) to (11) of section 19 serve as a reminder that the consumer may—instead of (or, in some cases, in addition to) pursuing the statutory remedies set out in section 19 and subsequent sections—seek common law or other (equitable) remedies. These may include damages, specific performance or (in Scotland) specific implement, or a right to treat the contract as terminated for breach of an express term in some cases (see also paragraph 94).

103. 'Damages' refers to the common law remedy of financial compensation paid by one party to the other. For example, where a trader is in breach of a term that this Part requires to be treated as included in a contract, the court may order the trader to pay damages to the consumer. Generally, an award of damages for breach of contract is intended to compensate the injured party for loss suffered. In some, less frequent, cases the court may award damages which go beyond simply compensating the consumer for loss suffered—e.g. a court can sometimes award nominal damages, where there is a breach of contract but no loss, or aggravated damages to compensate for mental distress. For a breach of a term that this Part requires to be treated as included in the contract, the general rule is that damages are intended to put the consumer in the same position as if there had not been a breach. The level of damages awarded will depend on the specific circumstances and the term which the trader has breached. Typically, damages would cover the estimated loss directly resulting from the breach, in the ordinary course of events: if the consumer keeps the goods, this would generally be the difference between the value of the goods, service or digital content received by the consumer and the value had there not been a breach. Damages may cover loss or damage caused by the faulty goods, for example, where a faulty washing machine damages clothing while in use. There are legal tests to be satisfied for a consumer to recover damages: a person can only recover damages for loss which was caused by the breach (of the term required by the Act) and which was sufficiently foreseeable; and the consumer cannot recover for loss which they could reasonably have acted to limit or mitigate.

104. 'Specific performance' is a direction a court can make, to compel a party to perform their obligations under a contract. It is an equitable remedy, meaning it is not available to consumers as a right, but at the court's discretion. It will not be ordered if damages (see above) are adequate to compensate the consumer—generally, damages will be adequate unless the subject matter of the contract is unique, as the consumer can use damages to buy a replacement. 'Specific implement' is similar to 'specific performance' for Scotland, and there are likewise

specific circumstances where that may be used. In referring to specific performance or specific implement, this section does not seek to codify the law as to when specific performance or specific implement might be available, but the references serve as a reminder that it may be an alternative remedy to the statutory remedies. Section 58 gives more detail on the powers of the court in proceedings where a remedy is sought.

105. Under the law of England and Wales and of Northern Ireland, claims for breach of contract are subject to a limitation period of six years from the date of the breach of contract, whereas in Scottish law the limitation period is five years. Because the protections provided under this Part of the Act operate on the basis of contract law, the consumer has 6 years (or 5 years in Scotland) within which they may pursue remedies for breach of one of the statutory rights. This does not mean that a consumer may seek a remedy under the Act for any fault arising in goods at any time in the six (or five) years following delivery, but only if one of the statutory rights is breached. The statutory right under section 9 (goods to be of satisfactory quality) will only be breached if goods are not of the standard which a reasonable person would consider to be satisfactory, taking into account circumstances including the price and any description given. This test of reasonableness is provided under section 9(2). For example, the statutory right may not be breached and so a consumer would not be able to obtain a remedy if, say, a very cheap kettle stopped working fully after four years, as a reasonable person might not expect a bottom of the range kettle to last that long.

Section 20: Right to reject

106. This section serves to explain the remedies of short-term right to reject, final right to reject and the right to reject under section 19(6), and how these operate.

107. The section establishes that when the consumer has one of these rights to reject and chooses to exercise it, this means rejecting the goods and terminating the contract. The section also provides what the consumer must do to exercise the right.

108. *Subsection* (5) sets out what the consumer must do to exercise one of these rights: they must indicate to the trader that they are rejecting the goods and treating the contract as at an end.

109. *Subsection* (6) clarifies that, as long as the meaning of the indication is clear, it does not matter what form it takes.

110. *Subsection* (7) provides that when the right to reject is exercised by the consumer, the trader has a duty to refund the consumer and from this time the consumer must make the goods available for collection by the trader, or if agreed, return the rejected goods to the trader.

111. *Subsection* (8) clarifies that any reasonable costs of returning rejected goods to the trader (except where the consumer returns the goods in person to where they obtained physical possession of them) is to be borne by the trader. This includes the trader paying postal costs. This applies whether or not the consumer has agreed to return the goods, as mentioned in subsection (7).

112. Subsection (8) does not prevent a consumer from pursuing a damages claim. For example, a consumer might wish to do so in circumstances where returning the goods to the place that the consumer obtained physical possession of them does incur quite substantial costs for the consumer.

113. *Subsection* (10) provides that where a refund is to be provided and the original payment (or part of it) was made with money, the consumer is entitled to money back for the money they paid, so the trader may not substitute store vouchers, credit or an equivalent in place of the required monetary refund.

114. If money was not used to pay for the goods, under *subsections* (11) and (12), the consumer is not entitled to money back but the 'refund' would be a return of whatever the consumer gave in exchange for the goods (see examples below). If this cannot be returned to the consumer due to the nature of the exchange, then, under *subsection* (18) and (19), the consumer may not demand a refund but may pursue a damages claim. The consumer still has a 'right to reject' (that is, to reject the goods and treat the contract as at an end) in this situation, but the means

of obtaining money back is different. Examples of situations where these subsections may apply include:

- A toy 'bought' with vouchers collected from cereal packets. In this case it would be possible to return equivalent vouchers (even though they would not necessarily be the actual vouchers that the consumer cut out) and a 'refund' could therefore take that form under subsection (11).
- A microwave supplied to the consumer by a trader specialising in refurbishment of white-goods, in exchange for the consumer's old fridge-freezer. In this case, if the fridge-freezer was still available in an unchanged state, then this could be returned to the consumer as a 'refund' under subsection (12), but if it was no longer available, or had been refurbished, then a refund would not be possible.

115. Where money formed part of what the consumer used to pay for the goods but the rest was 'paid for' with something else (something non-monetary), the consumer is still entitled to a refund for the money that they paid and return of the other property transferred if possible. The consumer may pursue a damages claim for any loss for which they cannot claim a 'refund' (of money or property) under section 20.

116. *Subsection* (13) provides that, in the specific case of hired goods, the consumer may not claim a refund on any money paid (or whatever was transferred in place of money) for hire that the consumer enjoyed. Any refund will only cover money paid for a period of hire that was lost due to the contract being ended. For example, if a consumer hired goods for 1 month and paid in advance, but after 3 weeks a fault manifested so the consumer exercised their short-term right to reject, the consumer would only be able to seek a refund for the remaining 1 week when the goods would not be used. The consumer may also have a claim in damages to compensate them for some of the hire charges paid during the period in which the consumer had the faulty goods but before they rejected them. Under *subsection* (18)(c), if something other than money was transferred in exchange for the hire of the goods, and this cannot be divided to account for the time that the consumer has not had use of the goods, no refund may be pursued. The consumer could instead claim damages. If what the consumer transferred can be divided but not into the portion to which the consumer would be entitled under subsection (13), a refund of the division can be pursued, even if this is less than the proportional amount transferred by the consumer for the period of use of the goods. The consumer could then claim damages for the remainder.

117. *Subsection* (14) establishes that for contracts other than hire, and where payments for the goods are made over time (conditional sale and hire purchase contracts), any claim for a refund can only be made against money that has already been paid up to that point. For example if a £500 washing machine was found to be faulty after the consumer had paid £350, the maximum refund would be £350.

118. *Subsection* (15) requires a trader to provide any refund due to the consumer without undue delay and at the latest within 14 days from when the trader agrees that the consumer is entitled to it. For example, if a consumer rejects goods because of a technical fault which cannot be seen without testing or detailed examination, the 14-day period would start once the trader had carried out the appropriate tests and found the goods were indeed faulty. In contrast, if it was clear from looking at the goods that they breached the relevant requirement under the Act, there is unlikely to be any reason for the trader not to agree immediately that the consumer is entitled to a refund. In any case, there must be no undue delay, so the trader could not delay payment unnecessarily, for example in order to wait for time-consuming tests which are completely irrelevant. *Subsection* (16) provides that, where the consumer paid money under the contract, the refund must be given in the same form as the original payment unless the consumer agrees otherwise. For example, a consumer who paid cash should receive cash rather than, say, a cheque

unless they agree to this. Under *subsection* (17), no fee may be charged for the provision of a refund.

119. *Subsections* (20) and (21) clarify how rejection of goods works where a contract is severable. That is where the contract was intended to be divisible, so different parts of the consideration can be assigned to different parts of the performance—e.g. an agreement to pay pro-rata for some goods supplied, no matter whether others are supplied.

120. Where a contract is severable, if the fault is with goods in one part of the contract, the consumer has a right to reject those goods and effectively terminate that part of the contract. Beyond that it is a question of the circumstances as to whether the consumer may or may not reject other goods and effectively terminate the whole of the contract.

121. Subsections (20) and (21) do not apply in relation to Scotland.

Section 21: Partial rejection of goods

122. This section clarifies the consumer's rights around partial rejection of goods. If the consumer has the right to reject the goods because some or all of them do not conform to the contract then the consumer can reject some or all of them. If the consumer rejects only some of the goods they cannot reject any of the goods which do conform to the contract. That is, the consumer can:

- reject all of the goods (conforming and non-conforming);
- reject all of the non-conforming goods (but none of the conforming goods); or
- reject some of the non-conforming goods (and keep some of the non-conforming goods and all of the conforming goods).

123. If the consumer has the right to reject an instalment of goods because some or all of them do not conform to the contract, then the consumer can reject some or all of the goods in the instalment. If the consumer rejects some of the goods they cannot reject any of the goods in the instalment which do conform to the contract.

124. If the contract is severable and the consumer has the right to reject goods supplied under one part of the contract because they do not conform to the contract, then the consumer can reject some or all of those goods. If the consumer chooses to reject only some of the goods they are entitled to reject, they cannot reject any of those goods which do conform to the contract.

125. In this section, conforming to the contract means conforming to any of the requirements of the contract. This includes conforming to all of the terms which the Act requires to be treated as included in a contract to supply goods, including under section 17. In this way, conforming to the contract has a wider meaning than in sections 19 and 22-24, which do not cover conformity to the terms required by section 17.

126. The provision is in effect consistent with section 35A of SGA, although section 35A provides that acceptance of some goods does not prevent rejection of others, whereas that concept of acceptance does not apply under the Act. This section therefore provides clarity that the consumer nonetheless has equivalent rights to reject in part.

127. *Subsections* (3) and (4) correspond to section 35(7) of the SGA and provide that where the goods form part of a 'commercial unit' (defined in subsection (4)) the consumer may not reject some of the goods in that unit but keep others. For example, if furniture was sold as a three-piece-suite, but there was a fault with one of the chairs, the consumer would not be entitled to reject only the chair.

Section 22: Time limit for short-term right to reject

128. This section establishes the minimum time limit of 30 days for the short-term right to reject. The one exception (established under *subsection* (4)) is that for perishable goods which

would not be reasonably expected to last longer than 30 days, the period for exercising the short-term right to reject lasts only as long as it would be reasonable to expect those goods to last.

129. The 30 day period begins the day after the latest of the following:

- The consumer obtains ownership of the goods (i.e. the consumer buys the goods) or, for hire, hire-purchase or conditional sales, obtains possession.
- The goods have been delivered.
- If applicable, the trader has notified the consumer that any actions required before the goods may be used (including installation, if needed) have been completed by the trader.

130. This section also provides that the 30 day period will not run during any repair or replacement (the waiting period). On return of the goods to the consumer, the consumer has the remainder of the 30-day period, or 7 days (whichever is longer), within which they can still exercise the short-term right to reject if the goods still breach the standards set by the Act.

131. *Subsection* (8) details when the waiting period starts and ends. The period starts on the day the consumer requests the repair or replacement and ends on the day that the consumer receives the repaired or replacement goods.

Section 23: Right to repair or replacement

132. This section details a consumer's right to insist on repair or replacement of faulty goods, the cost of which must be borne by the trader. This includes the trader bearing any costs involved in the removal of an installed item and reinstallation of a replacement. A replacement would usually need to be identical, that is of the same make and model and if the goods were bought new then the replacement would need to be new.

133. Once the consumer has opted for a repair or replacement of the goods, he or she may not ask for the other of these, or exercise the short-term right to reject, without first allowing the trader a reasonable time to complete that chosen remedy. However, if waiting a reasonable time would cause the consumer significant inconvenience then the consumer can pursue an alternative remedy without doing so.

Section 24: Right to price reduction or final right to reject

134. This section provides for the consumer's rights to reduction of the purchase price or to reject the goods and obtain a (partial) refund. These are generally available if repair or replacement of the goods has not been possible or has not corrected the fault. Under *subsection* (4), if the consumer transferred something other than money for the goods, and the thing transferred cannot be returned in the same state or divided sufficiently to give back to the consumer the appropriate amount the consumer may not seek a reduction in the purchase price.

135. This section largely corresponds to section 48C of the SGA and section 11P of the SGSA, but there are some changes as outlined below.

136. The section provides that, if repair or replacement was impossible or if the consumer's goods continue to be substandard after the consumer has either:

- already undergone one repair or replacement of the goods by the trader; or
- sought a repair or replacement but this was not carried out within a reasonable time or without significant inconvenient to the consumer,

the consumer may either:

- keep the goods and insist on a reduction in the price; or
- reject the goods and obtain a refund which may, in some circumstances, be subject to a deduction to take account of any use the consumer has had of the goods.

137. For the purposes of determining when one repair has been carried out, *subsection* (7) provides that, where the repair is carried out on the consumer's premises, the repair is not complete until the trader indicates to the consumer that the repairs are finished. This means that a single repair may be carried out over more than one visit, without triggering the right to a price reduction or the final right to reject until the trader notifies the consumer that it is complete.

138. Where the consumer requests that a number of faults be repaired, and these repairs are provided together, this counts as a single repair.

139. If the consumer opts to keep the goods and require a reduction in price the question of what is an appropriate amount will depend on the circumstances and the remaining functionality of the goods. It is intended that the reduction in price should reflect the difference in value between what the consumer paid for and the value of what they actually receive, and could be as much as a full refund or the full amount already paid.

140. Where the trader is required to provide a refund because the consumer had paid more than the reduced price, the refund must be provided to the consumer without undue delay and at the latest within 14 days from when the trader agrees that the consumer is entitled to it. Where the consumer paid money under the contract, the refund must be given in the same form as the original payment unless the consumer agrees otherwise. No fee may be charged for the provision of a refund. (See paragraph 118 for further details.)

141. *Subsections* (10) to (13) provide that if the final right to reject is exercised within 6 months of delivery of the goods (or, if later, transfer of ownership or the trader having completed and notified the consumer of any required action), the trader must generally give the consumer a full refund. After the first 6 months, the trader may apply a deduction to the refund to account for the use that the consumer has had. There is an exception if the goods consist of a motor vehicle (as defined in *subsections* (12) and (13)). In this case a deduction for use may be made in the first 6 months. Vehicles such as mobility scooters (referred to as invalid carriages in other legislation) are excepted from the definition of motor vehicle for these purposes.

142. Subsection (10)(b) provides an order making power to extend the exemption to the 6 month rule to other types of goods. Under *subsections* (14) and (15), the power would be exercisable if the inability to apply a deduction for use to those goods in the first 6 months causes significant detriment to traders. It is subject to the affirmative resolution procedure.

Other rules about remedies under goods contracts

Section 25: Delivery of wrong quantity

143. This section corresponds to section 30 of the SGA, but is not limited to sales contracts and as with all of this Part it only relates to trader to consumer contracts.

144. This section provides that the consumer may reject the goods if the wrong quantity is delivered, but if they choose to accept the goods then they must pay the contract rate for what they receive. If more is delivered than was contracted for, the consumer has the additional option to reject the excess and keep the contracted amount.

145. This section only entitles the consumer to reject goods: rules of contract law will determine whether or not the contract can be treated as at an end. This reflects the existing position under the SGA.

Section 26: Instalment deliveries

146. This section corresponds substantively to section 31 of the SGA, but is not limited to sales contracts and as with all of this Part it only relates to trader to consumer contracts.

147. Under this section the consumer is not required to accept delivery in instalments unless they agree to it. If they do agree and one or more of the deliveries is defective (for example because

the goods in that instalment are substandard), depending on the circumstances, the consumer may have a right to damages or to reject the goods in the relevant instalment(s), or to treat the whole contract as ended. Which of these rights applies depends on the specific circumstances and must be judged on a case-by-case basis. However, *subsection* (5) provides that, if a delivery of an instalment fails to comply with section 28, it is section 28 that applies, and not section 26.

Section 27: Consignation, or payment into court, in Scotland

148. This section is based on section 58 of the SGA, but is not limited to sales contracts and as with all of this Part it only relates to trader to consumer contracts.

149. This section applies where a trader is pursuing payment from a consumer for goods that a consumer could otherwise have opted to reject but chose not to, including where the consumer argues, in answer to a demand for payment, that the price should be reduced due to the trader's breach. It provides that a Scottish court may require that consumer to pay the outstanding price (or part of it) to the court or a third party under court authority, or to provide other security. This serves to provide comfort for the trader, that the consumer will pay if the court finds that the consumer is obliged to pay the price.

Other rules about goods contracts

Section 28: Delivery of goods

150. This section implements Article 18 of the CRD and will replace regulation 42 of the 2013 Regulations. It applies only to sales contracts between traders and consumers for goods. Sales contracts are defined in section 5. If the parties have agreed that the goods are to be delivered in instalments, this section applies to delivery of each instalment. 'Delivery' is defined in section 59. In addition to section 28, the rules about delivery in section 29 of SGA apply to sales contracts, with the exception of section 29(3) SGA.

151. Under this section, unless a separate agreement is reached between the consumer and trader, the trader must deliver the goods to the consumer and must do so without undue delay and within 30 days after the contract is made.

152. Where the goods are to be delivered immediately at the time the contract is made, this counts as an agreement between the parties as to the time for delivery. Therefore, if goods are not delivered immediately, the consumer is able to terminate the contract if immediate delivery was essential; otherwise, the trader may deliver again within a period specified by the consumer. It is expected that in most cases where a consumer purchases goods expecting to receive them immediately, that immediate delivery will be essential in the circumstances.

153. Where the trader refuses to deliver the goods or delivery within the initial timeframe was essential (either because the consumer told the trader that it was essential or this was implicit from the circumstances) then the consumer may treat the contract as at an end if the trader fails to meet the initial delivery period. The consumer does not have to give the trader a further opportunity to deliver in these circumstances. Examples of goods for which delivery within the initial delivery period might be taken to be essential would include a wedding dress or birthday cake.

154. In cases other than those above then, if the trader fails to deliver the goods on an agreed date or within the 30 days, under *subsection* (7), the consumer may state a further reasonable timeframe within which the trader is required to deliver the goods.

155. If the trader again fails to deliver the goods in this time frame, then the consumer may treat the contract as at an end.

156. The consumer may choose to reject some of the goods rather than treating the contract as at an end, or, where the goods have not been delivered, the consumer may cancel their order for some or all of those goods. For example, if goods are delivered after the periods required by this section, the consumer may wish to reject some of the goods but keep others, as some may no

longer be of use to the consumer. If some goods are delivered on time but others are outstanding, the consumer may wish to cancel the order for some or all of the outstanding goods.

157. *Subsection (14)* makes clear that the provisions of this section apply to a contract for sale of second hand goods which are sold at a public auction, if individuals can attend the auction sale in person. Most of the provisions of Chapter 2 do not apply in these circumstances, as explained further in relation to section 2(5).

Section 29: Passing of risk

158. This section determines where risk relating to the goods supplied under a sales contract lies before and after transfer of physical possession of the goods to the consumer. Under the section, the risk lies with the trader until the consumer has physical possession of the goods, at which point risk is transferred to the consumer. However, if the consumer stipulates that the trader must use a carrier of the consumer's choosing, and that carrier was not offered by the trader as an option, the risk transfers to the consumer at the time that the goods are passed to the carrier.

159. *Subsection (6)* makes clear that the provisions of this section apply to a contract for sale of second hand goods which are sold at a public auction, if individuals can attend the auction sale in person. Most of the provisions of Chapter 2 do not apply in these circumstances, as explained further in relation to section 2(5).

Section 30: Goods offered with a guarantee

160. This section replaces regulation 15 of the Sale and Supply of Goods to Consumers Regulations 2002. These regulations transposed the CSD and regulation 15 implemented Article 6 of the CSD. This section therefore serves to transpose Article 6 again. Under this section, a guarantee provided alongside the goods without extra charge is legally binding. In particular, the guarantee must:

- be written in plain, intelligible language and, if the goods are offered in the UK, in English,
- include the name and address of the guarantor,
- state that the consumer has statutory rights (under this Act) regarding the goods which are not affected by the guarantee,
- state the duration and territorial scope of the guarantee,
- state the essential details for making claims under the guarantee, and
- be made available to the consumer in writing and within a reasonable time.

Can a trader contract out of statutory rights and remedies under a goods contract?

Section 31: Liability that cannot be excluded or restricted

161. This section serves to prevent traders from contracting out of the consumer's statutory rights under sections 9 to 16, as well as sections 28 and 29 on time of delivery and the passing of risk and, for contracts other than hire, the requirement on right to title contained in section 17. This section also has the effect that any term in a contract which seeks to prevent the consumer from having access to the statutory rights and remedies or to make exercising these rights less attractive to the consumer by either making it more difficult and onerous to do so, or by placing the consumer at a disadvantage after doing so, will also be void. For hire contracts, *subsections* (5) and (6) provide that section 31 does not prevent the parties from contracting out of the protection that the trader must have the right to transfer possession or that the consumer must enjoy quiet possession (under section 17), but a term seeking to exclude or limit these protections is subject to the test of fairness in section 62.

162. This section corresponds to sections 6 and 7 of the UCTA, but as with all of this Part it only relates to trader to consumer contracts. The section also serves to implement Article 25 of the CRD (in relation to those Articles of the CRD implemented in this Chapter) and Article 7(1) of the CSD.

163. This section also provides that an agreement to submit disputes to arbitration is not covered by this bar on excluding or restricting liability. It should be noted however that paragraph 20 of Schedule 2 makes clear that a term requiring the consumer to take disputes exclusively to arbitration may be regarded as unfair. Furthermore, the Arbitration Act 1996 provides that a term which constitutes an arbitration agreement is automatically unfair (under Part 2 of the Act, once it comes into force), if the claim is for less than an amount specified in an Order made under section 91 of the Arbitration Act. This amount is currently set at £5000 in the Unfair Arbitration Agreements (Specified Amount) Order 1999 (SI 1999/2167). It is possible that this amount may change from time to time.

Section 32: Contracts applying law of non-EEA state

164. The parties to a contract may agree that the contract is to be governed by the law of a particular country. This might be because the trader is based in a country other than the UK. The Rome I Regulation governs which laws apply to those contracts. In some circumstances, despite another law being chosen, laws of the consumer's habitual residence apply if they cannot be derogated from by agreement. See paragraph 27 for further details.

165. This section provides that most of Chapter 2 will apply to protect a consumer under a sales contract (as defined in section 5), where a contract has a close connection with the UK, even if the contract states the law of a non-EEA State applies (the EEA is the European Economic Area of the EU plus Iceland, Liechtenstein and Norway). The provision is included to comply with Article 7(2) of the CSD, which requires that the consumer should not be deprived of its protection, where a contract has a close connection with a Member State, even if the contract states the law of a non-Member State applies. It does not cover section 28 and 29, nor restriction of liability under sections 28 and 29, as these derive from the CRD which does not have this requirement.

CHAPTER 3 DIGITAL CONTENT

Summary and Background

166. Chapter 3 concerns contracts where a trader agrees to supply digital content to a consumer. 'Digital content' is a key definition in Part 1 and as such is defined in section 2 (Key definitions). It is defined as data which are produced and supplied in digital form and includes software, music, computer games and applications or 'apps'. In the case of digital content which is supplied under contract from a trader to a consumer, and largely or wholly stored and processed remotely, such as software supplied via cloud computing, some digital content will always be transmitted to the consumer's device so that they can interact with the digital content product that they have contracted for. This digital content falls within the scope of the definition of digital content as set out in section 2 and, as long as it is provided pursuant to the types of contract set out in section 33 or 46, Chapter 3 applies. The definition of digital content would also cover the digital content supplied to a consumer as the result of a service which produced bespoke digital content, such as a website design service. The Chapter does not apply where a trader supplies a service merely to enable consumers to access digital content, such as Internet or mobile service provision.

167. For contracts involving digital content that has been paid for, Chapter 3 sets out:

• The rights consumers have when they pay a trader to supply digital content to them under contract; these are in effect contractual rights and if they are breached it is a breach of contract;
• when the rights apply;

- what the consumer is entitled to request (and the trader must offer) if these rights are breached: where the trader has no right to supply the digital content the consumer has a right of refund; where other statutory rights about the digital content are breached, the consumer has a right that the trader repairs or replaces the digital content and a subsequent right to a reduction in the price of the digital content; these are the 'statutory remedies';
- that the statutory remedies do not prevent the consumer claiming other actions from the trader where they are available according to general contract law (e.g. a claim for damages); and
- that the trader cannot 'contract out' of these provisions.

168.   For digital content supplied under contract (whether free or paid for), this Chapter sets out:

- that if digital content has damaged the consumer's other digital content, or the consumer's device, and the consumer can prove that the damage was caused because of the trader's lack of reasonable care and skill, then the trader has either to repair the damage or give the consumer some financial compensation for the damage.

169.   A legal research paper commissioned by BIS examined core consumer protections relating to digital content and found that it was not clear what, if any, legal rights the consumer has if digital content proves defective or fails to live up to the consumer's expectations. This is because it is not clear whether digital content would be described as goods, services, or something else. The paper concluded that the law in respect of consumer rights in digital content should be clarified and that 'in short, digital products should be treated exactly as physical goods, so far as that is possible'.

170.   The Consumer Contracts (Information, Cancellation and Additional Charges) Regulations 2013 ('the 2013 Regulations'), which implement the CRD, introduce a definition of digital content which is used in this Act. The 2013 Regulations also set out when the consumer has a right to withdraw from digital content contracts that are concluded at a distance (e.g. over the internet), or off premises. They also introduce requirements for digital content traders to provide pre-contractual information on the functionality and interoperability of digital content as well as information on the main characteristics of the digital content (amongst other things). The 2013 Regulations set out the obligation to provide the information but, once it is provided, the Act makes clear that the information will form part of the contract. Where the information is concerned with the digital content itself it will be treated the same as any other description of the digital content.

171.   The Government consulted formally on proposals to clarify consumer rights in relation to digital content from July to October 2012 and, since 2010, has also informally consulted a number of consumer and business stakeholders on various aspects of the proposals.

172.   The Government published a response to its consultation in June 2013. Most responses to the consultation supported the creation of a new category of digital content in consumer law with a bespoke set of rights and remedies appropriate for the unique nature of digital content.

173.   A draft Bill was published in June 2013 and scrutinised by the House of Commons Business Innovation and Skills Committee. The Committee published its report in December 2013.

What digital content contracts are covered?

Section 33: Contracts covered by this chapter

174.   This section sets out which contracts to supply digital content are covered by this Chapter. It clarifies that this Chapter will apply to contracts between a trader and a consumer where a trader agrees to supply digital content that has been:

- Paid for with money,
- Associated with any paid for goods, digital content or services (e.g. free software given away with a paid-for magazine), and not generally available to consumers for free (that is, the consumer must pay something in order to get the digital content), and/or

• Paid for with a facility, such as a token, virtual currency, or gift voucher, that was originally purchased with money (e.g. a magic sword bought within a computer game that was paid for within the game using 'jewels' but those jewels were originally purchased with money).

175. Section 46 (Remedy for damage to device or to other digital content) applies to all digital content supplied under contract, including where no money is paid.

176. The Government retains a reserve power to extend the coverage of the digital content provisions to digital content contractually supplied in exchange for something else of value other than money (e.g. in exchange for personal data) in the future, should the Secretary of State be satisfied that there is significant consumer detriment resulting from these sorts of contracts.

What statutory rights are there under a digital content contract?

177. In line with the recommendations of the Bradgate Report, consumers' statutory rights for digital content follow a similar approach to that taken for goods (Chapter 2).

Section 34: Digital content to be of satisfactory quality

178. This section requires that digital content sold to consumers must be of satisfactory quality according to the expectations of a reasonable person. There are several different factors that will affect whether the quality expectations of a reasonable person are met. These are any description of the digital content, the price paid as well as any other relevant circumstances (which includes any public statement about the characteristics of the digital content made by the trader or the manufacturer). This means that, as with goods, this quality standard is flexible to allow for the many different types of digital content. For example, the reasonable expectations of quality for a 69p app would not be as high as for one worth £5.99.

179. The section sets out in *subsection (3)* that the state and condition of the digital content is always an aspect of quality and sets out other matters that can be aspects of quality for the purposes of assessing whether the digital content is satisfactory—fitness for the purposes for which the type of digital content in question is usually supplied; freedom from minor defects, safety and durability (e.g. the lifespan of the digital content). A reasonable person's expectations as to quality are likely to vary according to the nature of the content and some aspects of quality set out in subsection (3) may not be relevant in particular cases. So for example a reasonable person might expect a simple music file to be free from minor defects so that a track which failed to play to the end would not be of satisfactory quality. However, it is the norm to encounter some bugs in a complex game or piece of software on release so a reasonable person might not expect that type of digital content to be free from minor defects. Consequently the application of the quality aspect 'freedom from minor defects' to digital content will depend on reasonable expectations as to quality.

180. As with goods, quality does not refer to subjective judgements as to the artistic value of the content itself (e.g. whether or not a book was interesting or well written).

181. Digital content will not be in breach of this section if the consumer was made aware of the aspect of the digital content that makes it unsatisfactory before the contract was concluded—either because it was specifically drawn to their attention or would have been apparent from inspection of the digital content or a trial version. These provisions and those relating to public statements about specific characteristics of the digital content are the same as those for goods (section 9).

Section 35: Digital content to be fit for a particular purpose

182. If the consumer specifies that the digital content will be used for a particular purpose, the digital content must be fit for that particular purpose. This section corresponds to section 10

in relation to goods. For example, if a consumer tells a trader he wants a piece of educational software so that his/her pre-school child can use it then, if it is only suitable for an older child, it would not be fit for that particular purpose (i.e. use by a pre-school child). The section states that the consumer must 'make known' to the trader the particular purpose for which it is intended. This implies that the trader must be aware of the consumer's intentions. For example, an email sent to a trader immediately before downloading an app is unlikely to fulfil the 'makes known' requirement, whereas an email discussion with a trader would.

183. *Subsection (2)* covers digital content supplied that is sold to a trader by a credit broker but the consumer does all the negotiations with the credit broker. For example, a consumer may talk to a salesperson working for a particular shop about which software would be appropriate to edit a film they are making on their personal computer. The consumer may then buy the digital content on a payment plan (paying in instalments) from a finance company introduced by the shop's salesperson. What may actually happen here is that the store sells the digital content to the finance company who then sells it to the consumer. This section makes sure that the digital content can be held to be fit for the purpose the consumer told the credit broker (i.e. the shop's salesperson), even though the consumer does not contract with the shop directly.

Section 36: Digital content to be as described

184. The right for digital content to be as described is similar to the right for goods (section 11). Section 36 clarifies that the digital content must match any description of it given by the trader to the consumer. This is an important right in the digital content context where people may not be able to view the digital content before buying the full version. Even when the digital content matches a trial version, if it does not meet the description (where they differ), then the digital content will be in breach of this section.

185. The policy intention is that matching the description should mean that the digital content should at least do what it is described as doing. It is not intended that 'matches the description' should mean that the digital content must be exactly the same in every aspect. This section would not, for example prevent the digital content going beyond the description, as long as it also continues to match the description. This is particularly relevant for updates that may enhance features or add new features. As clarified in section 40, as long as the digital content continued to match the original product description and conform to the pre-contractual information provided by the trader, improved or additional features would not breach this right.

186. The Consumer Contracts (Information, Cancellation and Additional Charges) Regulations 2013 require traders to provide certain information to consumers before consumers are bound by a contract. The type of information that is required can be split into two categories: information about the digital content (the main characteristics, interoperability and functionality) and other information (e.g. the trader's name and address). In order to implement the obligation to enforce these information requirements the Act makes clear that pre-contractual information will form part of the contract. This section makes clear that the former type of information (about the main characteristics of the digital content or the functionality or interoperability) also forms part of the description.

187. *Subsection (4)* provides that changes to information given pre-contractually about the digital content are only effective when expressly agreed between the consumer and the trader (although it may not be necessary to do so where the pre-contract information itself reflects the fact that the particular potential changes envisaged may be made). That is, if a trader and consumer do not expressly agree the change to the information then if the digital content provided was not in line with this information, this would be a breach of this section. Conversely, if the trader and consumer do expressly agree a change to the description of the digital content, the consumer would not subsequently be entitled to a remedy if the digital content did not meet the original description but did meet the agreed, changed description.

Section 37: Other pre-contract information included in the contract

188. This section establishes that the other type of information described above (e.g. information on the trader's name and address) provided by the trader pursuant to the obligation in the 2013 Regulations also forms part of the contract between the trader and the consumer. Like the provisions covered in paragraph 71 above, this implements the obligation to enforce relevant parts of the 2013 Regulations.

189. *Subsection (3)* provides that changes to this information are only effective when expressly agreed between the consumer and the trader (although it may not be necessary to do so where the pre-contract information itself reflects the fact that the particular potential changes envisaged may be made).

Section 38: No other requirement to treat term about quality or fitness as included

190. The section makes clear that no other terms about quality or fitness can be implied into the contract. Express terms (that is those that are expressly agreed and set out in the contract) about quality and fitness can be included. Furthermore, if another piece of legislation exists which implies terms into contracts for digital content, these too can be included in the contract (this section does not prevent those being included).

Section 39: Supply by transmission and facilities for continued transmission

191. This section concerns rights that apply when in order to access digital content it is transmitted to the consumer (for example, where digital content is bought or used via the internet or through a satellite transmission) and makes clear that digital content must be of satisfactory quality, fit for a particular purpose and as described at the point when it reaches either the consumer's device or, if earlier, a trader with whom the consumer has contracted, such as an internet service provider or mobile network operator.

192. Digital content can be supplied on a tangible medium (e.g. on a disk or preloaded on a device or embedded within other goods such as a washing machine which relies on software for its programming) or in other ways, such as through streaming or downloading. When it is not supplied on a tangible medium, it will usually travel through one or more intermediaries before it reaches the consumer's device. Some of these intermediaries, for example an Internet Service Provider ('ISP'), have been chosen by and are within the contractual control of the consumer. Other intermediaries, however, will be within the contractual control of the trader, or under arrangements initiated by the trader. For example, a supplier of streamed movies (the trader) may contract with a content delivery network who will deliver the data from the trader's server to the ISPs who will then deliver the content to the consumer.

193. *Subsection (2)* provides that the trader (T) from whom the consumer purchased the digital content supplies the content at the point that it reaches either the consumer's device (for example, directly to a consumer's satellite dish) or an independent trader within the contractual control of the consumer (such as an ISP), whichever is sooner. T is responsible for ensuring that it meets all the relevant quality standards. A trader which is in the contractual control of the consumer and which only provides a service by which the digital content reaches the consumer is not providing digital content for the purposes of Chapter 3 (see section 33(4)) but may be subject to the provision in Chapter 4 (Services)).

194. Where digital content fails to meet the quality standards because of a problem with the consumer's device or with the delivery service supplied by an independent trader with whom the consumer has contracted (e.g. ISP, mobile network provider, cable provider), T would not be liable for the failure to meet the quality standards as that trader (T) cannot be at fault in any way for the problem and has no way of rectifying it. If the problem is with the consumer's network

access provider, then this service provider is liable under the services provision of the Act if, for example, the service is not provided with reasonable care and skill (see Chapter 4). However, where the digital content fails to meet the quality standards because of a problem for which T or an intermediary in the contractual control of T (either directly or indirectly) is responsible, then T will be liable. This is similar to the rules on the passing of risk for goods (section 29) which provide that the trader carries the risk for the goods purchased until they come into the physical possession of the consumer, unless the delivery is arranged by the consumer in which case the consumer takes the risk for the delivery of the goods.

195. *Subsections (3) to (7)* apply to digital content where use of the content in line with the contract requires some digital content to be transferred via the internet between the consumer's device and a server (processing facility) operated by or within the contractual control of T. Examples of this type of digital content would be massively multiplayer online games ('MMOs') and software accessed on the Cloud such as a music streaming facility. *Subsection (5)* provides that for such types of digital content, the consumer should be able to use their digital content in the way described for a reasonable period of time. Where there is an express term in the contract relating to a specific period of time for the use of the digital content in this manner, the express term would apply (e.g. if a consumer expressly pays for 48 hours access to an online journal or for a one month trial period for an MMO game). *Subsection (7)* provides that breach of this provision will give the consumer access to the remedies under section 42. *Subsection (6)* also provides that for these types of contracts for digital content, the quality rights set out in sections 34 to 36 (satisfactory quality, fitness for purpose and meeting the description), should apply to the digital content for that period of time.

Section 40: Quality, fitness and description of content supplied subject to modifications

196. This section reflects a unique issue for digital content in that manufacturers and traders are technically able to change or update digital content after the initial provision of the digital content. This may be set out in the terms and conditions of the licence. In the majority of cases, this is to the benefit of consumers and often includes important updates to the digital content. Requiring consent for every update would create problems for business, both due to the logistics of contacting every consumer and getting their consent and the problems that would arise when some consumers do not accept updates, thus resulting in many different versions of software in circulation and unnecessary disputes with consumers when digital content stops working due to lack of updates.

197. This section therefore does not prevent a trader or a third party (such as the digital content manufacturer) updating digital content, as long as the contract stated that such updates would be supplied. However, such contract terms could be assessable for fairness under Part 2 (Unfair Terms). Furthermore, following any updates, the digital content must still meet the quality rights, (i.e. it must still be of satisfactory quality, be fit for purpose and match the description given). This does not prevent new features from being added or existing features from being enhanced, as long as the digital content continues to match the description and conform to the pre-contractual information provided by the trader. *Subsection (3)* makes clear that the time period for bringing a claim begins when the digital content was first supplied notwithstanding the fact that the modification itself must have occurred some time after the original supply. This means that any claim for breach of this provision must be brought within 6 years of the date the digital content was first supplied.

198. It is for a consumer to prove that the digital content is faulty. Where a consumer has not identified a fault (and therefore not requested a repair or replacement), but a general update is sent in any case to the consumer, this does not necessarily mean that the quality rights were breached nor that the update constitutes a repair or replacement.

Section 41: Trader's right to supply digital content

199. This section clarifies that a trader must have the right to supply the digital content to the consumer. Often where a consumer buys digital content from a trader there will be other traders who have rights over the digital content, particularly intellectual property rights.

200. This section is slightly different to the equivalent section for goods (section 17) to reflect the fact that (unless the contract states otherwise) the trader does not usually pass on (or sell) all property rights of the digital content (e.g. the ownership of any intellectual property rights to the digital content) to the consumer. More usually, the trader passes on a limited right to use the digital content in certain defined circumstances. The ownership of any rights to the digital content usually stays with the rights holder (usually the originator of the digital content).

201. If the trader does not have the right to supply the digital content at all, the consumer will be entitled to a refund (see section 45).

What remedies are there if statutory rights under a digital content contract are not met?

202. As set out above, Chapter 3 largely only covers those contracts where the consumer has paid some money towards the provision of digital content.

203. This, and following provisions, set out the remedies available to consumers: what consumers are entitled to if the statutory rights are not met.

Section 42: Consumer's rights to enforce terms about digital content

204. If the digital content is not of satisfactory quality, fit for purpose, or does not match the description, the digital content will not conform to the contract. If the digital content does not conform to the contract, the consumer is entitled to require that the trader repairs or replaces the digital content. They can also be entitled to a reduction in price. These two types of remedy are similar to some of those available to consumers of goods, with the notable difference that there is no right to reject digital content as there is when goods do not conform to with the contract (except where the digital content is included in goods—see section 16). The way the remedies fit together is also similar to the goods provisions—if the consumer asks for the digital content to be repaired or replaced, a trader must do so within a reasonable time and without causing significant inconvenience to a consumer. Here, there is a difference compared to the corresponding sections in relation to goods: for goods there are strict limits on the numbers of repairs or replacements a trader can provide (section 24(5)(a) sets out that after one repair or one replacement the trader must offer the consumer some money back). This is because it is the nature of some forms of digital content (such as games) that they may contain a few 'bugs' on release. Some consumers will request repairs in relation to the bugs whereas, for the majority of consumers, the same bugs will be fixed by updates which they agreed to in the contract but did not specifically request. Restricting the number of repairs could create an incentive for some consumers to report minor problems with the digital content in order to accumulate a target number of 'repairs' and thus proceed to a price reduction. A strict limit on the number of repairs allowable could therefore have the effect of restricting the availability of this type of product or raising its cost to consumers. However, it is possible that a consumer will be caused 'significant inconvenience' after a single repair or replacement.

205. Section 42 does not include a 'right to reject' (that is to say, a right to terminate the contract and obtain a refund) substandard digital content. The reason for this contrast with the goods remedies (see section 19) is because digital content cannot be returned in any meaningful sense. However for digital content sold on a tangible medium (e.g. on a disk or as part of a digital camera), section 16 provides that, where the digital content is substandard (as judged against the digital content quality rights), it will render the goods faulty and so the goods remedies

apply. *Subsection (3)* refers back to this section 16 so that consumers who may go directly to the Chapter of the Act that deals with contracts for the supply of digital content will know that they may also have rights under the Chapter that sets out their rights under contracts for the supply of goods. What section 16 makes clear is that consumers do have the right to reject substandard digital content sold on a tangible medium. It also means that there would be strict limits on the number of repairs or replacements that the consumer is required to accept before moving to a price reduction or the final right to reject.

206. Section 42(4) sets out the remedy that applies if the pre-contract information provided pursuant to section 37 is not complied with. This remedy is similar to the remedy of a price reduction (see paragraph 214 below) but as explained below we expect that a price reduction will usually be calculated on the basis of the difference in value between the digital content the consumer receives and what they actually paid. Given that section 37 concerns information that does not describe the digital content (such as the trader's name and address), if it is breached it is unlikely to affect the value of the digital content received and therefore it would not fit with the way it is anticipated a price reduction would be calculated. This subsection therefore provides that a consumer has the right to recover any costs which they incurred as a result of the breach, which could be any amount up to the full price of the digital content (so they could receive a full refund in appropriate cases). This applies equally to a facility for which money has been paid, such as a token, virtual currency, or gift voucher, that was originally purchased with money. Where the consumer has not incurred costs but has suffered other losses as a result of this breach, it may be open to them to claim damages in breach of contract (see below), although it is unlikely that these damages would amount to a significant amount.

207. This section (and sections 43 and 44) does not prevent the consumer seeking other remedies available to them. As set out in paragraph 167 above, the terms that are to be treated as included in the contract in sections 34-37 are contractual terms and if they are not met it means there is a breach of contract. The common law (that is, law that is set out in cases decided by judges) already provides certain remedies for breach of contract. This section serves as a reminder that the consumer may—instead of (or, in some cases, in addition to) pursuing the statutory remedies set out in this section (as explained further in subsequent sections) seek common law (and other) remedies of damages, specific performance or in Scotland specific implement but not so as to recover twice for the same loss.

208. 'Damages' refers to the common law remedy of financial compensation paid by one party to the other. For example, where a trader is in breach of a term that this Part requires to be treated as included in a contract, the court may order the trader to pay damages to the consumer. Generally, an award of damages for breach of contract is intended to compensate the injured party for loss suffered. In some, less frequent, cases the court may award damages which go beyond simply compensating the consumer for loss suffered—e.g. a court can sometimes award nominal damages, where there is a breach of contract but no loss, or aggravated damages to compensate for mental distress. For a breach of a term that this Part requires to be treated as included in the contract, the general rule is that damages are intended to put the consumer in the same position as if there had not been a breach. The level of damages awarded will depend on the specific circumstances and the term which the trader has breached. Typically, damages would cover the estimated loss directly resulting from the breach, in the ordinary course of events. This would generally be the difference between the value of the goods, service or digital content received by the consumer and the value had there not been a breach. There are legal tests to be satisfied for a consumer to recover damages: a person can only recover damages for loss which was caused by the breach (of the term required by the Act) and which was sufficiently foreseeable; and the consumer cannot recover for loss which they could reasonably have acted to limit or mitigate.

209. 'Specific performance' is a direction a court can make, to compel a party to perform their obligations under a contract. It is an equitable remedy, meaning it is not available to consumers as a right, but at the court's discretion. It will not be ordered if damages (see above) are adequate to compensate the consumer—generally, damages will be adequate unless the subject matter of the contract is unique as the consumer can use damages to buy a replacement. 'Specific implement' is similar to 'specific performance' for Scotland, and there are likewise specific circumstances where that may be used. In referring to specific performance or specific implement, this section does not seek to codify the law as to when specific performance or specific implement might be available, but the references serve as a reminder that it may be an alternative remedy to the statutory remedies. Section 58 gives more detail on the powers of the court in proceedings where a remedy is sought.

210. As is the normal position, the person who asserts a fault has to prove it. Therefore the burden of proof for proving digital content is faulty, as with goods and services, is on the consumer. However, during the first six months following the purchase if the consumer can prove that the digital content was faulty (it is not of satisfactory quality or does not meet the particular purpose the consumer wanted it for or it does not meet the description) it is assumed that the fault was present on the day the digital content was supplied unless this is inconsistent with the type of alleged fault or can be proven otherwise by the trader.

Section 43: Right to repair or replacement

211. A repair is not necessarily the same as an update to which section 40 applies. A repair means bringing the digital content into conformity with the contract—that is there must first be a breach of contract (the consumer must prove that the digital content does not meet the quality standards set in out in sections 34, 35 or 36—satisfactory quality, fitness for purpose and meets the description) and then the repair must make the digital content meet those standards. A repair (in response to a request from a consumer) may, in practice, be in the form of an update. Repairing digital content means bringing it back into conformity with the contract. If an update resolves a fault in this way, then it can be a repair (i.e. a repair does not have to be a bespoke solution). A repair or replacement has to be provided within a reasonable time or without significant inconvenience to the consumer.

212. A consumer cannot require the trader to repair or replace the digital content if it is impossible or if repair is disproportionate to replacement or vice versa. If repair or replacement is not provided within a reasonable time or without causing significant inconvenience to the consumer or is impossible, a consumer is entitled to a reduction in price. The reduction will be of an appropriate amount depending on the circumstances of each individual case.

213. For example, a downloaded music file is very low cost to the trader and can be delivered very quickly, and a replacement file would similarly be very quick and easy to provide. In this example, therefore, a reasonable time would be very short and any measure of inconvenience would similarly be very low. However, for an expensive, complicated piece of software which may require a patch to bring it in line with the contract (i.e. it may need to be repaired rather than replaced) the process might be expected to take longer. But, if the digital content was obtained with a specific purpose in mind, for example, when a consumer has paid an extra amount to have early access to an online multi-user game but the server crashed and so the consumer was not able to access the game early, a repair or replacement may not be possible so the consumer would be entitled to a price reduction of an appropriate amount.

Section 44: Right to price reduction

214. Section 44 sets out the circumstances in which the consumer is entitled to a price reduction and establishes that the price reduction could be as much as a full refund or the full amount

they already paid (if they had only paid in part for the digital content). What is an appropriate amount will depend on the circumstances. For example, for digital content such as a film that is fundamentally substandard and fails to play at all, this may be for a 100% refund because the consumer will have obtained no benefit or no substantial or meaningful benefit from the film. In contrast, for a game which the consumer has played for five months and which is exhibiting a minor bug at a later stage in the game play (e.g. a character 'floats' instead of 'runs'), the consumer has already had some enjoyment from playing the game and the bug does not prevent the game from being played, the appropriate amount might be quite a small proportion of the amount paid. If a single film failed to stream satisfactorily, as part of a monthly subscription, the appropriate amount may reflect the portion of the monthly subscription that could be ascribed to that film. For free digital content given away with, for example, a paid-for magazine, any price reduction would reflect the portion of the price paid that could be ascribed to the digital content instead of the magazine. We expect the reduction in price here to reflect the difference in value between what the consumer paid for the content and what they actually receive.

215. *Subsection (4)* requires a trader to provide any refund due to the consumer without undue delay and at the latest within 14 days from when the trader agrees the consumer is entitled to it. *Subsection (5)* makes clear that the refund must be given using the same means of payment as the consumer used to pay for the digital content, unless the consumer expressly agrees otherwise. If a consumer has paid a trader money to buy in-game currencies (a virtual currency) that can then only be used to buy other digital content from that trader, any digital content bought using the virtual currencies would still be covered by the digital content quality standards in out in sections 34, 35 or 36 (satisfactory quality, fitness for purpose and meets the description) by virtue of section 33(3). However, subsection (5) does not mean that a trader can refund the consumer by giving them back the virtual currency. Rather, to satisfy this requirement a trader must give the consumer back the money originally paid for the in-game currency, using the means of payment that the consumer used to buy that in-game currency (unless the consumer expressly agrees otherwise). However, digital currencies (or cryptocurrencies) that can be used in a variety of transactions with a number of traders, and exchanged for real money, are much more akin to real money (e.g. bitcoins). Where the consumer uses these types of digital currency to pay for digital content, the trader can (and must, unless the consumer agrees) repay the consumer in the digital currency. The trader cannot charge the consumer a fee for the payment of the refund.

Section 45: Right to a refund

216. In relation to this section, if the trader's right to supply the digital content (section 41) is breached, the consumer has a right to a full refund. Section 45 does not apply in any other cases (such as a breach of the quality rights). There is no corresponding duty for the consumer to return or delete the digital content for the following reasons. Firstly, the concept of return does not easily sit with digital content (data produced and supplied in digital form) and therefore to provide for a return of the digital content would not be practical; and many consumers would find it difficult to properly delete the digital content. In relation to intellectual property rights, there are other rules that protect these property rights and the Act's provisions in no way undermine those rules. Indeed, if anything, the provisions taken as a whole would support the intellectual property rights of others, since they will act as a disincentive to traders to supply digital content where they do not have the right to do so.

217. *Subsection (2)* of section 45 provides that, where the digital content that the trader did not have the right to supply was only part of the contract (e.g. a single film supplied as part of a subscription package), the refund would not be of the full amount paid, but an appropriate amount paid relating only to the portion of digital content affected.

218. Once the trader agrees a refund is due, the payment must be made without undue delay and at the latest within 14 calendar days. The refund must be in the same form as the original payment unless the consumer agrees otherwise. So for example if the consumer paid by credit card the refund should be to their credit card, unless the consumer agrees that a cheque is acceptable (see paragraph 215 for the situations where digital content has been paid for with in-game or digital currency). The trader cannot charge the consumer a fee for the payment of the refund.

Compensation for damage to device or to other digital content

Section 46: Remedy for damage to device or to other digital content

219. Currently, if a consumer downloads some software that contains a virus, he/she could seek to make a negligence claim against the trader if the virus caused loss or damage to the consumer's device or other digital content; claiming that the trader breached a duty of care and skill which caused the consumer loss. This may not be obvious to consumers, however, and this type of negligence claim does not have statutory underpinning. The intention behind this section is therefore to engage the principles behind a negligence claim but limit the type of loss that can be claimed. This section applies to all digital content contractually supplied, whether paid for with money, or free (as long as it is provided pursuant to a contract).

220. If the consumer can demonstrate that the digital content caused damage to the consumer's device or other digital content and the damage was caused because trader failed to use reasonable care and skill to prevent it, then the consumer is entitled to a remedy. The trader can either offer either to repair the damage (as long as that can be done within a reasonable time and without significantly inconveniencing the consumer), or to financially compensate the consumer for the damage. Once the trader agrees the consumer is entitled to compensation, the payment must be made without undue delay and at the latest within 14 calendar days. The trader cannot charge the consumer a fee for the payment of the compensation

221. What constitutes 'reasonable care and skill' will be judged against the standards of the profession. For example, it would not generally be reasonable to expect a trader to check every single possible configuration on a consumer's device before providing digital content. However, if the trader has not done something that other traders would do and this has caused damage, it is unlikely to meet the standard of reasonable care and skill. What is reasonable will also depend on the particular circumstances. For example, if an update is an emergency update in response to a security threat, then it may be that the necessary standard of care would be considered lower than the standard that would be reasonable for routine updates designed to fix bugs.

222. A negligence case could still be taken instead of the consumer claiming under this section.

223. In summary, the remedies that apply for breach of the consumer's statutory rights are as follows:

Consumer's statutory rights being breached	Remedies that may apply
Digital content to be of satisfactory quality (section 34)	• The right to repair or replacement (section 43) • If repair or replacement are not possible or do not resolve the fault within a reasonable time or without causing significant inconvenience to the consumer the right to a price reduction (section 44)

Digital content to be fit for particular purpose (section 35)	• The right to repair or replacement (section 43) • If repair or replacement are not possible or do not resolve the fault within a reasonable time or without causing significant inconvenience to the consumer, the right to a price reduction (section 44)
Digital content to be as described (section 36)	• The right to repair or replacement (section 43) • If repair or replacement are not possible or do not resolve the fault within a reasonable time or without causing significant inconvenience to the consumer, the right to a price reduction (section 44)
Other pre-contractual information (section 37)	• The right to recover costs incurred as a result of the breach (section 42)
Trader's right to supply digital content (section 41)	• The right to a refund (section 45)
Remedy for damage to device or other digital content (section 46)	The trader must either: • repair the damage; or • compensate the consumer with an appropriate payment (section 46)

Can a trader contract out of statutory rights and remedies under a digital content contract?

Section 47: Liability that cannot be excluded or restricted

224. This section prevents a trader 'contracting out' of the provisions in sections 34, 35, 36, 37, and 41. A trader can exclude or restrict their liability arising under section 46 (remedy for damage to device or to other digital content) to the extent that any limitation or exclusion is fair. Any such exclusions would be subject to section 62 (requirement for contract terms and notices to be fair).

225. Many forms of digital content are supplied subject to an End User Licence Agreement ('EULA'). This is because when a consumer contracts for digital content—for example software—it is usually protected by intellectual property law and the consumer needs the intellectual property owner's permission, or licence, to use it. These EULAs may therefore set out the consumer's right to use the digital content. EULAs may also contain terms relating to the quality of the digital content or terms limiting the trader's liability for remedies for faulty digital content. The Law Commissions suggest that some EULAs may have contractual status, for example the research suggests that a court would almost certainly find that those EULAs known as 'click-wrap licences', where the consumer has to tick a box to agree terms and conditions before buying a download, were contractual. This may mean that where a consumer has bought digital content from a retailer, as well as having a contract with the retailer, they may have a separate contract with the intellectual property rights holder. As long as the consumer has paid for the digital content (see section 33), the digital content will be subject to the provisions of Chapter 3, and under section 47, the trader from whom the consumer bought the digital content cannot exclude or restrict liability for the rights in Chapter 3—the consumer would always be able to enforce these rights against the trader from whom they bought the digital content. If there is a contract between the intellectual property rights holder and the consumer, for example the 'click wrapped licence' in the example set out above, but the consumer paid no money to the licence holder directly, it is unlikely they could enforce their rights in Chapter 3 against the rights holder since the contracts would not fall within the scope of section 33. However, these contracts would be subject to Part 2 of the Act and any terms in them relating to limiting liability could be held to be unfair. This is also true of other types of EULA such as those known as 'shrink-wrap' or 'browse-wrap' licences which may not have contractual status but may alternatively be consumer

notices. Such consumer notices would be subject to the provisions in Part 2, but the rights set out under Part 1 would not apply since there is no contract.

226. This section also provides that an agreement to submit disputes to arbitration is not covered by this bar on excluding or restricting liability. It should be noted however that paragraph 20 of Schedule 2 makes clear that a term requiring the consumer to take disputes exclusively to arbitration may be regarded as unfair. Furthermore, the Arbitration Act 1996 provides that a term which constitutes an arbitration agreement is automatically unfair under Part 2 of the Act (once in force) if the claim is for less than an amount specified in an Order made under section 91 of the Arbitration Act. This amount is currently set at £5000 in the Unfair Arbitration Agreements (Specified Amount) Order 1999 (SI 1999/2167). It is possible that this amount may change from time to time.

CHAPTER 4 SERVICES

Summary and Background

227. Chapter 4 concerns contracts where a trader supplies a service to a consumer. It sets out:

- the rights a consumer has when a trader provides a service to them under contract; these are, in effect, contractual rights and if they are breached it is therefore a breach of contract;
- what the consumer is entitled to request (and the trader must offer) if these rights are breached: that the trader re-performs the service or where that is not possible or feasible provides a reduction in the price paid for the service (we refer to these as 'statutory remedies');
- that the statutory remedies do not prevent the consumer claiming other actions from the trader where they are available according to general contract law (e.g. a claim for damages, termination of the contract); and
- that the trader cannot, in effect, limit its liability for less than the contract price.

228. Chapter 4 applies to all service sectors except where they are expressly excluded from one or all of its provisions. The provisions in this Chapter do not cover contracts of employment or apprenticeships and, where there is legislation that gives more detailed provision about rights or duties of particular services, that legislation will take precedence over the provisions in this Chapter. This Chapter also partially implements Articles 5 and 6 of the CRD; however certain sectors such as financial and gambling services are exempt from those provisions.

229. Currently (that is, until Chapter 4 comes into force) the SGSA provides some protection for recipients of services (whether they are consumers or not) in England, Wales and Northern Ireland (its provisions on services do not extend to Scotland). It sets out that a business supplier of a service must provide that service with 'reasonable care and skill' and, if the time and charge have not been agreed, the service must be provided within a 'reasonable time' and at a 'reasonable charge'. The way it does this is by saying that these matters are 'implied terms' of a contract. Implied terms are terms that are not expressly set out in a contract (those expressly set out in a contract are called 'express terms'). The effect of this is that, even if these matters are not expressly set out in the contract, these implied terms will still form part of the contract and a business supplier of a service must comply with them, unless they are excluded.

230. At the moment, there are no statutory remedies for breach of the SGSA in respect of its provisions relating solely to services.

231. Section 60 and Schedule 1 make provision for how this new legislation impacts on existing legislation. The SGSA will continue to apply to contracts between businesses.

232. Chapter 4 does not cover all legal rights and obligations surrounding the provision of services, for example there is a large amount of sector specific legislation that will affect contracts between traders and consumers.

233. In addition, the 2013 Regulations provide that, for all types of consumer contracts within scope, including most service contracts, a trader must provide certain information to the consumer before the contract is entered into.

234. In 2010, BIS commissioned a report, entitled 'Consolidation and Simplification of UK Consumer Law' to examine how existing consumer law might be consolidated and simplified to make it more accessible to consumers, business and their advisers. That report recommended that consumer contract law would be improved if many of the provisions could be brought together into a single consumer contract law that, so far as appropriate, subjected all consumer supply contracts to the same rights and remedies. The report recommended that this be done using simpler language, such as avoiding specialist legal language including references to 'implied terms'. The report suggested that remedies for services should be made clearer and more accessible by incorporating them into the legislation.

235. Following the 2010 report, BIS carried out a consultation, from 13 July to 5 October 2012, into proposals for reform of the law regarding contractual supplies to consumers of services, as well as of goods and digital content. This consultation covered most of the recommendations of the 2010 Report, including how to present 'implied terms' in easier and more accessible language, whether to introduce statutory remedies and whether to introduce a new 'satisfactory quality' standard for all or certain types of services.

236. Following the consultation, BIS published a government response. Most responses to the consultation supported simplification and removal of difficult to understand phrases, and the introduction of statutory remedies for when things go wrong in the provision of services. A draft Bill was published in June 2013 and scrutinised by the House of Commons Business Innovation and Skills Committee. The Committee published its report in December 2013.

What services contracts are covered?

Section 48: Contracts covered by this Chapter

237. This section sets out which contracts are covered by Chapter 4. It follows the structure of the corresponding provision of the SGSA but makes clear that Chapter 4 is only concerned with contracts where a trader provides a service to a consumer (and not where a trader provides a service to another trader or where a consumer provides a service to a consumer or a trader). It also sets out that contracts of employment are not covered by this Chapter.

238. In contrast to the relevant Part of the SGSA, Chapter 4, like the rest of the Act, applies to the whole of the UK, including Scotland.

239. In keeping with the SGSA, Chapter 4 also covers contracts in which the trader does not undertake to provide the service personally, but rather uses a subcontractor (or agent) to perform the service. For example, a house-building firm may engage a specialist glazing firm to perform part of the work that they have contracted with the consumer to perform, and the house-builder would still be bound by the provisions in this Chapter for the performance of the service by the glazing firm.

240. This section includes a power exercisable by statutory instrument to dis-apply the provisions to a particular service or particular services. There is a similar power in the SGSA, which has been used to dis-apply section 13 (implied term to take reasonable care and skill) of SGSA to the services provided by an advocate in a court or tribunal, by a company director, by a director of a building society and the management of a provident society to that building or provident society and finally to services rendered by an arbitrator in their capacity as such. Contracts of

employment are also excluded from the scope of SGSA. Employees are protected by employment specific legislation, such as the Employment Rights Act 1996.

241. This Chapter applies whether the service is supplied immediately or the parties agree that the trader will supply it at a future time.

What statutory rights are there under a services contract?

Section 49: Service to be performed with reasonable care and skill

242. This Section corresponds to section 13 of the SGSA but, as with all the provisions in Part 1 of the Act, it only relates to contracts between traders and consumers, specifically here, where a trader supplies a service to a consumer. It removes the legalistic reference to an 'implied term' that is in the SGSA and simply says that every contract where a trader supplies a service to a consumer includes a term that the service must be performed with reasonable care and skill. The standard that the trader must meet in section 49 and in section 13 of the SGSA however is the same and if the trader does not meet the test of 'reasonable care and skill', the trader will be in breach of contract.

243. 'Reasonable care and skill' focuses on the way a service has been carried out, rather than the end result of the service. This means that, if a trader has not provided a service with reasonable care and skill, they will be in breach of this right, whatever the end result.

244. This provision does not include a definition of 'reasonable care and skill'. This is to allow the standard to be flexible between sectors and industries. It is also to reflect that current case law provides guidance on this meaning and, further, that future case law might elaborate on that guidance. It is generally accepted that relevant to whether a person has met the standard of reasonable care and skill are industry standards or codes of practice. The price paid for the service can also be a factor in determining the level of care and skill that needs to be exercised in order to be reasonable. For example, a consumer might expect a lower standard of care and skill from a quick and cheap repair service than from a more expensive and thorough one.

245. For example, if an individual engages a high-cost, specialized gardener to landscape his/her garden, that gardening service must be provided with reasonable care and skill. If the gardener does not cut and treat the grass to the industry standard, it is likely that a court would find that the gardener did not exercise reasonable care and skill and the consumer would have the right to remedies (explained below).

Section 50: Information about the trader or service to be binding

246. This is a new provision in that there is no corresponding provision in the SGSA. It is incorporated here for two reasons:

- Firstly, there may be consumer detriment where a trader may say something to a consumer, which the consumer then relies on, but which the trader later does not comply with. Whilst it may be the case that the proper legal construction is that these statements are validly incorporated into the contract as express terms, a trader may try to argue that they are not contractually bound by the statement; and
- Secondly, for certain contracts, the 2013 Regulations mandate that certain information must be made available by a trader to a consumer before the consumer is bound by a contract. To enable enforcement of those Regulations, the Act makes clear that these pieces of information will form part of the contract—so that the service must be provided as stated in the information—which cannot be altered unless the parties expressly agree otherwise (although it may not be necessary to do so where the pre-contract information itself reflects the fact that the particular potential changes envisaged may be made). This part of the 2013 Regulations aims to ensure that consumers are properly informed of key information before they are

bound by a contract. Certain services are excluded from the scope of the 2013 Regulations and therefore from this provision, such as financial and gambling services.

247. Section 50 may be considered in two parts to deal with these two objectives above.

248. Firstly, the section requires that that the trader providing the service must comply with information it has provided, orally or in writing (e.g. a description it has given of the service to be provided), where the consumer has taken this information into account when making any decision about the service (including whether to enter into the contract). This information must be read in the context of everything else in the contract and other information given. This is to prevent the consumer being able to rely on some information, where the trader clearly qualified that information when giving it to the consumer. *Subsection* (2) makes this clear.

249. The information given covers both information about the service and other information the trader gives about the trader itself (e.g. information about its trading practices, such as a commitment to paying its workers the minimum wage). Different remedies apply depending on whether the information is about the service or is other information that the trader gives (see below).

250. Secondly, the section explains that information provided which was required under the 2013 Regulations is also to be treated as included in the contract. Therefore, the trader must comply with the information it has provided or be in breach of contract.

251. For both types of information (that required under 2013 Regulations and information provided by the trader voluntarily) this section also makes clear that the trader and consumer can later agree a change to the contract if, for example, circumstances change. A trader will not however be able to change the effect of this information without the agreement of the consumer, unless the information itself reflects the fact that the particular potential changes envisaged may be made (or, in the case of information provided voluntarily by the trader, the trader otherwise qualified the information on the same occasion as providing it). Variation provisions in a contract between a trader and a consumer must also comply with Part 2 of the Act on unfair terms. For neither type of information can the parties agree a change which would deprive the consumer of his or her rights under this Chapter (see section 57).

252. For example, a consumer invites a trader to their home where they agree a contract for the fitting of windows. The consumer chooses that trader to fit wooden windows on the basis that the trader said that it would install and fully finish the frames. If, after fitting the windows, the fitter would only prime the frame and told the consumer to paint them him/herself, the trader would not have complied with the information it gave the consumer, and which the consumer had taken into account. Under the 2013 Regulations, for services within scope, the trader must give the consumer the 'main characteristics' of the service and the service must comply with those characteristics. This is in addition to the right that the service must generally comply with any information given to the consumer by the trader which the consumer takes into account when deciding to enter into the contract

Section 51: Reasonable price to be paid for a service

253. In most cases, a contract will set out the price for the service, and indeed following the 2013 Regulations, traders who are not excluded will be under an obligation to provide information about the price before the consumer is bound by the contract. In addition, the price could be paid up-front when the contract is agreed, in which case the consumer will know the price. If for any reason the price is not known from the outset, this provision sets out that the consumer must pay a reasonable price. What is 'reasonable' is a question of fact. This means that if the question of what is a reasonable price comes before a court and the court makes a decision, the ability of the parties to appeal that decision will be limited once it has been made.

254. This section corresponds to section 15 of the SGSA but updates the language in line with the rest of Part 1.

255. For example, if a home owner engages a plumber to fix an urgent leak, he/she may not take the time to discuss the price before fixing the problem. The price might not be in the contract if the plumber did not know the problem before he/she arrived to fix it. If the leak was fixed in ten minutes and with only a £50 replacement part, £1000 is unlikely to be a reasonable price to pay.

Section 52: Service to be performed within a reasonable time

256. Like the price of the service (discussed above), the time for performance of the service is not always agreed in advance. For situations where a time for performance of the service has not been agreed, this section gives the consumer the right to have the service provided within a reasonable time after the contract is agreed.

257. For example, an individual engages a builder to rebuild a 1 metre high, 25 metre long garden wall. At the outset, the individual agrees the price with the builder, but not a deadline for completion of the work. If, six months later, the work had not been completed, the builder would most likely not have carried out the work within a reasonable time.

258. There is a similar provision in section 14 of the SGSA.

Section 53: Relation to other law on contract terms

259. The provision in this section corresponds to section 16 of the SGSA. It recognises that certain types of contract to provide services are regulated by sector specific legislation (e.g. financial services). In most of those cases, this provision means that the sector specific legislation applies alongside or instead of this Chapter.

260. *Subsection* (1) preserves any enactments or rules of law which impose stricter duties than those imposed by sections 49-52. 'Rules of law' means a rule of the common law.

261. *Subsection* (2) means that where Parliament has turned its mind to a particular type of service, and has decided that that service should be subject to particular rules, those rules take precedence over those in the Act. 'Enactment' is defined in section 59 to cover primary legislation and also 'subordinate legislation', which is defined in the Interpretation Act 1978 as 'Orders in Council, orders, rules, regulations, schemes, warrants, byelaws and other instruments made or to be made under any Act'.

What remedies are there if statutory rights under a services contract are not met?

Section 54: Consumer's rights to enforce terms about services; section 55: Right to repeat performance; and section 56: Right to price reduction

262. The provisions in these sections set out the remedies available to consumers if the statutory rights set out in Chapter 4 are not met. Section 54 also clarifies that there might be other remedies available, for example, seeking of damages (which may be available under common law).

263. If the service is not provided with reasonable care and skill (and so breaches the provision in section 49) or where the service is not performed in line with information given about the service (and so in breach of section 50), the service will not conform to the contract. If the service does not conform to the contract, the consumer is entitled to require that the service is properly performed, through it (or part of it) being done again. The consumer can also be entitled to request a reduction in price in certain circumstances. These two statutory remedies are available as alternatives (or, in some cases in addition) to remedies available under common law or equity, for example damages and specific performance (see paragraphs 271-273 below). So a consumer does not have to ask for a statutory remedy of re-performance if they would prefer to seek damages, for example. The two statutory remedies are similar to those available to consumers of goods (in section 19 onwards). The way the remedies fit together is also similar to the regime for goods as set out in Chapter 2—if the consumer asks for the service to be re-performed, a

trader must do so within a reasonable time and without causing significant inconvenience to the consumer. A consumer cannot require re-performance if it is impossible, for example this might apply if the service was time specific. If re-performance is not provided within a reasonable time or without causing significant inconvenience to the consumer or is impossible, the consumer is entitled to a reduction in price. The reduction will be of an appropriate amount depending on the circumstances of each individual case.

264. If the information provided about the trader is not complied with (and there is a breach of section 50), the consumer has the right to a reduction in price of an appropriate amount. This is in addition to potentially having access to remedies at common law and equity (see paragraphs 271-273 below).

265. If the service is not provided within a reasonable time (and so breaches the provision in section 52), the consumer has the right to a reduction in price of an appropriate amount. This is in addition to potentially having access to remedies at common law and equity (see paragraphs 271-273 below).

266. A 'reduction in price of an appropriate amount' will normally mean that the price is reduced by the difference in value between the service the consumer paid for and the value of the service as provided. In practice, this will mean that the reduction in price from the full amount takes into account the benefit which the consumer has derived from the service. Depending on the circumstances, the reduction in price could mean a full refund. This could be, for example, where the consumer has derived no benefit from the service and the consumer would have to employ another trader to repeat the service 'from scratch' to complete the work.

267. In relation to services, however, there may be some cases consumer is able to ask for a reduction in price even where it may be argued that the value of the service as provided has not been reduced by the breach of the consumer's rights. This could occur, for example, where the trader has not complied with information they gave about themselves. For example, if the trader tells the consumer that they will pay their workers the living wage and this is important to the consumer and a reason why they decided to go with this particular trader, arguably this does not affect the value of the service but the consumer would still have the right to request a reduction of an 'appropriate amount' to account for the breach.

268. Where a consumer has the right to ask the trader to re-perform the service the trader must re-perform all or part of the service as needed to bring it into conformity with the contract.

269. Where the consumer has the right to a reduction in price, once the trader and consumer have agreed the consumer is entitled to a reduction in price, any refund for anything paid above the reduced amount must be made without undue delay. In many cases, a trader will be able to give money back at the time of agreeing that the consumer is entitled to a reduction in price. For example, in a hairdressers, if a consumer had already paid in cash, the owner would be able quickly to provide money back from the till. However, where a refund cannot be given at the time of agreeing that the consumer is entitled to that reduction, the refund must be given without undue delay and within 14 days of that agreement at the latest. For example, for a design service provided online, it may take 3-4 days to process the payment to the consumer. To be without 'undue delay' the refund should be given as soon as the trader is able to give it. A factor out of the trader's control, such as a bank processing time, would be unlikely to be considered an 'undue delay'.

270. The refund must be in the same form as the original payment unless the consumer agrees otherwise. So for example if the consumer paid for the service by credit card the refund should be to their credit card, unless the consumer agrees that a cheque is acceptable. The trader cannot charge the consumer a fee for the payment of the refund.

271. As set out in paragraph 227 above, the terms that are to be treated as included in the contract in sections 49-52 are contractual terms and if they are not met it means there is a breach of contract. The common law (that is, law that is set out in cases decided by judges) already provides certain remedies for breach of contract. Section 54 provides a reminder that the consumer may, instead of (or, in some cases, in addition to) pursuing the statutory remedies set out in this

section and subsequent sections, seek common law remedies of damages or treating the contract as at an end where for example the breach is very serious, or the equitable remedy of specific performance or (in Scotland) specific implement.

272. 'Damages' refers to the common law remedy of financial compensation paid by one party to the other. For example, where a trader is in breach of a term that this Part requires to be treated as included in a contract, the court may order the trader to pay damages to the consumer. Generally, an award of damages for breach of contract is intended to compensate the injured party for loss suffered. In some, less frequent, cases the court may award damages which go beyond simply compensating the consumer for loss suffered—e.g. a court can sometimes award nominal damages, where there is a breach of contract but no loss, or aggravated damages to compensate for mental distress. For a breach of a term that this Part requires to be treated as included in the contract, the general rule is that damages are intended to put the consumer in the same position as if there had not been a breach. The level of damages awarded will depend on the specific circumstances and the term which the trader has breached. Typically, damages would cover the estimated loss directly resulting from the breach, in the ordinary course of events. This would generally be the difference between the value of the goods, service or digital content received by the consumer and the value had there not been a breach. There are legal tests to be satisfied for a consumer to recover damages: a person can only recover damages for loss which was caused by the breach (of the term required by the Act) and which was sufficiently foreseeable; and the consumer cannot recover for loss which they could reasonably have acted to limit or mitigate.

273. 'Specific performance' is a direction a court can make, to compel a party to perform their obligations under a contract. It is an equitable remedy, meaning it is not available to consumers as a right, but at the court's discretion. It will not be ordered if damages (see above) are adequate to compensate the consumer—generally, damages will be adequate unless the subject matter of the contract is unique as the consumer can use damages to buy a replacement. 'Specific implement' is similar to 'specific performance' for Scotland, and there are likewise specific circumstances where that may be used. In referring to specific performance or specific implement, this section does not seek to codify the law as to when specific performance or specific implement might be available, but the references serve as a reminder that it may be an alternative remedy to the statutory remedies. Section 58 gives more detail on the powers of the court in proceedings where a remedy is sought.

274. In summary (see above and the sections themselves for more detail), the remedies that apply for breach of the consumer's statutory rights are as follows:

Consumers' statutory right being breached	Remedies that apply
Service not performed with reasonable care and skill (section 49)	• The right to ask for a repeat performance (sections 54 and 55) • And, if that is impossible, or not done in a reasonable time or without significant inconvenience: • The right to a reduction in price (sections 54 and 56)
Service not performed within a reasonable time (section 52)	• The right to a reduction in price (sections 54 and 56)
Service not performed in-line with information provided concerning the service (section 50)	• The right to ask for a repeat performance (sections 54 and 55) • And, if that is impossible, or not done in a reasonable time without inconvenience: • The right to a reduction in price (sections 54 and 56)
Service not performed in-line with information provided concerning the trader (section 50)	• The right to a reduction in price (sections 54 and 56)

275. For example, a consumer has his/her house treated for subsidence, with a new kitchen floor laid and bedrooms redecorated. But, whilst the bedrooms are fine, in the kitchen the builder has just papered over cracks, and the kitchen floor is uneven. The builder accepts that the job in the kitchen was not done with reasonable care and skill. In this case, the consumer can insist that the builder re-does the relevant work without any extra cost to the consumer. If the builder does not do that within a reasonable time, the consumer would be entitled to a price reduction of an appropriate amount. The amount would reflect that only some of the work was not done with reasonable care and skill.

276. For example, if a decorator is engaged to paint a room in a certain high quality paint, stating in advance that he/she will do so, and the consumer took this into account when deciding whether to enter into the contract with this decorator, and the decorator uses lower quality paint, the consumer would be entitled to have the room repainted in the agreed paint and, if that was impossible or couldn't be done for another (say) ten weeks, the consumer would be entitled to a reduction in price. If the decorator claimed to have a certain qualification and the consumer only wanted to contract with someone with this qualification, which the decorator did not in fact have, the consumer would be entitled to a price reduction. If the decorator were to arrive to paint the room one year after being engaged to do so, that delay would entitle the consumer to a reduction in price. A reduction in price could be of the full amount.

Can a trader contract out of statutory rights and remedies under a services contract?

Section 57: Liability that cannot be excluded or restricted

277. This section addresses 'contracting out' of the consumer's statutory rights as established under sections 49, 50, 51 and 52. It also makes clear that a trader cannot limit its liability for breach of these sections to less than the contract price.

278. As regards the consumer's statutory rights as established under section 49 (service to be performed with reasonable care and skill) and section 50 (information about the trader or service to be binding) the trader cannot 'contract out' of complying with those rights. That is, the parties cannot agree in their contract that the trader has no responsibility in relation to those rights. They also cannot limit their liability for breach of those sections to less than the contract price.

279. As regards the consumer's statutory rights as established under section 51 (reasonable price to be paid for a service) and section 52 (service to be provided within a reasonable time) the trader can dis-apply these sections by specifying the price (so that section 51 and the default rule which it imposes does not apply) or time (so that section 52 and the default rule which it imposes does not apply) for providing the service. Where these sections do apply, the trader cannot limit their liability for breach of those sections to less than the contract price.

280. Even if a term does not contravene this section (i.e. does not limit its liability to less than the contract price) it is still subject to Part 2 (Unfair Terms).

281. For example, a decorator cannot get around complying with the statutory rights by asking a consumer to sign a contract to paint a room where the contract includes a term such as 'the decorator accepts no responsibility if the paint work is not completed with reasonable care and skill'. If this is in the contract, that term will be invalid.

282. This section also provides that an agreement to submit disputes to arbitration is not covered by the bars on excluding or restricting liability. It should be noted however that paragraph 20 of Schedule 2 makes clear that a term requiring the consumer to take disputes exclusively to arbitration may be regarded as unfair. Furthermore, the Arbitration Act 1996 provides that a term which constitutes an arbitration agreement is automatically unfair (under Part 2 of the Act) if the claim is for less than an amount specified in an Order made under section 91 of the Arbitration Act. This amount is currently set at £5000 in the Unfair Arbitration Agreements

(Specified Amount) Order 1999 (SI 1999/2167). It is possible that this amount may change from time to time.

CHAPTER 5 GENERAL AND SUPPLEMENTARY PROVISIONS

283. Section 58 sets out powers that a court may use to enforce the remedies of repair, replacement or repeat performance and final right to reject or price reduction (as applicable). *Subsection* (1) sets out the types of dispute between a consumer and trader in which the powers can be used. For goods, the section is similar in effect to section 48E of the SGA and section 11R of the SGSA for contracts between a trader and consumer, but reflects the limits on deduction for use under section 24(9)-(10). This section makes similar provision for services and digital content to that for goods.

284. Paragraphs 104, 209 and 273 above provide explanation of specific performance and specific implement.

285. Under *subsections* (3) and (4), a court may substitute a remedy under the provisions specified in *subsection* (8), in accordance with the hierarchy and conditions to exercising the remedies within the Act. So, for example, in relation to a contract to supply goods, a court could only order price reduction when the consumer had requested repair, if repair and replacement were impossible (as required by section 23(3)).

286. Section 59 provides definitions of terms used in the Act other than the key definitions set out in section 2 and section 60 gives effect to Schedule 1 which details consequential amendments to existing legislation resulting from the implementation of Part 1.

PART 2: UNFAIR TERMS

Background and overview

287. Part 2 of the Act clarifies and consolidates existing consumer legislation on unfair terms.

288. In 2005, the Law Commissions concluded, following an earlier consultation, that the law on unfair contract terms is particularly complex. It is contained in two separate pieces of legislation—the UCTA and the UTCCRs—that have inconsistent and overlapping provisions.

289. The UCTA applies to a broad range of contracts, including those between two businesses, contracts between businesses and consumers and even, to a limited extent, to contracts between two consumers. It applies to individually negotiated as well as non-negotiated terms. It focuses on exclusions, that is to say terms or notices which aim to exclude or restrict liability for: negligence causing death or personal injury; negligence causing other loss; and breach of contract. As a result, for example, traders are not permitted to exclude their liability for negligence causing death or personal injury. Other exclusions are only binding if they meet the 'reasonableness requirement'. Some types of contracts are exempted, for example those relating to insurance contracts, interests in land or, other than in Scotland, intellectual property rights.

290. The UTCCRs implement the Unfair Terms in Consumer Contracts Directive (Council Directive 93/13/EEC) ('UTCCD'), and only apply to non-negotiated (standard term) contract terms between a trader and a consumer. They provide that contract terms must be 'fair' and written in 'plain, intelligible language'. The definition of fairness differs from the reasonableness test in the UCTA, and while overall both pieces of legislation may in some cases achieve a similar effect, they do so in different ways. In their 2005 report, the Law Commissions concluded that the two overlapping and inconsistent pieces of unfair terms legislation have led to complexity and confusion about how the law should be applied.

291. A transposition note setting out how the main elements of this Directive are transposed in the Act is annexed to these explanatory notes—please see Annex B.

292. In 2012, BIS asked the Law Commissions to look again at how the legislation could be clarified in the light of some high profile legal cases. They therefore undertook a consultation in 2012, to obtain up-to-date evidence and views on their proposals for reform.

293. The focus of the consultation was on two particular areas:

- contract terms that are exempted from an assessment of fairness by the courts because they concern the essential bargain of the contract—the subject matter and the adequacy of the price (this is commonly referred to as 'the exemption'); and
- an indicative and non-exhaustive schedule of types of terms that may be considered unfair (this is commonly referred to as 'the grey list').

294. Part 2 consolidates the UCTA and the UTCCRs, to remove conflicting overlapping provisions and, in particular, to clarify and amend the law on the above-mentioned exemption and the 'grey list'.

What contracts and notices are covered by this Part?

Section 61: Contracts and notices covered by this Part

295. This section sets out the scope of Part 2 of the Act:

- It covers contracts between a trader and a consumer. For ease of reference, trader to consumer contracts are called 'consumer contracts' in this Part.
- Whilst Part 2 concerns contracts, it also includes consumer notices—both contractual and non-contractual consumer notices. A consumer notice includes an announcement or other communication which it is reasonable to assume is intended to be read by a consumer. Non-contractual consumer notices (e.g. a sign in a car park) do not include an exchange of something in return for something else of value (known as 'consideration') as a contract does.
- This Part does not cover employment contacts, as they are regulated by specific employment legislation.

296. This Part covers terms in End User Licence Agreements to the extent that they are either consumer contracts or consumer notices. Research suggests that some End User Licence Agreements, for example those known as 'click-wrap licences', which the consumer must explicitly agree to before they are able to download digital content, may have contractual status. Consumer contracts are subject to the provisions of Part 2 and if they contain terms listed in Schedule 2, those terms are assessable for fairness. Other types of End User Licence Agreements, such as those known as 'shrink-wrap' or 'browse-wrap' licences, may not have contractual status but may alternatively be consumer notices, and therefore also be subject to the provisions in Part 2. End User Licence Agreements may also set out for the consumer legal provisions in other pieces of legislation, such as those in relation to intellectual property. Section 73 makes clear that the Act's unfair terms provisions do not override legal requirements in other legislation, therefore if a term reflects other law, then it will be exempt from the provisions in Part 2.

What are the general rules about fairness of contract terms and notices?

Section 62: Requirement for contract terms and notices to be fair

297. The effect of this section is that terms used in contracts and notices will only be binding upon the consumer if they are fair. It defines 'unfair' terms as those which put the consumer at a disadvantage, by limiting the consumer's rights or disproportionately increasing their obligations as compared to the trader's rights and obligations.

298. This section also sets out factors that a court should take into account when determining whether a term is fair, notably that it should consider the specific circumstances existing when the term was agreed, other terms in the contract and the nature of the subject matter of the contract. This assessment is known as the 'fairness test' (see also section 63 as regards the list of terms that may be used to assist a court when considering the application of the fairness test).

299. For example, a contract to subscribe to a magazine could contain a term allowing the publisher to cancel the subscription at short notice. In deciding whether this is fair or not, the court could consider issues such as whether the subscriber can also cancel at short notice or obtain a refund if the publisher cancels the contract.

300. *Subsection* (8) explains that terms which are void will still be void regardless of the fairness test explained in this section. Terms which are void may still be subject to the fairness test and found to be unfair, however if they are found to be fair that does not prevent them from being void.

301. This section brings together sections 4 and 11 of the UCTA (for England, Wales and Northern Ireland), sections 17 and 18 of the UCTA (for Scotland), and regulations 5 and 6 of the UTCCRs. This section also implements Articles 3, 4 and 6 of the UTCCD.

Section 63: Contract terms which may or must be regarded as unfair

302. This section introduces Schedule 2, which lists examples of terms which may be regarded as unfair (this list is known as the 'grey list'). Schedule 2 is an indicative and non-exhaustive list. The terms on the list are not automatically unfair, but may be used to assist a court when considering the application of the fairness test in section 62 to a particular case. Equally, terms not found on the list in the Schedule may be found by a court to be unfair by application of the fairness test. This section and the Schedule are based on a copy-out of Article 3(3) of, and the Annex to, the UTCCD. Part 2 of the Schedule explains the scope of the list such that terms in Part 2 are not considered as part of the Schedule but are still assessable for fairness unless section 64 or section 73 applies. Part 2 of the 'grey list' accounts, for example, for the specific nature of financial services contracts where fluctuations in the market may influence the price.

303. Terms on the 'grey list' are assessable for fairness even if they would otherwise qualify for an exemption under section 64. Terms on the 'grey list' are assessable even if they are 'transparent' and 'prominent' as defined in section 64.

304. For example, if a contract to subscribe to a magazine included a term which provided that the publisher, but not the subscriber, could cancel the delivery at short notice, that term may be regarded as unfair, as it is covered by paragraph 7 of the Schedule (which gives a term which authorises 'the trader to dissolve the contact on a discretionary basis where the same facility is not granted to the consumer' as an example of a term which may be unfair). This does not mean that the term is automatically unfair, but the court must take this into account when assessing the term under the fairness test in section 62.

305. This reflects the case law of the EU Court of Justice on the effect of the list of terms in the Annex to the UTCCD. In Case C-478/99 *Commission v Sweden* (2002) ECR I-4147, the Court stated:

> "It is not disputed that a term appearing in the list need not necessarily be considered unfair and, conversely, a term that does not appear in the list may none the less be regarded as unfair... In so far as it does not limit the discretion of the national authorities to determine the unfairness of a term, the list contained in the annex to the Directive does not seek to give consumers rights going beyond those that result from Articles 3 to 7 of the Directive... Inasmuch as the list contained in the annex to the Directive is of indicative and illustrative value, it constitutes a source of information both for the national authorities responsible for applying the implementing measures and for individuals affected by those measures."

(paras.20-22)

306. In Case C-472/10 *Nemzeti* (judgment of 26 April 2012) the Court emphasised the importance of the list:

"If the content of the annex does not suffice in itself to establish automatically the unfair nature of a contested term, it is nevertheless an essential element on which the competent court may base its assessment as to the unfair nature of that term."

(para.26)

307. Part 1 of Schedule 2 is as included in the UTCCRs and in the UTCCD, however the terminology has been brought in-line with the Act as a whole. In addition, three additional items have been added to the list (paragraphs 5, 12 and 14) as recommended by the Law Commissions in their report of March 2013.

308. Paragraph 5 adds to the grey list terms of a contract which have the object or effect of requiring that a consumer pay a disproportionate amount if they decide not to continue the contract. In this paragraph the phrase 'decides not to conclude or perform' includes where a consumer cancels a contract (and is charged a so-called 'termination fee').

309. Paragraph 12 adds to the grey list terms which have the object or effect of allowing the trader to determine the subject matter of the contract after the contract has been agreed with the consumer. In certain circumstances, defined in paragraph 23, this does not apply to contracts which last indefinitely.

310. Paragraph 14 adds to the grey list terms which have the object or effect of allowing the trader to set (for the first time) the price under a contract (or the method for calculating the price), after that contract has been agreed with the consumer. The paragraph expressly provides that, in certain circumstances, defined in paragraphs 23, 24, and 25, it does not apply to contracts which last indefinitely, contracts for the sale of securities and foreign currency (etc), and price index clauses. This is only for the avoidance of doubt, because in most of these situations the price of the contract, or the method for calculating it, will be determined before the contract is agreed, so paragraph 14 would not be relevant.

311. This section also implements Article 15 of the Distance Marketing Directive (Directive 2002/65/EC concerning the distance marketing of consumer financial services, implemented in the UK in the Financial Services (Distance Marketing) Regulations 2004 (SI 2004/2095)). That Directive sets common minimum standards for the information that must be given to a consumer prior to a distance contract for financial services being concluded. There are also provisions for rights of withdrawal ('cancellation rights') in many circumstances, and provisions to protect consumers in relation to misuse of payment cards in connection with distance contracts for financial services, unsolicited supplies of financial services and unsolicited communications about such services. Article 15 provides that any contractual term or condition that puts the burden of proof on the consumer (rather than the trader) to show non-compliance with the Directive is an unfair term.

Section 64: Exclusion from assessment of fairness

312. This section describes how the assessment of fairness of price and subject matter terms in consumer contracts is limited.

313. If a term is of the type listed in Part 1 of Schedule 2, it can be assessed for fairness. Other terms in a consumer contract can be assessed for fairness except to the extent that:

a)   they specify the main subject matter of the contract (usually the goods, services or digital content being purchased); or

b)   the assessment is of the appropriateness (usually the level) of the price payable under the contract compared with what is supplied under it.

However, if such price or subject matter terms are not transparent and prominent (e.g. if they are in the small print) they are assessable for fairness.

314. Then, in order to determine whether it is assessable for fairness, the court will first consider whether a price or subject matter term is transparent and prominent. If such a term is not transparent and prominent (e.g. if it is in the 'small print'), it is assessable for fairness. If the term is transparent and prominent, it is exempt from assessment for fairness.

315. This provision replaces regulation 6(2) of the UTCCRs, and implements the exemption in Article 4(2) of the UTCCD. Regulation 6(2) was considered in *Office of Fair Trading v Abbey National plc* [2009] UKSC 6. The Supreme Court concluded that the concepts of main subject matter and price are to be narrowly construed as '*the two sides of the* quid pro quo *inherent in any consumer contract*', that is, the goods or service that the trader agrees to provide, and the price that the consumer agrees to pay (Lord Walker at para.39). Lord Walker explained that the fact that other types of price terms appeared on the grey list reinforced this narrow construction of the exemption:

> "This House's decision in First National Bank shows that not every term that is in some way linked to monetary consideration falls within Regulation 6(2)(b). Paras (d), (e), (f) and (l) of the 'grey list' in Schedule 2 to the 1999 Regulations are an illustration of that."
>
> (Lord Walker, para.43)

316. Reflecting this case law, the effect of this section is that, if a term concerns other aspects of the price other than the amount, for example the timing of payment, the term may be assessed for fairness, but the amount of the price cannot be assessed (if it is transparent and prominent as defined here).

317. For example, if an individual contracts with a catering company to provide a buffet lunch, and the contract includes a term that the individual will pay £100 for a 3 course meal, the court cannot look at whether it is fair to pay £100 for 3 courses. It may, however, look at other things, such as the rights of the company and the individual to cancel the lunch, and when the price is due to be paid.

Section 65: Bar on exclusion or restriction of negligence liability and
Section 66: Scope of section 65

318. Section 65 provides that a trader cannot, in a consumer contract or consumer notice, limit liability for death or personal injury resulting from negligence.

319. With regard to other loss or damage (such as death or personal injury not resulting from negligence), the trader can only limit its liability if the clause is 'fair'. Whether a term is fair is determined by the fairness test, set out in section 62.

320. For example, if an individual contracts with a catering company to provide a buffet lunch, and a term in that contract states that the catering company accepts no responsibility for death by food poisoning caused by their negligence, that term is not binding. The catering company can, however, and providing the clause is fair, limit liability if it breaks kitchen equipment.

321. This bar does not apply to a discharge or indemnity given as part of a compensation settlement. This allows parties to settle disputes which have arisen concerning the performance of an earlier contract. Section 66 expressly provides that this bar does not apply to agreements mentioned in section 4(2)(a) of the Damages (Scotland) Act 2011, because not all agreements to discharge liability will include compensation.

322. Section 65 does not affect section 5 of the Damages (Scotland) Act 2011, which sets out special rules for settlement of mesothelioma claims in Scotland, and provides that relatives can still claim certain damages in some cases even if the original liability were discharged.

323. In some cases, under common law, if an individual is aware of a risk, but ignores it, he/she may be deemed to have taken on that risk. However, this provision explains that, in contrast,

a consumer cannot be assumed to have taken on any risk by agreeing to a term which limits a trader's liability.

324. Terms which are barred under this section are still assessable for fairness under section 62.

325. This section reflects section 2 (for England, Wales and Northern Ireland) and section 16 (for Scotland) of the UCTA.

Section 67: Effect of an unfair term on the rest of a contract

326. As explained above, a court can find a particular term to be unfair, rendering it unenforceable. However, it may not be in the interests of the consumer or the business for the entire contract not to be binding any more. Therefore, in so far as is practical, the contract will continue even if one or more terms within it are deemed unfair.

327. This section reflects regulation 6(1) of the UTCCD, which is implemented by Article 8(2) of the UTCCRs.

Section 68: Requirement for transparency

328. Whilst previous sections explain that a term in a consumer contract or a consumer notice must be fair, and how that is determined, this section states that, in addition, written terms and written notices must be transparent (defined as legible and in plain and intelligible language). The trader has an obligation to ensure that such terms are transparent.

329. This requirement, like others in this Act, may be enforced by public bodies under the relevant provisions, including under Part 8 of the EA, if the conditions in that Act are met (for example, if the term harms the collective interest of consumers). It may also be enforced under Schedule 3.

330. This section reflects regulation 7(1) of the UTCCRs, which implements Article 5 of the UTCCD.

Section 69: Contract terms that may have different meanings

331. Contract terms can be ambiguous and capable of being interpreted in different ways, especially if they are not in writing or in an accessible format. In these cases, this section ensures that the interpretation that is most beneficial to the consumer, rather than the trader, is the interpretation that is used.

332. This section reflects regulation 7(2) of the UTCCRs, which implements Article 5 of the UTCCD.

How are the general rules enforced?

Section 70: Enforcement of the law on unfair contract terms

333. If traders do use (or propose to use or recommend the use of) unfair, void and/or non-transparent terms in consumer contracts or consumer notices, there are a number of means of enforcing this Part.

334. This section introduces Schedule 3 which sets out how this Part can be enforced. Schedule 3 explains that the Competition and Markets Authority ('CMA') and other Regulators (coordinated by the CMA) can investigate and apply for injunctions to prevent the use of certain terms. These are terms which the CMA or other Regulator considers might be unfair, not transparent or void (for example if they purport to exclude liability for death or personal injury through negligence). The CMA or other Regulator may take action if it thinks that a term or notice falls into one or more of those three categories.

335. Schedule 3 includes provisions for the CMA to collate and if appropriate make public information about actions taken against certain terms and notices. It also provides that the CMA may issue guidance if it considers it appropriate to do so.

336. There are other means of enforcement available, for example private action by the consumer through the courts or enforcement by a public body through Part 8 of the EA.

337. Schedule 5 also includes one additional power made available to Unfair Terms enforcers. This is the power to require the production of information (Part 3 of Schedule 5). As set out in paragraph 6 of Schedule 5, this power is only available to those enforcers listed in Schedule 3 which are also public authorities (within the meaning of the Human Rights Act 1998). So, for example, this power is not available to the Consumers' Association (known as Which?).

338. This section reflects regulations 10 to 15 of the UTCCRs, which implement Article 7 of the UTCCD.

Supplementary provisions

Section 71: Duty of court to consider fairness of term

339. Courts hear a wide variety of disputes between traders and consumers concerning contracts. However, courts are not always specifically asked to look at the fairness of a term in a consumer contract. This provision places a duty upon the courts to look at the fairness of terms even if the parties do not specifically ask the court to do so.

340. This section reflects the view of the EUCJ in Case C-168/05 *Mostaza Claro* (2006) ECR I-10421 that 'the nature and importance of the public interest underlying the protection which the Directive confers on consumers justify, moreover, the national court being required to assess of its own motion whether a contractual term is unfair' (paragraph 38).

341. In fulfilling this duty, the courts would not have to look at the fairness of the term if they do not have adequate information to do so, as was emphasised by the Court of Justice in Case C-243/08 *Pannon*(2009) ECR I-4713 (at para.35). In addition, the courts would only have to look at the term or terms in question, not the entire contract; this reflects the principle in Case C-137/08 *VB Penzugyi v Schneider* in 2010.

Section 72: Application of rules to secondary contracts

342. This section clarifies that the requirement for terms to be fair, as set out above, extends to contracts agreed in addition to the original contract, whether or not they are contracts between a trader and a consumer. This provides additional protection for consumers, by ensuring that any agreements made after, before or in addition to the signing of a contract are also covered by these rules.

Section 73: Disapplication of rules to mandatory terms and notices

343. This section ensures that the new and amended provisions on unfair terms do not override legal requirements in other legislation. This may be relevant, for example, where several pieces of legislation affect a trader's business.

344. This section reflects regulation 4(2) of the UTCCRs, which implements Article 1(2) of the UTCCD.

Section 74: Contracts applying law of non-EEA State

345. The parties to a contract may agree that it is to be governed by the law of a particular country. This might be because the trader is based in a country other than the UK. This

section provides that the consumer may not be deprived of the protection of this Part, where a contract has a close connection with the UK, even if the contract states that the law of a non-EEA State applies (the EEA is the EU Member States plus Iceland, Liechtenstein and Norway).

346. The Rome I Regulation (Regulation (EC) No 593/2008 of the European Parliament and of the Council of 17 June 2008 on the law applicable to contractual obligations), governs which law applies to a consumer contract. See paragraph 27 above for more information on the Rome I Regulation.

347. Section 74 is based on regulation 9 of the UTCCRs, which implements Article 6(2) of the UTCCD; and sections 26 and 27 of the UCTA.

Section 75: Changes to other legislation

348. This section gives effect to Schedule 4 which lists amendments required to other legislation, including the UCTA, as a result of this Part.

PART 3 MISCELLANEOUS AND GENERAL
CHAPTER 1:
ENFORCEMENT ETC.

Section 77: Investigatory powers etc.

349. This section makes provision for the investigatory powers of consumer law enforcers. Consumer law, which includes enforcers' investigatory powers, has built up piecemeal, resulting in the investigatory powers, contained in around 60 pieces of consumer legislation, being unclear, inconsistent and overlapping each other. In its consultation published in March 2012 entitled 'Enhancing Consumer Confidence Through Effective Enforcement – Consultation on consolidating and modernising consumer law enforcement powers,' BIS proposed simplifying the powers by consolidating them into one generic set.

350. This section gives effect to Schedule 5 on Investigatory Powers and Schedule 6 which details the consequential amendments in relation to the investigatory powers.

SCHEDULE 5: INVESTIGATORY POWERS ETC.

351. This Schedule contains a generic set of powers, which is based on those currently contained in Part 4 of the Consumer Protection from Unfair Trading Regulations 2008 (CPRs). This is because CPRs are relatively modern; reflect current business practices; build on similar existing legislation and can be used to investigate breaches which may lead to criminal or civil proceedings. Some specific powers contained in weights and measures and product safety legislation will be retained in that legislation alongside the generic set.

352. As well as consolidating powers that already exist, stronger safeguards have been added to the use of some powers in order to reduce the burdens on businesses. For example, subject to a number of exemptions, the power of entry into premises without a warrant cannot be exercised unless a notice in writing has been given to the occupier at least two working days before an inspection is carried out and the power exercised. This requirement applies to routine inspections only and the Schedule sets out those circumstances that would not amount to a routine inspection.

353. As a consequence of consolidating these powers, some modification has been necessary to the existing powers, either to ensure compliance with EU obligations, or to align powers across consumer law in order to ensure that the powers contained in the generic set are simple and consistent. For example, the generic set includes a power to require production of information under paragraph 14 of Part 3 of the Schedule, which is based on Part 8 of the EA dealing with civil enforcement but which will now apply to both civil and criminal consumer law enforcement.

354. In some instances, a limitation has been specifically placed on the use of a particular power. For example, the power to require production of information can only be used if the enforcer reasonably suspects a breach of legislation. This limitation does not apply, or apply in the same way, for all types of enforcer.

355. The generic set of powers applies to all enforcers detailed in the Schedule except where access to powers is specifically limited for particular enforcers. For example, the powers of unfair contract terms enforcers and public designated enforcers, are restricted to the power to require production of information.

356. Paragraph 1 of Part 1 provides an overview of the Parts of Schedule 5.

357. Paragraphs 2 to 6 detail the types of enforcers that have access to the powers in the Schedule and define the terms used to refer to those enforcers, e.g. EU and domestic enforcers. Paragraph 7 details what is meant by the term 'officer' in relation to enforcers whilst Paragraph 8 defines other terms used in the Schedule.

358. Paragraphs 9 to 11 of Part 2 of the Schedule specify the legislation to which the generic set of powers applies.

359. Paragraph 12 introduces a power for the Secretary of State by order to amend the list of legislation to which the generic set of powers applies. This is to ensure that the generic set of powers can be used to enforce any new duties that may in future be prescribed.

360. The order making power would also allow other legislation to be amended, repealed or revoked as a consequence of amending this list. The safeguards on the use of the powers of entry that replace those being repealed must be greater than those that existed before.

361. Paragraphs 13 to 17 of Part 3 of the Schedule detail the power in relation to the production of information. These paragraphs set out the purposes for which the power can be used, the procedure to be followed when using it and how the power can be enforced, as well as limitations on the use of the information obtained.

362. Paragraph 18 clarifies that Part 3 of the Schedule applies to the Crown to the same extent that the relevant powers in Part 8 of the EA (which are being replaced by the powers in the Schedule) applied to the Crown.

363. Paragraph 19 to 20 of Part 4 of the Schedule sets out the purposes for which the further powers in the generic set detailed in this Part may be exercised by domestic and EU enforcers. These further powers are detailed in paragraphs 21 to 34. Table 1 and Table 2 below summarises how the powers in the generic set have been modified compared to those in the CPRs and other relevant legislation. The new safeguards that have been added are highlighted in bold.

364. These provisions in the Act give effect in part to certain EU legislation by providing domestic regulators with the necessary powers for enforcing such legislation. This includes the Regulation on Consumer Protection Cooperation, the Regulation on Accreditation and Market Surveillance and the General Product Safety Directive.

365. The existing investigatory powers are being repealed or revoked in order to ensure that only the generic set of powers apply in relation to the consumer legislation within the scope of this Schedule.

Table 1: Summary of main modifications from existing investigative powers in the new generic set in Part 3 of Schedule 5 (New safeguards are highlighted in bold)

Power/Provision	Modelled on	Main modifications from existing provisions
Paragraphs 13 to 17 – Power to require production of information (by way of a written notice only)	Section 224 to 227 EA	Certain enforcers, such as unfair contract terms enforcers and public designated enforcers, have access to this power only.
		Some enforcers are required to reasonably suspect a breach before exercising the power.
		Clarifies that it includes a power to require the creation of documents.
		Clarifies that local weights and measures authorities have access to this power specifically for the purposes of fulfilling duties conferred by the Estate Agents Act 1979.
		Can be used for both criminal and civil enforcement purposes.
		Provision is made regarding protection from self-incrimination.
Paragraph 18 Application to the Crown		Clarifies that Part 3 of the Schedule applies to the Crown when an enforcer is acting for certain purposes.

Table 2: Summary of main modifications from existing investigative powers in the new generic set in Part 4 of Schedule 5 (New safeguards are highlighted in bold)

Power/Provision	Modelled on	Main modifications from existing provisions
Paragraph 19 – Exercise of powers in this Part: Domestic enforcers	Regulation 21(1) CPRs and section 9 Estate Agents Act 1979	Details the purposes and circumstances in which the powers in this Part can be exercised by domestic enforcers.
		Clarifies that for the power to require production of documents, the enforcer need not have reasonable suspicion where there is a statutory duty to hold the documents sought or when the enforcer is a market surveillance authority as defined by the Regulation on Accreditation and Market Surveillance (EC 765/2008).
		Clarifies that the powers can be used to investigate undesirable practices under Estate Agents Act 1979 as well as breaches of it.
Paragraph 20 – Exercise of powers in this Part: EU Enforcers		Details the purposes and circumstances in which the powers in this Part can be exercised by EU enforcers.
Paragraph 21 – Power to purchase products	Regulation 20 CPRs	A new express provision is added to clarify that enforcers may enter premises normally open to the public and inspect products.
		The definition of officer in paragraph 7(1)(d) extends this power to authorised persons (e.g. volunteers).Clarification that power may be exercised at all reasonable times.
		Clarification that this power can be exercised without first giving notice or obtaining a warrant.

(Continued)

Table 2 (*Continued*)

Power/Provision	Modelled on	Main modifications from existing provisions
Paragraph 22 – Power to observe the carrying on of a business	Section 227B(1)(a) EA	A new express provision is added to clarify that enforcers may enter premises accessible to the public to observe businesses. Clarification that the power may be exercised at all reasonable times. Clarification that this power can be exercised without first giving notice or obtaining a warrant.
Paragraph 23 – Power to enter premises without warrant	Regulation 21(1)(a) CPRs (Currently excludes premises used only as a dwelling)	The power excludes entry to premises which are wholly or mainly private dwellings. **In relation to routine inspections there is a requirement to give written notice. There must be two working days between the date of receipt of the notice by the occupier and the date of entry by the enforcer. A routine inspection is defined in Schedule 5 as one where none of the circumstances in sub-paragraph (6) apply. These include circumstances where notice would defeat the purpose of the entry, e.g. because an officer reasonably suspects that evidence may be lost or destroyed if notice is given, such as where counterfeit goods are suspected. Notice also need not be given where the occupier has waived the requirement.** **If advance notice is not given, enforcers are required to give notice to occupiers when entering the premises.** **Enforcers are required to provide evidence of their authorisation and identity, whether or not advance notice has been given.** Clarification that proceedings are not invalid where there is a failure to provide notice or evidence of authorisation.
Paragraph 24 – Application of paragraphs 25 to 31		Clarifies that the powers in paragraphs 25–31 are only exercisable when the enforcer has entered premises under paragraph 23(1) or under a warrant under paragraph 32–33.
Paragraph 25 – Power to inspect products etc.	Regulation 21(1)(a) CPRs	This includes the power to inspect products, records and to examine any procedure on the premises, as well as inspecting any apparatus or fixed installation as defined in Electromagnetic Compatibility Regulations 2006 (SI 2006/3418).
Paragraph 26 – Power to test equipment	Weights and Measures Act 1985 and Weights and Measures (Packaged Goods) Regulations 2006	This power enables enforcers to test weighing and measuring instruments on the premises.
Paragraph 27 – Power to require production of documents	Regulation 21(1)(b) CPRs	Clarifies that this power includes requiring an explanation of documents. **Clarification that the power does not permit an officer to require a person to create a document except where documents are held electronically.** Clarification that the power can be applied to a business under investigation or another person.

Power/Provision	Modelled on	Main modifications from existing provisions
Paragraph 28 – Power to seize and detain goods	Regulation 21(c) CPRs	**Requirement for enforcers to provide evidence of their authorisation and identity, whether or not it is requested by the occupier, unless it is impractical to do so.**
		Requirement to issue a written record of goods seized.
		The power is available where an enforcer reasonably suspects goods may disclose a breach of legislation; that goods are liable to be forfeited or that they may be required as evidence in proceedings.
		The time limit on detention for goods is three months, unless they are reasonably needed for longer, e.g. for use in proceedings.
		Requirement for certain enforcers to have regard to any relevant provision on property seizure in a code of practice under section 66 Police and Criminal Evidence Act 1984 or Article 65 Police and Criminal Evidence (Northern Ireland) Order 1989 (SI 1989/1341 (NI 12)).
Paragraph 29 – Power to seize and detain documents required as evidence	Regulation 21(d) CPRs	**Requirement for enforcers to provide evidence of their authorisation and identity, whether or not it is requested by the occupier, unless it is impractical to do so.**
		Requirement to issue a written record of documents seized.
		The power is available where an enforcer reasonably suspects they may be required as evidence in proceedings.
		The time limit on detention for documents is three months, unless they are reasonably needed for longer for use in proceedings.
		Requirement for certain enforcers to have regard to any relevant provision on property seizure in a code of practice under section 66 Police and Criminal Evidence Act 1984 or Article 65 Police and Criminal Evidence (Northern Ireland) Order 1989 (SI 1989/1341 (NI 12)).
Paragraph 30 – Power to decommission or switch off fixed installations	Regulation 37 Electromagnetic Compatibility Regulations 2006	Confers a power to decommission or switch off fixed installations (as defined in the Electromagnetic Compatibility Regulations 2006).
Paragraph 31 – Power to break open a container/ vending machine	Regulation 21(2) CPRs	Clarification that the power includes access to information held on electronic devices, such as computers including those on a network.
		Clarification on what constitutes a container.
Paragraphs 32 to 33 – Power to enter premises with a warrant	Combination of Regulation 22 CPRs and 227C EA	Includes a condition that a Justice of the Peace must be satisfied that certain conditions have been met, such as that it is likely that goods or documents may be concealed or interfered with, if notice of entry were given.
		Where premises are unoccupied or occupier is temporally absent, officers will be required to issue a notice on leaving the premises stating that the premises have been entered under warrant and to leave the premises secured as found.

(Continued)

Table 2 (*Continued*)

Power/Provision	Modelled on	Main modifications from existing provisions
Paragraph 34 – Power to require assistance from persons on the premises	Provision under Weights and Measures legislation	Requirement for persons on premises to provide assistance or information reasonably required by the officer.
		Clarification that the power includes requiring a person on the premises to provide information about the name and address of the packer or importer of a package which the officer finds on the premises.

Table 3: Supplementary provisions in Part 5 of Schedule 5 (New safeguards are highlighted in bold)

Provision	Modelled on	Main modifications from existing provisions in CPRs
Paragraph 36 – Offence of obstruction	Combination of Regulation 23 CPRs and regulation 24(2)(b) General Product Safety Regulations 2005	Clarification that this offence applies in relation to powers exercised under Part 4.
		Includes an offence of recklessly making a statement which is false. Maximum penalties are aligned at level 3 on the standard scale.
		Clarification that a person commits an offence if they give misleading information.
Paragraph 37 – Offence of purporting to act as officer	Regulation 21(11) CPRs	Clarification that the level of the maximum penalty for this offence may be subject to amendment by section 85 of the Legal Aid, Sentencing and Punishment of Offenders Act 2012 and regulations made under that provision.
Paragraph 38 – Access to seized goods and documents	–	**Enforcers must grant reasonable access to goods and documents seized, e.g. so that copies of seized documents can be made. Enforcers may recover the reasonable costs of complying with such a request.**
Paragraph 39 – Notice of testing goods	Combination of Regulation 24 CPRs and Consumer Protection Act 1987 (CPA) and Electromagnetic Compatibility Regulations 2006	Clarification that there is a requirement for notice also to be given where the test leads to issuing of a suspension notice or the forfeiture of the goods.
Paragraph 40 – Appeals against detention of goods	Section 33 CPA	None.
Paragraph 41 – Compensation	Regulation 25 CPRs	None.

366. Additionally, Part 5 of the Schedule provides supplementary provisions. Paragraphs 36 and 37 respectively designate the acts of obstructing officers of enforcers and purporting to act as such an officer when not so authorised as offences. These and other provisions in the generic set are detailed in Table 3 above.

367. Also in Part 6 of this Schedule, the law in relation to the ability of Trading Standards Services is clarified to ensure that they are able to operate across local authority boundaries efficiently and effectively. This is set out at paragraphs 44 to 46 of the Schedule.

Section 78: Amendment of the Weights and Measures (Packaged Goods) Regulations 2006

368. This section provides an automatic exemption from keeping records of checks for packers of bread which is sold unwrapped or in open packs.

Section 79: Enterprise Act 2002: enhanced consumer measures and other enforcement

Introduction

369. The intention of this part of the Act is to amend Part 8 of the EA to allow the courts to attach a range of enhanced consumer measures to enforcement orders and undertakings. Public enforcers will also be able to agree undertakings under Part 8 that include enhanced consumer measures.

370. The main aim of the section is to give the civil courts and public enforcers flexibility when dealing with persons who have given undertakings or who are subject to enforcement orders. The section will allow a range of enhanced consumer measures that are just, reasonable and proportionate, to be attached to enforcement orders and undertakings.

371. The section will also introduce a power for the Secretary of State to extend the use of the enhanced consumer measures to private designated enforcers.

Background

372. When there is a breach or potential breach of consumer law, the measures available to public enforcers are limited and there is a lack of flexibility in the ways that they can achieve better outcomes for consumers and compliant businesses. The main formal sanction is a criminal prosecution of the trader by an enforcer. While this can benefit consumers as it prevents the spread of instances of illegal trading, in practice there is generally no direct remedy for victims of the breach.

373. As an alternative to criminal prosecution, certain enforcers can seek civil injunctive relief under Part 8 of the EA against infringements of consumer protection legislation. The key mechanism is an enforcement order. Through an enforcement order, a civil court can order that the infringer stop engaging in the conduct in question. It can also order that the infringer publish the enforcement order and a corrective statement, aiming to eliminate the continued effect of an infringement. Alternatively, a court or an enforcer may accept an undertaking from the business that they will not engage in conduct that involves an infringement. However, civil enforcement will not generally give remedies to individual consumers or secure positive action by businesses.

374. The Government's response to the consultation 'Extending the Range of Remedies Available to Public Enforcers of Consumer Law' sets out further information on the measures in this section. The response also confirms the Government's intention that the new enhanced consumer measures should always be just, reasonable and proportionate and aimed at achieving one or more of the following:

• redress for consumers who have suffered loss from breaches of consumer law;
• improved compliance and a reduction in the likelihood of future breaches; and
• more information being provided to consumers so they can exercise greater choice and in doing so improve the functioning of the market for consumers and businesses generally.

375. Details of possible measures are not included in the legislation as this may risk taking away flexibility from the courts and enforcers of consumer law to identify the most suitable measure or measures to deal with a person subject to enforcement orders or undertakings. It may also take away the flexibility for a person who is subject to enforcement orders or undertakings to put forward their own measures, which could be deemed suitable, to the court or enforcer of consumer law.

Part 8 Enterprise Act 2002

376. Part 8 of the EA enables certain enforcers to take civil action in respect of infringements of specified domestic/Community consumer legislation which harm the collective interests of consumers.

377. The enforcement procedure is set out at sections 214 to 223 of the EA. Key to this procedure is an application for an enforcement order (under section 215), following consultation with the business and notification of the CMA which can then be issued by the court (under section 217). As an alternative to issuing an enforcement order, the court may accept undertakings (section 217(9)). Similarly, as an alternative to making an application for an enforcement order the enforcer may accept undertakings (section 219).

Enforcers

378. There are a number of enforcers who are able to use this enforcement procedure. Some enforcers are specialist, within a particular market, for example the CAA; whereas others, like Trading Standards Services have a broader remit. The EA (section 213) provides for the following categories of enforcer: general; designated; community; and CPC.

379. Under section 213(4), the Secretary of State may designate a person or body which is not a public body only if the person or body (as the case may be) satisfies such criteria as the Secretary of State specifies by Order. Currently only the Consumers' Association (Which?) is designated as such.

380. The new enhanced consumer measures will only be available where the enforcer is a public body. A power is included to extend the use of the measures to private designated enforcers if certain conditions are met.

381. The section amends Part 8 of the EA to enable enforcement orders or undertakings to include new enhanced consumer measures, in addition to requirements that could be made under the existing legislation (i.e. generally a requirement to stop, or to not engage in the conduct that constitutes a breach of consumer law).

382. Section 79 introduces Schedule 7 and limits the use of the enhanced consumer measures to breaches or potential breaches of consumer law that occur, or are likely to occur, after the commencement of this section.

SCHEDULE 7: ENTERPRISE ACT 2002: ENHANCED CONSUMER
MEASURES AND OTHER ENFORCEMENT

383. The aim of Schedule 7 is to provide greater flexibility for public enforcers and the civil courts in relation to the contents of enforcement orders and undertakings made under Part 8 of the EA. If they are deemed suitable for a particular case, public enforcers and the civil courts will be able to attach (where they consider it just and reasonable) enhanced consumer measures to enforcement orders and undertakings. The enhanced consumer measures will need to fall into at least one of three specified categories (referred to as the redress, compliance and choice categories). Measures in the redress category will offer compensation or other redress to consumers who have suffered loss as a result of the breach of consumer law. Compliance measures are intended to increase business compliance with the law and to reduce the likelihood of further breaches. Measures in the choice category will help consumers obtain relevant market information to enable them to make better purchasing decisions.

384. Paragraphs 2 and 3 amend sections 210 and 211 of the EA to widen the injunctive regime under Part 8. This will enable enforcers to use it for infringements of domestic legislation that harm the collective interests of consumers where either the supplier or the consumer is in the UK.

385. Paragraph 4 updates the list of enforcers in the EA.

386. Paragraph 5 amends section 214 (consultation), and sub-paragraph (2) extends from 14 to 28 days the consultation period for enforcers of consumer law before they can take action against a person for an enforcement order or undertaking in cases where the new subsection (4A) applies (see paragraph 389 below).

387. Sub paragraph (3) inserts a new subsection (4A) that describes when the extended 28 day period applies. It applies in those cases where the person that may be subjected to the enforcement

order or undertaking is a member of, or represented by, a trade association or other business representative body that operates a consumer code of practice that has been approved by a public enforcement body or a community interest company whose role includes the approval of consumer codes.

388. In practice, the extended consultation period may be used, for example, by the person that may be subject to the enforcement order or undertaking to propose their own measures which may include addressing the detriment caused and be based on the requirements of the relevant consumer code. Depending on the circumstances of the case, this may be an indicator that the infringement will not be repeated. At the end of the 28 day period, the enforcer of consumer law may take further action if they consider it appropriate. They can either commence court action to seek an enforcement order and/or seek to work with the person to agree undertakings.

389. Paragraph 6 amends section 217 (enforcement orders) inserting new subsections (10A) to (10D). New subsection (10A) provides a power for the court to attach enhanced consumer measures defined in section 219A (paragraph 395 below) to an enforcement order and for the court to specify an appropriate time period for the person to comply with the enhanced consumer measures.

390. New subsection (10B) allows the court to attach enhanced consumer measures to an undertaking accepted under section (9) and for the court to specify an appropriate time period for the person to comply with the enhanced consumer measures.

391. New subsection (10C) restricts the court from attaching enhanced consumer measures to an enforcement order or undertaking sought by a private enforcer unless the conditions in new section 219C are met.

392. New subsection (10D) allows the court to include in an enforcement order or undertaking a requirement that the person subject to the enforcement order or undertaking provide information or documentation to the court to show that they have complied with the enhanced consumer measures.

393. Paragraph 7 amends section 219 (undertakings) inserting new subsections (5ZA) and (5ZB). New subsection (5ZA) enables public enforcers to include enhanced consumer measures in undertakings and to be provided with documentation from the person subject to the undertaking and to specify an appropriate time period for the person to comply with the enhanced consumer measures. Subsection (5ZA) also requires the person subject to the undertaking to provide information or documents to the enforcer to enable them to determine if the person is carrying out the enhanced consumer measures agreed in the undertaking.

394. New subsection (5ZB) restricts private enforcers from agreeing an undertaking with enhanced consumer measures unless the conditions in new section 219C are met.

395. Paragraph 8 inserts new sections 219A (definition of enhanced consumer measures) and 219B (inclusion of enhanced consumer measures etc) and 219C (availability of enhanced consumer measures to private enforcers). New section 219A(1) lists the three categories of enhanced consumer measures—redress, compliance and choice. Subsections (2) to (5) describe those measures.

396. New subsection (2) describes the first category of measures—the redress category. New subsection (2)(a) limits compensation or redress to those consumers who have suffered loss as a result of the breach of consumer law. This is mirrored in new section 219B(4)(a). Consumers retain the right to refuse offers of redress, whether in an enforcement order or undertaking, and instead take their own civil action against the person that has caused them detriment. Where the infringing conduct relates to a contract, new subsection (2)(b) states that measures in the redress category can include giving consumers the option to terminate that contract. New subsection (2)(c) allows for measures intended to be in the collective interests of consumers in cases where consumers who have suffered detriment cannot be identified or it would require a disproportionate cost to do so. Measures in these circumstances could include, for example, the non-compliant business making a charitable donation equivalent to the value of the detriment caused to consumers (where that charity acts in the interests of consumers). New subsection (2)(c) only applies in the circumstances outlined above. It does not apply in

circumstances where consumers who have been identified as suffering detriment choose to decline the redress offered.

397. New subsections (3) and (4) describe the measures in the second and third categories—the compliance and choice categories. Measures in these categories might include the person subject to the enforcement order or undertaking:

- appointing a compliance officer;
- introducing a complaints handling process;
- improving their record keeping;
- signing up to an established customer review/feedback site; or
- publicising details of the breach or potential breach, and what they have done to put the situation right in the local or national press or on social media.

398. New subsection (5) excludes the existing publication requirements within Part 8 of the EA from the scope of the new enhanced consumer measures.

399. New section 219B sets out the requirements that apply to the inclusion of enhanced consumer measures within an enforcement order or undertaking. New subsection (1) confirms that only just and reasonable enhanced consumer measures can be attached to enforcement orders or undertakings under this Part. New subsections (2) and (3) set out the factors the court or enforcer must take into account. This includes a specific requirement that the measures must be proportionate, taking into account the costs of the measures (to business and consumers) and the benefit to consumers.

400. New subsections (4) to (5) make provision in relation to a loss case (which is defined in new subsections (9) and (10)). These provisions restrict the imposition of enhanced consumer measures in the redress category to cases where there has been a loss suffered by consumers and require that in those cases, the court or enforcer must be satisfied that the cost to the person subject to the enforcement order or undertaking of complying with the measures is unlikely to exceed the loss suffered by consumers. However, the administrative costs (i.e. the cost of setting up and running the redress scheme) should not be included in this calculation.

401. New subsections (6) and (7) limit any waiver sought by the person who is subject to an enforcement order or undertaking, from consumers as part of a compensation scheme, so that the waiver is not valid to the extent that it seeks to cover conduct which is not covered by the enforcement order or undertaking. For example, the waiver will not be valid if it relates to additional goods or services that were not covered by the enforcement order or undertaking.

402. New section 219C sets out the conditions that must be met before enhanced consumer measures can be sought in an undertaking or order sought by a private enforcer.

403. New subsection (3) sets out the first condition, which is that the enforcer must have been specified by the Secretary of State in an Order under this section.

404. New subsection (4) sets out the second condition, which is that the enhanced consumer measures must not directly benefit the enforcer or an associated undertaking. New subsection (5) sets out particular types of measure that would be considered as directly benefitting the enforcer or an associated undertaking. These include requiring a person to pay money to the private enforcer, requiring a person to participate in a scheme designed to recommend goods or services that is administered by the private enforcer or where the measure would give the private enforcer a commercial advantage over any of its competitors.

405. New subsection (6) provides that the Secretary of State can only exercise the power in subsection (3) to extend the use of the enhanced consumer measures to a private enforcer if they are satisfied that it will result in:

- more redress being paid to consumers;
- more information being provided to consumers to enable them to make better informed purchasing decisions; and/or
- more compliance by business with the law.

406. New subsection (7) provides that the Secretary of State can only use the power in subsection (3) if the private enforcer is subject to the principles of good regulation in the Regulators Code and section 21 of the Legislative and Regulatory Reform Act 2006 (transparency, accountability, proportionality, consistency and targeting cases that need action).

407. New subsections (9) and (10) set out a requirement on private enforcers that when using enhanced consumer measures they must act consistently with advice or guidance given by a primary authority.

408. New subsection (11) defines 'associated undertaking'.

409. Paragraph 9 makes amendments to section 220 of the EA (further proceedings), which makes provision for further applications to the court where there has been a failure to comply with an enforcement order or undertaking made under sections 217 and 218 of the EA. Sub-paragraph (2) inserts a new subsection (1A) which provides that section 220 does not apply where the only failure is a failure to comply with the information requirement in new subsection 217(10D).

410. Subsection 220(2) of the EA gives the CMA the same right to apply to the court in respect of a failure to comply with an order or undertaking as the enforcer that made the application for the order. Sub-paragraph (3) amends subsection 220(2) to provide that any CPC enforcer (defined in section 213(5A)) has that right, not just the CMA.

411. Sub-paragraph (4) contains related or consequential amendments to Part 8 of the EA.

412. Paragraph 10 updates the EA to reflect the enforcement of Schedule 5 in the Consumer Rights Act 2015.

Section 80: Contravention of code regulating premium rate services

413. Under sections 120 to 123 of the Communications Act 2003, providers of premium rate services are obliged to comply with the code published by the regulator, PhonepayPlus, and approved by Ofcom for the purposes of regulating such services. Premium rate services are a form of micro-payment for content, data services and value added services charged to a telephone bill. They include services such as directory inquiries, voting in competitions and quizzes, business information lines, making charity donations by text and making payment for digital goods and services.

414. PhonepayPlus may impose a maximum penalty of £250,000 in respect of a contravention of the code. For example, some providers may use intentionally misleading promotional material or fail to provide clear pricing information, leaving consumers out of pocket.

415. This section amends these provisions to make clear that the maximum penalty of £250,000 can be imposed in respect of each breach of the code and not, as has been argued by some providers, just once regardless of the number of provisions of the code that have been breached in any one set of proceedings against a provider.

416. This will allow PhonepayPlus to impose penalties of more than £250,000 in appropriate cases and where it is proportionate to do so.

CHAPTER 2:
COMPETITION

Summary and Background

417. This Chapter deals with the scope and operation of the Competition Appeals Tribunal. It introduces provisions to make it easier for consumers and businesses to gain access to redress where there has been an infringement of antitrust provisions ('competition law'), and addresses the unintended barriers in the current process to the appointment of Scottish and Northern Irish judges to sit as chairmen in the Competition Appeal Tribunal (CAT).

Section 81: Private actions in competition law

418. Section 81 and Schedule 8 have three main aims:

• To widen the types of the competition cases that the Competition Appeal Tribunal hears ('CAT') (see paragraph 420 to 433 below) and to make other changes to the procedure of bringing a private action before the CAT;
• To provide for opt-out collective actions and opt-out collective settlements (see paragraphs 434 to 445 below);
• To provide for voluntary redress schemes (see paragraph 446 to 450 below).

419. The Government's response to the consultation 'Private Actions in Competition Law', explains the proposals for reform of claims for damages under the private actions framework in Part 3 of this Act. There are also further proposed changes accompanying these sections in the CAT's rules which govern how it deals with cases.

Widen the types of cases which the CAT can hear

420. The CAT is a specialist tribunal whose function is to hear cases involving competition issues. However, at present, the CAT is restricted in which competition law cases it can consider. The CAT is able to hear follow-on cases. A follow-on action is brought after an infringement has been found by 'a relevant competition authority', which are the Competition and Markets Authority ('CMA'), European Commission and the following relevant sector regulators with competition powers:

• The Office of Gas and Electricity Markets ('Ofgem');
• The Office of Communications ('Ofcom');
• The Water Service Regulation Authority ('Ofwat');
• Civil Aviation Authority ('CAA');
• Office of the Rail Regulator ('ORR');
• Northern Ireland Authority for Utility Regulation ('NIAUR');
• Monitor.

421. In contrast, a stand-alone claim requires the party which brings the action to prove an infringement. In *Enron v EWS* (I), the Court of Appeal ruled that the scope for the CAT to go beyond the findings of the initial infringement decision is extremely limited. This judgment is widely thought to be one of the contributing factors restricting the role of the CAT in competition law actions in the current regime. Businesses or consumers who wish to bring stand-alone cases must bring their case in the High Court of England and Wales, the Court of Session or the Sheriff Court in Scotland or the High Court of Northern Ireland.

422. In addition, whilst the CAT may award damages for follow-on actions, it does not have the power to grant injunctions (an order which prohibits a party from doing a particular act). This restriction prevents a party from obtaining redress from the CAT in the form of an order prohibiting, for example, anti-competitive pricing. At present, a party seeking an injunction would need to apply to the High Court.

423. Paragraph 4 replaces section 47A of the Competition Act 1998 ('CA') which currently only provides for follow-on cases to be brought before the CAT. Paragraph 4 enables the CAT to hear a stand-alone claim as well as a follow-on claim and also to have the power to grant injunctions.

424. Paragraph 31 inserts paragraph 15A of the EA to allow rules to be made providing for a fast-track procedure for claims brought under s.47A of the CA. The purpose of this is to enable simpler cases brought by small and medium enterprises ('SMEs') to be resolved more quickly and at a lower cost.

425. Paragraph 7 introduces a new section 47D of the CA, This provides that an injunction granted under s.47A and in respect of collective proceedings is enforceable as if it were granted

by the High Court. This means that if the injunction is breached, a party may bring proceedings for breach of the injunction, such as contempt proceedings which could result in a penalty such as a fine.

426. Paragraph 24 amends Schedule 4 of the EA providing for enforcement of injunctions granted under section 47A of the CA. It does this by providing that where a party fails to comply with an injunction, the CAT may certify the matter to the High Court, i.e. sets out the facts and evidence of the matter.

427. Paragraph 34 amends Schedule 4 of EA to enable rules to be made about the grant of injunctions by the CAT.

428. Paragraph 8 introduces a new section 47E of the CA. This provides that the limitation/prescription periods (the time limit for claims to be brought) for claims before the CAT are the same as the relevant limitation/prescription period for claims before the High Court in England and Wales, the Court of Session in Scotland, the High Court in Northern Ireland. At present, the limitation period for claims before the CAT is two years, compared with six years for a claim before the High Court of England and Wales and the High Court in Northern Ireland and five years for the Court of Session in Scotland. See paragraph 442 below for how the limitation/prescription periods may be suspended in the case of collective actions.

429. Paragraph 13 amends section 58 of the CA to make clear that the CAT is bound by a finding of fact of the CMA, unless it directs otherwise. This is to ensure the CAT has sufficient flexibility when dealing with case and is in the same position as a court which hears a competition case. A court is already able to make such a direction.

430. Paragraph 9 amends section 49 of the CA to provide for a right of appeal against a decision of the CAT in proceedings brought under section 47A of the CA (stand-alone or follow-on actions) or 47B of the CA (collective proceedings). Where the appeal concerns section 47B, it may only be brought by the representative in those proceedings.

431. Paragraph 14 replaces existing section 58A of the CA. The purpose of this is to make clear when a court or the CAT is bound by a decision that there has been an infringement of competition law. This ensures the position is the same for the court and the CAT. New section 58A ensures that once an infringement decision has become final, the court or the CAT is bound by it. New section 58A sets out when a decision becomes final, for example when the time for appealing against the decision has expired without an appeal having been brought.

432. Paragraph 32 amends paragraph 17 of Schedule 4 to the EA, to enable rules to be made to enable the CAT to order payments to a legal party who has been acting on behalf of a business or consumer for free (i.e. on a pro bono basis).

433. Paragraph 33 inserts paragraph 20A of Schedule 4 to the EA which enables rules to be made which enable the CAT to stay or sist proceedings under section 47A and 47B. This is because the CAT may wish to stay (or sist) proceedings, for example if the original infringement decision is subject to appeal and that appeal has not yet been decided.

Collective actions and opt-out collective settlements

434. The second aim is to introduce an opt-out collective actions regime and an opt-out collective settlement regime (both of which involve a case being brought forward on behalf of a group of claimants to obtain compensation for their losses). Cases would be able to be brought by representatives on behalf of individuals and/or businesses.

435. The CAT can already hear opt-in collective actions under the existing section 47B of the CA. An opt-in regime requires claimants to 'opt-in' to the legal action to be able to obtain any damages. However, the CAT does not currently have the power to hear opt-out collective actions. An opt-out regime means claimants are automatically included into the action unless they 'opt-out' in a manner as decided by the CAT on a case by case basis. The purpose of introducing opt-out collective actions is to allow consumers and businesses to easily achieve redress for losses they have suffered as a result of breaches of competition law.

436. The function of a collective settlement regime is to introduce a procedure for infringements of competition law, where those who have suffered a loss and the alleged infringer may jointly apply to the CAT to approve the settlement of a dispute on an opt-out basis. The collective settlement regime will operate on the same opt-out principles as the opt-out collective proceedings.

437. Paragraph 5 replaces section 47B of the CA so as to provide for opt-out collective proceedings, as well as continuing to provide for opt-in collective proceedings. Subsection (11) defines opt-out collective proceedings and also provides that a person who is not domiciled in the United Kingdom must opt-in to become part of the proceedings. Subsection (10) defines opt-in collective proceedings. Subsection (4) provides that collective proceedings may only be progressed if the CAT makes a collective proceedings order. Subsection (5) provides that that CAT may only make a collective proceedings order if it considers the person who brought the proceedings meets the requirements of subsection (8) and the claims are eligible for inclusion in collective proceedings (they fall within the claims provided for in section 47A of the CA, so the proceedings may either be stand-alone or follow-on). Subsection (8) provides that a representative must be a person whom the Tribunal considers it is just and reasonable to appoint as a representative. The current section 47B of the CA only allows for named representative bodies to bring opt-in collective actions. Currently, this only includes the consumer organization Which?. The new subsection (8) will enable any appropriate representative, such as a consumer body or trade association to bring claims on behalf of consumers or businesses, as long all the claims raise the same, similar or related issues of fact or law under section 49B(6).

438. Paragraph 6 introduces new section 47C of the CA. Subsection (1) prohibits the CAT from awarding exemplary damages in collective proceedings, i.e. damages which are designed to be punitive rather than simply compensate for the actual loss suffered. This is to avoid very large damages being awarded which do not reflect the losses suffered. Subsection (2) enables the CAT to determine the damages due in collective proceedings without being required to consider each claim which forms part of the action. This is designed the avoid the CAT having to spend time assessing many individual claims and instead enables the CAT to group the claims together for the purpose of assessing damages. Subsection (5) provides that damages not claimed in opt-out collective proceedings must be paid to a charity specified by section 194(8) of the Legal Services Act 2007, unless under subsection (6) the Tribunal decides to award part or all of any unclaimed damages to the claimant's representative to cover their costs. Currently, the charity is the Access to Justice Foundation as recommended by the Jackson Review of Costs, the Civil Justice Council and HM Treasury's Financial Services Rules committee as a suitable body to receive unclaimed sums. Subsection (7) allows the Secretary of State to make regulations to substitute a different a different charity for one being prescribed at the time. Subsection (8) provides that damages-based agreements are not allowed in opt-out collective actions. A damages-based agreement is where some of the damages are paid to the legal representatives. Paragraph 37 amends section 58AA of the Courts and Legal Services Act 1990, to make clear this restriction on damages-based agreements applies, notwithstanding the other provisions of that Act.

439. Paragraph 25 amends Schedule 4 of the EA to allow representatives in a collective action to be able to take action to enforce an order concerning damages in collective proceedings.

440. Paragraph 26 replaces paragraph 6(a) and amends paragraph 6(b) of Schedule 4 EA to provide that where damages are awarded in a collective action to a person who is not a party to the order (i.e. they are not the representative or another person who the CAT considers are suitable to hold the damages and then distribute) or costs or expenses are awarded to a person in respect of a claim made under section 47A of the CA before it became part of the collective proceedings, it may only be enforced if permission is granted by the High Court or the Court of Session. This is to provide some judicial control over the volume of enforcement claims being made by persons who are not the representative or another person who the CAT considers is suitable to hold the damages.

441. Paragraph 27 amends paragraph 7 of Schedule 4 of the EA so that where any award of costs is made against a representative in collective proceedings, the person who is being represented (i.e. a particular business or consumer) may not be held responsible for those costs. This provision is designed to prevent legal costs being passed on from the representative to the persons who are being represented.

442. Paragraph 8 (see paragraph 428 above) introduces new section 47E of the CA which makes provisions about the limitation/prescription periods for claims before the CAT. Subsection (4) provides for there to be a suspension of the limitation/prescription period where claims are made under section 47B of the CA (collective proceedings). The purpose of this is to discourage parties from also commencing separate section 47A proceedings before the CAT, so as to protect their position. This is because the collective proceedings may only progress if a collective proceedings order is made. As this may not be made for some time, a party may be tempted to bring separate section 47A proceedings before the CAT to avoid the limitation/prescription period expiring before it knows whether the collective proceedings can be continued. The suspension of the limitation/prescription period offers protection to claimants who might otherwise be time-barred in bringing a single claim if the collective proceedings fail. Subsection (5) sets out when the limitation/prescription period will resume, such as where the Tribunal declines to make a collective proceedings order. Paragraph 29 replaces paragraph 11(2)(a) of Schedule 4 EA to enable rules to be made about the operation of the limitation and prescription periods.

443. The Government is also keen to encourage parties to settle disputes. To do this it is providing for collective settlements in opt-out collective proceedings where a collective proceedings order has been made as well as in cases where a collective proceedings order has not been made. The Government is also introducing voluntary redress schemes (see paragraphs 446 – 450 below). Paragraph 10 provides for a new section 49A of the CA which provides for collective settlements where a collective proceedings order has been made. Subsection (2) provides that the representative and the defendant must apply for approval of the proposed collective settlement. Subsection (4) provides that where there are multiple defendants, the defendants who want to be bound by an approved collective settlement must apply to the CAT. Subsection (5) provides that the CAT may approve the collective settlement if it is satisfied the terms are just and reasonable. Subsections (6) to (10) describes which persons are bound by the collective settlement.

444. Paragraph 11 introduces a new section 49B of the CA which enables a collective settlement to be made where a collective proceedings order has not been made. This procedure may be relevant if parties are at an early stage of the litigation. Subsection (4) requires that the CAT may only approve the collective settlement if it makes a collective settlement order. Subsection (5) provides that this requires the CAT to consider the person who proposes to be the settlement representative is a person who the CAT could approve as being a settlement representative and that if collective proceedings were brought, the claims would be suitable for inclusion in such proceedings. Subsection (8) provides the CAT may only approve the collective settlement if it considers its terms are just and reasonable. Subsections (9) and (10) provide for who is bound by a collective settlement order.

445. Paragraph 31 introduces paragraph 15C to Schedule 4 of the EA to provide that rules can be made about collective settlements. It also enables rules to be made to provide for costs to be paid by an underlying claimant who is not the representative in a collective action, in limited circumstances where he or she makes an application. For example, where a claimant makes an application to have their representative removed.

Voluntary redress schemes

446. The third aim is to define a voluntary redress scheme (referred to in legislation as a 'redress scheme') so as to put it on a statutory footing. The government is keen for parties who are found liable for a breach of competition law to enter into negotiations with consumers or businesses where possible rather than the first route being a private action proceeding through

the courts. The intention is to provide suitable, alternative mechanisms to allow for alternative dispute resolution. One mechanism is to allow the CMA to certify voluntary redress schemes that are entered into by businesses that have been found to have infringed competition law.

447. To support this goal, Government is introducing a new power enabling the CMA to certify redress schemes. Even without the certification, voluntary redress schemes can still be offered. However, Government wishes to place voluntary redress schemes on a firmer legal footing by allowing the CMA to approve binding, voluntary undertakings as to a compensation scheme. The intention would be that the CMA could take into account whether a business had bound themselves to provide redress when assessing the level of fine for the competition law breach.

448. Accordingly, paragraph 12 introduces new section 49C, which provides that the CMA may decide to approve a voluntary redress scheme (which may be put forward to the CMA prior to an infringement decision or after the decision has been made). Where a scheme is submitted prior to the CMA making an infringement decision, the CMA may approve an outline of the voluntary redress scheme, if it makes an infringement decision. The CMA may then require the business to create the full scheme afterwards which complies with any conditions imposed, such as the provision for further information by a set date. If the business does not comply with the conditions, the CMA may withdraw its approval of the voluntary redress scheme. Although the CMA will not determine the level of compensation that should be paid under the scheme, subsection (3) allows the CMA to take into account the amount or value of compensation when deciding whether or not to approve a voluntary redress scheme. This is to permit the CMA to reject a scheme, if the compensation on offer seems exceptionally low. Subsection (8) provides that the Secretary of State may make regulations about the approval of voluntary redress schemes. These regulations may make provisions about the procedure for approval, including the information to be provided. In addition, they may set out the factors the CMA should or should not take into account when considering applications for approval.

449. Paragraph 12 also inserts new section 49D to the CA. Section 49D provides that the CMA may require a person who applies for the approval of a voluntary redress scheme to pay the CMA's reasonable costs. The CMA will incur costs in considering an application for approval. In addition, paragraph 12 also inserts new section 49E to CA which provides in subsection (1) that a party who has a voluntary redress scheme approved has a duty to comply with its terms. Subsection (3) provides that if a business or consumer suffers as a result of a breach by a business of the terms of voluntary redress scheme, they may bring legal proceedings before a court for damages or another remedy, such as an injunction. This is to ensure there are remedies available for a breach of a voluntary redress scheme.

450. Paragraph 17 amends Schedule 8 of CA to allow for a business to appeal to the CAT against any costs imposed by the CMA in respect of a voluntary redress scheme.

Section 82: Appointment of Judges to the Competition Appeal Tribunal

451. This section changes the current process for appointing judges to the CAT to make it easier for judges from Scotland and Northern Ireland to be able to sit in the Tribunal as chairmen. It does this by providing for the Lord Chief Justices of England and Wales, and Northern Ireland and the Lord President of the Court of Session to be able to nominate judges sitting in their respective High Courts or the Court of Session for deployment as CAT chairmen.

452. Under the new provisions, the Lord Chief Justice of England and Wales will be able to nominate suitably qualified judges sitting in any Division of the High Court to be deployed as a judge in the CAT to sit as a chairman; currently, only judges appointed to the Chancery Division are appointed as CAT Chairs.

453. As a consequence of the change, the current eight year limit on appointment of judges in the CAT to sit as chairmen will not apply to those judges nominated to sit in the CAT and they will be able to sit until their retirement from the judiciary.

CHAPTER 3:
DUTY OF LETTING AGENTS TO PUBLICISE FEES ETC.

Summary and background

454. This Chapter imposes a duty on letting agents to publicise their fees, whether or not they are a member of a client money protection scheme and which redress scheme they have joined (fees etc). It explains which letting agents and which fees etc the duty applies to and details the enforcement of the duty.

455. Currently, although consumer rights legislation and guidance recommend that traders are clear and upfront about the fees which they charge, there is no specific duty for letting agents to display or publish their fees.

Section 83: Duty of letting agents to publicise fees etc

456. This section imposes a duty on letting agents to publicise 'relevant fees' (see commentary on section 85) and sets out how they must do this.

457. *Subsection (2)* requires agents to display a list of their fees at each of their premises where they deal face to face with customers and *subsection (3)* requires them to also publish a list of their fees on their website where they have a website.

458. *Subsection (4)* sets out what must be included in the list as follows. Subsection (4)(a) requires the fees to be described in such a way that a person who may have to pay the fee can understand what service or cost is covered by the fee or the reason why the fee is being imposed. For example, it will not be sufficient to call something an 'administration fee' without further describing what administrative costs or services that fee covers.

459. Subsection (4)(b) requires that where fees are charged to tenants the list should make clear whether the fee relates to each tenant under a tenancy or to the property. Finally, subsection (4)(c) requires the list to include the amount of each fee inclusive of tax, or, where the amount of the fee cannot be determined in advance a description of how that fee will be calculated. An example might be where a letting agent charges a landlord based on a percentage of rent.

460. *Subsection (6)* applies to letting agents who hold money on behalf of their clients as part of their letting agent or property management work. As well as publicising their fees, the agent must publish a statement which states whether or not that agent is a member of a client money protection scheme.

461. *Subsection (7)* means that agents who are required to belong to a redress scheme for dealing with complaints must publish which redress scheme they are a member of.

462. *Subsection (8)* enables the appropriate national authority to specify in regulations other ways in which letting agents must publicise details of their fees and the details that must be published. This could be used, for instance, to require letting agents to include information about fees in advertisements.

463. *Subsection (9)* defines a client money protection scheme and a redress scheme. A client money protection scheme is defined as a scheme which enables a client on whose behalf a letting agent holds money to be compensated by that scheme if all or part of that money is not repaid in circumstances where the scheme applies. A redress scheme is defined as a scheme which has been approved by the Secretary of State by order under section 83 or 84 of the Enterprise and Regulatory Reform Act 2013.

Section 84: Letting agents to which the duty applies

464. This section defines who is a 'letting agent' and explains when someone who could be regarded as a letting agent is exempt from the requirements of this Chapter.

465. *Subsection (1)* defines a letting agent as someone who engages in 'letting agency work', which is defined in section 86.

466. *Subsection (2)* excludes a person who carries out letting agency work as part of their employment contract. This is to ensure that a salaried employee is not held responsible for publishing the fees.

467. *Subsection (3)* gives powers to the appropriate national authority to exclude other persons and activities in regulations.

Section 85: Fees to which the duty applies

468. This section defines 'relevant fees' for the purposes of the duty to publicise fees.

469. *Subsection (1)* provides that 'relevant fees' are the fees, charges or penalties which a landlord or tenant pays to the agent in relation to letting agency work, property management work or otherwise in connection with an assured tenancy or a dwelling-house let under an assured tenancy. *Subsection (2)* excludes certain payments from the definition of 'relevant fees'. Subsection (2)(a) excludes the rent payable to a landlord (many agents collect the rent on behalf of the landlord). Subsection (2)(b) excludes fees, charges or penalties which a landlord has to pay the agent but which the agent simply passes onto another person. For example, an agent may pay a gardener on behalf of a landlord and then reclaim this money from the landlord. Subsection (2)(c) excludes the deposit which is paid by the tenant in respect of the tenancy. Subsection (2)(d) gives the appropriate national authority the power to exclude other payments from the definition of 'relevant fees'.

Section 86: Letting agency work and property management work

470. This section defines letting agency work and property management work for the purposes of this Chapter.

471. *Subsection (1)* defines letting agency work as work undertaken on behalf of prospective landlords and prospective tenants and covers the process both of finding a tenant for the landlord or a property for a tenant and the work done to put the tenancy in place. It applies only to the letting of privately rented homes. *Subsection (2)* excludes from the definition of letting agency work those businesses that simply allow landlords and tenants to find and communicate with one another, provided they do not otherwise participate in the transaction.

472. *Subsection (3)* provides that local authorities are not included and thereby ensures that, for example, any local letting agency business established by local authorities is not caught by the duty in section 83.

473. *Subsection (4)* defines property management work for the purposes of this Chapter. The premises managed must consist of a dwelling-house let under an assured tenancy. As with letting agency work, property management work applies only to privately rented homes (see commentary on section 88 below).

Section 87: Enforcement of the duty

474. *Subsection (1)* places a duty on every local weights and measures authority in England and Wales to enforce the requirement for letting agents to publicise their fees etc in its area.

475. *Subsection (2)* sets out that, if an agent breaches the duty in section 83(3) to publicise fees on its website, that breach is taken to have occurred in the area in which the property to which the fees relate is located.

476. *Subsection (3)* enables local weights and measures authorities who are satisfied on the balance of probabilities that a letting agent has breached the requirement to impose a financial penalty on the agent in respect of that breach.

477. *Subsection (4)* provides that while it is the duty of local weights and measures authorities to enforce the requirement in their area, they may also impose a penalty in respect of a breach which occurs in England and Wales but outside that authority's area. However, *subsection (6)* ensures that an agent may only be fined once in respect of the same breach.

478. *Subsection (5)* requires a local weights and measures authority who wants to impose a fine in respect of a breach outside its own area but in the area of a Welsh authority, to seek the consent of that authority.

479. *Subsection (7)* provides that local weights and measures authorities may fine letting agents in breach of the requirement up to £5,000. When imposing a fine, *subsection (8)* states that authorities must follow the process described in Schedule 9.

480. *Subsection (9)* requires a local weights and measures authority in England to have regard to any guidance issued by the Secretary of State about how letting agents should comply with the duty to publicise their fees etc and on how the authority should carry out its enforcement duties.

481. Similarly *subsection (10)* requires a local weights and measures authority in Wales to have regard to any guidance issued by the Welsh Ministers about how letting agents should comply with the duty to publicise their fees etc and on how the authority should carry out its enforcement duties.

482. *Subsection (11) and (12)* give both the Secretary of State and the Welsh Ministers the power to make secondary legislation which amends the enforcement provisions and make the necessary consequential amendments for England and Wales respectively.

Section 88: Supplementary provisions

483. *Subsections (1) to (4)* provide the remaining definitions of the terms used in this Chapter. The definition of an assured tenancy is relevant to determining firstly who is a letting agent for the purposes of this Chapter and, secondly, the fees to which the duty applies. *Subsection (1)* defines an assured tenancy (which is the most common type of tenancy in the private rented sector) for these purposes. In particular, the definition of an assured tenancy excludes assured tenancies granted by a private registered provider of social housing and any assured tenancy that is a long lease. This ensures that the duty applies to agents who let properties in the private rented sector and to the fees, penalties and charges that they charge in connection with the letting, management etc. of such properties.

484. *Subsections (5) to (9)* set out the Parliamentary procedures for making the regulations detailed in this Chapter and *subsections (10) and (11)* provide a power for incidental provision to be made.

CHAPTER 4:
STUDENT COMPLAINTS SCHEME

Section 89: Qualifying Institutions for the purposes of the student complaints scheme

485. The section expands the list of higher education providers which are required to join the higher education complaints handling scheme. All those delivering courses which are specifically or automatically designated to receive student support funding in England and Wales and providers with degree awarding powers will be required to join. This scheme was set up under the provisions of the Higher Education Act 2004 and is operated by the Office of the Independent Adjudicator for Higher Education.

CHAPTER 5:
SECONDARY TICKETING

Summary and Background

486. This Chapter concerns the online secondary ticketing market. That is, the market where tickets for sporting, recreational and cultural events are re-sold having been first bought or otherwise acquired on the primary market from an event organiser. It concerns:

- Information which must be provided in respect of a ticket to its buyer, when that ticket is resold online;
- The original terms and conditions of a ticket;
- Reporting of criminal activity on online ticket marketplaces; and
- A review of the online secondary ticketing market.

487. Currently, there are no provisions in statute specifically regulating the online secondary ticketing market. There is, however, other legislation which applies generally and in so doing covers the market, including:

- The Consumer Contracts (Information, Cancellation and Additional Charges) Regulations 2013 (SI 2013/3134) which provide that certain information must be provided when goods, a service or digital content are sold by a trader to a consumer, including sales concluded at a distance (e.g. online);
- Section 166 of the Criminal Justice and Public Order Act 1994 which regulates the re-selling of tickets for certain football matches;
- The Fraud Act 2006 and the Consumer Protection from Unfair Trading Regulations 2008 (SI 2008/1277) which aim to protect buyers from misleading or fraudulent sales; and
- The Unfair Terms in Consumer Contracts Regulations 1999 (SI 1999/2083) (which are to be replaced by Part 2 of the Act once Part 2 comes into force) which provide that terms in a consumer contract must be fair.

488. This Chapter applies to tickets for all recreational, sporting and cultural events taking place in the UK.

Duty to provide information about tickets

Section 90: Duty to provide information about tickets

489. Section 90 sets out the information which is to be provided when a ticket is re-sold online by virtue of these provisions. As noted above, additional statutory information requirements may also apply. This section applies when a ticket is re-sold through an online secondary ticketing facility. This might be a website but could equally be a web based application (or other type of online facility). This section applies to tickets first offered for re-sale after the entry into force of the section.

490. The duty to provide information rests on both the seller of the ticket and the person operating the online facility through which it is being sold. In practice, it will be for the seller to give the information when they go to list their tickets online, and for the operator then to ensure that this information is given to the buyer.

491. There are four pieces of information which must be given. Firstly, *subsection (3)(a)* requires information to enable the buyer to identify the particular seat or standing area of the venue to which the ticket applies. This includes, where applicable, the name of the relevant area of the venue, the block in which the seat or relevant area is located, and the row and number of the seat. Where the seat and row are identified by something other than a number, this identifier must also be given.

492. Secondly, under *subsection (3)(b)* the buyer must be given information about any restrictions that apply to the ticket and concern who can use it. For example, the ticket might be for a specific area reserved for disabled persons, or it might only be able to be used by those under 12 years old.

493. Thirdly, *subsection (3)(c)* requires the face value of the ticket to be given. This is the price printed on the ticket itself. This will likely be the price at which the seller originally bought the ticket for.

494. Fourthly, where the seller has a connection with the online facility on which they are selling, or the organiser of the event for which the ticket is being sold, under *subsection (6)* they must state that this is the case, and what that connection is. For example, if the seller is an employee of the facility which they are using to sell the tickets, they must give the buyer that information. Where the seller is the operator of the facility itself, this information must be given.

495. In each case, the seller only has to provide this information where it is applicable to them or the ticket they are selling. For example, where a ticket is for a standing section of a venue, the seller does not have to give a seat number. The seller must make reasonable attempts to obtain and then provide this information to the buyer, however it is acknowledged that there are circumstances where this might not be possible, such as where the ticket is resold before the event organiser has allocated seat numbers.

496. *Subsection (8)* requires the information to be provided in a clear and comprehensible manner, and before the buyer purchases the ticket. For example, the information would be clearly displayed in a legible font before the buyer clicks on a button marked 'confirm purchase'.

Section 91: Prohibition on cancellation or blacklisting

497. Section 91 sites alongside section 90 and provides for consumer protections when the information required by section 90 is given. Information provided under section 90 could be used by an event organiser to cancel a ticket or blacklist a seller. An event organiser may also seek to cancel a ticket or blacklist a seller for other reasons or based on other information.

498. Section 91 provides that an event organiser cannot cancel a ticket (*subsection (2)*) or blacklist a seller (*subsection (3)*) merely because that ticket is resold or offered for resale unless two conditions are met:

499. Firstly, it must be a term of the contract under which the original buyer purchased the ticket from the event organiser that cancellation of the ticket and/or blacklisting of the seller may occur as a consequence of that ticket being resold or offered for resale.

500. Secondly, that term of the contract under which the original buyer purchased the ticket from the event organiser must not be unfair. The fairness of terms in consumer contracts is assessable under Part 2 of this Act (see paragraphs 287 to 348 of these notes) and, before the coming into force of those provisions, under the Unfair Terms in Consumer Contracts Regulations 1999. Unfair terms are not enforceable against consumers.

501. Blacklisting of a seller includes not just the placing of the seller on a list of those sellers who cannot, or cannot without restriction, purchase further tickets. Blacklisting covers any steps taken by an event organiser to prevent or restrict that seller buying tickets, in any form.

502. *Subsection (9)* applies this prohibition to actions taken by event organisers after this section comes into force. The ticket in question may have, however, been resold or offered for resale before that time.

Section 92: Duty to report criminal activity

503. This section provides that, where the operator of a secondary ticketing facility is aware of criminal activity on that facility, a relevant report must be made to the police and to the event organiser. This section applies to criminal activity related to the resale of tickets (though there may be other reporting requirements which apply where this is not the case).

504. Criminal activity means where an offence is committed, under the law of any part of the UK. There are several pieces of legislation breach of which could lead to an offence being committed. However this provision is intended to cover legislation for which the authorities listed here (that is, the police) are one of the principal enforcers. This includes offences under the Fraud Act 2006 and the Theft Act 1968.

505. *Subsection (3)* specifies that the information to be reported is—where this is known to the operator—the identity of the person committing the offence (for example their company name or an individual's name) and the fact that the operator knows that a criminal offence is or has been committed.

506. The report must be made to a police force within the United Kingdom. Where, for example, the facility is aware that the person is based in England the report could be made to a police constable in England. Where there is a lead police force for a particular crime (for example fraud) that force might be the appropriate police force to which the report can be made. A report must also be made to the organiser of the relevant event(s), that is, where the criminal activity involves tickets for a particular event, the organiser of that event must be informed. However, under *subsection (5)* such a report is not required if it would prejudice the investigation of an offence (not just the one being reported). In practice, this might mean that—where the facility has some doubt—the report is first made to the police who can advise whether a report to an event organiser would prejudice an investigation.

507. The criminal activity can be either ongoing or have already occurred, however the operator of the facility need only report offences which it became aware of after this provision comes into force.

Section 93: Enforcement of this Chapter

508. This section provides for enforcement of sections 90, 91 and 92. Enforcement is by local weights and measures authorities in Great Britain (known as Trading Standards) and by the Department of Enterprise, Trade and Investment in Northern Ireland.

509. *Subsection (4)* allows these enforcers to levy a fine of up to £5000 for a breach of the requirements in those sections. That fine can be levied on a private individual or a business, depending on the nature of the breach.

510. This sanction is, however, limited by *subsection (5)* which states that an enforcer may not impose a fine for a breach of the duty in section 90 or the prohibition in section 91 if it is satisfied that the breach was the result of circumstances beyond a person's control, for example a mistake or accident, and the person had taken reasonable precautions and undertaken due diligence. For example, where an online ticket marketplace had been supplied with false information by a seller, and had taken reasonable steps to ensure that that information was correct, they would not be liable for a fine.

511. This section also gives effect to Schedule 10 (secondary ticketing: financial penalties) which provides for the procedure to be followed when enforcing the provisions in this Chapter:

a) Before a fine is levied, paragraph 1 of this Schedule requires a relevant enforcer to give a notice of intent. This must be given within 6 months of the enforcer having evidence of a breach. Within 28 days of receiving that notice, the person on whom it is served can make representations. Once the 28 day period has expired, the enforcer can issue a final notice giving details of the level of the fine and how it is to be paid. The notice can be withdrawn at any time.

b) Once a final notice has been issued, the person on whom it is served can appeal on the grounds given in paragraph 5 of this Schedule.

c) Should the final notice not be appealed, or be upheld on appeal, and the fine not be paid, the enforcer can ask the county court (or in Scotland, a sheriff court) for an order to recover that fine under paragraph 6 of this Schedule.

Section 94: Duty to review measures relating to secondary ticketing

512. This section provides for a review of the online secondary ticketing market. The review must either be carried out by the Secretary of State or arranged by the Secretary of State to be carried out, e.g. by an external reviewer.

513. The review:

a) must cover the online secondary ticketing market for recreational, sporting and cultural events in the UK;

b) must cover consumer protection measures in the secondary market, defined as such legislation, rules of law, codes of practice and guidance which the Secretary of State deems relevant;

c) must prepare and publish a report within 12 months of this section coming into force; and

d) must be presented to Parliament.

Section 95: Interpretation of this Chapter

514. This section gives the definitions that apply to terms used in this Chapter. It includes a power for the Secretary of State to change by regulations who this Chapter applies to through changing the definition of the operator of a secondary ticketing facility.

COMMENCEMENT

515. The provisions of the Act listed in section 100(2) come into force on the day of Royal Assent. For the most part these are powers to make secondary legislation, but the general provisions in Chapter 6 of Part 3 also come into force on Royal Asset. Chapter 5 of Part 3 comes into force at the end of the period of two months beginning with the day of Royal Assent.

516. The remaining provisions of this Act, apart from Chapters 3 and 4 of Part 3, will come into force on such day as the Secretary of State may appoint by order made by Statutory Instrument. Chapters 3 and 4 will be brought into force by the Secretary of State in relation to England and the Welsh Ministers in relation to Wales. Different days may be appointed for different purposes.

HANSARD REFERENCE

517. The following table sets out the dates and Hansard reference for each stage of this Act's passage through Parliament. Links to the Hansard extracts can be found here: http://services.parliament.uk/bills/2014-15/consumerrights/stages.html

Stage	Date	Hansard reference
House of Commons		
Introduction	23 January 2014	Vol 574; Col 478
Second Reading	28 January 2014	Vol 574; Col 768
Public Bill Committee on the Consumer Rights Bill	11 February 2014	Morning: Col 3-38
		Afternoon: Col 41-77
	13 February 2014	Morning: Col 81-106
		Afternoon: Col 109-162
	25 February 2014	Morning: Col 165-208
		Afternoon: Col 211-266
	27 February 2014	Morning: Col 269-294
		Afternoon: Col 297-336
	4 March 2014	Morning: Col 339-380
		Afternoon: Col 383-446
	6 March 2014	Morning: Col 449-474
		Afternoon: Col 477-525
	11 March 2014	Morning: Col 529-572
		Afternoon: Col 575-628
	13 March 2014	Col 631-658

(Continued)

*(**Continued**)*

Stage	Date	Hansard reference
Report and Third Reading	13 May 2014 (1st day)	Vol 580; Col 600
	16 June 2014 (2nd day)	Vol 582; Col 873
	16 June 2014 (3rd Reading)	Vol 582; Col 915
House of Lords		
Introduction	17 June 2014	Vol 754; Col 764
Second Reading	1 July 2014	Vol 754; Col 1645
Committee	13 October 2014	Vol 756; GC1
	15 October 2014	Vol 756; GC99
	20 October 2014	Vol 756; GC163
	22 October 2014	Vol 756; GC215
	27 October 2014	Vol 756; GC307
	29 October 2014	Vol 756; GC441
	3 November 2014	Vol 756; GC561
	5 November 2014	Vol 756; GC689
Report	19 November 2014	Vol 757; Col 455
	24 November 2014	Vol 757; Col 701
	26 November 2014	Vol 757; Col 890
Third Reading	8 December 2014	Vol 757; Col 1601
Ping Pong		
Commons Consideration of Lords Amendments	12 January 2015	Vol 590; Col 625
Lords Consideration of Commons Reason	24 February 2015	Vol 759; Col 1539
Commons Consideration of Lords Non-Instance and Amendments in Lieu	9 March 2015	Vol 594; Col 55
Royal Assent		
Commons	26 March 2015	Vol 594; Col 1682
Lords	26 March 2015	Vol 760; Col 1589

Schedule 5

Investigatory Powers etc.

PART 1

BASIC CONCEPTS

Overview

1 (1) This Schedule confers investigatory powers on enforcers and specifies the purposes for which and the circumstances in which those powers may be exercised.

(2) Part 1 of this Schedule contains interpretation provisions; in particular paragraphs 2 to 6 explain what is meant by an 'enforcer'.

(3) Part 2 of this Schedule explains what is meant by 'the enforcer's legislation'.

(4) Part 3 of this Schedule contains powers in relation to the production of information; paragraph 13 sets out which enforcers may exercise those powers, and the purposes for which they may do so.

(5) Part 4 of this Schedule contains further powers; paragraphs 19 and 20 set out which enforcers may exercise those powers, and the purposes for which they may do so.

(6) Part 5 of this Schedule contains provisions that are supplementary to the powers in Parts 3 and 4 of this Schedule.

(7) Part 6 of this Schedule makes provision about the exercise of functions by certain enforcers outside their area or district and the bringing of proceedings in relation to conduct outside an enforcer's area or district.

Enforcers

2 (1) In this Schedule 'enforcer' means—
   (a) a domestic enforcer,
   (b) an EU enforcer,
   (c) a public designated enforcer, or
   (d) an unfair contract terms enforcer.

(2) But in Part 4 and paragraphs 38 and 41 of this Schedule 'enforcer' means—
   (a) a domestic enforcer, or
   (b) an EU enforcer.

(3) In paragraphs 13, 19 and 20 of this Schedule, a reference to an enforcer exercising a power includes a reference to an officer of the enforcer exercising that power.

Domestic enforcers

3 (1) In this Schedule 'domestic enforcer' means—
   (a) the Competition and Markets Authority,
   (b) a local weights and measures authority in Great Britain,

    (c) a district council in England,
    (d) the Department of Enterprise, Trade and Investment in Northern Ireland,
    (e) a district council in Northern Ireland,
    (f) the Secretary of State,
    (g) the Gas and Electricity Markets Authority,
    (h) the British Hallmarking Council,
    (i) an assay office within the meaning of the Hallmarking Act 1973, or
    (j) any other person to whom the duty in subsection (1) of section 27 of the Consumer Protection Act 1987 (duty to enforce safety provisions) applies by virtue of regulations under subsection (2) of that section.

(2) But the Gas and Electricity Markets Authority is not a domestic enforcer for the purposes of Part 4 of this Schedule.

(3) The reference to the Department of Enterprise, Trade and Investment in Northern Ireland includes a person with whom the Department has made arrangements, under paragraph 3(1) of Schedule 15 to the Lifts Regulations 1997 (SI 1997/831) for enforcement of those regulations.

EU enforcers

4 In this Schedule 'EU enforcer' means—
    (a) the Competition and Markets Authority,
    (b) a local weights and measures authority in Great Britain,
    (c) the Department of Enterprise, Trade and Investment in Northern Ireland,
    (d) the Financial Conduct Authority,
    (e) the Civil Aviation Authority,
    (f) the Secretary of State,
    (g) the Department of Health, Social Services and Public Safety in Northern Ireland,
    (h) the Office of Communications,
    (i) an enforcement authority within the meaning of section 120(15) of the Communications Act 2003 (regulation of premium rate services), or
    (j) the Information Commissioner.

Public designated enforcers

5 In this Schedule 'public designated enforcer' means a person or body which—
    (a) is designated by order under subsection (2) of section 213 of the Enterprise Act 2002, and
    (b) has been designated by virtue of subsection (3) of that section (which provides that the Secretary of State may designate a public body only if satisfied that it is independent).

Unfair contract terms enforcer

6 In this Schedule 'unfair contract terms enforcer' means a person or body which—
    (a) is for the time being listed in paragraph 8(1) of Schedule 3 (persons or bodies that may enforce provisions about unfair contract terms), and
    (b) is a public authority within the meaning of section 6 of the Human Rights Act 1998.

Officers

7 (1) In this Schedule 'officer', in relation to an enforcer, means—
    (a) an inspector appointed by the enforcer to exercise powers under this Schedule, or authorised to do so,

(b) an officer of the enforcer appointed by the enforcer to exercise powers under this Schedule, or authorised to do so,

(c) an employee of the enforcer (other than an inspector or officer) appointed by the enforcer to exercise powers under this Schedule, or authorised to do so, or

(d) a person (other than an inspector, officer or employee of the enforcer) authorised by the enforcer to exercise powers under this Schedule.

(2) But references in this Schedule to an officer in relation to a particular power only cover a person within sub-paragraph (1) if and to the extent that the person has been appointed or authorised to exercise that power.

(3) A person who, immediately before the coming into force of this Schedule, was appointed or authorised to exercise a power replaced by a power in this Schedule is to be treated as having been appointed or authorised to exercise the new power.

(4) In this paragraph 'employee', in relation to the Secretary of State, means a person employed in the civil service of the State.

Interpretation of other terms

8 In this Schedule—

• 'Community infringement' has the same meaning as in section 212 of the Enterprise Act 2002;

• 'document' includes information recorded in any form;

• 'enforcement order' means an order under section 217 of the Enterprise Act 2002;

• 'interim enforcement order' means an order under section 218 of that Act;

• 'the Regulation on Accreditation and Market Surveillance' means Regulation (EC) No 765/2008 of the European Parliament and of the Council of 9 July 2008 setting out the requirements for accreditation and market surveillance relating to the marketing of products and repealing Regulation (EEC) No 339/93.

PART 2
THE ENFORCER'S LEGISLATION

Enforcer's legislation

9 (1) In this Schedule 'the enforcer's legislation', in relation to a domestic enforcer, means—

(a) legislation or notices which, by virtue of a provision listed in paragraph 10, the domestic enforcer has a duty or power to enforce, and

(b) where the domestic enforcer is listed in an entry in the first column of the table in paragraph 11, the legislation listed in the corresponding entry in the second column of that table.

(2) References in this Schedule to a breach of or compliance with the enforcer's legislation include a breach of or compliance with a notice issued under—

(a) the enforcer's legislation, or

(b) legislation under which the enforcer's legislation is made.

(3) References in this Schedule to a breach of or compliance with the enforcer's legislation are to be read, in relation to the Lifts Regulations 1997 (SI 1997/831), as references to a breach of or compliance with the Regulations as they apply to relevant products (within the meaning of Schedule 15 to the Regulations) for private use or consumption.

Enforcer's legislation: duties and powers mentioned in paragraph 9(1)(a)

10 The duties and powers mentioned in paragraph 9(1)(a) are those arising under any of the following provisions—

- 'section 26(1) or 40(1)(b) of the Trade Descriptions Act 1968 (including as applied by regulation 8(3) of the Crystal Glass (Descriptions) Regulations 1973 (SI 1973/1952) and regulation 10(2) of the Footwear (Indication of Composition) Labelling Regulations 1995 (SI 1995/2489));
- section 9(1) or (6) of the Hallmarking Act 1973;
- paragraph 6 of the Schedule to the Prices Act 1974 (including as read with paragraph 14(1) of that Schedule);
- section 161(1) of the Consumer Credit Act 1974;
- section 26(1) of the Estate Agents Act 1979;
- Article 39 of the Weights and Measures (Northern Ireland) Order 1981 (SI 1981/231 (NI 10));
- section 16A(1) or (4) of the Video Recordings Act 1984;
- section 27(1) of the Consumer Protection Act 1987 (including as applied by section 12(1) of the Fireworks Act 2003 to fireworks regulations under that Act);
- section 215(1) of the Education Reform Act 1988;
- section 107A(1) or (3) or 198A(1) or (3) of the Copyright, Designs and Patents Act 1988;
- paragraph 3(a) of Schedule 5 to the Simple Pressure Vessels (Safety) Regulations 1991 (SI 1991/2749);
- paragraph 1 of Schedule 3 to the Package Travel, Package Holidays and Package Tours Regulations 1992 (SI 1992/3288);
- section 30(4) or (7) or 31(4)(a) of the Clean Air Act 1993;
- paragraph 1 of Schedule 2 to the Sunday Trading Act 1994;
- section 93(1) or (3) of the Trade Marks Act 1994;
- section 8A(1) or (3) of the Olympic Symbol etc (Protection) Act 1995;
- paragraph 2(a) or 3(1) of Schedule 15 to the Lifts Regulations 1997 (SI 1997/831);
- paragraph 2(a) or 3(3)(a) of Schedule 8 to the Pressure Equipment Regulations 1999 (SI 1999/2001);
- regulation 5C(5) of the Motor Fuel (Composition and Content) Regulations 1999 (SI 1999/3107);
- paragraph 1(1)(b) or (2)(b) or 2 of Schedule 9 to the Radio Equipment and Telecommunications Terminal Equipment Regulations 2000 (SI 2000/730);
- paragraph 1(a) of Schedule 10 to the Personal Protective Equipment Regulations 2002 (SI 2002/1144);
- paragraph 1 of Schedule 4 to the Packaging (Essential Requirements) Regulations 2003 (SI 2003/1941);
- section 3(1) of the Christmas Day Trading Act 2004;
- regulation 10(1) of the General Product Safety Regulations 2005 (SI 2005/1803);
- regulation 10(1) of the Weights and Measures (Packaged Goods) Regulations 2006 (SI 2006/659);
- regulation 17 of the Measuring Instruments (Automatic Discontinuous Totalisers) Regulations 2006 (SI 2006/1255);
- regulation 18 of the Measuring Instruments (Automatic Rail-weighbridges) Regulations 2006 (SI 2006/1256);
- regulation 20 of the Measuring Instruments (Automatic Catchweighers) Regulations 2006 (SI 2006/1257);

- regulation 18 of the Measuring Instruments (Automatic Gravimetric Filling Instruments) Regulations 2006 (SI 2006/1258);
- regulation 18 of the Measuring Instruments (Beltweighers) Regulations 2006 (SI 2006/1259);
- regulation 16 of the Measuring Instruments (Capacity Serving Measures) Regulations 2006 (SI 2006/1264);
- regulation 17 of the Measuring Instruments (Liquid Fuel and Lubricants) Regulations 2006 (SI 2006/1266);
- regulation 16 of the Measuring Instruments (Material Measures of Length) Regulations 2006 (SI 2006/1267);
- regulation 17 of the Measuring Instruments (Cold-water Meters) Regulations 2006 (SI 2006/1268);
- regulation 18 of the Measuring Instruments (Liquid Fuel delivered from Road Tankers) Regulations 2006 (SI 2006/1269);
- regulation 37(1)(a)(ii) or (b)(ii) of the Electromagnetic Compatibility Regulations 2006 (SI 2006/3418);
- regulation 13(1) or (1A) of the Business Protection from Misleading Marketing Regulations 2008 (SI 2008/1276);
- regulation 19(1) or (1A) of the Consumer Protection from Unfair Trading Regulations 2008 (SI 2008/1277);
- paragraph 2 or 5 of Schedule 5 to the Supply of Machinery (Safety) Regulations 2008 (SI 2008/1597);
- regulation 32(2) or (3) of the Timeshare, Holiday Products, Resale and Exchange Contracts Regulations 2010 (SI 2010/2960);
- regulation 10(1) of the Weights and Measures (Packaged Goods) Regulations (Northern Ireland) 2011 (SR 2011/331);
- regulation 11 of the Textile Products (Labelling and Fibre Composition) Regulations 2012 (SI 2012/1102);
- regulation 6(1) of the Cosmetic Products Enforcement Regulations 2013 (SI 2013/1478);
- section 87(1) of this Act;
- section 93(1) or (2) of this Act.'

Enforcer's legislation: legislation mentioned in paragraph 9(1)(b)

11 Here is the table mentioned in paragraph 9(1)(b)—

Enforcer	Legislation
A local weights and measures authority in Great Britain or the Department of Enterprise, Trade and Investment in Northern Ireland	Section 35ZA of the Registered Designs Act 1949
A local weights and measures authority in Great Britain or the Department of Enterprise, Trade and Investment in Northern Ireland	The Measuring Container Bottles (EEC Requirements) Regulations 1977 (SI 1977/932)
The Secretary of State	The Alcoholometers and Alcohol Hydrometers (EEC Requirements) Regulations 1977 (SI 1977/1753)
A local weights and measures authority in Great Britain	The Weights and Measures Act 1985 and regulations and orders made under that Act
A local weights and measures authority in Great Britain or the Department of Enterprise, Trade and Investment in Northern Ireland	The Measuring Instruments (EEC Requirements) Regulations 1988 (SI 1988/186)

(Continued)

(*Continued*)

Enforcer	Legislation
A local weights and measures authority in Great Britain or the Department of Enterprise, Trade and Investment in Northern Ireland	The Financial Services and Markets Act 2000 so far as it relates to a relevant regulated activity within the meaning of section 107(4)(a) of the Financial Services Act 2012
A local weights and measures authority in Great Britain or the Department of Enterprise, Trade and Investment in Northern Ireland	The Non-Automatic Weighing Instruments Regulations 2000 (SI 2000/3236)

Powers to amend paragraph 10 or 11

12 (1) The Secretary of State may by order made by statutory instrument—
   (a) amend paragraph 10 or the table in paragraph 11 by adding, modifying or removing any entry in it;
   (b) in consequence of provision made under paragraph (a), amend, repeal or revoke any other legislation (including this Act) whenever passed or made.
   (2) The Secretary of State may not make an order under this paragraph that has the effect that a power of entry, or an associated power, contained in legislation other than this Act is replaced by a power of entry, or an associated power, contained in this Schedule unless the Secretary of State thinks that the condition in sub-paragraph (3) is met.
   (3) That condition is that, on and after the changes made by the order, the safeguards applicable to the new power, taken together, provide a greater level of protection than any safeguards applicable to the old power.
   (4) In sub-paragraph (2) 'power of entry' and 'associated power' have the meanings given by section 46 of the Protection of Freedoms Act 2012.
   (5) An order under this paragraph may contain transitional or transitory provision or savings.
   (6) A statutory instrument containing an order under this paragraph that amends or repeals primary legislation may not be made unless a draft of the instrument containing the order has been laid before, and approved by a resolution of, each House of Parliament.
   (7) Any other statutory instrument containing an order under this paragraph is subject to annulment in pursuance of a resolution of either House of Parliament.
   (8) In this paragraph 'primary legislation' means—
   (a) an Act of Parliament,
   (b) an Act of the Scottish Parliament,
   (c) an Act or Measure of the National Assembly for Wales, or
   (d) Northern Ireland legislation.

PART 3
POWERS IN RELATION TO THE PRODUCTION OF INFORMATION

Exercise of powers in this Part

13 (1) An enforcer of a kind mentioned in this paragraph may exercise a power in this Part of this Schedule only for the purposes and in the circumstances mentioned in this paragraph in relation to that kind of enforcer.

(2) The Competition and Markets Authority may exercise the powers in this Part of this Schedule for any of the following purposes—

    (a) to enable the Authority to exercise or to consider whether to exercise any function it has under Part 8 of the Enterprise Act 2002;

    (b) to enable a private designated enforcer to consider whether to exercise any function it has under that Part;

    (c) to enable a Community enforcer to consider whether to exercise any function it has under that Part;

    (d) to ascertain whether a person has complied with or is complying with an enforcement order or an interim enforcement order;

    (e) to ascertain whether a person has complied with or is complying with an undertaking given under section 217(9), 218(10) or 219 of the Enterprise Act 2002.

(3) A public designated enforcer, a local weights and measures authority in Great Britain, the Department of Enterprise, Trade and Investment in Northern Ireland or an EU enforcer other than the Competition and Markets Authority may exercise the powers in this Part of this Schedule for any of the following purposes—

    (a) to enable that enforcer to exercise or to consider whether to exercise any function it has under Part 8 of the Enterprise Act 2002;

    (b) to ascertain whether a person has complied with or is complying with an enforcement order or an interim enforcement order made on the application of that enforcer;

    (c) to ascertain whether a person has complied with or is complying with an undertaking given under section 217(9) or 218(10) of the Enterprise Act 2002 following such an application;

    (d) to ascertain whether a person has complied with or is complying with an undertaking given to that enforcer under section 219 of that Act.

(4) A domestic enforcer may exercise the powers in this Part of this Schedule for the purpose of ascertaining whether there has been a breach of the enforcer's legislation.

(5) But a domestic enforcer may not exercise the power in paragraph 14 (power to require the production of information) for the purpose in sub-paragraph (4) unless an officer of the enforcer reasonably suspects a breach of the enforcer's legislation.

(6) Sub-paragraph (5) does not apply if the enforcer is a market surveillance authority within the meaning of Article 2(18) of the Regulation on Accreditation and Market Surveillance and the power is exercised for the purpose of market surveillance within the meaning of Article 2(17) of that Regulation.

(7) An unfair contract terms enforcer may exercise the powers in this Part of this Schedule for either of the following purposes—

    (a) to enable the enforcer to exercise or to consider whether to exercise any function it has under Schedule 3 (enforcement of the law on unfair contract terms and notices);

    (b) to ascertain whether a person has complied with or is complying with an injunction or interdict (within the meaning of that Schedule) granted under paragraph 5 of that Schedule or an undertaking given under paragraph 6 of that Schedule.

(8) But an unfair contract terms enforcer may not exercise the power in paragraph 14 for a purpose mentioned in sub-paragraph (7)(a) unless an officer of the enforcer reasonably suspects that a person is using, or proposing or recommending the use of, a contractual term or notice within paragraph 3 of Schedule 3.

(9) A local weights and measures authority in Great Britain may exercise the powers in this Part of this Schedule for either of the following purposes—

    (a) to enable it to determine whether to make an order under section 3 or 4 of the Estate Agents Act 1979;

    (b) to enable it to exercise any of its functions under section 5, 6, 8, 13 or 17 of that Act.

(10) In this paragraph—
- 'Community enforcer' has the same meaning as in the Enterprise Act 2002 (see section 213(5) of that Act);
- 'private designated enforcer' means a person or body which—
  - (a) is designated by order under subsection (2) of section 213 of that Act, and
  - (b) has been designated by virtue of subsection (4) of that section (which provides that the Secretary of State may designate a person or body which is not a public body only if it satisfies criteria specified by order).

Power to require the production of information

14 An enforcer or an officer of an enforcer may give notice to a person requiring the person to provide the enforcer with the information specified in the notice.

Procedure for notice under paragraph 14

15 (1) A notice under paragraph 14 must be in writing and specify the purpose for which the information is required.
   (2) If the purpose is to enable a person to exercise or to consider whether to exercise a function, the notice must specify the function concerned.
   (3) The notice may specify—
      (a) the time within which and the manner in which the person to whom it is given must comply with it;
      (b) the form in which information must be provided.
   (4) The notice may require—
      (a) the creation of documents, or documents of a description, specified in the notice, and
      (b) the provision of those documents to the enforcer or an officer of the enforcer.
   (5) A requirement to provide information or create a document is a requirement to do so in a legible form.
   (6) A notice under paragraph 14 does not require a person to provide any information or create any documents which the person would be entitled to refuse to provide or produce—
      (a) in proceedings in the High Court on the grounds of legal professional privilege, or
      (b) in proceedings in the Court of Session on the grounds of confidentiality of communications.
   (7) In sub-paragraph (6) 'communications' means—
      (a) communications between a professional legal adviser and the adviser's client, or
      (b) communications made in connection with or in contemplation of legal proceedings or for the purposes of those proceedings.

Enforcement of notice under paragraph 14

16 (1) If a person fails to comply with a notice under paragraph 14, the enforcer or an officer of the enforcer may make an application under this paragraph to the court.
   (2) If it appears to the court that the person has failed to comply with the notice, it may make an order under this paragraph.

(3) An order under this paragraph is an order requiring the person to do anything that the court thinks it is reasonable for the person to do, for any of the purposes for which the notice was given, to ensure that the notice is complied with.

(4) An order under this paragraph may require the person to meet the costs or expenses of the application.

(5) If the person is a company, partnership or unincorporated association, the court in acting under sub-paragraph (4) may require an official who is responsible for the failure to meet the costs or expenses.

(6) In this paragraph—
- 'the court' means—
  (a) the High Court,
  (b) in relation to England and Wales, the county court,
  (c) in relation to Northern Ireland, a county court,
  (d) the Court of Session, or
  (e) the sheriff;
- 'official' means—
  (a) in the case of a company, a director, manager, secretary or other similar officer,
  (b) in the case of a limited liability partnership, a member,
  (c) in the case of a partnership other than a limited liability partnership, a partner, and
  (d) in the case of an unincorporated association, a person who is concerned in the management or control of its affairs.

Limitations on use of information provided in response to a notice under paragraph 14

17 (1) This paragraph applies if a person provides information in response to a notice under paragraph 14.

(2) This includes information contained in a document created by a person in response to such a notice.

(3) In any criminal proceedings against the person—
(a) no evidence relating to the information may be adduced by or on behalf of the prosecution, and
(b) no question relating to the information may be asked by or on behalf of the prosecution.

(4) Sub-paragraph (3) does not apply if, in the proceedings—
(a) evidence relating to the information is adduced by or on behalf of the person providing it, or
(b) a question relating to the information is asked by or on behalf of that person.

(5) Sub-paragraph (3) does not apply if the proceedings are for—
(a) an offence under paragraph 36 (obstruction),
(b) an offence under section 5 of the Perjury Act 1911 (false statutory declarations and other false statements without oath),
(c) an offence under section 44(2) of the Criminal Law (Consolidation) (Scotland) Act 1995 (false statements and declarations), or
(d) an offence under Article 10 of the Perjury (Northern Ireland) Order 1979 (SI 1979/1714 (NI 19)) (false statutory declarations and other false unsworn statements).

Application to Crown

18 In its application in relation to—
(a) an enforcer acting for a purpose within paragraph 13(2) or (3), or
(b) an enforcer acting for the purpose of ascertaining whether there has been a breach of the Consumer Protection from Unfair Trading Regulations 2008 (SI 2008/1277), this Part binds the Crown.

PART 4
FURTHER POWERS EXERCISABLE BY DOMESTIC ENFORCERS AND EU ENFORCERS

Exercise of powers in this Part: domestic enforcers

19 (1) A domestic enforcer may exercise a power in this Part of this Schedule only for the purposes and in the circumstances mentioned in this paragraph in relation to that power.
(2) A domestic enforcer may exercise any power in paragraphs 21 to 26 and 31 to 34 for the purpose of ascertaining compliance with the enforcer's legislation.
(3) A domestic enforcer may exercise the power in paragraph 27 (power to require the production of documents) for either of the following purposes—
(a) subject to sub-paragraph (4), to ascertain compliance with the enforcer's legislation;
(b) to ascertain whether the documents may be required as evidence in proceedings for a breach of, or under, the enforcer's legislation.
(4) A domestic enforcer may exercise the power in paragraph 27 for the purpose mentioned in sub-paragraph (3)(a) only if an officer of the enforcer reasonably suspects a breach of the enforcer's legislation, unless—
(a) the power is being exercised in relation to a document that the trader is required to keep by virtue of a provision of the enforcer's legislation, or
(b) the enforcer is a market surveillance authority within the meaning of Article 2(18) of the Regulation on Accreditation and Market Surveillance and the power is exercised for the purpose of market surveillance within the meaning of Article 2(17) of that Regulation.
(5) A domestic enforcer may exercise the power in paragraph 28 (power to seize and detain goods) in relation to—
(a) goods which an officer of the enforcer reasonably suspects may disclose (by means of testing or otherwise) a breach of the enforcer's legislation,
(b) goods which an officer of the enforcer reasonably suspects are liable to forfeiture under that legislation, and
(c) goods which an officer of the enforcer reasonably suspects may be required as evidence in proceedings for a breach of, or under, that legislation.
(6) A domestic enforcer may exercise the power in paragraph 29 (power to seize documents required as evidence) in relation to documents which an officer of the enforcer reasonably suspects may be required as evidence—
(a) in proceedings for a breach of the enforcer's legislation, or
(b) in proceedings under the enforcer's legislation.
(7) A domestic enforcer may exercise the power in paragraph 30 (power to decommission or switch off fixed installations)—
(a) if an officer of the enforcer reasonably suspects a breach of the Electromagnetic Compatibility Regulations 2006 (SI 2006/3418), and

    (b) for the purpose of ascertaining (by means of testing or otherwise) whether there has been such a breach.

(8) For the purposes of the enforcement of the Estate Agents Act 1979—

    (a) the references in sub-paragraphs (2) and (3)(a) to ascertaining compliance with the enforcer's legislation include ascertaining whether a person has engaged in a practice mentioned in section 3(1)(d) of that Act (practice in relation to estate agency work declared undesirable by the Secretary of State), and

    (b) the references in sub-paragraph (4) and paragraphs 23(6)(a) and 32(3)(a) to a breach of the enforcer's legislation include references to a person's engaging in such a practice.

Exercise of powers in this Part: EU enforcers

20 (1) Any power in this Part of this Schedule which is conferred on an EU enforcer may be exercised by such an enforcer only for the purposes and in the circumstances mentioned in this paragraph in relation to that power.

(2) If the condition in sub-paragraph (3) is met, an EU enforcer may exercise any power conferred on it by paragraphs 21 to 25 and 31 to 34 for any purpose relating to the functions that the enforcer has under Part 8 of the Enterprise Act 2002 in its capacity as a CPC enforcer under that Part.

(3) The condition is that an officer of the EU enforcer reasonably suspects—

    (a) that there has been, or is likely to be, a Community infringement,

    (b) a failure to comply with an enforcement order or an interim enforcement order made on the application of that enforcer,

    (c) a failure to comply with an undertaking given under section 217(9) or 218(10) of the Enterprise Act 2002 following such an application, or

    (d) a failure to comply with an undertaking given to that enforcer under section 219 of that Act.

(4) An EU enforcer may exercise the power in paragraph 27 (power to require the production of documents) for either of the following purposes—

    (a) the purpose mentioned in sub-paragraph (2), if the condition in sub-paragraph (3) is met;

    (b) to ascertain whether the documents may be required as evidence in proceedings under Part 8 of the Enterprise Act 2002.

(5) An EU enforcer may exercise the power in paragraph 28 (power to seize and detain goods) in relation to goods which an officer of the enforcer reasonably suspects—

    (a) may disclose (by means of testing or otherwise) a Community infringement or a failure to comply with a measure specified in sub-paragraph (3)(b), (c) or (d), or

    (b) may be required as evidence in proceedings under Part 8 of the Enterprise Act 2002.

(6) An EU enforcer may exercise the power in paragraph 29 (power to seize documents required as evidence) in relation to documents which an officer of the enforcer reasonably suspects may be required as evidence in proceedings under Part 8 of the Enterprise Act 2002.

Power to purchase products

21 (1) An officer of an enforcer may—

    (a) make a purchase of a product, or

    (b) enter into an agreement to secure the provision of a product.

(2) For the purposes of exercising the power in sub-paragraph (1), an officer may—
  (a) at any reasonable time, enter premises to which the public has access (whether or not the public has access at that time), and
  (b) inspect any product on the premises which the public may inspect.
(3) The power of entry in sub-paragraph (2) may be exercised without first giving notice or obtaining a warrant.

Power to observe carrying on of business etc

22 (1) An officer of an enforcer may enter premises to which the public has access in order to observe the carrying on of a business on those premises.
  (2) The power in sub-paragraph (1) may be exercised at any reasonable time (whether or not the public has access at that time).
  (3) The power of entry in sub-paragraph (1) may be exercised without first giving notice or obtaining a warrant.

Power to enter premises without warrant

23 (1) An officer of an enforcer may enter premises at any reasonable time.
  (2) Sub-paragraph (1) does not authorise the entry into premises used wholly or mainly as a dwelling.
  (3) In the case of a routine inspection, the power of entry in sub-paragraph (1) may only be exercised if a notice has been given to the occupier of the premises in accordance with the requirements in sub-paragraph (4), unless sub-paragraph (5) applies.
  (4) Those requirements are that—
    (a) the notice is in writing and is given by an officer of the enforcer,
    (b) the notice sets out why the entry is necessary and indicates the nature of the offence under paragraph 36 (obstruction), and
    (c) there are at least two working days between the date of receipt of the notice and the date of entry.
  (5) A notice need not be given if the occupier has waived the requirement to give notice.
  (6) In this paragraph 'routine inspection' means an exercise of the power in sub-paragraph (1) other than where—
    (a) the power is exercised by an officer of a domestic enforcer who reasonably suspects a breach of the enforcer's legislation,
    (b) the officer reasonably considers that to give notice in accordance with sub-paragraph (3) would defeat the purpose of the entry,
    (c) it is not reasonably practicable in all the circumstances to give notice in accordance with that sub-paragraph, in particular because the officer reasonably suspects that there is an imminent risk to public health or safety, or
    (d) the enforcer is a market surveillance authority within the meaning of Article 2(18) of the Regulation on Accreditation and Market Surveillance and the entry is for the purpose of market surveillance within the meaning of Article 2(17) of that Regulation.
  (7) If an officer of an enforcer enters premises under sub-paragraph (1) otherwise than in the course of a routine inspection, and finds one or more occupiers on the premises, the officer must provide to that occupier or (if there is more than one) to at least one of them a document that—

    (a) sets out why the entry is necessary, and

    (b) indicates the nature of the offence under paragraph 36 (obstruction).

(8) If an officer of an enforcer enters premises under sub-paragraph (1) and finds one or more occupiers on the premises, the officer must produce evidence of the officer's identity and authority to that occupier or (if there is more than one) to at least one of them.

(9) An officer need not comply with sub-paragraph (7) or (8) if it is not reasonably practicable to do so.

(10) Proceedings resulting from the exercise of the power under sub-paragraph (1) are not invalid merely because of a failure to comply with sub-paragraph (7) or (8).

(11) An officer entering premises under sub-paragraph (1) may be accompanied by such persons, and may take onto the premises such equipment, as the officer thinks necessary.

(12) In this paragraph—

- 'give', in relation to the giving of a notice to the occupier of premises, includes delivering or leaving it at the premises or sending it there by post;
- 'working day' means a day other than—
  - (a) Saturday or Sunday,
  - (b) Christmas Day or Good Friday, or
  - (c) a day which is a bank holiday under the Banking and Financial Dealings Act 1971 in the part of the United Kingdom in which the premises are situated.

Application of paragraphs 25 to 31

24 Paragraphs 25 to 31 apply if an officer of an enforcer has entered any premises under the power in paragraph 23(1) or under a warrant under paragraph 32.

Power to inspect products etc

25 (1) The officer may inspect any product on the premises.

(2) The power in sub-paragraph (3) is also available to an officer of a domestic enforcer acting pursuant to the duty in section 27(1) of the Consumer Protection Act 1987 or regulation 10(1) of the General Product Safety Regulations 2005 (SI 2005/1803).

(3) The officer may examine any procedure (including any arrangements for carrying out a test) connected with the production of a product.

(4) The powers in sub-paragraph (5) are also available to an officer of a domestic enforcer acting pursuant to—

    (a) the duty in regulation 10(1) of the Weights and Measures (Packaged Goods) Regulations 2006 (SI 2006/659) ('the 2006 Regulations'), or

    (b) the duty in regulation 10(1) of the Weights and Measures (Packaged Goods) Regulations (Northern Ireland) 2011 (SR 2011/331) ('the 2011 Regulations').

(5) The officer may inspect and take copies of, or of anything purporting to be—

    (a) a record of a kind mentioned in regulation 5(2) or 9(1), or

    (b) evidence of a kind mentioned in regulation 9(3).

(6) The references in sub-paragraph (5) to regulations are to regulations in the 2006 Regulations in the case of a domestic enforcer in Great Britain or the 2011 Regulations in the case of a domestic enforcer in Northern Ireland.

(7) The powers in sub-paragraph (8) are also available to an officer of a domestic enforcer acting pursuant to the duty in regulation 37(1)(a)(ii) or (b)(ii) of the Electromagnetic Compatibility Regulations 2006 (SI 2006/3418).

(8) The officer may—
  (a) inspect any apparatus or fixed installation (as defined in those Regulations), or
  (b) examine any procedure (including any arrangements for carrying out a test) connected with the production of apparatus.

Power to test equipment

26 (1) An officer of a domestic enforcer may test any weighing or measuring equipment—
  (a) which is, or which the officer has reasonable cause to believe may be, used for trade or in the possession of any person or on any premises for such use, or
  (b) which has been, or which the officer has reasonable cause to believe to have been, passed by an approved verifier, or by a person purporting to act as such a verifier, as fit for such use.
(2) Expressions used in sub-paragraph (1) have the same meaning—
  (a) as in the Weights and Measures Act 1985, in the case of a domestic enforcer in Great Britain;
  (b) as in the Weights and Measures (Northern Ireland) Order 1981 (SI 1981/231 (NI 10)), in the case of a domestic enforcer in Northern Ireland.
(3) The powers in sub-paragraph (4) are available to an officer of a domestic enforcer acting pursuant to—
  (a) the duty in regulation 10(1) of the Weights and Measures (Packaged Goods) Regulations 2006 (SI 2006/659) ('the 2006 Regulations'), or
  (b) the duty in regulation 10(1) of the Weights and Measures (Packaged Goods) Regulations (Northern Ireland) 2011 (SR 2011/331) ('the 2011 Regulations').
(4) The officer may test any equipment which the officer has reasonable cause to believe is used in—
  (a) making up packages (as defined in regulation 2) in the United Kingdom, or
  (b) carrying out a check mentioned in paragraphs (1) and (3) of regulation 9.
(5) The references in sub-paragraph (4) to regulations are to regulations in the 2006 Regulations in the case of a domestic enforcer in Great Britain or the 2011 Regulations in the case of a domestic enforcer in Northern Ireland.

Power to require the production of documents

27 (1) The officer may, at any reasonable time—
  (a) require a trader occupying the premises, or a person on the premises acting on behalf of such a trader, to produce any documents relating to the trader's business to which the trader has access, and
  (b) take copies of, or of any entry in, any such document.
(2) The power in sub-paragraph (1) is available regardless of whether—
  (a) the purpose for which the documents are required relates to the trader or some other person, or
  (b) the proceedings referred to in paragraph 19(3)(b) or 20(4)(b) could be taken against the trader or some other person.
(3) That power includes power to require the person to give an explanation of the documents.
(4) Where a document required to be produced under sub-paragraph (1) contains information recorded electronically, the power in that sub-paragraph includes power to require

the production of a copy of the document in a form in which it can easily be taken away and in which it is visible and legible.

(5) This paragraph does not permit an officer to require a person to create a document other than as described in sub-paragraph (4).

(6) This paragraph does not permit an officer to require a person to produce any document which the person would be entitled to refuse to produce—

(a) in proceedings in the High Court on the grounds of legal professional privilege, or

(b) in proceedings in the Court of Session on the grounds of confidentiality of communications.

(7) In sub-paragraph (6) 'communications' means—

(a) communications between a professional legal adviser and the adviser's client, or

(b) communications made in connection with or in contemplation of legal proceedings or for the purposes of those proceedings.

(8) In this paragraph 'trader' has the same meaning as in Part 1 of this Act.

Power to seize and detain goods

28 (1) The officer may seize and detain goods other than documents (for which see paragraph 29).

(2) An officer seizing goods under this paragraph from premises which are occupied must produce evidence of the officer's identity and authority to an occupier of the premises before seizing them.

(3) The officer need not comply with sub-paragraph (2) if it is not reasonably practicable to do so.

(4) An officer seizing goods under this paragraph must take reasonable steps to—

(a) inform the person from whom they are seized that they have been seized, and

(b) provide that person with a written record of what has been seized.

(5) If, under this paragraph, an officer seizes any goods from a vending machine, the duty in sub-paragraph (4) also applies in relation to—

(a) the person whose name and address are on the vending machine as the owner of the machine, or

(b) if there is no such name and address on the machine, the occupier of the premises on which the machine stands or to which it is fixed.

(6) In determining the steps to be taken under sub-paragraph (4), an officer exercising a power under this paragraph in England and Wales or Northern Ireland must have regard to any relevant provision about the seizure of property made by—

(a) a code of practice under section 66 of the Police and Criminal Evidence Act 1984, or

(b) a code of practice under Article 65 of the Police and Criminal Evidence (Northern Ireland) Order 1989 (SI 1989/1341 (NI 12)), (as the case may be).

(7) Goods seized under this paragraph (except goods seized for a purpose mentioned in paragraph 19(5)(b)) may not be detained—

(a) for a period of more than 3 months beginning with the day on which they were seized, or

(b) where the goods are reasonably required to be detained for a longer period by the enforcer for a purpose for which they were seized, for longer than they are required for that purpose.

Power to seize documents required as evidence

29 (1) The officer may seize and detain documents.

(2) An officer seizing documents under this paragraph from premises which are occupied must produce evidence of the officer's identity and authority to an occupier of the premises before seizing them.

(3) The officer need not comply with sub-paragraph (2) if it is not reasonably practicable to do so.

(4) An officer seizing documents under this paragraph must take reasonable steps to—

(a) inform the person from whom they are seized that they have been seized, and

(b) provide that person with a written record of what has been seized.

(5) In determining the steps to be taken under sub-paragraph (4), an officer exercising a power under this paragraph in England and Wales or Northern Ireland must have regard to any relevant provision about the seizure of property made by—

(a) a code of practice under section 66 of the Police and Criminal Evidence Act 1984, or

(b) a code of practice under Article 65 of the Police and Criminal Evidence (Northern Ireland) Order 1989 (SI 1989/1341 (NI 12)), (as the case may be).

(6) This paragraph does not confer any power on an officer to seize from a person any document which the person would be entitled to refuse to produce—

(a) in proceedings in the High Court on the grounds of legal professional privilege, or

(b) in proceedings in the Court of Session on the grounds of confidentiality of communications.

(7) In sub-paragraph (6) 'communications' means—

(a) communications between a professional legal adviser and the adviser's client, or

(b) communications made in connection with or in contemplation of legal proceedings or for the purposes of those proceedings.

(8) Documents seized under this paragraph may not be detained—

(a) for a period of more than 3 months beginning with the day on which they were seized, or

(b) where the documents are reasonably required to be detained for a longer period by the enforcer for the purposes of the proceedings for which they were seized, for longer than they are required for those purposes.

Power to decommission or switch off fixed installations

30 (1) The power in sub-paragraph (2) is available to an officer of a domestic enforcer acting pursuant to the duty in regulation 37(1)(a)(ii) or (b)(ii) of the Electromagnetic Compatibility Regulations 2006 (SI 2006/3418).

(2) The officer may decommission or switch off any fixed installation (as defined in those Regulations) or part of such an installation.

Power to break open container etc

31 (1) The officer may, for the purpose of exercising any of the powers in paragraphs 28 to 30, require a person with authority to do so to—

(a) break open any container,

(b) open any vending machine, or

    (c) access any electronic device in which information may be stored or from which it may be accessed.

(2) Where a requirement under sub-paragraph (1) has not been complied with, the officer may, for the purpose of exercising any of the powers in paragraphs 28 to 30—

    (a) break open the container,

    (b) open the vending machine, or

    (c) access the electronic device.

(3) Sub-paragraph (1) or (2) applies if and to the extent that the exercise of the power in that sub-paragraph is reasonably necessary for the purposes for which that power may be exercised.

(4) In this paragraph 'container' means anything in which goods may be stored.

Power to enter premises with warrant

32 (1) A justice of the peace may issue a warrant authorising an officer of an enforcer to enter premises if satisfied, on written information on oath given by such an officer, that there are reasonable grounds for believing that—

    (a) condition A or B is met, and

    (b) condition C, D or E is met.

(2) Condition A is that on the premises there are—

    (a) products which an officer of the enforcer has power to inspect under paragraph 25, or

    (b) documents which an officer of the enforcer could require a person to produce under paragraph 27.

(3) Condition B is that, on the premises—

    (a) in the case of a domestic enforcer, there has been or is about to be a breach of the enforcer's legislation,

    (b) in the case of an EU enforcer, there has been or is about to be a Community infringement as defined in section 212 of the Enterprise Act 2002, or

    (c) in the case of an EU enforcer, there has been a failure to comply with a measure specified in paragraph 20(3)(b), (c) or (d).

(4) Condition C is that—

    (a) access to the premises has been or is likely to be refused, and

    (b) notice of the enforcer's intention to apply for a warrant under this paragraph has been given to the occupier of the premises.

(5) Condition D is that it is likely that products or documents on the premises would be concealed or interfered with if notice of entry on the premises were given to the occupier of the premises.

(6) Condition E is that—

    (a) the premises are unoccupied, or

    (b) the occupier of the premises is absent, and it might defeat the purpose of the entry to wait for the occupier's return.

(7) In the application of this paragraph to Scotland—

    (a) the reference in sub-paragraph (1) to a justice of the peace is to be read as a reference to a sheriff, and

    (b) the reference in that sub-paragraph to information on oath is to be read as a reference to evidence on oath.

(8) In the application of this paragraph to Northern Ireland—

    (a) the reference in sub-paragraph (1) to a justice of the peace is to be read as a reference to a lay magistrate, and

    (b) the reference in that sub-paragraph to written information is to be read as a reference to a written complaint.

Entry to premises under warrant

33 (1) A warrant under paragraph 32 authorises an officer of the enforcer to enter the premises at any reasonable time, using reasonable force if necessary.

(2) A warrant under that paragraph ceases to have effect at the end of the period of one month beginning with the day it is issued.

(3) An officer entering premises under a warrant under paragraph 32 may be accompanied by such persons, and may take onto the premises such equipment, as the officer thinks necessary.

(4) If the premises are occupied when the officer enters them, the officer must produce the warrant for inspection to an occupier of the premises.

(5) Sub-paragraph (6) applies if the premises are unoccupied or the occupier is temporarily absent.

(6) On leaving the premises the officer must—

(a) leave a notice on the premises stating that the premises have been entered under a warrant under paragraph 32, and

(b) leave the premises as effectively secured against trespassers as the officer found them.

Power to require assistance from person on premises

34 (1) If an officer of an enforcer has entered premises under the power in paragraph 23(1) or under a warrant under paragraph 32, the officer may require any person on the premises to provide such assistance or information as the officer reasonably considers necessary.

(2) Sub-paragraph (3) applies if an officer of a domestic enforcer has entered premises under the power in paragraph 23(1) or under a warrant under paragraph 32 for the purposes of the enforcement of—

(a) the Weights and Measures (Packaged Goods) Regulations 2006 (SI 2006/659), or

(b) the Weights and Measures (Packaged Goods) Regulations (Northern Ireland) 2011 (SR 2011/331).

(3) The officer may, in particular, require any person on the premises to provide such information as the person possesses about the name and address of the packer and of any importer of a package which the officer finds on the premises.

(4) In sub-paragraph (3) 'importer', 'package' and 'packer' have the same meaning as in—

(a) the Weights and Measures (Packaged Goods) Regulations 2006 (see regulation 2), in the case of a domestic enforcer in Great Britain, or

(b) the Weights and Measures (Packaged Goods) Regulations (Northern Ireland) 2011 (see regulation 2), in the case of a domestic enforcer in Northern Ireland.

Definitions for purposes of this Part

35 In this Part of this Schedule—

- 'goods' has the meaning given by section 2(8);
- 'occupier', in relation to premises, means any person an officer of an enforcer reasonably suspects to be the occupier of the premises;
- 'premises' includes any stall, vehicle, vessel or aircraft;
- 'product' means—
  (a) goods,
  (b) a service,

(c) digital content, as defined in section 2(9),

(d) immovable property, or

(e) rights or obligations.

PART 5
PROVISIONS SUPPLEMENTARY TO PARTS 3 AND 4

Offence of obstruction

36 (1) A person commits an offence if the person—

(a) intentionally obstructs an enforcer or an officer of an enforcer who is exercising or seeking to exercise a power under Part 4 of this Schedule in accordance with that Part,

(b) intentionally fails to comply with a requirement properly imposed by an enforcer or an officer of an enforcer under Part 4 of this Schedule, or

(c) without reasonable cause fails to give an enforcer or an officer of an enforcer any other assistance or information which the enforcer or officer reasonably requires of the person for a purpose for which the enforcer or officer may exercise a power under Part 4 of this Schedule.

(2) A person commits an offence if, in giving information of a kind referred to in sub-paragraph (1)(c), the person—

(a) makes a statement which the person knows is false or misleading in a material respect, or

(b) recklessly makes a statement which is false or misleading in a material respect.

(3) A person who is guilty of an offence under sub-paragraph (1) or (2) is liable on summary conviction to a fine not exceeding level 3 on the standard scale.

(4) Nothing in this paragraph requires a person to answer any question or give any information if to do so might incriminate that person.

Offence of purporting to act as officer

37 (1) A person who is not an officer of an enforcer commits an offence if the person purports to act as such under Part 3 or 4 of this Schedule.

(2) A person who is guilty of an offence under sub-paragraph (1) is liable on summary conviction to a fine not exceeding level 5 on the standard scale.

(3) If section 85(1) of the Legal Aid, Sentencing and Punishment of Offenders Act 2012 comes into force on or before the day on which this Act is passed—

(a) section 85 of that Act (removal of limit on certain fines on conviction by magistrates' court) applies in relation to the offence in this paragraph as if it were a relevant offence (as defined in section 85(3) of that Act), and

(b) regulations described in section 85(11) of that Act may amend or otherwise modify sub-paragraph (2).

Access to seized goods and documents

38 (1) This paragraph applies where anything seized by an officer of an enforcer under Part 4 of this Schedule is detained by the enforcer.

(2) If a request for permission to be granted access to that thing is made to the enforcer by a person who had custody or control of it immediately before it was seized, the

enforcer must allow that person access to it under the supervision of an officer of the enforcer.

(3) If a request for a photograph or copy of that thing is made to the enforcer by a person who had custody or control of it immediately before it was seized, the enforcer must—

    (a) allow that person access to it under the supervision of an officer of the enforcer for the purpose of photographing or copying it, or

    (b) photograph or copy it, or cause it to be photographed or copied.

(4) Where anything is photographed or copied under sub-paragraph (3), the photograph or copy must be supplied to the person who made the request within a reasonable time from the making of the request.

(5) This paragraph does not require access to be granted to, or a photograph or copy to be supplied of, anything if the enforcer has reasonable grounds for believing that to do so would prejudice the investigation for the purposes of which it was seized.

(6) An enforcer may recover the reasonable costs of complying with a request under this paragraph from the person by whom or on whose behalf it was made.

(7) References in this paragraph to a person who had custody or control of a thing immediately before it was seized include a representative of such a person.

Notice of testing of goods

39 (1) Sub-paragraphs (3) and (4) apply where goods purchased by an officer of a domestic enforcer under paragraph 21 are submitted to a test and as a result—

    (a) proceedings are brought for a breach of, or under, the enforcer's legislation or for the forfeiture of the goods by the enforcer, or

    (b) a notice is served by the enforcer preventing a person from doing any thing.

(2) Sub-paragraphs (3) and (4) also apply where goods seized by an officer of a domestic enforcer under paragraph 28 are submitted to a test.

(3) The enforcer must inform the relevant person of the results of the test.

(4) The enforcer must allow a relevant person to have the goods tested if it is reasonably practicable to do so.

(5) In sub-paragraph (3) 'relevant person' means the person from whom the goods were purchased or seized or, where the goods were purchased or seized from a vending machine—

    (a) the person whose name and address are on the vending machine as the owner of the machine, or

    (b) if there is no such name and address on the machine, the occupier of the premises on which the machine stands or to which it is fixed.

(6) In sub-paragraph (4) 'relevant person' means—

    (a) a person within sub-paragraph (5),

    (b) in a case within sub-paragraph (1)(a), a person who is a party to the proceedings, and

    (c) in a case within sub-paragraph (1)(b), a person with an interest in the goods.

Appeals against detention of goods and documents

40 (1) This paragraph applies where goods or documents are being detained as the result of the exercise of a power in Part 4 of this Schedule.

(2) A person with an interest in the goods or documents may apply for an order requiring them to be released to that or another person.

(3) An application under this paragraph may be made in England and Wales or Northern Ireland—

   (a) to any magistrates' court in which proceedings have been brought for an offence as the result of the investigation in the course of which the goods or documents were seized,

   (b) to any magistrates' court in which proceedings have been brought for the forfeiture of the goods or documents or (in the case of seized documents) any goods to which the documents relate, or

   (c) if no proceedings within paragraph (a) or (b) have been brought, by way of complaint to a magistrates' court.

(4) An application under this paragraph may be made in Scotland by summary application to the sheriff.

(5) On an application under this paragraph, the court or sheriff may make an order requiring goods to be released only if satisfied that condition A or B is met.

(6) Condition A is that—

   (a) no proceedings have been brought—

      (i) for an offence as the result of the investigation in the course of which the goods or documents were seized, or

      (ii) for the forfeiture of the goods or documents or (in the case of seized documents) any goods to which the documents relate, and

   (b) the period of 6 months beginning with the date the goods or documents were seized has expired.

(7) Condition B is that—

   (a) proceedings of a kind mentioned in sub-paragraph (6)(a) have been brought, and

   (b) those proceedings have been concluded without the goods or documents being forfeited.

(8) A person aggrieved by an order made under this paragraph by a magistrates' court, or by the decision of a magistrates' court not to make such an order, may appeal against the order or decision—

   (a) in England and Wales, to the Crown Court;

   (b) in Northern Ireland, to a county court.

(9) An order made under this paragraph by a magistrates' court may contain such provision as the court thinks appropriate for delaying its coming into force pending the making and determination of any appeal.

(10) In sub-paragraph (9) 'appeal' includes an application under section 111 of the Magistrates' Courts Act 1980 or Article 146 of the Magistrates' Courts (Northern Ireland) Order 1981 (SI 1981/1675 (NI 26)) (statements of case).

Compensation

41 (1) This paragraph applies where an officer of an enforcer has seized and detained goods under Part 4 of this Schedule for a purpose within paragraph 19(5)(a) or 20(5)(a).

   (2) The enforcer must pay compensation to any person with an interest in the goods in respect of any loss or damage caused by the seizure and detention, if the condition in sub-paragraph (3) or (4)that is relevant to the enforcer is met.

   (3) The condition that is relevant to a domestic enforcer is that—

      (a) the goods have not disclosed a breach of the enforcer's legislation, and

      (b) the power to seize and detain the goods was not exercised as a result of any neglect or default of the person seeking the compensation.

(4) The condition that is relevant to an EU enforcer is that—

    (a) the goods have not disclosed a Community infringement or a failure to comply with a measure specified in paragraph 20(3)(b), (c) or (d), and

    (b) the power to seize and detain the goods was not exercised as a result of any neglect or default of the person seeking the compensation.

(5) Any dispute about the right to or amount of any compensation payable under this paragraph is to be determined—

    (a) in England and Wales or Northern Ireland, by arbitration, or

    (b) in Scotland, by a single arbitrator appointed by the parties or, if there is no agreement between the parties as to that appointment, by the sheriff.

Meaning of 'goods' in this Part

42 In this Part of this Schedule 'goods' does not include a document.

PART 6

EXERCISE OF ENFORCEMENT FUNCTIONS BY AREA ENFORCERS

Interpretation of this Part

43 In this Part, 'area enforcer' means—

    (a) a local weights and measures authority in Great Britain,

    (b) a district council in England, or

    (c) a district council in Northern Ireland.

Investigatory powers

44 (1) Sub-paragraphs (3) to (6) apply in relation to an area enforcer's exercise, in accordance with this Schedule, of a power in Part 3 or 4 of this Schedule.

(2) Sub-paragraphs (3) to (6) also apply in relation to an area enforcer's exercise of an investigatory power—

    (a) conferred by legislation which, by virtue of a provision listed in paragraph 10 of this Schedule, the area enforcer has a duty or power to enforce, or conferred by legislation under which such legislation is made, or

    (b) conferred by legislation listed in the second column of the table in paragraph 11 of this Schedule,

for the purpose of ascertaining whether there has been a breach of that legislation or of any notice issued by the area enforcer under that legislation.

(3) A local weights and measures authority in England or Wales may exercise the power in a part of England or Wales which is outside that authority's area.

(4) A local weights and measures authority in Scotland may exercise the power in a part of Scotland which is outside that authority's area.

(5) A district council in England may exercise the power in a part of England which is outside that council's district.

(6) A district council in Northern Ireland may exercise the power in a part of Northern Ireland which is outside that council's district.

Civil proceedings

45 (1) Sub-paragraphs (4) to (7) apply in relation to civil proceedings which may be brought by an area enforcer under—
  (a) Part 8 of the Enterprise Act 2002,
  (b) Schedule 3 to this Act,
  (c) legislation which, by virtue of a provision listed in paragraph 10 of this Schedule, the area enforcer has a duty or power to enforce,
  (d) legislation under which legislation mentioned in paragraph (c) is made, or
  (e) legislation listed in the second column of the table in paragraph 11 of this Schedule.

  (2) Sub-paragraphs (4) to (7) also apply in relation to an application for forfeiture which may be made by an area enforcer, in circumstances where there are no related criminal proceedings—
  (a) under section 35ZC of the Registered Designs Act 1949,
  (b) under section 16 of the Consumer Protection Act 1987,
  (c) under section 97 of the Trade Marks Act 1994 (including as applied by section 11 of the Olympic Symbol etc (Protection) Act 1995), or
  (d) under legislation which, by virtue of a provision listed in paragraph 10 of this Schedule, the area enforcer has a duty or power to enforce.

  (3) In sub-paragraphs (4), (5), (6) and (7), the reference to civil proceedings includes a reference to an application mentioned in sub-paragraph (2).

  (4) A local weights and measures authority in England or Wales may bring civil proceedings in respect of conduct in a part of England or Wales which is outside that authority's area.

  (5) A local weights and measures authority in Scotland may bring civil proceedings in respect of conduct in a part of Scotland which is outside that authority's area.

  (6) A district council in England may bring civil proceedings in respect of conduct in a part of England which is outside that council's district.

  (7) A district council in Northern Ireland may bring civil proceedings in respect of conduct in a part of Northern Ireland which is outside that council's district.

Criminal proceedings

46 (1) A local weights and measures authority in England or Wales may bring proceedings for a consumer offence allegedly committed in a part of England or Wales which is outside that authority's area.

  (2) In sub-paragraph (1) 'a consumer offence' means—
  (a) an offence under legislation which, by virtue of a provision listed in paragraph 10 of this Schedule, a local weights and measures authority in England or Wales has a duty or power to enforce,
  (b) an offence under legislation under which legislation within paragraph (a) is made,
  (c) an offence under legislation listed in the second column of the table in paragraph 11 of this Schedule in relation to which a local weights and measures authority is listed in the corresponding entry in the first column of the table as an enforcer,
  (d) an offence originating from an investigation into a breach of legislation mentioned in paragraph (a), (b) or (c), or
  (e) an offence described in paragraph 36 or 37 of this Schedule.

(3) A district council in England may bring proceedings for a consumer offence allegedly committed in a part of England which is outside that council's district.

(4) In sub-paragraph (3) 'a consumer offence' means—

(a) an offence under legislation which, by virtue of a provision listed in paragraph 10 of this Schedule, a district council in England has a duty or power to enforce,

(b) an offence under legislation under which legislation within paragraph (a) is made,

(c) an offence originating from an investigation into a breach of legislation mentioned in paragraph (a) or (b), or

(d) an offence described in paragraph 36 or 37 of this Schedule.

(5) A district council in Northern Ireland may bring proceedings for a consumer offence allegedly committed in a part of Northern Ireland which is outside that council's district.

(6) In sub-paragraph (5) 'a consumer offence' means—

(a) an offence under legislation which, by virtue of a provision listed in paragraph 10 of this Schedule, a district council in Northern Ireland has a duty or power to enforce,

(b) an offence under legislation under which legislation within paragraph (a) is made,

(c) an offence originating from an investigation into a breach of legislation mentioned in paragraph (a) or (b), or

(d) an offence described in paragraph 36 or 37 of this Schedule.

Schedule 8

Private Actions in Competition Law

PART 1
COMPETITION ACT 1998

1 The Competition Act 1998 is amended in accordance with this Part.

2 For the heading of Chapter 4 of Part 1, substitute 'Appeals, proceedings before the Tribunal and settlements relating to infringements of competition law'.

3 For the cross-heading preceding section 46, substitute 'Appeals and proceedings before the Tribunal'.

4 (1) For section 47A substitute—

'47A Proceedings before the Tribunal: claims for damages etc.

(1) A person may make a claim to which this section applies in proceedings before the Tribunal, subject to the provisions of this Act and Tribunal rules.

(2) This section applies to a claim of a kind specified in subsection (3) which a person who has suffered loss or damage may make in civil proceedings brought in any part of the United Kingdom in respect of an infringement decision or an alleged infringement of—

  (a) the Chapter I prohibition,

  (b) the Chapter II prohibition,

  (c) the prohibition in Article 101(1), or

  (d) the prohibition in Article 102.

(3) The claims are—

  (a) a claim for damages;

  (b) any other claim for a sum of money;

  (c) in proceedings in England and Wales or Northern Ireland, a claim for an injunction.

(4) For the purpose of identifying claims which may be made in civil proceedings, any limitation rules or rules relating to prescription that would apply in such proceedings are to be disregarded.

(5) The right to make a claim in proceedings under this section does not affect the right to bring any other proceedings in respect of the claim.

(6) In this Part (except in section 49C) "infringement decision" means—

  (a) a decision of the CMA that the Chapter I prohibition, the Chapter II prohibition, the prohibition in Article 101(1) or the prohibition in Article 102 has been infringed,

  (b) a decision of the Tribunal on an appeal from a decision of the CMA that the Chapter I prohibition, the Chapter II prohibition, the prohibition in Article 101(1) or the prohibition in Article 102 has been infringed, or

  (c) a decision of the Commission that the prohibition in Article 101(1) or the prohibition in Article 102 has been infringed.'

(2) Section 47A of the Competition Act 1998 (as substituted by sub-paragraph (1)) applies to claims arising before the commencement of this paragraph as it applies to claims arising after that time.

5 (1) For section 47B substitute—

'47B Collective proceedings before the Tribunal

(1) Subject to the provisions of this Act and Tribunal rules, proceedings may be brought before the Tribunal combining two or more claims to which section 47A applies ("collective proceedings").

(2) Collective proceedings must be commenced by a person who proposes to be the representative in those proceedings.

(3) The following points apply in relation to claims in collective proceedings—
   (a) it is not a requirement that all of the claims should be against all of the defendants to the proceedings,
   (b) the proceedings may combine claims which have been made in proceedings under section 47A and claims which have not, and
   (c) a claim which has been made in proceedings under section 47A may be continued in collective proceedings only with the consent of the person who made that claim.

(4) Collective proceedings may be continued only if the Tribunal makes a collective proceedings order.

(5) The Tribunal may make a collective proceedings order only—
   (a) if it considers that the person who brought the proceedings is a person who, if the order were made, the Tribunal could authorise to act as the representative in those proceedings in accordance with subsection (8), and
   (b) in respect of claims which are eligible for inclusion in collective proceedings.

(6) Claims are eligible for inclusion in collective proceedings only if the Tribunal considers that they raise the same, similar or related issues of fact or law and are suitable to be brought in collective proceedings.

(7) A collective proceedings order must include the following matters—
   (a) authorisation of the person who brought the proceedings to act as the representative in those proceedings,
   (b) description of a class of persons whose claims are eligible for inclusion in the proceedings, and
   (c) specification of the proceedings as opt-in collective proceedings or opt-out collective proceedings (see subsections (10) and (11)).

(8) The Tribunal may authorise a person to act as the representative in collective proceedings—
   (a) whether or not that person is a person falling within the class of persons described in the collective proceedings order for those proceedings (a "class member"), but
   (b) only if the Tribunal considers that it is just and reasonable for that person to act as a representative in those proceedings.

(9) The Tribunal may vary or revoke a collective proceedings order at any time.

(10) "Opt-in collective proceedings" are collective proceedings which are brought on behalf of each class member who opts in by notifying the representative, in a manner and by a time specified, that the claim should be included in the collective proceedings.

(11) "Opt-out collective proceedings" are collective proceedings which are brought on behalf of each class member except—
   (a) any class member who opts out by notifying the representative, in a manner and by a time specified, that the claim should not be included in the collective proceedings, and
   (b) any class member who—

     (i) is not domiciled in the United Kingdom at a time specified, and

     (ii) does not, in a manner and by a time specified, opt in by notifying the representative that the claim should be included in the collective proceedings.

(12) Where the Tribunal gives a judgment or makes an order in collective proceedings, the judgment or order is binding on all represented persons, except as otherwise specified.

(13) The right to make a claim in collective proceedings does not affect the right to bring any other proceedings in respect of the claim.

(14) In this section and in section 47C, "specified" means specified in a direction made by the Tribunal.'

(2) Section 47B of the Competition Act 1998 (as substituted by sub-paragraph (1)) applies to claims arising before the commencement of this paragraph as it applies to claims arising after that time.

6 After section 47B (as substituted by paragraph 5) insert—

'47C Collective proceedings: damages and costs

(1) The Tribunal may not award exemplary damages in collective proceedings.

(2) The Tribunal may make an award of damages in collective proceedings without undertaking an assessment of the amount of damages recoverable in respect of the claim of each represented person.

(3) Where the Tribunal makes an award of damages in opt-out collective proceedings, the Tribunal must make an order providing for the damages to be paid on behalf of the represented persons to—

    (a) the representative, or

    (b) such person other than a represented person as the Tribunal thinks fit.

(4) Where the Tribunal makes an award of damages in opt-in collective proceedings, the Tribunal may make an order as described in subsection (3).

(5) Subject to subsection (6), where the Tribunal makes an award of damages in opt-out collective proceedings, any damages not claimed by the represented persons within a specified period must be paid to the charity for the time being prescribed by order made by the Lord Chancellor under section 194(8) of the Legal Services Act 2007.

(6) In a case within subsection (5) the Tribunal may order that all or part of any damages not claimed by the represented persons within a specified period is instead to be paid to the representative in respect of all or part of the costs or expenses incurred by the representative in connection with the proceedings.

(7) The Secretary of State may by order amend subsection (5) so as to substitute a different charity for the one for the time being specified in that subsection.

(8) A damages-based agreement is unenforceable if it relates to opt-out collective proceedings.

(9) In this section—

    (a) "charity" means a body, or the trustees of a trust, established for charitable purposes only;

    (b) "damages" (except in the term "exemplary damages") includes any sum of money which may be awarded by the Tribunal in collective proceedings (other than costs or expenses);

    (c) "damages-based agreement" has the meaning given in section 58AA(3) of the Courts and Legal Services Act 1990.'

7 After section 47C (inserted by paragraph 6) insert—

'47D Proceedings under section 47A or collective proceedings: injunctions etc.

(1) An injunction granted by the Tribunal in proceedings under section 47A or in collective proceedings—

    (a) has the same effect as an injunction granted by the High Court, and

    (b) is enforceable as if it were an injunction granted by the High Court.

(2) In deciding whether to grant an injunction in proceedings under section 47A or in collective proceedings, the Tribunal must—

(a) in proceedings in England and Wales, apply the principles which the High Court would apply in deciding whether to grant an injunction under section 37(1) of the Senior Courts Act 1981, and

(b) in proceedings in Northern Ireland, apply the principles that the High Court would apply in deciding whether to grant an injunction.

(3) Subsection (2) is subject to Tribunal rules which make provision of the kind mentioned in paragraph 15A(3) of Schedule 4 to the Enterprise Act 2002 (undertakings as to damages in relation to claims subject to the fast-track procedure).'

8 (1) After section 47D (inserted by paragraph 7) insert—

'47E Limitation or prescriptive periods for proceedings under section 47A and collective proceedings

(1) Subsection (2) applies in respect of a claim to which section 47A applies, for the purposes of determining the limitation or prescriptive period which would apply in respect of the claim if it were to be made in—

(a) proceedings under section 47A, or

(b) collective proceedings at the commencement of those proceedings.

(2) Where this subsection applies—

(a) in the case of proceedings in England and Wales, the Limitation Act 1980 applies as if the claim were an action in a court of law;

(b) in the case of proceedings in Scotland, the Prescription and Limitation (Scotland) Act 1973 applies as if the claim related to an obligation to which section 6 of that Act applies;

(c) in the case of proceedings in Northern Ireland, the Limitation (Northern Ireland) Order 1989 applies as if the claim were an action in a court established by law.

(3) Where a claim is made in collective proceedings at the commencement of those proceedings ("the section 47B claim"), subsections (4) to (6) apply for the purpose of determining the limitation or prescriptive period which would apply in respect of the claim if it were subsequently to be made in proceedings under section 47A.

(4) The running of the limitation or prescriptive period in respect of the claim is suspended from the date on which the collective proceedings are commenced.

(5) Following suspension under subsection (4), the running of the limitation or prescriptive period in respect of the claim resumes on the date on which any of the following occurs—

(a) the Tribunal declines to make a collective proceedings order in respect of the collective proceedings;

(b) the Tribunal makes a collective proceedings order in respect of the collective proceedings, but the order does not provide that the section 47B claim is eligible for inclusion in the proceedings;

(c) the Tribunal rejects the section 47B claim;

(d) in the case of opt-in collective proceedings, the period within which a person may choose to have the section 47B claim included in the proceedings expires without the person having done so;

(e) in the case of opt-out collective proceedings—

      (i)   a person domiciled in the United Kingdom chooses (within the period in which such a choice may be made) to have the section 47B claim excluded from the collective proceedings, or

      (ii) the period within which a person not domiciled in the United Kingdom may choose to have the section 47B claim included in the collective proceedings expires without the person having done so;

  (f) the section 47B claim is withdrawn;

  (g) the Tribunal revokes the collective proceedings order in respect of the collective proceedings;

  (h) the Tribunal varies the collective proceedings order in such a way that the section 47B claim is no longer included in the collective proceedings;

  (i) the section 47B claim is settled with or without the Tribunal's approval;

  (j) the section 47B claim is dismissed, discontinued or otherwise disposed of without an adjudication on the merits.

(6) Where the running of the limitation or prescriptive period in respect of the claim resumes under subsection (5) but the period would otherwise expire before the end of the period of six months beginning with the date of that resumption, the period is treated as expiring at the end of that six month period.

(7) This section has effect subject to any provision in Tribunal rules which defers the date on which the limitation or prescriptive period begins in relation to claims in proceedings under section 47A or in collective proceedings.'

(2) Section 47E of the Competition Act 1998 does not apply in relation to claims arising before the commencement of this paragraph.

9 (1) Section 49 (further appeals) is amended in accordance with this paragraph.

(2) In subsection (1)—

  (a) at the end of paragraph (a) insert 'and', and

  (b) omit paragraph (b) and the 'and' at the end of that paragraph.

(3) After subsection (1) insert—

  '(1A) An appeal lies to the appropriate court on a point of law arising from a decision of the Tribunal in proceedings under section 47A or in collective proceedings—

    (a) as to the award of damages or other sum (other than a decision on costs or expenses), or

    (b) as to the grant of an injunction.

  (1B) An appeal lies to the appropriate court from a decision of the Tribunal in proceedings under section 47A or in collective proceedings as to the amount of an award of damages or other sum (other than the amount of costs or expenses).

  (1C) An appeal under subsection (1A) arising from a decision in respect of a stand-alone claim may include consideration of a point of law arising from a finding of the Tribunal as to an infringement of a prohibition listed in section 47A(2).

  (1D) In subsection (1C) "a stand-alone claim" is a claim—

    (a) in respect of an alleged infringement of a prohibition listed in section 47A(2), and

    (b) made in proceedings under section 47A or included in collective proceedings.'

(4) In subsection (2)(a), at the beginning insert 'except as provided by subsection (2A),'.

(5) After subsection (2) insert—

  '(2A) An appeal from a decision of the Tribunal in respect of a claim included in collective proceedings may be brought only by the representative in those proceedings or by a defendant to that claim.'

10 (1) After section 49 insert—

'Settlements relating to infringements of competition law

49A Collective settlements: where a collective proceedings order has been made

(1) The Tribunal may, in accordance with this section and Tribunal rules, make an order approving the settlement of claims in collective proceedings (a "collective settlement") where—
(a) a collective proceedings order has been made in respect of the claims, and
(b) the Tribunal has specified that the proceedings are opt-out collective proceedings.

(2) An application for approval of a proposed collective settlement must be made to the Tribunal by the representative and the defendant in the collective proceedings.

(3) The representative and the defendant must provide agreed details of the claims to be settled by the proposed collective settlement and the proposed terms of that settlement.

(4) Where there is more than one defendant in the collective proceedings, "defendant" in subsections (2) and (3) means such of the defendants as wish to be bound by the proposed collective settlement.

(5) The Tribunal may make an order approving a proposed collective settlement only if satisfied that its terms are just and reasonable.

(6) On the date on which the Tribunal approves a collective settlement—
(a) if the period within which persons may opt out of or (in the case of persons not domiciled in the United Kingdom) opt in to the collective proceedings has expired, subsections (8) and (10) apply so as to determine the persons bound by the settlement;
(b) if that period has not yet expired, subsections (9) and (10) apply so as to determine the persons bound by the settlement.

(7) If the period within which persons may opt out of the collective proceedings expires on a different date from the period within which persons not domiciled in the United Kingdom may opt in to the collective proceedings, the references in subsection (6) to the expiry of a period are to the expiry of whichever of those periods expires later.

(8) Where this subsection applies, a collective settlement approved by the Tribunal is binding on all persons falling within the class of persons described in the collective proceedings order who—
(a) were domiciled in the United Kingdom at the time specified for the purposes of determining domicile in relation to the collective proceedings (see section 47B(11) (b)(i)) and did not opt out of those proceedings, or
(b) opted in to the collective proceedings.

(9) Where this subsection applies, a collective settlement approved by the Tribunal is binding on all persons falling within the class of persons described in the collective proceedings order.

(10) But a collective settlement is not binding on a person who—
(a) opts out by notifying the representative, in a manner and by a time specified, that the claim should not be included in the collective settlement, or
(b) is not domiciled in the United Kingdom at a time specified, and does not, in a manner and by a time specified, opt in by notifying the representative that the claim should be included in the collective settlement.

(11) This section does not affect a person's right to offer to settle opt-in collective proceedings.

(12) In this section and in section 49B, "specified" means specified in a direction made by the Tribunal.'

(2) Section 49A of the Competition Act 1998 applies to claims arising before the commencement of this paragraph as it applies to claims arising after that time.

11 (1) After section 49A (inserted by paragraph 10) insert—

'49B Collective settlements: where a collective proceedings order has not been made

(1) The Tribunal may, in accordance with this section and Tribunal rules, make an order approving the settlement of claims (a "collective settlement") where—

    (a) a collective proceedings order has not been made in respect of the claims, but

    (b) if collective proceedings were brought, the claims could be made at the commencement of the proceedings (disregarding any limitation or prescriptive period applicable to a claim in collective proceedings).

(2) An application for approval of a proposed collective settlement must be made to the Tribunal by—

    (a) a person who proposes to be the settlement representative in relation to the collective settlement, and

    (b) the person who, if collective proceedings were brought in respect of the claims, would be a defendant in those proceedings (or, where more than one person would be a defendant in those proceedings, such of those persons as wish to be bound by the proposed collective settlement).

(3) The persons applying to the Tribunal under subsection (2) must provide agreed details of the claims to be settled by the proposed collective settlement and the proposed terms of that settlement.

(4) The Tribunal may make an order approving a proposed collective settlement (see subsection (8)) only if it first makes a collective settlement order.

(5) The Tribunal may make a collective settlement order only—

    (a) if it considers that the person described in subsection (2)(a) is a person who, if the order were made, the Tribunal could authorise to act as the settlement representative in relation to the collective settlement in accordance with subsection (7), and

    (b) in respect of claims which, if collective proceedings were brought, would be eligible for inclusion in the proceedings (see section 47B(6)).

(6) A collective settlement order must include the following matters—

    (a) authorisation of the person described in subsection (2)(a) to act as the settlement representative in relation to the collective settlement, and

    (b) description of a class of persons whose claims fall within subsection (5)(b).

(7) The Tribunal may authorise a person to act as the settlement representative in relation to a collective settlement—

    (a) whether or not that person is a person falling within the class of persons described in the collective settlement order for that settlement, but

    (b) only if the Tribunal considers that it is just and reasonable for that person to act as the settlement representative in relation to that settlement.

(8) Where the Tribunal has made a collective settlement order, it may make an order approving a proposed collective settlement only if satisfied that its terms are just and reasonable.

(9) A collective settlement approved by the Tribunal is binding on all persons falling within the class of persons described in the collective settlement order.

(10) But a collective settlement is not binding on a person who—

    (a) opts out by notifying the settlement representative, in a manner and by a time specified, that the claim should not be included in the collective settlement, or

    (b) is not domiciled in the United Kingdom at a time specified, and does not, in a manner and by a time specified, opt in by notifying the settlement representative that the claim should be included in the collective settlement.

(11) In this section, "settlement representative" means a person who is authorised by a collective settlement order to act in relation to a collective settlement.'

(2) Section 49B of the Competition Act 1998 applies to claims arising before the commencement of this paragraph as it applies to claims arising after that time.

12 After section 49B (inserted by paragraph 11) insert—

'49C Approval of redress schemes by the CMA

(1) A person may apply to the CMA for approval of a redress scheme.

(2) The CMA may consider an application before the infringement decision to which the redress scheme relates has been made, but may approve the scheme only—

    (a) after that decision has been made, or

    (b) in the case of a decision of the CMA, at the same time as that decision is made.

(3) In deciding whether to approve a redress scheme, the CMA may take into account the amount or value of compensation offered under the scheme.

(4) The CMA may approve a redress scheme under subsection (2)(b) subject to a condition or conditions requiring the provision of further information about the operation of the scheme (including about the amount or value of compensation to be offered under the scheme or how this will be determined).

(5) If the CMA approves a redress scheme subject to such a condition, it may—

    (a) approve the scheme subject to other conditions;

    (b) withdraw approval from the scheme if any conditions imposed under subsection (4) or paragraph (a) are not met;

    (c) approve a redress scheme as a replacement for the original scheme (but may not approve that scheme subject to conditions).

(6) An approved scheme may not be varied by the CMA or the compensating party.

(7) But, where the CMA approves a redress scheme subject to a condition of the kind mentioned in subsection (4), subsection (6) does not prevent further information provided in accordance with the condition from forming part of the terms of the scheme.

(8) The Secretary of State may make regulations relating to the approval of redress schemes, and the regulations may in particular—

    (a) make provision as to the procedure governing an application for approval of a redress scheme, including the information to be provided with the application;

    (b) provide that the CMA may approve a redress scheme only if it has been devised according to a process specified in the regulations;

    (c) provide that the CMA may approve a redress scheme only if it is in a form, or contains terms, specified in the regulations (which may include terms requiring a settlement agreement under the scheme to be in a form, or contain terms, specified in the regulations);

    (d) provide that the CMA may approve a redress scheme only if (so far as the CMA can judge from facts known to it) the scheme is intended to be administered in a manner specified in the regulations;

    (e) describe factors which the CMA may or must take into account, or may not take into account, in deciding whether to approve a redress scheme.

(9) The CMA must publish guidance with regard to—

    (a) applications for approval of redress schemes,

    (b) the approval of redress schemes, and

    (c) the enforcement of approved schemes, and in particular as to the criteria which the CMA intends to adopt in deciding whether to bring proceedings under section 49E(4).

(10) Guidance under subsection (9) must be approved by the Secretary of State before it is published.

(11) In this section and sections 49D and 49E—

    • "approved scheme" means a redress scheme approved by the CMA,

- "compensating party" means a person offering compensation under an approved scheme,
- "infringement decision" means—
  (a) a decision of the CMA that the Chapter I prohibition, the Chapter II prohibition, the prohibition in Article 101(1) or the prohibition in Article 102 has been infringed, or
  (b) a decision of the Commission that the prohibition in Article 101(1) or the prohibition in Article 102 has been infringed, and
- "redress scheme" means a scheme under which a person offers compensation in consequence of an infringement decision made in respect of that person.

(12) For the purposes of this section and section 49E, "compensation"—
  (a) may be monetary or non-monetary, and
  (b) may be offered to persons who have not suffered a loss as a result of the infringement decision to which the redress scheme relates.

49D Redress schemes: recovery of costs

(1) The CMA may require a person making an application for approval of a redress scheme to pay some or all of the CMA's reasonable costs relating to the application.

(2) A requirement to pay costs is imposed by giving that person written notice specifying—
  (a) the amount to be paid,
  (b) how that amount has been calculated, and
  (c) by when that amount must be paid.

(3) A person required to pay costs under this section may appeal to the Tribunal against the amount.

(4) Where costs required to be paid under this section relate to an approved scheme, the CMA may withdraw approval from that scheme if the costs have not been paid by the date specified in accordance with subsection (2)(c).

(5) Costs required to be paid under this section are recoverable by the CMA as a debt.

49E Enforcement of approved schemes

(1) A compensating party is under a duty to comply with the terms of an approved scheme ("the duty").

(2) The duty is owed to any person entitled to compensation under the terms of the approved scheme.

(3) Where such a person suffers loss or damage as a result of a breach of the duty, the person may bring civil proceedings before the court for damages, an injunction or interdict or any other appropriate relief or remedy.

(4) Where the CMA considers that the compensating party is in breach of the duty, the CMA may bring civil proceedings before the court for an injunction or interdict or any other appropriate relief or remedy.

(5) Subsection (4) is without prejudice to any right that a person has to bring proceedings under subsection (3).

(6) In any proceedings brought under subsection (3) or (4), it is a defence for the compensating party to show that it took all reasonable steps to comply with the duty.

(7) Where the CMA considers that it is no longer appropriate for the compensating party to be subject to the duty, the CMA may give notice in writing to that party stating that it is released from the duty.

(8) Where a person has entered into a settlement agreement with the compensating party, that agreement remains enforceable notwithstanding the release of the compensating party under subsection (7) from the duty.

(9) In this section "the court" means—
  (a) in England and Wales, the High Court or the county court,
  (b) in Northern Ireland, the High Court or a county court,
  (c) in Scotland, the Court of Session or the sheriff.'

13 (1) Section 58 (findings of fact by CMA) is amended in accordance with this paragraph.
  (2) In subsection (1), after 'the court' insert 'or the Tribunal'.
  (3) In subsection (2)—
    (a) in the definition of 'Part I proceedings', before paragraph (a) insert—
      '(za) in respect of an infringement decision;', and
    (b) in the definition of 'relevant party', in paragraphs (a) and (b), for 'is alleged to have infringed the prohibition' substitute 'has been found to have infringed the prohibition or is alleged to have infringed the prohibition (as the case may be)'.
  (4) In subsection (3)—
    (a) after 'Rules of court' insert 'or Tribunal rules', and
    (b) after 'the court' insert 'or the Tribunal'.
  (5) After subsection (3) insert—
    '(4) In this section "the court" means—
      (a) in England and Wales or Northern Ireland, the High Court,
      (b) in Scotland, the Court of Session or the sheriff.'

14 (1) For section 58A substitute—

'58A Infringement decisions

  (1) This section applies to a claim in respect of an infringement decision which is brought in proceedings—
    (a) before the court, or
    (b) before the Tribunal under section 47A or 47B.
  (2) The court or the Tribunal is bound by the infringement decision once it has become final.
  (3) An infringement decision specified in section 47A(6)(a) or (b) becomes final—
    (a) when the time for appealing against that decision expires without an appeal having been brought;
    (b) where the decision is specified in section 47A(6)(a) and an appeal has been brought against the decision under section 46 or 47, when that appeal—
      (i) has been withdrawn, dismissed or otherwise discontinued, or
      (ii) has confirmed the infringement decision and the time for making any further appeal against that confirmatory decision expires without a further appeal having been brought;
    (c) where an appeal has been brought in relation to the decision under section 49, when that appeal—
      (i) in the case of an appeal against the infringement decision or against a decision which confirmed the infringement decision, has been withdrawn, dismissed or otherwise discontinued, or
      (ii) has confirmed the infringement decision and the time for making any further appeal to the Supreme Court against that confirmatory decision expires without a further appeal having been brought; or
    (d) where an appeal has been brought to the Supreme Court in relation to the decision, when that appeal—
      (i) in the case of an appeal against a decision which confirmed the infringement decision, has been withdrawn, dismissed or otherwise discontinued, or
      (ii) has confirmed the infringement decision.

(4) An infringement decision specified in section 47A(6)(c) becomes final—
    (a) when the time for appealing against that decision in the European Court expires without an appeal having been brought; or
    (b) where such an appeal has been brought against the decision, when that appeal—
        (i) has been withdrawn, dismissed or otherwise discontinued, or
        (ii) has confirmed the infringement decision.

(5) This section applies to the extent that the court or the Tribunal would not otherwise be bound by the infringement decision in question.

(6) In this section "the court" means—
    (a) in England and Wales or Northern Ireland, the High Court,
    (b) in Scotland, the Court of Session or the sheriff.'

(2) Section 58A of the Competition Act 1998 (as substituted by sub-paragraph (1)) does not apply in relation to decisions made before the commencement of this paragraph.

15 (1) Section 59 (interpretation of Part 1) is amended in accordance with this paragraph.

    (2) In subsection (1), at the appropriate places insert—
- ' "class member" has the meaning given in section 47B(8)(a);';
- ' "collective proceedings" has the meaning given in section 47B(1);';
- ' "collective proceedings order" means an order made by the Tribunal authorising the continuance of collective proceedings;';
- ' "infringement decision", except in section 49C, has the meaning given in section 47A(6);';
- ' "injunction" includes an interim injunction;';
- ' "opt-in collective proceedings" has the meaning given in section 47B(10);';
- ' "opt-out collective proceedings" has the meaning given in section 47B(11);';
- ' "representative" means a person who is authorised by a collective proceedings order to bring collective proceedings;';
- ' "represented person" means a class member who—
    (a) has opted in to opt-in collective proceedings,
    (b) was domiciled in the United Kingdom at the time specified for the purposes of determining domicile (see section 47B(11)(b)(i)) and has not opted out of opt-out collective proceedings, or
    (c) has opted in to opt-out collective proceedings;'.

    (3) In subsection (1), in the definition of 'the court', before '58' insert '49E,'.

    (4) After subsection (1) insert—
    '(1A) In this Part, in respect of proceedings in Scotland, "defendant" is to be read as "defender".
    (1B) Sections 41, 42, 45 and 46 of the Civil Jurisdiction and Judgments Act 1982 apply for the purpose of determining whether a person is regarded as "domiciled in the United Kingdom" for the purposes of this Part.'

16 In section 71 (regulations, orders and rules), after subsection (4)(ca) insert—

'(cb) section 47C(7),'.

17 (1) Schedule 8 (appeals) is amended in accordance with this paragraph.

    (2) In paragraph 2(1), for '46 or 47' substitute '46, 47 or 49D(3)'.

    (3) After paragraph 3A insert—
    '3B (1) This paragraph applies to an appeal under section 49D(3).
        (2) The Tribunal must determine the appeal on the merits by reference to the grounds of appeal set out in the notice of appeal.
        (3) The Tribunal may—
            (a) approve the amount of costs which is the subject of the appeal, or
            (b) impose a requirement to pay costs of a different amount.

(4) The Tribunal may also give such directions, or take such other steps, as the CMA could itself have given or taken.

(5) A requirement imposed by the Tribunal under sub-paragraph (3)(b) has the same effect, and may be enforced in the same manner, as a requirement imposed by the CMA under section 49D.'

PART 2
ENTERPRISE ACT 2002

18 The Enterprise Act 2002 is amended in accordance with this Part.

19 (1) Section 14 (constitution of Tribunal for particular proceedings and its decisions) is amended as follows.

(2) In subsection (1), after 'before it' insert ', including proceedings relating to the approval of a collective settlement under section 49A or 49B of the 1998 Act,'.

(3) After subsection (1) insert—

'(1A) But in the case of proceedings relating to a claim under section 47A of the 1998 Act which is subject to the fast-track procedure (as described in Tribunal rules), the Tribunal may consist of a chairman only.'

20 In section 15 (Tribunal rules), in subsection (1), at the end insert ', including proceedings relating to the approval of a collective settlement under section 49A or 49B of the 1998 Act.'

21 In section 16 (transfers of certain proceedings to and from Tribunal), in subsection (5), for 'High Court or the Court of Session of' substitute 'court of all or any part of'.

22 Schedule 4 (Tribunal: procedure) is amended in accordance with the following paragraphs of this Part.

23 In paragraph 1 (decisions of the Tribunal), for sub-paragraph (1)(a) substitute—

'(a) state the reasons for the decision;

(aa) state whether the decision was unanimous or taken by a majority or, where proceedings are heard by a chairman only, state that fact;'.

24 After paragraph 1 insert—

'Enforcement of injunctions in England and Wales and Northern Ireland

1A (1) Where a person ("A") fails to comply with an injunction granted by the Tribunal in proceedings under section 47A or 47B of the 1998 Act, the Tribunal may certify the matter to the High Court.

(2) The High Court may enquire into the matter.

(3) If, after hearing any witnesses who may be produced against or on behalf of A, and any statement made by or on behalf of A, the High Court is satisfied that A would have been in contempt of court if the injunction had been granted by the High Court, the High Court may deal with A as if A were in contempt.'

25 In each of paragraphs 4(c) and 5(1)(c)—

(a) for '47B(6)' substitute '47C(3) or (4)'; and

(b) for 'specified body concerned' substitute 'representative in the proceedings under section 47B of that Act'.

26 In paragraph 6—

(a) for sub-paragraph (a) substitute—

'(a) awards damages to a person in respect of a claim made or continued on behalf of that person (but is not the subject of an order under section 47C(3) or (4) of that Act); or';

(b) in sub-paragraph (b)—

      (i) for 'an individual' substitute 'a person',

      (ii) for 'his behalf' substitute 'behalf of that person'; and

  (c) in the full-out words at the end, for 'individual' substitute 'person'.

27 In paragraph 7—

  (a) for 'specified body' substitute 'representative'; and

  (b) for 'individual' substitute 'person'.

28 In paragraph 9—

  (a) the existing provision is numbered as sub-paragraph (1), and

  (b) after that provision insert—

    '(2) In this Schedule, where a paragraph is capable of applying to proceedings relating to the approval of a collective settlement under section 49A or 49B of the 1998 Act, any reference in that paragraph to "proceedings" includes a reference to those proceedings.'

29 In paragraph 11(2), for paragraph (a) substitute—

  '(a) make further provision as to procedural aspects of the operation of the limitation or prescriptive periods in relation to claims which may be made in proceedings under section 47A of the 1998 Act, as set out in section 47E(3) to (6) of that Act;'.

30 For paragraph 13 substitute—

  '13 (1) Tribunal rules may provide for the Tribunal—

      (a) to reject a claim made under section 47A of the 1998 Act or a section 47B claim if it considers that there are no reasonable grounds for making it;

      (b) to reject a section 47B claim if—

          (i) the Tribunal declines to make a collective proceedings order in respect of the proceedings under section 47B of the 1998 Act,

          (ii) the Tribunal makes a collective proceedings order in respect of the proceedings, but the order does not provide that the claim in question is eligible for inclusion in the proceedings,

          (iii) the Tribunal revokes the collective proceedings order in respect of the proceedings, or

          (iv) the Tribunal varies the collective proceedings order in such a way that the claim in question is no longer included in the proceedings;

      (c) to reject a section 47B claim if the claim had been previously made in proceedings under section 47A of the 1998 Act by a person who has not consented to its being continued in proceedings under section 47B of that Act.

    (2) In this paragraph, "a section 47B claim" means a claim made in proceedings under section 47B of the 1998 Act at the commencement of those proceedings.'

31 After paragraph 15 insert—

'Fast-track procedure

  15A (1) Tribunal rules may make provision in relation to a fast-track procedure for claims made in proceedings under section 47A of the 1998 Act, including describing the factors relevant to determining whether a claim is suitable to be dealt with according to that procedure.

    (2) Tribunal rules may make different provision for claims in proceedings under section 47A of the 1998 Act which are and which are not subject to the fast-track procedure.

    (3) Tribunal rules may, in particular, provide for the Tribunal to—

      (a) grant an interim injunction on a claim in proceedings under section 47A of the 1998 Act which is subject to the fast-track procedure to a person who has not given an undertaking as to damages, or

(b) impose a cap on the amount that a person may be required to pay under an undertaking as to damages given on the granting of such an interim injunction.

(4) In sub-paragraph (3) "an undertaking as to damages" means an undertaking to pay damages which a person sustains as a result of the interim injunction and which the Tribunal considers the person to whom the injunction is granted should pay.

Collective proceedings

15B (1) Tribunal rules may make provision in relation to collective proceedings under section 47B of the 1998 Act.

(2) Rules under sub-paragraph (1) must in particular make provision as to the following matters—

(a) the procedure governing an application for a collective proceedings order;

(b) the factors which the Tribunal must take into account in deciding whether a claim is suitable to be brought in collective proceedings (but rules need not make provision in connection with the determination as to whether claims raise the same, similar or related issues of fact or law);

(c) the factors which the Tribunal must take into account in deciding whether to authorise a person to act as a representative in collective proceedings;

(d) the procedure by which the Tribunal is to reach a decision as to whether to make a collective proceedings order;

(e) the procedure by which a person may opt in or opt out of collective proceedings;

(f) the factors which the Tribunal must take into account in deciding whether to vary or revoke a collective proceedings order;

(g) the assessment of damages in collective proceedings;

(h) the payment of damages in collective proceedings, including the procedure for publicising an award of damages;

(i) the effect of judgments and orders in collective proceedings.

Collective settlements

15C (1) Tribunal rules may make provision in relation to collective settlements under sections 49A and 49B of the 1998 Act.

(2) Rules under sub-paragraph (1) must in particular make provision as to the following matters—

(a) the procedure governing an application for approval of a proposed collective settlement;

(b) where section 49B applies, the factors which the Tribunal must take into account in deciding whether to make a collective settlement order (but rules need not make provision in connection with the determination as to whether claims raise the same, similar or related issues of fact or law);

(c) where section 49B applies, the factors which the Tribunal must take into account in deciding whether to authorise a person to act as a settlement representative in relation to a collective settlement;

(d) where section 49B applies, the procedure by which the Tribunal is to reach a decision as to whether to make a collective settlement order;

(e) the factors which the Tribunal must take into account in deciding whether to approve a proposed collective settlement;

(f) the procedure by which the Tribunal is to reach a decision as to whether to approve a collective settlement;

(g) the procedure by which a person may opt in or opt out of a collective settlement;

(h) the payment of compensation under a collective settlement, including the procedure for publicising a compensation award.'

32 In paragraph 17 (conduct of the hearing)—

(a) after sub-paragraph (1)(h) insert—

'(ha) allowing the Tribunal to order payments in respect of the representation of a party to proceedings under section 47A or 47B of the 1998 Act, where the representation by a legal representative was provided free of charge;';

(b) in sub-paragraph (2)—

(i) for 'an individual' substitute 'a person'; and

(ii) for 'that individual' substitute 'that person';

(c) after sub-paragraph (2) insert—

'(2A) Rules under sub-paragraph (1)(h) may provide for costs or expenses to be awarded to or against a person on whose behalf a claim is made or continued in proceedings under section 47B of the 1998 Act in respect of an application in the proceedings made by that person (where that application is not made by the representative in the proceedings on that person's behalf).'; and

(d) in sub-paragraph (3), for 'an individual' substitute 'a person'.

33 After paragraph 20 insert—

'*Stay or sist of proceedings*

20A (1) In relation to proceedings in England and Wales or Northern Ireland under section 47A or 47B of the 1998 Act, Tribunal rules may make provision as to the stay of the proceedings, including as to—

(a) the circumstances in which a stay may be ordered or removed at the request of a party to the proceedings,

(b) the circumstances in which the proceedings may be stayed at the instance of the Tribunal, and

(c) the procedure to be followed.

(2) In relation to proceedings in Scotland under section 47A or 47B of the 1998 Act, Tribunal rules may make provision as to the sist of the proceedings, including as to—

(a) the circumstances in which a sist may be granted or recalled at the request of a party to the proceedings,

(b) the circumstances in which the proceedings may be sisted at the instance of the Tribunal, and

(c) the procedure to be followed.

(3) Rules under sub-paragraph (1) or (2) may in particular make provision in relation to the stay or sist of proceedings under section 47A or 47B which relate to a claim in respect of an infringement decision (as defined in section 47A(6)) which has not become final (see section 58A of the 1998 Act).'

34 After paragraph 21 insert—

'*Injunctions*

21 A Tribunal rules may make provision in relation to the grant of injunctions (including interim injunctions) in proceedings under section 47A or 47B of the 1998 Act.'

35 In paragraph 23(3), for 'an individual' substitute 'a person'.

36 In paragraph 25, after 'transfer of' insert 'all or any part of'.

PART 3

COURTS AND LEGAL SERVICES ACT 1990

37 In the Courts and Legal Services Act 1990, in section 58AA (damages-based agreements), after subsection (10) insert—

'(11) Subsection (1) is subject to section 47C(8) of the Competition Act 1998.'

APPENDIX 5

A. Unfair Contract Terms Black List

Statutory right	Remedies for breach	What is blacklisted
Section 9 (Goods) – Goods to be of satisfactory quality.	Section 19(3) – • Short term right to reject; • Right to repair or replacement; • Right to a price reduction or final right to reject. Other remedies under general law (but note that there is no right to treat the contract as at an end except as indicated above).	Exclusion or restrictions of rights or remedies – section 31.
Section 10 (Goods) – Goods to be fit for a particular purpose.	Section 19(3) – • Short term right to reject; • Right to repair or replacement; • Right to a price reduction or final right to reject. Other remedies under general law (but note that there is no right to treat the contract as at an end except as indicated above).	Exclusion or restrictions of rights or remedies – section 31.
Section 11 (Goods) – • Goods to match description; • CCRs pre-contract information on main characteristics of goods treated as a binding term of the contract.	Section 19(3) – • Short term right to reject; • Right to repair or replacement; • Right to a price reduction or final right to reject. Other remedies under general law (but note that there is no right to treat the contract as at an end except as indicated above).	Exclusion or restrictions of rights or remedies – section 31.
Section 12 (Goods) – Other CCRs pre-contract information (not about the goods) treated as a binding term of the contract.	Section 19(5) – Right to recover costs incurred as a result of the breach up to a maximum of the contract price for the goods. Other remedies under general law, except there is no right to treat the contract as at an end.	Exclusion or restrictions of rights or remedies – section 31.

Statutory right	Remedies for breach	What is blacklisted
Section 13 (Goods) – Goods to match a sample.	Section 19(3) – • Short-term right to reject; • Right to repair or replacement; • Right to a price reduction or final right to reject. Other remedies under general law (but note that there is no right to treat the contract as at an end except as indicated above).	Exclusion or restrictions of rights or remedies – section 31.
Section 14 (Goods) – Goods to match a model.	Section 19(3) – • Short-term right to reject; • Right to repair or replacement; • Right to a price reduction or final right to reject. Other remedies under general law (but note that there is no right to treat the contract as at an end except as indicated above).	Exclusion or restrictions of rights or remedies – section 31.
Section 15 (Goods) – Goods must be installed correctly (in supply and installation contracts).	Section 19(4) – • Right to repair or replacement; • Right to a price reduction or final right to reject. Other remedies under general law (but note that there is no right to treat the contract as at an end except as indicated above).	Exclusion or restrictions of rights or remedies – section 31.
Section 16 (Goods) – Digital content must conform to the contract to supply digital content (where goods are an item including digital content).	Section 19(3) – • Short term right to reject; • Right to repair or replacement; • Right to a price reduction or final right to reject. Other remedies under general law (but note that there is no right to treat the contract as at an end except as indicated above).	Exclusion or restrictions of rights or remedies – section 31.
Section 17 (Goods) – Trader must have the right to supply the goods.	Section 19(6) – right to reject. Other remedies under general law (but note that there is no right to treat the contract as at an end except as indicated above).	Exclusion or restrictions of rights or remedies – section 31.

Statutory right	Remedies for breach	What is blacklisted
Section 28 (Goods) – • Trader to deliver goods to consumer unless otherwise agreed; • Goods to be delivered without undue delay an in any cases within 30 days of contracts if no time for delivery agreed.	Section 28 (6) to (8) – time for delivery. • Right to treat contract as at an end in some cases or to specify a further period for delivery; • If further delivery period missed, right to treat contract as at an end. Other remedies under general law.	Exclusion of restrictions of rights or remedies – section 31.
Section 29 (Goods) – Goods remain at trader risk until delivered to any of: • The consumer; • Someone nominated by the consumer; • A carrier arranged by the consumer.	N/A	Exclusion or restrictions of rights or remedies – section 31.
Section 34 (Digital content) – Digital content to be of satisfactory quality.	Section 42(2) – • Right to repair or replacement; • Right to a price reduction. Other remedies under general law except the right to treat the contract as at an end.	Exclusion or restrictions of rights or remedies – section 47.
Section 35 (Digital content) – Digital content to be fit for a particular purpose.	Section 42(2) – • Right to repair or replacement; • Right to a price reduction. Other remedies under general law except the right to treat the contract as at an end.	Exclusion or restrictions of rights or remedies – section 47.
Section 36 (Digital content) – Digital content: • To match description; • CCRs pre-contract information on main characteristics, functionality and compatibility of digital content treated as term of contract.	Section 42(2) – • Right to repair or replacement; • Right to a price reduction. Other remedies under general law except the right to treat the contract as at an end.	Exclusion or restrictions of rights or remedies – section 47.
Section 37 (Digital content) – Digital content: Other CCRs pre-contract information (not about the digital content) treated as a binding term of the contract.	Section 42(4) – Right to recover costs as a result of the breach up to a maximum of the contract price for the digital content or facility. Other remedies under general law except the right to treat the contract as at an end.	Exclusion or restrictions of rights or remedies – section 47.

(Continued)

(*Continued*)

Statutory right	Remedies for breach	What is blacklisted
Section 40 (Digital content) – Statutory rights of satisfactory quality, fitness for a particular purpose and description apply to modified digital content as they do to original digital content.	Section 42(2) – • Right to repair or replacement; • Right to a price reduction. Other remedies under general law except that there is no right to treat the contract as at an end.	Exclusion or restrictions of rights or remedies – section 47.
Section 41 (Digital content) – Trader must have the right to supply the digital content.	Section 45 – right to a refund. Other remedies under general law (but note that there is no right to treat the contract as at an end except as indicated above).	Exclusion or restrictions of rights or remedies – section 47.
Section 46 (Digital content) – Right to a remedy for damage to the consumer's device or other digital content (whether paid for or not).	Section 46 – right to repair or compensation. Other remedies under general law.	Exclusion or restriction of rights and remedies is not blacklisted (but is assessable for fairness) – section 47(6).
Section 49 (Services) – Service must be performed with reasonable care and skill.	Section 54(3) – • Right to require repeat performance; • Right to a price reduction. Other remedies under general law including the right to treat the contract as at an end.	Exclusion or restriction of rights or remedies – section 57.
Section 50 (Services) – Anything said or written about the trade or service treated as a term of contract (subject to conditions). CCRs pre-contract information treated as term of contract.	Section 54 (3) – For breach of information about performance of the service: • Right to repeat performance; • Right to a price reduction. Section 55(4) – for breach of information not about the service: • Right to price reduction. Other remedies under general law including the right to treat the contract as at an end.	Exclusion of liability – section 57(2). Restriction of liability where that prevents the consumer recovering the price paid – section 57(3).

Statutory right	Remedies for breach	What is blacklisted
Section 51 (Services) – If no price has been agreed, a reasonable price is payable.	N/A	Exclusion of liability is not blacklisted (but would be assessable for fairness). Restriction of liability where that prevents the consumer recovering the price paid – section 57(3).
Section 53 (Services) – If no time for performance has been agreed, the service must be performed within a reasonable time.	Section 54 (5) – right to a price reduction. Other remedies under general law including the right to treat the contract as at an end.	Exlcusion of liability is *not* blacklisted. Restriction of liability where that prevents the consumer recovering the price paid – section 57(3).

A. Table of Consumer Protection Enforcement Powers

1. DOMESTIC ENFORCERS

POWER	REASON FOR USE	PRECONDITION FOR USE	PARAGRAPH OF SCHEDULE 5
Test purchase.	Ascertain compliance with enforcer's legislation.	None	21
Observation of a business.	Ascertain compliance with enforcer's legislation.	None	22
Entry into premises without a warrant.	Ascertain compliance with enforcer's legislation.	None	23
To inspect products.	Ascertain compliance with enforcer's legislation.	None	25
To examine any procedure connected with the production of a product.	Ascertain compliance with enforcer's legislation.	None	25
To test weighing or measuring equipment.	Ascertain compliance with enforcer's legislation.	(a) Equipment is used for trade or officer has a reasonable belief that equipment is used for trade; (b) Equipment has been verified or officer believes equipment verified as fit for use.	26
To produce documents.	(a) Ascertain compliance with enforcer's legislation; (b) Ascertain whether documents may be required as evidence in proceedings for breach under the enforcer's legislation.	Reasonable suspicion that a breach of enforcer's legislation has taken place unless there is a legal duty to keep certain documents.	27

To seize and detain goods.	(a) If goods would disclose (by testing or otherwise) a breach of legislation; (b) If goods are liable to forfeiture; (c) Goods may be required as evidence in proceedings for breach of legislation.	There must be a reasonable suspicion that (a), (b), or (c) applies.	28
To seize documents required as evidence.	Proceedings for a breach of enforcer's legislation or proceedings under enforcer's legislation.	Reasonable suspicion on part of enforcer that documents are required.	29
To decommission or switch off fixed installations.	Ascertain via testing or otherwise whether the Electromagnetic Compatibility Regulations 2006 have been breached.	Enforcer has reasonable suspicion of a breach of Electromagnetic Compatibility Regulations 2006.	30
To break open containers.	Ascertain compliance with enforcer's legislation.	Must be exercising powers in paragraphs 28, 29, or 30, and must be reasonably necessary in order to exercise the powers.	31
Enter premises with a warrant.	Ascertain compliance with enforcer's legislation.	(1) Justice of the Peace must have issued warrant. Officer must have reasonable grounds for believing the following: (a) condition A or B is met, and (b) condition C, D, or E is met.	

			32

(2) Condition A is that on the premises there are—
   (a) products which an officer of the enforcer has power to inspect under paragraph 25, or
   (b) documents which an officer of the enforcer could require a person to produce under paragraph 27.

(3) Condition B is that, on the premises—
   (a) in the case of a domestic enforcer, there has been or is about to be a breach of the enforcer's legislation,

…

(4) Condition C is that—
   (a) access to the premises has been or is likely to be refused, and
   (b) notice of the enforcer's intention to apply for a warrant under this paragraph has been given to the occupier of the premises.

(5) Condition D is that it is likely that products or documents on the premises would be concealed or interfered with if notice of entry on the premises were given to the occupier of the premises.

(6) Condition E is that—
   (a) the premises are unoccupied, or
   (b) the occupier of the premises is absent, and it might defeat the purpose of the entry to wait for the occupier's return.

| To require assistance from a person on the premises. | Ascertain compliance with enforcer's legislation. | Must have entered premises. Officer must have reasonable belief that the information or assistance is necessary. | 34 |

364

2. EU ENFORCERS

POWER	REASON FOR USE	PRECONDITION FOR USE	PARAGRAPH OF SCHEDULE 5.
Test purchase.	Any purpose relating to functions under Part 8 of the Enterprise Act 2002 in its capacity as a CPC enforcer.	Reasonable suspicion of the following – (a) that there has been, or is likely to be, a Community infringement; (b) a failure to comply with an enforcement order or an interim enforcement order made on the application of that enforcer; (c) a failure to comply with an undertaking given under section 217(9) or 218(10) of the Enterprise Act 2002 following such an application; or (d) a failure to comply with an undertaking given to that enforcer under section 219 of that Act.	21
Observation of a business.	Any purpose relating to functions under Part 8 of the Enterprise Act 2002 in its capacity as a CPC enforcer.	Reasonable suspicion of the following – (a) that there has been, or is likely to be, a Community infringement; (b) a failure to comply with an enforcement order or an interim enforcement order made on the application of that enforcer; (c) a failure to comply with an undertaking given under section 217(9) or 218(10) of the Enterprise Act 2002 following such an application; or (d) a failure to comply with an undertaking given to that enforcer under section 219 of that Act.	22
Entry into premises without a warrant.	Any purpose relating to functions under Part 8 of the Enterprise Act 2002 in its capacity as a CPC enforcer.	Reasonable suspicion of the following – (a) that there has been, or is likely to be, a Community infringement; (b) a failure to comply with an enforcement order or an interim enforcement order made on the application of that enforcer; (c) a failure to comply with an undertaking given under section 217(9) or 218(10) of the Enterprise Act 2002 following such an application; or (d) a failure to comply with an undertaking given to that enforcer under section 219 of that Act.	23

To inspect products.	Any purpose relating to functions under Part 8 of the Enterprise Act 2002 in its capacity as a CPC enforcer.	Reasonable suspicion of the following – (a) that there has been, or is likely to be, a Community infringement; (b) a failure to comply with an enforcement order or an interim enforcement order made on the application of that enforcer; (c) a failure to comply with an undertaking given under section 217(9) or 218(10) of the Enterprise Act 2002 following such an application; or (d) a failure to comply with an undertaking given to that enforcer under section 219 of that Act.	25
To examine any procedure connected with the production of a product.	Any purpose relating to functions under Part 8 of the Enterprise Act 2002 in its capacity as a CPC enforcer.	Reasonable suspicion of the following – (a) that there has been, or is likely to be, a Community infringement; (b) a failure to comply with an enforcement order or an interim enforcement order made on the application of that enforcer; (c) a failure to comply with an undertaking given under section 217(9) or 218(10) of the Enterprise Act 2002 following such an application; or (d) a failure to comply with an undertaking given to that enforcer under section 219 of that Act.	25
To produce documents.	(a) Any purpose relating to functions under Part 8 of the Enterprise Act 2002 in its capacity as a CPC enforcer. (b) Ascertain whether documents are required as evidence in proceedings brought under Part 8 of the Enterprise Act 2002.	Reasonable suspicion of the following – (a) that there has been, or is likely to be, a Community infringement; (b) a failure to comply with an enforcement order or an interim enforcement order made on the application of that enforcer; (c) a failure to comply with an undertaking given under section 217(9) or 218(10) of the Enterprise Act 2002 following such an application; or (d) a failure to comply with an undertaking given to that enforcer under section 219 of that Act.	27

Power	Conditions	Grounds	Para
To seize and detain goods.	(a) a community infringement; or a (b) a failure to comply with an enforcement order or an interim enforcement order made on the application of that enforcer; (c) a failure to comply with an undertaking given under section 217(9) or 218(10) of the Enterprise Act 2002 following such an application; or (d) a failure to comply with an undertaking given to that enforcer under section 219 of that Act,¹ or that the goods are required as evidence in proceedings brought under Part 8 of the Enterprise Act 2002.	Reasonable suspicion	28
To seize documents required as evidence.	Proceedings must be under Part 8 of the Enterprise Act 2002.	Reasonable suspicion on part of enforcer that documents are required as evidence.	29
To break open containers.	Any purpose relating to functions under Part 8 of the Enterprise Act 2002 in its capacity as a CPC enforcer.	Must be exercising powers in paragraphs 28, 29, or 30, and must be reasonably necessary in order to exercise the powers.	31
Enter premises with a warrant.	Any purpose relating to functions under Part 8 of the Enterprise Act 2002 in its capacity as a CPC enforcer.	(1) Justice of the Peace must have issued warrant. Officer must have reasonable grounds for believing the following: (a) condition A or B is met; and (b) condition C, D, or E is met. (2) Condition A is that on the premises there are – (a) products which an officer of the enforcer has power to inspect under paragraph 25; or (b) documents which an officer of the enforcer could require a person to produce under paragraph 27.	32

¹ Sch. 5 para. 20(5)(a).

(3) Condition B is that, on the premises—

...

(b) there has been or is about to be a Community infringement as defined in section 212 of the Enterprise Act 2002, or

(c) there has been a failure to comply with a measure specified in paragraph 20(3)(b), (c), or (d).

(4) Condition C is that –

(a) access to the premises has been or is likely to be refused; and

(b) notice of the enforcer's intention to apply for a warrant under this paragraph has been given to the occupier of the premises.

(5) Condition D is that it is likely that products or documents on the premises would be concealed or interfered with if notice of entry on the premises were given to the occupier of the premises.

(6) Condition E is that –

(a) the premises are unoccupied; or

(b) the occupier of the premises is absent, and it might defeat the purpose of the entry to wait for the occupier's return.

To require assistance from a person on the premises.

Any purpose relating to functions under Part 8 of the Enterprise Act 2002 in its capacity as a CPC enforcer.

34

Index